300道独家定量推理试题

GMAT™

定量推理复习官方指南

2018版

 书籍 +  在线学习

GMAT®
考试历年真题的唯一来源

此版本包含

45道从未公布过的试题

Graduate Management Admission Council® (GMAC®) mba.com

GMAT® OFFICIAL GUIDE 2018 QUANTITATIVE REVIEW

Published by John Wiley & Sons, Inc., Hoboken, New Jersey.

For general information on our other products and services or to obtain technical support please contact our Customer Care Department within the U.S. at (877) 762-2974, outside the U.S. at (317) 572-3993 or fax (317) 572-4002.

Wiley also publishes its books in a variety of electronic formats. Some content that appears in print may not be available in electronic books. For more information about Wiley products, please visit our Web site at www.wiley.com.

ISBN 978-1-119-40619-8 (pbk); ISBN 978-1-119-40238-1 (ePDF); ISBN 978-1-119-40237-4 (ePub)

Printed in Singapore

10 9 8 7 6 5 4 3

Table of Contents

Dear GMAT Test-Taker,

Thank you for your interest in graduate management education. Taking the GMAT® exam lets schools know that you're serious about your graduate business education. By using the *Official Guide* to prepare for the GMAT, you're taking a very important step toward achieving your goals and pursuing admission to a high-quality business school or master's program.

This book, *GMAT® Official Guide 2018 Quantitative Review,* is designed to help you prepare for and build confidence to do your best on the GMAT exam. It's the only guide of its kind on the market that includes real GMAT exam questions published by the Graduate Management Admission Council (GMAC), the makers of the exam.

GMAC was founded by the world's leading business schools in 1953. The GMAT exam was developed to help people who aspire to careers in management demonstrate their command of the skills needed for success in the classroom. Schools use and trust the GMAT exam as part of their admissions process because it's an excellent predictor of classroom success and your ability to excel in your chosen program.

Today more than 6,500 graduate programs around the world use the GMAT exam to establish their MBA, graduate-level management degrees and specialized programs as hallmarks of excellence. Nine out of 10 new MBA enrollments at Top 50 US full-time MBA programs are made using a GMAT score.

These facts make us proud and drive us to keep improving the GMAT as well as play a role in helping you find and gain admission to the best school or program for you. We're committed to ensuring that no talent goes undiscovered, and that more people around the world can pursue opportunities in graduate management education.

I applaud your commitment to educational success, and I know that this book and the other Official GMAT preparation materials available at mba.com will give you the confidence to achieve your personal best on the GMAT exam and launch or reinvigorate a rewarding career.

I wish you the best success on all your educational and professional endeavors in the future.

Sincerely,

Sangeet Chowfla
CEO of the Graduate Management Admission Council

GMAC 首席心理测评专家对于“机经”的看法：

使用“机经”不仅是得不偿失的复习方法，考生更可能因此被取消 GMAT 成绩，甚至构成刑事犯罪。GMAC 鼓励考生端正心态，正确备考。

虽然许多人可能认为使用“机经”是备考 GMAT 的捷径，但实际上这是对“机经”和 GMAT 考试的认识误区，而且这是直接违反《中华人民共和国著作权法》和其他知识产权法律法规，以及国际知识产权法规的行为，严重违反者将受到刑罚处罚。在 GMAT 考试中，使用“机经”属于舞弊行为，GMAC 严禁考生使用“机经”帮助他们备考 GMAT。

如果考生一旦被发现使用“机经”，将会承担严重的后果。虽然考生可能认为这类作弊行为不容易被发现，但是 GMAC 有能力识别这些违反考试规章的行为。GMAC 打击“机经”的法律行动从未停止。例如，GMAC 曾经将一家把“机经”公布于自己网站上的网络公司告上法庭。公司的所有者被法院起诉并被判违反当地法律以及国际知识产权法规。因此，GMAC 没收了这家公司的数据库，进行了数据取证，识别曾经使用“机经”的每个考生并取消了他们的分数，他们的考试资格也被永久剥夺，GMAC 还通知了那些已经收到这些作弊考生分数的学校。

实际上“机经”面对 GMAT 考试这种自适应机制，几乎很难发挥作用。在 2009 年的一份研究报告《量化泄露的 CAT 考试题目对最终成绩的影响》(Quantifying the Impact of Compromised Items in CAT) 中，我发现如果已知五道题目，对考生的定量推理或者文本逻辑推理部分成绩几乎没有影响。以下图表列出了已知五道 GMAT 定量推理或者文本逻辑推理题目，对于考生分数变化的平均影响。

定量推理

% 的考生	分数变化
0.5%	≤ -1 point
94.7%	**= 0 points**
2.2%	= +1 point
1.3%	= +2 points
1.2%	≥ +3 points

文本逻辑推理

% 的考生	分数变化
0.4%	≤ -1 point
94.8%	**= 0 points**
2.5%	= +1 point
1.4%	= +2 points
0.9%	≥ +3 points

为什么参考“机经”得不偿失？

像GMAT考试这样的计算机自适应式考试（CAT），通常会从一个巨大的题库中根据考生具体的考试表现为其匹配适合其答题能力的考题。碰见预知的题目的几率非常小。

CAT考试具备自我纠正的能力。如果一位考生碰巧答对了一道难度大于他/她真实能力的题目，那下一道题目会更难，这样这位考生就会倾向于答错。考试的难度就会在两至三道这样的错题之后恢复到这位考生真实的水平。

在CAT计分系统中，并不是每道答对的题目都会有相同的得分。

GMAC 承诺将维持 GMAT 考试的公正性和有效性。我们邀请您和我们一起加入到抵制“机经”的努力当中，并且鼓励其他考生也一起加入。如果您发现任何组织或个人使用或者鼓励他人使用机经，请通过电子邮箱 testsecurity@gmac.com 向 GMAC 举报。

郭凡民 博士
GMAC 测评研究部副总裁

GMAT® 定量推理复习官方指南 2018 版

1.0 什么是 GMAT® 考试？

1.0 什么是 GMAT® 考试?

GMAT® 考试 (Graduate Management Admission Test®) 是一项标准化考试，被全球超过 6,500 个管理专业研究生项目用于做出招生决策。GMAT 考试可帮助考生进行自我评估，并向所申请的院校展示您具备能够顺利完成管理专业研究生项目的学术潜力。

考试分为四个部分，分别考查分析性写作、文本逻辑推理、定量推理和综合推理技能。世界各地的管理学院均认为这些高阶推理技能对于入学新生来说至关重要。“高阶”推理技能涉及复杂的判断，包括批判性思维、分析和问题求解。本科成绩和课程在不同地区及院校的标准会有所不同，GMAT 则并非如此。对考生在管理专业研究生项目核心课程中可能具有的学术表现，GMAT 成绩可进行标准化、统计学上有效且可靠的衡量。经过大量的学术研究，GMAT 考试的有效性、公正性以及在招生方面的价值已得到广泛认可.

GMAT 考试是一项全程用计算机完成的全英文考试。该考试并不测试商学知识、学科掌握程度、英语词汇或高级计算技能。它也不评估与顺利完成管理专业研究生阶段学习相关的其他因素，比如工作经验、领导能力、自我激励和人际交往技能等。除了申请文书和面试表现等其他更主观的标准外，您的 GMAT 成绩也将用作一项录取标准。

1.1 为什么要参加 GMAT® 考试?

GMAT 考试由九所商学院于 1954 年共同设立，旨在提供一个统一的考查标准，考查顺利完成其学业项目所需的学术技能。如今，全球大约有 2,100 所院校的超过 6,500 个管理专业研究生项目采用该考试。

参加 GMAT 考试可帮助您从招生流程中脱颖而出，展现您对管理专业研究生教育充满热忱并且已经做好准备。院校使用 GMAT 成绩来帮助选择最符合资格的申请者，因为他们知道，参加 GMAT 考试的考生是真心希望获得商学硕士学位。该成绩也是一项经过验证的预测指标，可用于预测学生是否能够顺利完成所选项目。当您考虑要申请哪些项目时，您可将院校对 GMAT 考试的使用情况作为一项教学质量参考指标。使用 GMAT 考试的院校通常会在其班级介绍中列出分数范围或平均分数。您会发现这些介绍有助于您衡量所考虑项目的学术竞争力，还可与该项目录取学生的分数进行比较，了解自己的分数处于哪一水平。

误区 -与- 真相

误区 – **如果我在 GMAT 中没有取得高分，我将不能被首选院校录取。**

真相 – **取得任何 GMAT 成绩的考生，都有很棒的院校可供选择。**

每年参加 GMAT 考试的 250,000 多名考生中，取得满分 800 分的不到 50人；但每年都有许多人被全球顶级的商学院项目录取。招生官在做出招生决策时，GMAT 成绩只是其考虑的一个方面，他们在决定录取哪些申请者加入项目时，还会结合本科成绩、申请文书、面试表现、推荐信及其他信息。访问 mba.com 上的“School Finder（院校查找器）工具，了解最适合您的院校。

无论您在 GMAT 考试中表现如何，您都应当主动联系您感兴趣的院校了解更多信息，询问他们在招生流程中如何使用 GMAT 成绩和其他标准（比如您的本科成绩、申请文书和推荐信）。当您研究想就读哪所商学院时，您可从院校的招生办公室、网站和院校发布的资料中搜索相关信息，这些都是重要的信息来源。

如需关于 GMAT、备考资料、注册报名、如何使用 GMAT 成绩并将其发送给院校，以及申请商学院的更多信息，请访问 mba.com。

1.2 GMAT® 考试形式

GMAT 考试由四个独立计时的考核部分组成（见下一页中的表格）。在分析性写作 (AWA) 部分，您将有 30 分钟的时间通过计算机键盘输入您的作文。综合推理部分时长为 30 分钟，包含 4 种不同题型，共 12 道大题。定量推理和文本逻辑推理部分的试题为多项选择题，时长均为 75 分钟，定量推理部分包含 37 道试题，文本逻辑推理部分包含 41 道试题。

GMAT 考试的文本逻辑推理和定量推理部分采用计算机自适应性考试形式，这意味着计算机会根据您的能力水平，从包含大量试题的题库中选择与您能力相当的试题。因此，您不会遇到太多对您而言难度过高或过低的试题。第一道试题难度适中。当您解答每道试题时，计算机将对您的答案进行计分，使用该答案并结合您之前试题的作答情况，为您选择下一题。

根据计算机自适应性机制，您正确回答的试题数量越多，接下来的试题就会越难。但是如果您遇到的试题似乎比上一题简单，也不一定意味着上一题您答错了。考试必须涵盖一定范围的内容，包括要求的题型和涉及的学科知识。

由于计算机使用您的回答来为您选择下一题，所以您不能跳过某道试题，也不能返回之前的试题修改答案。如果您不知道某个试题的答案，请尽量多排除几个选项，然后选择您认为最佳的答案。

虽然单个的试题不尽相同，但每次 GMAT 考试所包含的题型是相同的。您的成绩取决于您所解答试题的难度和统计特征，以及您答对的试题数量。GMAT 考试通过适应每位考生的能力，能准确有效地考查其在各种能力上所具备的技能水平，从极高到极低。

误区 -与- 真相

误区 – **遇到更简单的试题意味着我上一题答错了。**

真相 – 您不应该因试题的难度水平而分心。

大部分人并不擅长评估试题难度，所以参加考试时不要担心，也不要将宝贵的时间浪费在判断试题难度上面。

为确保每位考生被考查的范围一致，考试针对每种题型选择特定数量的试题。例如，考试系统需要调取一道相对较难的涉及算术运算的数据充分性分析试题，但题库中已经没有此类试题，那么可能会为您提供一道更简单的试题。

考试包含本书和在线综合推理部分中的题型，但计算机屏幕上的试题形式和呈现方式会有所不同。当您参加考试时：

- 计算机屏幕上一次仅会显示一道试题。
- 多项选择题的答案选项前为圆圈而不是字母。
- 在多项选择题部分，将随机出现不同的题型。
- 您必须使用计算机选择您的答案。
- 您必须选择一个答案并进行确认，然后才能继续解答下一题。
- 您不能返回到前面的试题更改答案。

GMAT® 考试形式

	题量	考试时间
分析性写作 论证分析写作	1	30 分钟
综合推理 多源推理 表格分析 图表解读 二段式分析	12	30 分钟
休息（可选）		最多 8 分钟
定量推理 问题求解 数据充分性分析	37	75 分钟
休息（可选）		最多 8 分钟
文本逻辑推理 阅读理解 批判性推理 句子改错	41	75 分钟
	考试时长：	210 分钟

1.3 考试内容介绍

GMAT 考试会考查包含几种推理能力在内的高阶分析技能。分析性写作部分要求您进行论证推理分析，并以写作的形式作答；综合推理部分要求您阐述并整合以不同形式出现的多源信息，得出合理的结论；定量推理部分要求您运用基本算术、代数和几何知识来进行定量推理；文本逻辑推理部分要求您阅读并理解书面材料，进行推理并评估论点。

考试试题可能涉及多类学科知识，但解答试题所需的全部信息都会在考试中提供，您无需具备学科知识以外的信息。GMAT 考试并不考查商学知识、英语词汇或高级计算技能。要在考试中良好发挥，您需要具备英语阅读和写作能力以及基本的数学和英语技能。然而，真正的考试难点在于英语分析和批判性思维能力。

本书中的试题按照题型由易到难进行编排，但请记住，当您参加考试时，每个部分中的各类题型会以任意顺序出现。

1.4 综合推理部分

在如今数据驱动的世界中，企业管理者需要分析复杂的数据流和解决复杂的问题。综合推理部分重点考查与此相关的技能。综合推理部分考查您以下方面的能力：理解和评估不同来源和不同形式信息的能力，比如图表、数字和文本；使用定量推理和文本逻辑推理来解决复杂问题的能力；以及解决彼此相关的多个问题的能力。

综合推理部分包含 4 种题型：

- 多源推理
- 表格分析
- 图表解读
- 二段式分析

综合推理部分的试题可能是定量推理、文本逻辑推理或两者的结合。您需要解读图表并对表格进行排序，从数据中提取有价值的信息，但您无需具备高级统计学知识和电子表格操作技能。在综合推理部分，您将可以使用具有基本功能的在线计算器，但请注意，定量推理部分不提供计算器。

1.5 定量推理部分

GMAT 定量推理部分考查您进行定量推理、解决量化问题和解读图表数据的能力。

定量推理部分包含两类多项选择题：

- 问题求解
- 数据充分性分析

这两种题型将在定量推理部分混合出现，需要的基础知识包括：算术、初等代数和一般的几何概念。

如需查看 GMAT 定量推理试题会考查的基本数学概念，请参阅第 3 章的“数学复习”部分。如需针对 GMAT 考试定量推理部分特定题型的应试技巧、例题和答案解析，请参阅第 4 章和第 5 章。

1.6 文本逻辑推理部分

GMAT 文本逻辑推理部分考查您阅读和理解书面材料、推理和评估论点以及纠正书面材料中的错误以使其符合标准书面英语规范的能力。由于文本逻辑推理部分涉及几个不同内容领域的阅读材料，您可能会对某些材料有一定了解。但是在阅读篇章或试题中，均不会涉及有关该主题的任何详细知识点。

文本逻辑推理部分包含以下三类多项选择题：

- 阅读理解
- 批判性推理
- 句子改错

这三种题型均需您掌握基本的英语知识，但文本逻辑推理部分并非考查高级词汇。

如需针对文本逻辑推理部分特定题型的应试技巧、例题和答案解析，请参阅《*GMAT® 官方指南 2018 版*》或《*GMAT® 文本逻辑推理复习官方指南 2018 版*》；两本指南均可通过 mba.com 网站购买。

1.7 分析性写作部分

分析性写作部分 (AWA) 的考试时间为 30 分钟，您需要完成一篇论证分析作文。该部分考查您进行批判性思考、表达自己的想法以及提出恰当且具建设性的批判观点的能力。您需要通过计算机键盘输入您的作文。

1.8 我需要具备哪些计算机技能？

GMAT 考试仅需具备基本的计算机技能。您需要通过计算机键盘，使用标准的文字处理击键输入您的分析性写作文章。在综合推理和多项选择题部分，您可以使用计算机鼠标或者键盘来选择答案。综合推理部分涉及基本的计算机导航和功能，如点击选项卡、使用下拉菜单来对表格进行排序及选择答案。

1.9 考试中心环境

GMAT 考试是在全球考试中心标准化的环境下进行的。每个考试中心的考场均有监考，并为每位考生配备个人机位，让您能在安静和拥有一定隐私的环境中完成整场考试。考试期间，您有两次可选择的休息时间，每次时长为 8 分钟。您不能将笔记或草稿纸带入考场，但考试中心会为您提供一个可擦性记事本和一支记号笔，供您在考试过程中使用。

1.10 成绩计算方式

文本逻辑推理部分和定量推理部分的分数范围在 0 分到 60 分之间，6 分以下或 51 分以上的分数都非常少见。GMAT 总分根据您在上述两部分的表现得出，分数区间为 200 分到 800 分。您的分数由以下几方面决定：

- 您所解答的试题总数
- 您正确或错误回答的试题数量
- 每道试题的难度和其他统计特征

您的文本逻辑推理部分分数、定量推理部分分数和 GMAT 总分根据复杂的计算程序得出，该程序会综合考虑呈现给您的试题的难度和您的答题表现。如果您正确解答了难度较低的试题，便有机会解答更高难度的试题，从而可能得到一个更高的分数。当您完成整场考试的所有试题后，或者当考试时间结束时，计算机便会计算您的分数。计算机会结合您在文本逻辑推理部分和定量推理部分的得分计算出您的总分，分数区间为 200 分到 800 分，分数递增单位为 10 分。

分析性写作部分仅包含一项写作任务，即论证分析写作，您的作文会经过两次独立评分。作文部分的阅卷者是来自管理学教育等多个学科的院校教师，他们会评估您的批判性思维能力和作文的整体质量。（如需更多关于阅卷者资质的信息，请访问 mba.com。）此外，您的作文还可能被具备阅卷专家判断能力的自动评分程序进行评分。

作文的分数范围在 0 分到 6 分之间，分数递增单位为 0.5 分，6 分为最高分，0 分为最低分。在以下情况下会给 0 分：答案跑题、未采用英语作答、只是抄写试题题目、答案中仅包含击键字符或交白卷。您在分析性写作部分的得分通常取两次独立评分的平均分。如果两次独立评分结果相差 1 分以上，那么第三位阅卷者会进行最终判定。然而，由于阅卷者长期接受培训和监督，出现这类差异的情况非常少。

综合推理部分的分数范围在 1 分到 8 分之间，分数递增单位为 1 分。您必须正确回答单个试题下的所有问题才能得分。部分回答正确不计分。同分析性写作部分一样，综合推理部分的分数也不会计入总分。

分析性写作部分和综合推理部分的分数将与其他考试部分分开计算和报告，对文本逻辑推理、定量推理部分的分数及总分无任何影响。您指定的成绩单接收院校可能会收到一份成绩单外加您的分析性写作作文副本。您自己的成绩单将不会随附作文副本。

您的 GMAT 成绩单包含一项成绩百分位排名，该排名根据您的技能水平与过去三年所有其他考生的技能水平比较得出。成绩百分位排名显示了成绩在您之下的考生百分比数。每年 7 月，百分位排名表都会更新。如需查看最新的百分位排名表，请访问 mba.com。

1.11 考试的开发过程

开发 GMAT 考试的专家们运用标准化流程来确保考试材料的高质量和广泛适用性。所有试题均经过独立审阅，并会根据需要进行修改或废弃。多项选择题会在 GMAT 考试期间进行考察。分析性写作部分通过 mba.com 网站注册进行考察，然后评估分数的公正性和可靠性。如需更多关于考试开发的信息，请访问 mba.com。

2.0 如何备考

2.0 如何备考

2.1 如何准备应试？

GMAT® 考试专门用于考查管理学教育所需的推理技能，考试涉及 GMAT 考试独有的几种题型。参加考试前，您至少应该熟悉考试形式和各类题型。由于 GMAT 考试有时间限制，您应练习模拟答题。这不仅能帮助您更好地了解题型及相应应试技能，还有助于您在参加考试时调整答题节奏，顺利完成各个部分。

由于考试考查的是推理能力，而不是对学科知识的掌握，所以您很可能会发现牢记知识点并没有什么帮助。您不需要学习高等数学概念，但您需要确保对基本算术、代数和几何有很好的掌握，足以使用这些技能来解答定量问题。同样，您无需学习高阶词汇，但您应该牢固掌握基本英语词汇和语法，以应对阅读、写作和推理部分。

本书及管理专业研究生入学考试委员会 (GMAC) 发布的其他学习资料是 GMAT 考试历年真题的唯一来源。GMAT 考试中出现或出现过的所有试题的版权及所有权归 GMAC 所有，严禁在其他地方转载和重印这些内容。提前获取综合推理、定量推理或文本逻辑推理部分的试题，或在考试期间或之后分享考试内容，均属于严重违规行为。这可能导致您的考试成绩被取消，我们还将会通知您所申请的院校。如果情节恶劣，可能会禁止您参加今后的考试，并追究相关法律责任。

误区 -与- 真相

误区 – **需要具备非常高级的数学技能才能在 GMAT 考试中取得高分。**

真相 – GMAT 主要考查推理和批判性思维能力，而非高等数学技能。

GMAT 考试只需要运用基本的定量分析技能。您需要查看本指南（第 3 章）及*《GMAT® 官方指南 2018 版》*中列出的数学技能（代数、几何、基本算术）。GMAT 定量推理试题的难度来自于解决问题所需要运用的逻辑与分析能力，而非基本的数学技能。

2.2 如何进行模考练习？

GMAT 考试的定量推理部分和文本逻辑推理部分是计算机自适应性考试，综合推理部分的某些试题需要您使用计算机对表格进行排序以及浏览不同的信息来源。我们的官方练习资料将帮助您熟悉考试形式，更好地为考试当天做好准备。在 mba.com 上创建帐户的考生可免费进行两次完整的 GMAT 模考练习。模考练习包含计算机自适应性的定量推理和文本逻辑推理部分、额外的练习题、考试信息以及一些教程，这些教程可帮助您熟悉 GMAT 考试在考试中心计算机屏幕上的呈现方式。

在进行免费模考练习时，为了使学习效果最大化，您应该在开始备考时使用官方练习资料。您可以先进行一次模考练习，熟悉考试流程，了解自己能取得的大致成绩。在您学完本书和其他学习资料后，可以进行第二次模考练习，以判断是否需要将重点放在其他仍需加强的部分。请注意，免费的模考练习中可能包含本书中出现过的试题。随着考试日期临近，您可以考虑进行更多的官方模考练习，检测一下自己的进度，对考试当天的表现有更好的把握。

2.3 从哪里可以获得更多的练习？

如果您完成了本指南中的所有试题，并希望进行更多的练习，您可以购买《*GMAT® 官方指南 2018 版*》和 / 或《*GMAT® 文本逻辑推理复习官方指南 2018 版*》。您还可在 mba.com 上找到这些指南，以及更多的定量推理、文本逻辑推理和综合推理练习题、完整的计算机自适应性模考练习及其他有用的学习资料。

2.4 一般性应试建议

针对不同题型的具体应试策略将在本书后面部分进行介绍。以下是帮助您在考试中发挥最佳水平的一般性建议：

1. 合理运用您的时间。

尽管 GMAT 考试更强调准确性而非速度，但是，合理运用您的时间仍然相当重要。平均来说，您有大约 1 分 45 秒的时间解答一道文本逻辑推理试题，大约 2 分钟的时间解答一道定量推理试题，大约 2 分 30 秒的时间解答一道综合推理试题（部分试题包含多个问题）。一旦您开始考试，屏幕上的时钟会持续显示您还剩下的时间。您可以选择隐藏时间显示，但非常建议您定期查看时钟，密切关注进程。在每个部分规定时间结束前 5 分钟时，时钟会自动提醒。

2. 提前完成练习题。

在您熟悉所有的题型之后，可以使用本书中的例题来准备实战考试。您可以在解答练习题时自行计时，大概估算一下真正参加 GMAT 考试时每道试题所需的时间，判断您是否能够在规定时间内完成相应试题。

3. 仔细阅读各部分的考试说明。

考试说明准确阐述了解答每种题型的注意事项。如果您读得很匆忙，可能会忽略重要提示并影响正确作答。如需在考试过程中重温考试说明，请点击“Help”（帮助）图标。但请注意，您查看考试说明所花费的时间将计入该部分考试的答题时间。

4. 认真仔细地阅读每一道试题。

在您解答每一道多项选择题前，请明确试题问的到底是什么，然后排除错误答案并选出最佳选项。请不要只是粗略地浏览试题或任何可能的答案，这么做可能会让您遗漏重要信息或细微差别。

5. 不要在任何一道试题上花费过多时间。

如果您不知道某道试题的正确答案，或者在某道试题上已耗时太长，请尽可能多地排除您认为错误的选项，在余下选项中选出相对最佳的答案，然后继续解答下一题。未完成某些部分，以及在各部分即将结束时随机猜测试题答案，可能会显著降低您的成绩。得分以完成题目为准，即使没有在规定时间内完成整个部分，回答准确的题目还是能够得分的。如果您连试题都没看到，自然无法得分。

6. 只有在您准备好继续进行下一题时才确认答案。

在定量推理和文本逻辑推理部分，一旦您选择了某道单项选择题的答案，您会被要求进行确认。一旦确认答案，您将不能返回和更改。您不能够跳过任何试题。在综合推理部分，同一题目下面可能会有多个小问题。当一个屏幕上有多个回答时，您可以在进入下一个屏幕前，更改当前屏幕上的任一试题答案。但是，您不能返回之前的屏幕更改任何答案。

误区 -与- 真相

误区 – **正确回答试题比完成考试更为重要。**

真相 – **未答完 GMAT 考题的考生在分数上将受到严重的影响。**

考试节奏非常重要。如果您被某一道试题难住了，尽量猜测最有可能的答案并继续进行下一题。如果您猜错了，计算机程序接下来很可能会给出一道相对容易的试题，并且您也容易正确作答。计算机也会迅速调整，根据您的实际能力匹配出题。如果未能完成考试，将会扣分。例如，如果您未能回答 5 道文本逻辑推理试题，您的成绩百分位数就会从 91 降到 77。

7. 在开始写作前构思您的作文。

应对论证分析写作的最佳方法是仔细阅读试题说明，花几分钟时间审清题目，在作答之前构思清楚。花些时间组织好想法并充分展开，但记得留些时间重读一遍文章，并进行任何您认为可提升行文质量的修改。

误区 -与- 真相

误区 – **前10道试题尤其重要，应该在这些试题上投入更多时间。**

真相 – **所有试题都同样重要。**

计算机自适应性考试算法使用所有已解答的试题来对您的能力做出初步评估。但是，随着您继续解答接下来的试题，该算法会根据您已解答的所有试题，实时评估并自行调整，进而给出最符合您当时能力水平的试题。您的最终成绩取决于您作答的准确性及所解答试题的难度水平。在前 10 道试题上花费额外的时间并不能影响计分系统，却可能导致您没有足够的时间完成考试，得不偿失。

3.0 Math Review

3.0 Math Review

Although this chapter provides a review of some of the mathematical concepts of arithmetic, algebra, and geometry, it is not intended to be a textbook. You should use this chapter to familiarize yourself with the kinds of topics that may be tested in the GMAT® exam. You may wish to consult an arithmetic, algebra, or geometry book for a more detailed discussion of some of the topics.

Section 3.1, "Arithmetic," includes the following topics:

1. Properties of Integers
2. Fractions
3. Decimals
4. Real Numbers
5. Ratio and Proportion
6. Percents
7. Powers and Roots of Numbers
8. Descriptive Statistics
9. Sets
10. Counting Methods
11. Discrete Probability

Section 3.2, "Algebra," does not extend beyond what is usually covered in a first-year high school algebra course. The topics included are as follows:

1. Simplifying Algebraic Expressions
2. Equations
3. Solving Linear Equations with One Unknown
4. Solving Two Linear Equations with Two Unknowns
5. Solving Equations by Factoring
6. Solving Quadratic Equations
7. Exponents
8. Inequalities
9. Absolute Value
10. Functions

Section 3.3, "Geometry," is limited primarily to measurement and intuitive geometry or spatial visualization. Extensive knowledge of theorems and the ability to construct proofs, skills that are usually developed in a formal geometry course, are not tested. The topics included in this section are the following:

1. Lines
2. Intersecting Lines and Angles
3. Perpendicular Lines
4. Parallel Lines
5. Polygons (Convex)
6. Triangles
7. Quadrilaterals
8. Circles
9. Rectangular Solids and Cylinders
10. Coordinate Geometry

Section 3.4, "Word Problems," presents examples of and solutions to the following types of word problems:

1. Rate Problems
2. Work Problems
3. Mixture Problems
4. Interest Problems
5. Discount
6. Profit
7. Sets
8. Geometry Problems
9. Measurement Problems
10. Data Interpretation

3.1 Arithmetic

1. Properties of Integers

An *integer* is any number in the set $\{\ldots -3, -2, -1, 0, 1, 2, 3, \ldots\}$. If x and y are integers and $x \neq 0$, then x is a *divisor* (*factor*) of y provided that $y = xn$ for some integer n. In this case, y is also said to be *divisible* by x or to be a *multiple* of x. For example, 7 is a divisor or factor of 28 since $28 = (7)(4)$, but 8 is not a divisor of 28 since there is no integer n such that $28 = 8n$.

If x and y are positive integers, there exist unique integers q and r, called the *quotient* and *remainder*, respectively, such that $y = xq + r$ and $0 \leq r < x$. For example, when 28 is divided by 8, the quotient is 3 and the remainder is 4 since $28 = (8)(3) + 4$. Note that y is divisible by x if and only if the remainder r is 0; for example, 32 has a remainder of 0 when divided by 8 because 32 is divisible by 8. Also, note that when a smaller integer is divided by a larger integer, the quotient is 0 and the remainder is the smaller integer. For example, 5 divided by 7 has the quotient 0 and the remainder 5 since $5 = (7)(0) + 5$.

Any integer that is divisible by 2 is an *even integer*; the set of even integers is $\{\ldots -4, -2, 0, 2, 4, 6, 8, \ldots\}$. Integers that are not divisible by 2 are *odd integers*; $\{\ldots -3, -1, 1, 3, 5, \ldots\}$ is the set of odd integers.

If at least one factor of a product of integers is even, then the product is even; otherwise the product is odd. If two integers are both even or both odd, then their sum and their difference are even. Otherwise, their sum and their difference are odd.

A *prime* number is a positive integer that has exactly two different positive divisors, 1 and itself. For example, 2, 3, 5, 7, 11, and 13 are prime numbers, but 15 is not, since 15 has four different positive divisors, 1, 3, 5, and 15. The number 1 is not a prime number since it has only one positive divisor. Every integer greater than 1 either is prime or can be uniquely expressed as a product of prime factors. For example, $14 = (2)(7)$, $81 = (3)(3)(3)(3)$, and $484 = (2)(2)(11)(11)$.

The numbers $-2, -1, 0, 1, 2, 3, 4, 5$ are *consecutive integers*. Consecutive integers can be represented by $n, n + 1, n + 2, n + 3, \ldots$, where n is an integer. The numbers 0, 2, 4, 6, 8 are *consecutive even integers*, and 1, 3, 5, 7, 9 are *consecutive odd integers*. Consecutive even integers can be represented by $2n, 2n + 2, 2n + 4, \ldots$, and consecutive odd integers can be represented by $2n + 1, 2n + 3, 2n + 5, \ldots$, where n is an integer.

Properties of the integer 1. If n is any number, then $1 \cdot n = n$, and for any number $n \neq 0$, $n \cdot \frac{1}{n} = 1$.

The number 1 can be expressed in many ways; for example, $\frac{n}{n} = 1$ for any number $n \neq 0$.

Multiplying or dividing an expression by 1, in any form, does not change the value of that expression.

Properties of the integer 0. The integer 0 is neither positive nor negative. If n is any number, then $n + 0 = n$ and $n \cdot 0 = 0$. Division by 0 is not defined.

2. Fractions

In a fraction $\frac{n}{d}$, n is the *numerator* and d is the *denominator*. The denominator of a fraction can never be 0, because division by 0 is not defined.

Two fractions are said to be *equivalent* if they represent the same number. For example, $\frac{8}{36}$ and $\frac{14}{63}$ are equivalent since they both represent the number $\frac{2}{9}$. In each case, the fraction is reduced to lowest terms by dividing both numerator and denominator by their *greatest common divisor* (gcd). The gcd of 8 and 36 is 4 and the gcd of 14 and 63 is 7.

Addition and subtraction of fractions.

Two fractions with the same denominator can be added or subtracted by performing the required operation with the numerators, leaving the denominators the same. For example, $\frac{3}{5}+\frac{4}{5}=\frac{3+4}{5}=\frac{7}{5}$ and $\frac{5}{7}-\frac{2}{7}=\frac{5-2}{7}=\frac{3}{7}$. If two fractions do not have the same denominator, express them as equivalent fractions with the same denominator. For example, to add $\frac{3}{5}$ and $\frac{4}{7}$, multiply the numerator and denominator of the first fraction by 7 and the numerator and denominator of the second fraction by 5, obtaining $\frac{21}{35}$ and $\frac{20}{35}$, respectively; $\frac{21}{35}+\frac{20}{35}=\frac{41}{35}$.

For the new denominator, choosing the *least common multiple* (lcm) of the denominators usually lessens the work. For $\frac{2}{3}+\frac{1}{6}$, the lcm of 3 and 6 is 6 (not $3 \times 6 = 18$), so $\frac{2}{3}+\frac{1}{6}=\frac{2}{3}\times\frac{2}{2}+\frac{1}{6}=\frac{4}{6}+\frac{1}{6}=\frac{5}{6}$.

Multiplication and division of fractions.

To multiply two fractions, simply multiply the two numerators and multiply the two denominators.

For example, $\frac{2}{3}\times\frac{4}{7}=\frac{2\times4}{3\times7}=\frac{8}{21}$.

To divide by a fraction, invert the divisor (that is, find its *reciprocal*) and multiply. For example, $\frac{2}{3}\div\frac{4}{7}=\frac{2}{3}\times\frac{7}{4}=\frac{14}{12}=\frac{7}{6}$.

In the problem above, the reciprocal of $\frac{4}{7}$ is $\frac{7}{4}$. In general, the reciprocal of a fraction $\frac{n}{d}$ is $\frac{d}{n}$, where n and d are not zero.

Mixed numbers.

A number that consists of a whole number and a fraction, for example, $7\frac{2}{3}$, is a mixed number: $7\frac{2}{3}$ means $7+\frac{2}{3}$.

To change a mixed number into a fraction, multiply the whole number by the denominator of the fraction and add this number to the numerator of the fraction; then put the result over the denominator of the fraction. For example, $7\frac{2}{3}=\frac{(3\times7)+2}{3}=\frac{23}{3}$.

3. Decimals

In the decimal system, the position of the period or *decimal point* determines the place value of the digits. For example, the digits in the number 7,654.321 have the following place values:

Thousands		Hundreds	Tens	Ones or units		Tenths	Hundredths	Thousandths
7	,	6	5	4	.	3	2	1

Some examples of decimals follow.

$$0.321 = \frac{3}{10} + \frac{2}{100} + \frac{1}{1,000} = \frac{321}{1,000}$$

$$0.0321 = \frac{0}{10} + \frac{3}{100} + \frac{2}{1,000} + \frac{1}{10,000} = \frac{321}{10,000}$$

$$1.56 = 1 + \frac{5}{10} + \frac{6}{100} = \frac{156}{100}$$

Sometimes decimals are expressed as the product of a number with only one digit to the left of the decimal point and a power of 10. This is called *scientific notation.* For example, 231 can be written as 2.31×10^2 and 0.0231 can be written as 2.31×10^{-2}. When a number is expressed in scientific notation, the exponent of the 10 indicates the number of places that the decimal point is to be moved in the number that is to be multiplied by a power of 10 in order to obtain the product. The decimal point is moved to the right if the exponent is positive and to the left if the exponent is negative. For example, 2.013×10^4 is equal to 20,130 and 1.91×10^{-4} is equal to 0.000191.

Addition and subtraction of decimals.

To add or subtract two decimals, the decimal points of both numbers should be lined up. If one of the numbers has fewer digits to the right of the decimal point than the other, zeros may be inserted to the right of the last digit. For example, to add 17.6512 and 653.27, set up the numbers in a column and add:

$$\begin{array}{r} 17.6512 \\ +\,653.2700 \\ \hline 670.9212 \end{array}$$

Likewise for 653.27 minus 17.6512:

$$\begin{array}{r} 653.2700 \\ -17.6512 \\ \hline 635.6188 \end{array}$$

Multiplication of decimals.

To multiply decimals, multiply the numbers as if they were whole numbers and then insert the decimal point in the product so that the number of digits to the right of the decimal point is equal to the sum of the numbers of digits to the right of the decimal points in the numbers being multiplied. For example:

$$\begin{array}{rl} 2.09 & \text{(2 digits to the right)} \\ \times\,1.3 & \text{(1 digit to the right)} \\ \hline 627 & \\ 2090 & \\ \hline 2.717 & (2+1=3 \text{ digits to the right}) \end{array}$$

Division of decimals.

To divide a number (the dividend) by a decimal (the divisor), move the decimal point of the divisor to the right until the divisor is a whole number. Then move the decimal point of the dividend the same number of places to the right, and divide as you would by a whole number. The decimal point in the quotient will be directly above the decimal point in the new dividend. For example, to divide 698.12 by 12.4:

$$12.4\overline{)698.12}$$

will be replaced by:

$$124\overline{)6981.2}$$

and the division would proceed as follows:

$$\begin{array}{r} 56.3 \\ 124\overline{)6981.2} \\ \underline{620} \\ 781 \\ \underline{744} \\ 37\,2 \\ \underline{37\,2} \\ 0 \end{array}$$

4. Real Numbers

All *real* numbers correspond to points on the number line and all points on the number line correspond to real numbers. All real numbers except zero are either positive or negative.

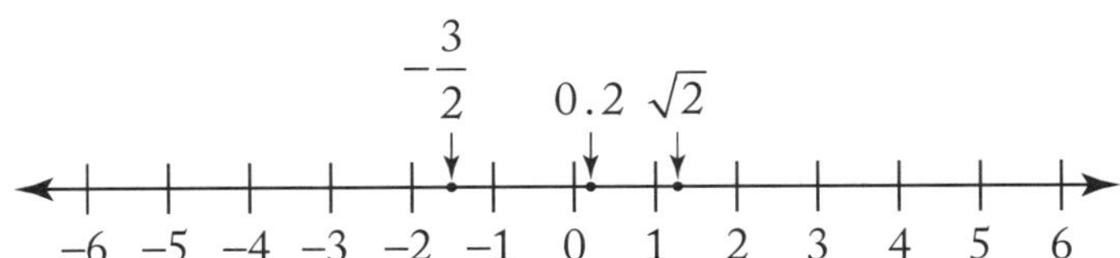

On a number line, numbers corresponding to points to the left of zero are negative and numbers corresponding to points to the right of zero are positive. For any two numbers on the number line, the number to the left is less than the number to the right; for example, $-4 < -3 < -\frac{3}{2} < -1$, and $1 < \sqrt{2} < 2$.

To say that the number n is between 1 and 4 on the number line means that $n > 1$ and $n < 4$, that is, $1 < n < 4$. If n is "between 1 and 4, inclusive," then $1 \le n \le 4$.

The distance between a number and zero on the number line is called the *absolute value* of the number. Thus 3 and −3 have the same absolute value, 3, since they are both three units from zero. The absolute value of 3 is denoted $|3|$. Examples of absolute values of numbers are

$$|-5| = |5| = 5, \left|-\frac{7}{2}\right| = \frac{7}{2}, \text{ and } |0| = 0.$$

Note that the absolute value of any nonzero number is positive.

Here are some properties of real numbers that are used frequently. If x, y, and z are real numbers, then

(1) $x + y = y + x$ and $xy = yx$.
For example, $8 + 3 = 3 + 8 = 11$, and $(17)(5) = (5)(17) = 85$.

(2) $(x + y) + z = x + (y + z)$ and $(xy)z = x(yz)$.
For example, $(7 + 5) + 2 = 7 + (5 + 2) = 7 + (7) = 14$, and $\left(5\sqrt{3}\right)\left(\sqrt{3}\right) = (5)\left(\sqrt{3}\sqrt{3}\right) = (5)(3) = 15$.

(3) $xy + xz = x(y + z)$.
For example, $718(36) + 718(64) = 718(36 + 64) = 718(100) = 71{,}800$.

(4) If x and y are both positive, then $x + y$ and xy are positive.

(5) If x and y are both negative, then $x + y$ is negative and xy is positive.

(6) If x is positive and y is negative, then xy is negative.

(7) If $xy = 0$, then $x = 0$ or $y = 0$. For example, $3y = 0$ implies $y = 0$.

(8) $|x + y| \le |x| + |y|$. For example, if $x = 10$ and $y = 2$, then $|x + y| = |12| = 12 = |x| + |y|$; and if $x = 10$ and $y = -2$, then $|x + y| = |8| = 8 < 12 = |x| + |y|$.

5. Ratio and Proportion

The *ratio* of the number a to the number b ($b \neq 0$) is $\frac{a}{b}$.

A ratio may be expressed or represented in several ways. For example, the ratio of 2 to 3 can be written as 2 to 3, 2:3, or $\frac{2}{3}$. The order of the terms of a ratio is important. For example, the ratio of the number of months with exactly 30 days to the number with exactly 31 days is $\frac{4}{7}$, not $\frac{7}{4}$.

A *proportion* is a statement that two ratios are equal; for example, $\frac{2}{3} = \frac{8}{12}$ is a proportion. One way to solve a proportion involving an unknown is to cross multiply, obtaining a new equality. For example, to solve for n in the proportion $\frac{2}{3} = \frac{n}{12}$, cross multiply, obtaining $24 = 3n$; then divide both sides by 3, to get $n = 8$.

6. Percents

Percent means *per hundred* or *number out of 100.* A percent can be represented as a fraction with a denominator of 100, or as a decimal. For example:

$$37\% = \frac{37}{100} = 0.37.$$

To find a certain percent of a number, multiply the number by the percent expressed as a decimal or fraction. For example:

$$20\% \text{ of } 90 = 0.2 \times 90 = 18$$

or

$$20\% \text{ of } 90 = \frac{20}{100} \times 90 = \frac{1}{5} \times 90 = 18.$$

Percents greater than 100%.

Percents greater than 100% are represented by numbers greater than 1. For example:

$$300\% = \frac{300}{100} = 3$$
$$250\% \text{ of } 80 = 2.5 \times 80 = 200.$$

Percents less than 1%.

The percent 0.5% means $\frac{1}{2}$ of 1 percent. For example, 0.5% of 12 is equal to $0.005 \times 12 = 0.06$.

Percent change.

Often a problem will ask for the percent increase or decrease from one quantity to another quantity. For example, "If the price of an item increases from $24 to $30, what is the percent increase in price?" To find the percent increase, first find the amount of the increase; then divide this increase by the original amount, and express this quotient as a percent. In the example above, the percent increase would be found in the following way: the amount of the increase is $(30 - 24) = 6$. Therefore, the percent increase is $\frac{6}{24} = 0.25 = 25\%$.

Likewise, to find the percent decrease (for example, the price of an item is reduced from $30 to $24), first find the amount of the decrease; then divide this decrease by the original amount, and express this quotient as a percent. In the example above, the amount of decrease is $(30 - 24) = 6$.

Therefore, the percent decrease is $\frac{6}{30} = 0.20 = 20\%$.

Note that the percent increase from 24 to 30 is not the same as the percent decrease from 30 to 24.

In the following example, the increase is greater than 100 percent: If the cost of a certain house in 1983 was 300 percent of its cost in 1970, by what percent did the cost increase?

If n is the cost in 1970, then the percent increase is equal to $\frac{3n - n}{n} = \frac{2n}{n} = 2$, or 200%.

7. Powers and Roots of Numbers

When a number k is to be used n times as a factor in a product, it can be expressed as k^n, which means the nth power of k. For example, $2^2 = 2 \times 2 = 4$ and $2^3 = 2 \times 2 \times 2 = 8$ are powers of 2.

Squaring a number that is greater than 1, or raising it to a higher power, results in a larger number; squaring a number between 0 and 1 results in a smaller number. For example:

$$3^2 = 9 \qquad (9 > 3)$$
$$\left(\frac{1}{3}\right)^2 = \frac{1}{9} \qquad \left(\frac{1}{9} < \frac{1}{3}\right)$$
$$(0.1)^2 = 0.01 \qquad (0.01 < 0.1)$$

A *square root* of a number n is a number that, when squared, is equal to n. The square root of a negative number is not a real number. Every positive number n has two square roots, one positive and the other negative, but $\sqrt{n}$ denotes the positive number whose square is n. For example, $\sqrt{9}$ denotes 3. The two square roots of 9 are $\sqrt{9} = 3$ and $-\sqrt{9} = -3$.

Every real number r has exactly one real *cube root*, which is the number s such that $s^3 = r$. The real cube root of r is denoted by $\sqrt[3]{r}$. Since $2^3 = 8$, $\sqrt[3]{8} = 2$. Similarly, $\sqrt[3]{-8} = -2$, because $(-2)^3 = -8$.

8. Descriptive Statistics

A list of numbers, or numerical data, can be described by various statistical measures. One of the most common of these measures is the *average,* or *(arithmetic) mean,* which locates a type of "center" for the data. The average of n numbers is defined as the sum of the n numbers divided by n. For example, the average of 6, 4, 7, 10, and 4 is $\frac{6+4+7+10+4}{5}=\frac{31}{5}=6.2$.

The *median* is another type of center for a list of numbers. To calculate the median of n numbers, first order the numbers from least to greatest; if n is odd, the median is defined as the middle number, whereas if n is even, the median is defined as the average of the two middle numbers. In the example above, the numbers, in order, are 4, 4, 6, 7, 10, and the median is 6, the middle number.

For the numbers 4, 6, 6, 8, 9, 12, the median is $\frac{6+8}{2}=7$. Note that the mean of these numbers is 7.5.

The median of a set of data can be less than, equal to, or greater than the mean. Note that for a large set of data (for example, the salaries of 800 company employees), it is often true that about half of the data is less than the median and about half of the data is greater than the median; but this is not always the case, as the following data show.

3, 5, 7, 7, 7, 7, 7, 7, 8, 9, 9, 9, 9, 10, 10

Here the median is 7, but only $\frac{2}{15}$ of the data is less than the median.

The *mode* of a list of numbers is the number that occurs most frequently in the list. For example, the mode of 1, 3, 6, 4, 3, 5 is 3. A list of numbers may have more than one mode. For example, the list 1, 2, 3, 3, 3, 5, 7, 10, 10, 10, 20 has two modes, 3 and 10.

The degree to which numerical data are spread out or dispersed can be measured in many ways. The simplest measure of dispersion is the *range,* which is defined as the greatest value in the numerical data minus the least value. For example, the range of 11, 10, 5, 13, 21 is $21-5=16$. Note how the range depends on only two values in the data.

One of the most common measures of dispersion is the *standard deviation.* Generally speaking, the more the data are spread away from the mean, the greater the standard deviation. The standard deviation of n numbers can be calculated as follows: (1) find the arithmetic mean, (2) find the differences between the mean and each of the n numbers, (3) square each of the differences, (4) find the average of the squared differences, and (5) take the nonnegative square root of this average. Shown below is this calculation for the data 0, 7, 8, 10, 10, which have arithmetic mean 7.

x	$x-7$	$(x-7)^2$
0	−7	49
7	0	0
8	1	1
10	3	9
10	3	9
	Total	68

Standard deviation $\sqrt{\frac{68}{5}}\approx 3.7$

Notice that the standard deviation depends on every data value, although it depends most on values that are farthest from the mean. This is why a distribution with data grouped closely around the mean will have a smaller standard deviation than will data spread far from the mean. To illustrate this, compare the data 6, 6, 6.5, 7.5, 9, which also have mean 7. Note that the numbers in the second set of data seem to be grouped more closely around the mean of 7 than the numbers in the first set. This is reflected in the standard deviation, which is less for the second set (approximately 1.1) than for the first set (approximately 3.7).

There are many ways to display numerical data that show how the data are distributed. One simple way is with a *frequency distribution,* which is useful for data that have values occurring with varying frequencies. For example, the 20 numbers

–4	0	0	–3	–2	–1	–1	0	–1	–4
–1	–5	0	–2	0	–5	–2	0	0	–1

are displayed in a frequency distribution by listing each different value x and the frequency f with which x occurs.

Data Value x	Frequency f
–5	2
–4	2
–3	1
–2	3
–1	5
0	7
Total	20

From the frequency distribution, one can readily compute descriptive statistics:

Mean: $= \dfrac{(-5)(2)+(-4)(2)+(-3)(1)+(-2)(3)+(-1)(5)+(0)(7)}{20} = -1.6$

Median: –1 (the average of the 10th and 11th numbers)

Mode: 0 (the number that occurs most frequently)

Range: $0 - (-5) = 5$

Standard deviation: $\sqrt{\dfrac{(-5+1.6)^2(2)+(-4+1.6)^2(2)+\ldots+(0+1.6)^2(7)}{20}} \approx 1.7$

9. Sets

In mathematics a *set* is a collection of numbers or other objects. The objects are called the *elements* of the set. If S is a set having a finite number of elements, then the number of elements is denoted by $|S|$. Such a set is often defined by listing its elements; for example, $S = \{-5, 0, 1\}$ is a set with $|S| = 3$.
The order in which the elements are listed in a set does not matter; thus $\{-5, 0, 1\} = \{0, 1, -5\}$.
If all the elements of a set S are also elements of a set T, then S is a *subset* of T; for example, $S = \{-5, 0, 1\}$ is a subset of $T = \{-5, 0, 1, 4, 10\}$.

For any two sets A and B, the *union* of A and B is the set of all elements that are in A *or* in B *or* in both. The *intersection* of A and B is the set of all elements that are both in A *and* in B. The union is denoted by $A \cup B$ and the intersection is denoted by $A \cap B$. As an example, if $A = \{3, 4\}$ and $B = \{4, 5, 6\}$, then $A \cup B = \{3, 4, 5, 6\}$ and $A \cap B = \{4\}$. Two sets that have no elements in common are said to be *disjoint* or *mutually exclusive.*

The relationship between sets is often illustrated with a *Venn diagram* in which sets are represented by regions in a plane. For two sets S and T that are not disjoint and neither is a subset of the other, the intersection $S \cap T$ is represented by the shaded region of the diagram below.

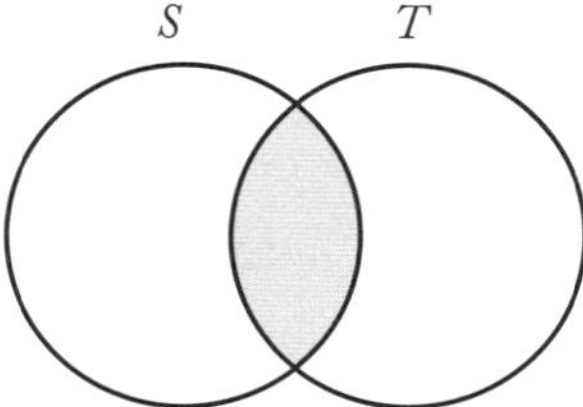

This diagram illustrates a fact about any two finite sets S and T: the number of elements in their union equals the sum of their individual numbers of elements minus the number of elements in their intersection (because the latter are counted twice in the sum); more concisely,

$$|S \cup T| = |S| + |T| - |S \cap T|.$$

This counting method is called the general addition rule for two sets. As a special case, if S and T are disjoint, then

$$|S \cup T| = |S| + |T|$$

since $|S \cap T| = 0$.

10. Counting Methods

There are some useful methods for counting objects and sets of objects without actually listing the elements to be counted. The following principle of multiplication is fundamental to these methods.

If an object is to be chosen from a set of m objects and a second object is to be chosen from a different set of n objects, then there are mn ways of choosing both objects simultaneously.

As an example, suppose the objects are items on a menu. If a meal consists of one entree and one dessert and there are 5 entrees and 3 desserts on the menu, then there are $5 \times 3 = 15$ different meals that can be ordered from the menu. As another example, each time a coin is flipped, there are two possible outcomes, heads and tails. If an experiment consists of 8 consecutive coin flips, then the experiment has 2^8 possible outcomes, where each of these outcomes is a list of heads and tails in some order.

A symbol that is often used with the multiplication principle is the *factorial.* If n is an integer greater than 1, then n factorial, denoted by the symbol $n!$, is defined as the product of all the integers from 1 to n. Therefore,

$$2! = (1)(2) = 2,$$
$$3! = (1)(2)(3) = 6,$$
$$4! = (1)(2)(3)(4) = 24, \text{ etc.}$$

Also, by definition, $0! = 1! = 1$.

The factorial is useful for counting the number of ways that a set of objects can be ordered. If a set of n objects is to be ordered from 1st to nth, then there are n choices for the 1st object, $n - 1$ choices for the 2nd object, $n - 2$ choices for the 3rd object, and so on, until there is only 1 choice for the nth object. Thus, by the multiplication principle, the number of ways of ordering the n objects is

$$n(n-1)(n-2)\cdots(3)(2)(1) = n!.$$

For example, the number of ways of ordering the letters A, B, and C is 3!, or 6:

ABC, ACB, BAC, BCA, CAB, and CBA.

These orderings are called the *permutations* of the letters A, B, and C.

A permutation can be thought of as a selection process in which objects are selected one by one in a certain order. If the order of selection is not relevant and only k objects are to be selected from a larger set of n objects, a different counting method is employed.

Specifically, consider a set of n objects from which a complete selection of k objects is to be made without regard to order, where $0 \le k \le n$. Then the number of possible complete selections of k objects is called the number of *combinations* of n objects taken k at a time and is denoted by $\binom{n}{k}$.

The value of $\binom{n}{k}$ is given by $\binom{n}{k} = \frac{n!}{k!(n-k)!}$.

Note that $\binom{n}{k}$ is the number of k-element subsets of a set with n elements. For example, if $S = \{A, B, C, D, E\}$, then the number of 2-element subsets of S, or the number of combinations of 5 letters taken 2 at a time, is $\binom{5}{2} = \frac{5!}{2!3!} = \frac{120}{(2)(6)} = 10$.

The subsets are {A, B}, {A, C}, {A, D}, {A, E}, {B, C}, {B, D}, {B, E}, {C, D}, {C, E}, and {D, E}. Note that $\binom{5}{2} = 10 = \binom{5}{3}$ because every 2-element subset chosen from a set of 5 elements corresponds to a unique 3-element subset consisting of the elements *not* chosen.

In general, $\binom{n}{k} = \binom{n}{n-k}$.

11. Discrete Probability

Many of the ideas discussed in the preceding three topics are important to the study of discrete probability. Discrete probability is concerned with *experiments* that have a finite number of *outcomes*. Given such an experiment, an *event* is a particular set of outcomes. For example, rolling a number cube with faces numbered 1 to 6 (similar to a 6-sided die) is an experiment with 6 possible outcomes: 1, 2, 3, 4, 5, or 6. One event in this experiment is that the outcome is 4, denoted $\{4\}$; another event is that the outcome is an odd number: $\{1, 3, 5\}$.

The probability that an event E occurs, denoted by $P(E)$, is a number between 0 and 1, inclusive. If E has no outcomes, then E is *impossible* and $P(E) = 0$; if E is the set of all possible outcomes of the experiment, then E is *certain* to occur and $P(E) = 1$. Otherwise, E is possible but uncertain, and $0 < P(E) < 1$. If F is a subset of E, then $P(F) \le P(E)$. In the example above, if the probability of each of the 6 outcomes is the same, then the probability of each outcome is $\frac{1}{6}$, and the outcomes are said to be *equally likely*. For experiments in which all the individual outcomes are equally likely, the probability of an event E is

$$P(E) = \frac{\text{The number of outcomes in } E}{\text{The total number of possible outcomes}}.$$

In the example, the probability that the outcome is an odd number is

$$P(\{1,3,5\}) = \frac{|\{1,3,5\}|}{6} = \frac{3}{6} = \frac{1}{2}.$$

Given an experiment with events E and F, the following events are defined:
"*not* E" is the set of outcomes that are not outcomes in E;
"E *or* F" is the set of outcomes in E or F or both, that is, $E \cup F$;
"E *and* F" is the set of outcomes in both E and F, that is, $E \cap F$.

The probability that E does not occur is $P(\text{not } E) = 1 - P(E)$. The probability that "$E$ or F" occurs is $P(E \text{ or } F) = P(E) + P(F) - P(E \text{ and } F)$, using the general addition rule at the end of section 3.1.9 ("Sets"). For the number cube, if E is the event that the outcome is an odd number, $\{1, 3, 5\}$, and F is the event that the outcome is a prime number, $\{2, 3, 5\}$, then $P(E \text{ and } F) = P(\{3,5\}) = \frac{2}{6} = \frac{1}{3}$ and so $P(E \text{ or } F) = P(E) + P(F) - P(E \text{ and } F) = \frac{3}{6} + \frac{3}{6} - \frac{2}{6} = \frac{4}{6} = \frac{2}{3}$.
Note that the event "E or F" is $E \cup F = \{1, 2, 3, 5\}$, and hence $P(E \text{ or } F) = \frac{|\{1,2,3,5\}|}{6} = \frac{4}{6} = \frac{2}{3}$.

If the event "E and F" is impossible (that is, $E \cap F$ has no outcomes), then E and F are said to be *mutually exclusive* events, and $P(E \text{ and } F) = 0$. Then the general addition rule is reduced to $P(E \text{ or } F) = P(E) + P(F)$.

This is the special addition rule for the probability of two mutually exclusive events.

Two events A and B are said to be *independent* if the occurrence of either event does not alter the probability that the other event occurs. For one roll of the number cube, let $A = \{2, 4, 6\}$ and let $B = \{5, 6\}$. Then the probability that A occurs is $P(A) = \frac{|A|}{6} = \frac{3}{6} = \frac{1}{2}$, while, *presuming B occurs,* the probability that A occurs is

$$\frac{|A \cap B|}{|B|} = \frac{|\{6\}|}{|\{5,6\}|} = \frac{1}{2}.$$

Similarly, the probability that B occurs is $P(B) = \frac{|B|}{6} = \frac{2}{6} = \frac{1}{3}$, while, *presuming A occurs,* the probability that B occurs is

$$\frac{|B \cap A|}{|A|} = \frac{|\{6\}|}{|\{2,4,6\}|} = \frac{1}{3}.$$

Thus, the occurrence of either event does not affect the probability that the other event occurs. Therefore, A and B are independent.

The following multiplication rule holds for any independent events E and F: $P(E \text{ and } F) = P(E)P(F)$.

For the independent events A and B above, $P(A \text{ and } B) = P(A)P(B) = \left(\frac{1}{2}\right)\left(\frac{1}{3}\right) = \left(\frac{1}{6}\right)$.

Note that the event "A and B" is $A \cap B = \{6\}$, and hence $P(A \text{ and } B) = P(\{6\}) = \frac{1}{6}$. It follows from the general addition rule and the multiplication rule above that if E and F are independent, then

$$P(E \text{ or } F) = P(E) + P(F) - P(E)P(F).$$

For a final example of some of these rules, consider an experiment with events A, B, and C for which $P(A) = 0.23$, $P(B) = 0.40$, and $P(C) = 0.85$. Also, suppose that events A and B are mutually exclusive and events B and C are independent. Then

$$\begin{aligned} P(A \text{ or } B) &= P(A) + P(B) \text{ (since } A \text{ or } B \text{ are mutually exclusive)} \\ &= 0.23 + 0.40 \\ &= 0.63 \\ P(B \text{ or } C) &= P(B) + P(C) - P(B)P(C) \text{ (by independence)} \\ &= 0.40 + 0.85 - (0.40)(0.85) \\ &= 0.91 \end{aligned}$$

Note that $P(A \text{ or } C)$ and $P(A \text{ and } C)$ cannot be determined using the information given. But it can be determined that A and C are *not* mutually exclusive since $P(A) + P(C) = 1.08$, which is greater than 1, and therefore cannot equal $P(A \text{ or } C)$; from this it follows that $P(A \text{ and } C) \geq 0.08$. One can also deduce that $P(A \text{ and } C) \leq P(A) = 0.23$, since $A \cap C$ is a subset of A, and that $P(A \text{ or } C) \geq P(C) = 0.85$ since C is a subset of $A \cup C$. Thus, one can conclude that $0.85 \leq P(A \text{ or } C) \leq 1$ and $0.08 \leq P(A \text{ and } C) \leq 0.23$.

3.2 Algebra

Algebra is based on the operations of arithmetic and on the concept of an *unknown quantity,* or *variable.* Letters such as x or n are used to represent unknown quantities. For example, suppose Pam has 5 more pencils than Fred. If F represents the number of pencils that Fred has, then the number of pencils that Pam has is $F + 5$. As another example, if Jim's present salary S is increased by 7%, then his new salary is $1.07S$. A combination of letters and arithmetic operations, such as $F + 5$, $\frac{3x^2}{2x-5}$, and $19x^2 - 6x + 3$, is called an *algebraic expression.*

The expression $19x^2 - 6x + 3$ consists of the *terms* $19x^2$, $-6x$, and 3, where 19 is the *coefficient* of x^2, -6 is the coefficient of x^1, and 3 is a *constant term* (or coefficient of $x^0 = 1$). Such an expression is called a *second degree* (or *quadratic*) *polynomial in x* since the highest power of x is 2. The expression $F + 5$ is a *first degree* (or *linear*) *polynomial in F* since the highest power of F is 1. The expression $\frac{3x^2}{2x-5}$ is not a polynomial because it is not a sum of terms that are each powers of x multiplied by coefficients.

1. Simplifying Algebraic Expressions

Often when working with algebraic expressions, it is necessary to simplify them by factoring or combining *like* terms. For example, the expression $6x + 5x$ is equivalent to $(6 + 5)x$, or $11x$.
In the expression $9x - 3y$, 3 is a factor common to both terms: $9x - 3y = 3(3x - y)$. In the expression $5x^2 + 6y$, there are no like terms and no common factors.

If there are common factors in the numerator and denominator of an expression, they can be divided out, provided that they are not equal to zero.

For example, if $x \neq 3$, then $\frac{x-3}{x-3}$ is equal to 1; therefore,

$$\begin{aligned}\frac{3xy-9y}{x-3} &= \frac{3y(x-3)}{x-3}\\ &= (3y)(1)\\ &= 3y\end{aligned}$$

To multiply two algebraic expressions, each term of one expression is multiplied by each term of the other expression. For example:

$$\begin{aligned}(3x-4)(9y+x) &= 3x(9y+x)-4(9y+x)\\ &= (3x)(9y)+(3x)(x)+(-4)(9y)+(-4)(x)\\ &= 27xy+3x^2-36y-4x\end{aligned}$$

An algebraic expression can be evaluated by substituting values of the unknowns in the expression. For example, if $x = 3$ and $y = -2$, then $3xy - x^2 + y$ can be evaluated as

$$3(3)(-2)-(3)^2+(-2) = -18-9-2 = -29$$

2. Equations

A major focus of algebra is to solve equations involving algebraic expressions. Some examples of such equations are

$5x - 2 = 9 - x$ (a linear equation with one unknown)

$3x + 1 = y - 2$ (a linear equation with two unknowns)

$5x^2 + 3x - 2 = 7x$ (a quadratic equation with one unknown)

$\frac{x(x-3)(x^2+5)}{x-4} = 0$ (an equation that is factored on one side with 0 on the other)

The *solutions* of an equation with one or more unknowns are those values that make the equation true, or "satisfy the equation," when they are substituted for the unknowns of the equation. An equation may have no solution or one or more solutions. If two or more equations are to be solved together, the solutions must satisfy all the equations simultaneously.

Two equations having the same solution(s) are *equivalent equations.* For example, the equations

$$2 + x = 3$$
$$4 + 2x = 6$$

each have the unique solution $x = 1$. Note that the second equation is the first equation multiplied by 2. Similarly, the equations

$$3x - y = 6$$
$$6x - 2y = 12$$

have the same solutions, although in this case each equation has infinitely many solutions. If any value is assigned to x, then $3x - 6$ is a corresponding value for y that will satisfy both equations; for example, $x = 2$ and $y = 0$ is a solution to both equations, as is $x = 5$ and $y = 9$.

3. Solving Linear Equations with One Unknown

To solve a linear equation with one unknown (that is, to find the value of the unknown that satisfies the equation), the unknown should be isolated on one side of the equation. This can be done by performing the same mathematical operations on both sides of the equation. Remember that if the same number is added to or subtracted from both sides of the equation, this does not change the equality; likewise, multiplying or dividing both sides by the same nonzero number does not change the equality. For example, to solve the equation $\frac{5x-6}{3} = 4$ for x, the variable x can be isolated using the following steps:

$$5x - 6 = 12 \quad \text{(multiplying by 3)}$$
$$5x = 18 \quad \text{(adding 6)}$$
$$x = \frac{18}{5} \quad \text{(dividing by 5)}$$

The solution, $\frac{18}{5}$, can be checked by substituting it for x in the original equation to determine whether it satisfies that equation:

$$\frac{5\left(\frac{18}{5}\right)-6}{3} = \frac{18-6}{3} = \frac{12}{3} = 4$$

Therefore, $x = \frac{18}{5}$ is the solution.

4. Solving Two Linear Equations with Two Unknowns

For two linear equations with two unknowns, if the equations are equivalent, then there are infinitely many solutions to the equations, as illustrated at the end of section 3.2.2 ("Equations"). If the equations are not equivalent, then they have either one unique solution or no solution. The latter case is illustrated by the two equations:

$$3x + 4y = 17$$
$$6x + 8y = 35$$

Note that $3x + 4y = 17$ implies $6x + 8y = 34$, which contradicts the second equation. Thus, no values of x and y can simultaneously satisfy both equations.

There are several methods of solving two linear equations with two unknowns. With any method, if a contradiction is reached, then the equations have no solution; if a trivial equation such as $0 = 0$ is reached, then the equations are equivalent and have infinitely many solutions. Otherwise, a unique solution can be found.

One way to solve for the two unknowns is to express one of the unknowns in terms of the other using one of the equations, and then substitute the expression into the remaining equation to obtain an equation with one unknown. This equation can be solved and the value of the unknown substituted into either of the original equations to find the value of the other unknown. For example, the following two equations can be solved for x and y.

$$(1)\quad 3x + 2y = 11$$
$$(2)\quad x - y = 2$$

In equation (2), $x = 2 + y$. Substitute $2 + y$ in equation (1) for x:

$$3(2 + y) + 2y = 11$$
$$6 + 3y + 2y = 11$$
$$6 + 5y = 11$$
$$5y = 5$$
$$y = 1$$

If $y = 1$, then $x - 1 = 2$ and $x = 2 + 1 = 3$.

There is another way to solve for x and y by eliminating one of the unknowns. This can be done by making the coefficients of one of the unknowns the same (disregarding the sign) in both equations and either adding the equations or subtracting one equation from the other. For example, to solve the equations

$$(1)\quad 6x + 5y = 29$$
$$(2)\quad 4x - 3y = -6$$

by this method, multiply equation (1) by 3 and equation (2) by 5 to get

$$18x + 15y = 87$$
$$20x - 15y = -30$$

Adding the two equations eliminates y, yielding $38x = 57$, or $x = \frac{3}{2}$. Finally, substituting $\frac{3}{2}$ for x in one of the equations gives $y = 4$. These answers can be checked by substituting both values into both of the original equations.

5. Solving Equations by Factoring

Some equations can be solved by factoring. To do this, first add or subtract expressions to bring all the expressions to one side of the equation, with 0 on the other side. Then try to factor the nonzero side into a product of expressions. If this is possible, then using property (7) in section 3.1.4 ("Real Numbers"), each of the factors can be set equal to 0, yielding several simpler equations that possibly can be solved. The solutions of the simpler equations will be solutions of the factored equation. As an example, consider the equation $x^3 - 2x^2 + x = -5(x - 1)^2$:

$$\begin{aligned} x^3 - 2x^2 + x + 5(x-1)^2 &= 0 \\ x(x^2 - 2x + 1) + 5(x-1)^2 &= 0 \\ x(x-1)^2 + 5(x-1)^2 &= 0 \\ (x+5)(x-1)^2 &= 0 \\ x + 5 = 0 \text{ or } (x-1)^2 &= 0 \\ x = -5 \text{ or } x &= 1. \end{aligned}$$

For another example, consider $\frac{x(x-3)(x^2+5)}{x-4} = 0.$ A fraction equals 0 if and only if its numerator equals 0. Thus, $x(x - 3)(x^2 + 5) = 0$:

$$\begin{aligned} x = 0 \text{ or } x - 3 = 0 \text{ or } x^2 + 5 = 0 \\ x = 0 \text{ or } x = 3 \text{ or } x^2 + 5 = 0. \end{aligned}$$

But $x^2 + 5 = 0$ has no real solution because $x^2 + 5 > 0$ for every real number. Thus, the solutions are 0 and 3.

The solutions of an equation are also called the *roots* of the equation. These roots can be checked by substituting them into the original equation to determine whether they satisfy the equation.

6. Solving Quadratic Equations

The standard form for a *quadratic equation* is

$$ax^2 + bx + c = 0,$$

where a, b, and c are real numbers and $a \neq 0$; for example:

$$\begin{aligned} x^2 + 6x + 5 &= 0 \\ 3x^2 - 2x &= 0, \text{ and} \\ x^2 + 4 &= 0 \end{aligned}$$

Some quadratic equations can easily be solved by factoring. For example:

(1)
$$x^2+6x+5=0$$
$$(x+5)(x+1)=0$$
$$x+5=0 \text{ or } x+1=0$$
$$x=-5 \text{ or } x=-1$$

(2)
$$3x^2-3=8x$$
$$3x^2-8x-3=0$$
$$(3x+1)(x-3)=0$$
$$3x+1=0 \text{ or } x-3=0$$
$$x=-\frac{1}{3} \text{ or } x=3$$

A quadratic equation has at most two real roots and may have just one or even no real root. For example, the equation $x^2-6x+9=0$ can be expressed as $(x-3)^2=0$, or $(x-3)(x-3)=0$; thus the only root is 3. The equation $x^2+4=0$ has no real root; since the square of any real number is greater than or equal to zero, x^2+4 must be greater than zero.

An expression of the form a^2-b^2 can be factored as $(a-b)(a+b)$.

For example, the quadratic equation $9x^2-25=0$ can be solved as follows.

$$(3x-5)(3x+5)=0$$
$$3x-5=0 \text{ or } 3x+5=0$$
$$x=\frac{5}{3} \text{ or } x=-\frac{5}{3}$$

If a quadratic expression is not easily factored, then its roots can always be found using the *quadratic formula:* If $ax^2+bx+c=0$ $(a \neq 0)$, then the roots are

$$x=\frac{-b+\sqrt{b^2-4ac}}{2a} \text{ and } x=\frac{-b-\sqrt{b^2-4ac}}{2a}$$

These are two distinct real numbers unless $b^2-4ac \le 0$. If $b^2-4ac=0$, then these two expressions for x are equal to $-\frac{b}{2a}$, and the equation has only one root. If $b^2-4ac<0$, then $\sqrt{b^2-4ac}$ is not a real number and the equation has no real roots.

7. Exponents

A positive integer exponent of a number or a variable indicates a product, and the positive integer is the number of times that the number or variable is a factor in the product. For example, x^5 means $(x)(x)(x)(x)(x)$; that is, x is a factor in the product 5 times.

Some rules about exponents follow.

Let x and y be any positive numbers, and let r and s be any positive integers.

(1) $(x^r)(x^s) = x^{(r+s)}$; for example, $(2^2)(2^3) = 2^{(2+3)} = 2^5 = 32$.

(2) $\frac{x^r}{x^s} = x^{(r-s)}$; for example, $\frac{4^5}{4^2} = 4^{5-2} = 4^3 = 64$.

(3) $(x^r)(y^r) = (xy)^r$; for example, $(3^3)(4^3) = 12^3 = 1{,}728$.

(4) $\left(\frac{x}{y}\right)^r = \frac{x^r}{y^r}$; for example, $\left(\frac{2}{3}\right)^3 = \frac{2^3}{3^3} = \frac{8}{27}$.

(5) $(x^r)^s = x^{rs} = (x^s)^r$; for example, $(x^3)^4 = x^{12} = (x^4)^3$.

(6) $x^{-r} = \frac{1}{x^r}$; for example, $3^{-2} = \frac{1}{3^2} = \frac{1}{9}$.

(7) $x^0 = 1$; for example, $6^0 = 1$.

(8) $x^{\frac{r}{s}} = \left(x^{\frac{1}{s}}\right)^r = \left(x^r\right)^{\frac{1}{s}} = \sqrt[s]{x^r}$; for example, $8^{\frac{2}{3}} = \left(8^{\frac{1}{3}}\right)^2 = \left(8^2\right)^{\frac{1}{3}} = \sqrt[3]{8^2} = \sqrt[3]{64} = 4$ and $9^{\frac{1}{2}} = \sqrt{9} = 3$.

It can be shown that rules 1 – 6 also apply when r and s are not integers and are not positive, that is, when r and s are any real numbers.

8. Inequalities

An *inequality* is a statement that uses one of the following symbols:

$\neq$ not equal to

$>$ greater than

$\geq$ greater than or equal to

$<$ less than

$\leq$ less than or equal to

Some examples of inequalities are $5x - 3 < 9$, $6x \geq y$, and $\frac{1}{2} < \frac{3}{4}$. Solving a linear inequality with one unknown is similar to solving an equation; the unknown is isolated on one side of the inequality. As in solving an equation, the same number can be added to or subtracted from both sides of the inequality, or both sides of an inequality can be multiplied or divided by a positive number without changing the truth of the inequality. However, multiplying or dividing an inequality by a negative number reverses the order of the inequality. For example, $6 > 2$, but $(-1)(6) < (-1)(2)$.

To solve the inequality $3x - 2 > 5$ for x, isolate x by using the following steps:

$$3x - 2 > 5$$

$$3x > 7 \quad \text{(adding 2 to both sides)}$$

$$x > \frac{7}{3} \quad \text{(dividing both sides by 3)}$$

To solve the inequality $\frac{5x-1}{-2} < 3$ for x, isolate x by using the following steps:

$$\frac{5x-1}{-2} < 3$$

$5x-1 > -6$ (multiplying both sides by -2)

$5x > -5$ (adding 1 to both sides)

$x > -1$ (dividing both sides by 5)

9. Absolute Value

The absolute value of x, denoted $|x|$, is defined to be x if $x \geq 0$ and $-x$ if $x < 0$. Note that $\sqrt{x^2}$ denotes the nonnegative square root of x^2, and so $\sqrt{x^2} = |x|$.

10. Functions

An algebraic expression in one variable can be used to define a *function* of that variable. A function is denoted by a letter such as f or g along with the variable in the expression. For example, the expression $x^3 - 5x^2 + 2$ defines a function f that can be denoted by

$$f(x) = x^3 - 5x^2 + 2.$$

The expression $\frac{2z+7}{\sqrt{z+1}}$ defines a function g that can be denoted by

$$g(z) = \frac{2z+7}{\sqrt{z+1}}.$$

The symbols "$f(x)$" or "$g(z)$" do not represent products; each is merely the symbol for an expression, and is read "f of x" or "g of z."

Function notation provides a short way of writing the result of substituting a value for a variable. If $x = 1$ is substituted in the first expression, the result can be written $f(1) = -2$, and $f(1)$ is called the "value of f at $x = 1$." Similarly, if $z = 0$ is substituted in the second expression, then the value of g at $z = 0$ is $g(0) = 7$.

Once a function $f(x)$ is defined, it is useful to think of the variable x as an input and $f(x)$ as the corresponding output. In any function there can be no more than one output for any given input. However, more than one input can give the same output; for example, if $h(x) = |x + 3|$, then $h(-4) = 1 = h(-2)$.

The set of all allowable inputs for a function is called the *domain* of the function. For f and g defined above, the domain of f is the set of all real numbers and the domain of g is the set of all numbers greater than -1. The domain of any function can be arbitrarily specified, as in the function defined by "$h(x) = 9x - 5$ for $0 \leq x \leq 10$." Without such a restriction, the domain is assumed to be all values of x that result in a real number when substituted into the function.

The domain of a function can consist of only the positive integers and possibly 0. For example, $a(n) = n^2 + \frac{n}{5}$ for $n = 0, 1, 2, 3, \ldots$ . .

Such a function is called a *sequence* and $a(n)$ is denoted by a_n. The value of the sequence a_n at $n = 3$ is $a_3 = 3^2 + \frac{3}{5} = 9.60$. As another example, consider the sequence defined by $b_n = (-1)^n(n!)$ for $n = 1, 2, 3, \ldots$ . . . A sequence like this is often indicated by listing its values in the order $b_1, b_2, b_3, \ldots, b_n, \ldots$ as follows:

$-1, 2, -6, \ldots, (-1)^n(n!), \ldots$, and $(-1)^n(n!)$ is called the nth term of the sequence.

3.3 Geometry

1. Lines

In geometry, the word "line" refers to a straight line that extends without end in both directions.

The line above can be referred to as line PQ or line ℓ. The part of the line from P to Q is called a *line segment*. P and Q are the *endpoints* of the segment. The notation $\overline{PQ}$ is used to denote line segment PQ and PQ is used to denote the length of the segment.

2. Intersecting Lines and Angles

If two lines intersect, the opposite angles are called *vertical angles* and have the same measure. In the figure

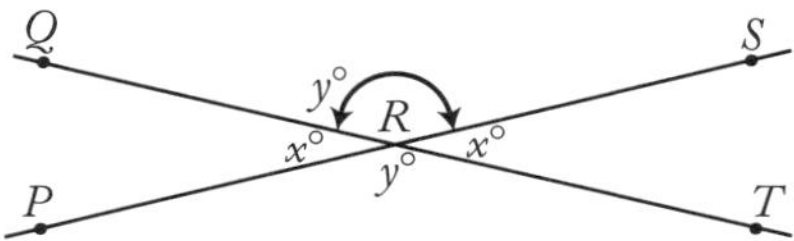

$\angle PRQ$ and $\angle SRT$ are vertical angles and $\angle QRS$ and $\angle PRT$ are vertical angles. Also, $x + y = 180°$ since PRS is a straight line.

3. Perpendicular Lines

An angle that has a measure of 90° is a *right angle*. If two lines intersect at right angles, the lines are *perpendicular*. For example:

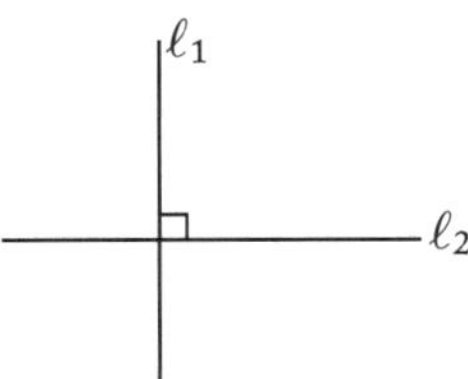

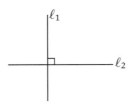

ℓ_1 and ℓ_2 above are perpendicular, denoted by $\ell_1 \perp \ell_2$. A right angle symbol in an angle of intersection indicates that the lines are perpendicular.

4. Parallel Lines

If two lines that are in the same plane do not intersect, the two lines are *parallel*. In the figure

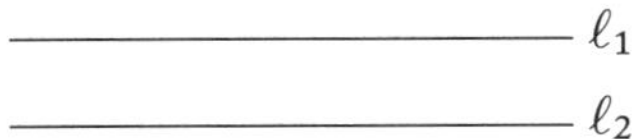

lines ℓ_1 and ℓ_2 are parallel, denoted by $\ell_1 \parallel \ell_2$. If two parallel lines are intersected by a third line, as shown below, then the angle measures are related as indicated, where $x + y = 180°$.

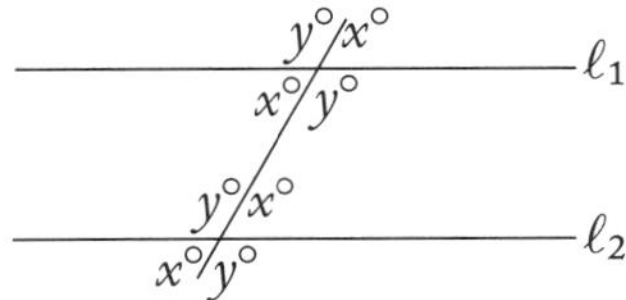

5. Polygons (Convex)

A *polygon* is a closed plane figure formed by three or more line segments, called the *sides* of the polygon. Each side intersects exactly two other sides at their endpoints. The points of intersection of the sides are *vertices*. The term "polygon" will be used to mean a convex polygon, that is, a polygon in which each interior angle has a measure of less than 180°.

The following figures are polygons:

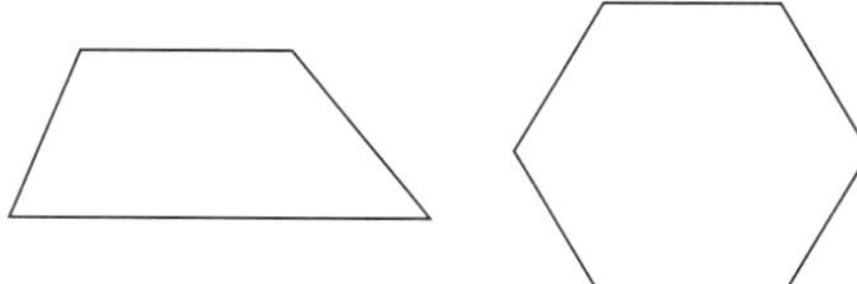

The following figures are not polygons:

A polygon with three sides is a *triangle*; with four sides, a *quadrilateral*; with five sides, a *pentagon*; and with six sides, a *hexagon*.

The sum of the interior angle measures of a triangle is 180°. In general, the sum of the interior angle measures of a polygon with n sides is equal to $(n - 2)180°$. For example, this sum for a pentagon is $(5 - 2)180° = (3)180° = 540°$.

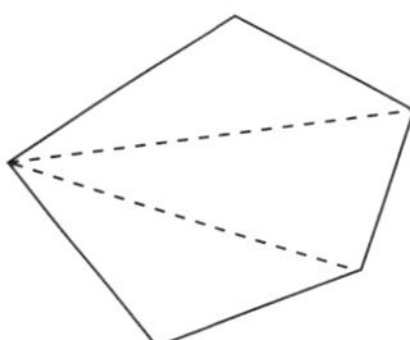

Note that a pentagon can be partitioned into three triangles and therefore the sum of the angle measures can be found by adding the sum of the angle measures of three triangles.

The *perimeter* of a polygon is the sum of the lengths of its sides.

The commonly used phrase "area of a triangle" (or any other plane figure) is used to mean the area of the region enclosed by that figure.

6. Triangles

There are several special types of triangles with important properties. But one property that all triangles share is that the sum of the lengths of any two of the sides is greater than the length of the third side, as illustrated below.

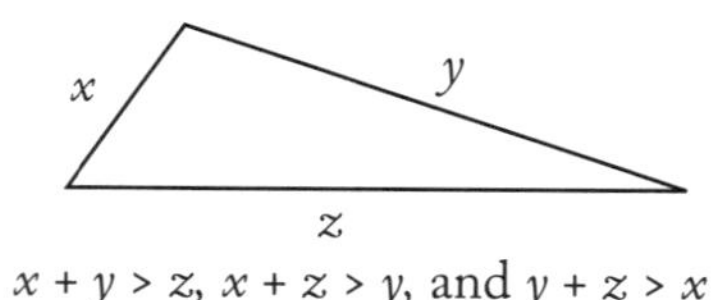

$x + y > z$, $x + z > y$, and $y + z > x$

An *equilateral* triangle has all sides of equal length. All angles of an equilateral triangle have equal measure. An *isosceles* triangle has at least two sides of the same length. If two sides of a triangle have the same length, then the two angles opposite those sides have the same measure. Conversely, if two angles of a triangle have the same measure, then the sides opposite those angles have the same length. In isosceles triangle PQR below, $x = y$ since $PQ = QR$.

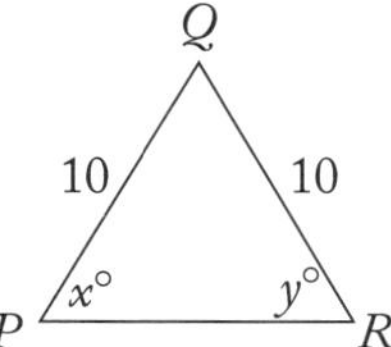

A triangle that has a right angle is a *right* triangle. In a right triangle, the side opposite the right angle is the *hypotenuse,* and the other two sides are the *legs.* An important theorem concerning right triangles is the *Pythagorean theorem,* which states: In a right triangle, the square of the length of the hypotenuse is equal to the sum of the squares of the lengths of the legs.

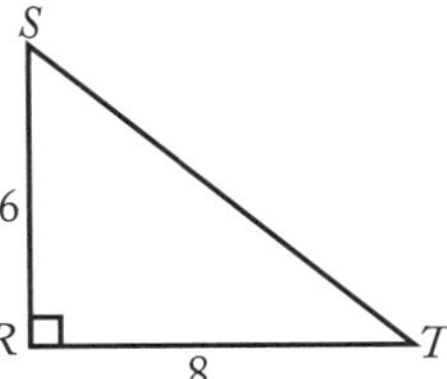

In the figure above, ΔRST is a right triangle, so $(RS)^2 + (RT)^2 = (ST)^2$. Here, $RS = 6$ and $RT = 8$, so $ST = 10$, since $6^2 + 8^2 = 36 + 64 = 100 = (ST)^2$ and $ST = \sqrt{100}$. Any triangle in which the lengths of the sides are in the ratio 3:4:5 is a right triangle. In general, if a, b, and c are the lengths of the sides of a triangle and $a^2 + b^2 = c^2$, then the triangle is a right triangle.

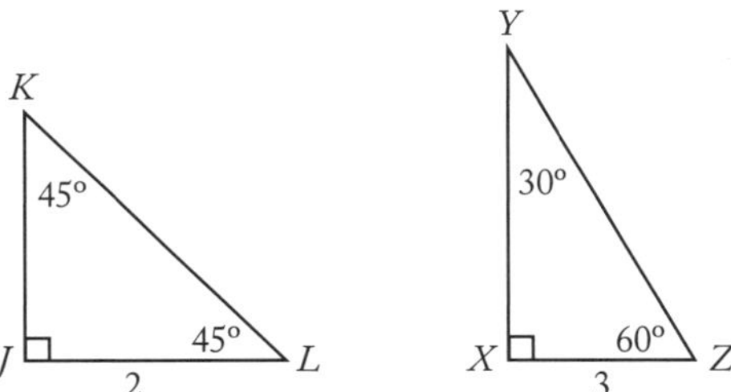

In 45°– 45°– 90° triangles, the lengths of the sides are in the ratio $1:1:\sqrt{2}$. For example, in ΔJKL, if $JL = 2$, then $JK = 2$ and $KL = 2\sqrt{2}$. In 30°– 60°– 90° triangles, the lengths of the sides are in the ratio $1:\sqrt{3}:2$. For example, in ΔXYZ, if $XZ = 3$, then $XY = 3\sqrt{3}$ and $YZ = 6$.

The *altitude* of a triangle is the segment drawn from a vertex perpendicular to the side opposite that vertex. Relative to that vertex and altitude, the opposite side is called the *base.*

The area of a triangle is equal to:

$$\frac{(\text{the length of the altitude}) \times (\text{the length of the base})}{2}$$

$BD = 5$

In ΔABC, $\overline{BD}$ is the altitude to base $\overline{AC}$ and $\overline{AE}$ is the altitude to base $\overline{BC}$. The area of ΔABC is equal to

$$\frac{BD \times AC}{2} = \frac{5 \times 8}{2} = 20.$$

The area is also equal to $\frac{AE \times BC}{2}$. If ΔABC above is isosceles and $AB = BC$, then altitude $\overline{BD}$ bisects the base; that is, $AD = DC = 4$. Similarly, any altitude of an equilateral triangle bisects the side to which it is drawn.

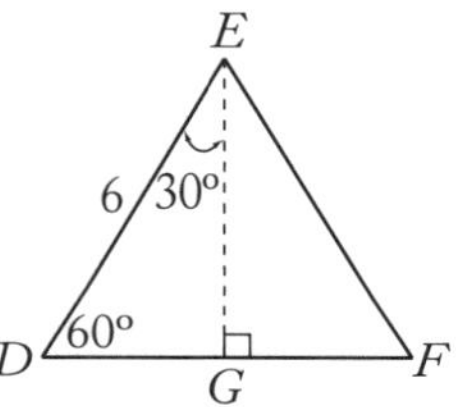

In equilateral triangle DEF, if $DE = 6$, then $DG = 3$ and $EG = 3\sqrt{3}$. The area of ΔDEF is equal to $\frac{3\sqrt{3} \times 6}{2} = 9\sqrt{3}$.

7. Quadrilaterals

A polygon with four sides is a *quadrilateral*. A quadrilateral in which both pairs of opposite sides are parallel is a *parallelogram*. The opposite sides of a parallelogram also have equal length.

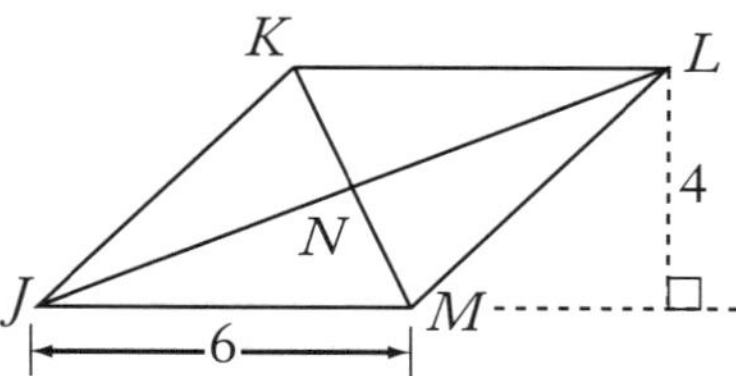

In parallelogram $JKLM$, $\overline{JK} \parallel \overline{LM}$ and $JK = LM$; $\overline{KL} \parallel \overline{JM}$ and $KL = JM$.

The diagonals of a parallelogram bisect each other (that is, $KN = NM$ and $JN = NL$).

The area of a parallelogram is equal to

(the length of the altitude) $\times$ (the length of the base).

The area of $JKLM$ is equal to $4 \times 6 = 24$.

A parallelogram with right angles is a *rectangle,* and a rectangle with all sides of equal length is a *square.*

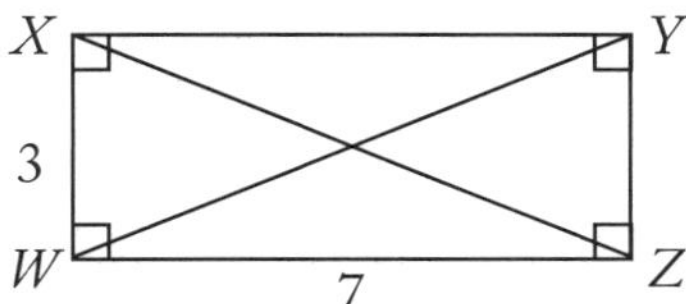

The perimeter of $WXYZ = 2(3) + 2(7) = 20$ and the area of $WXYZ$ is equal to $3 \times 7 = 21$. The diagonals of a rectangle are equal; therefore $WY = XZ = \sqrt{9+49} = \sqrt{58}$.

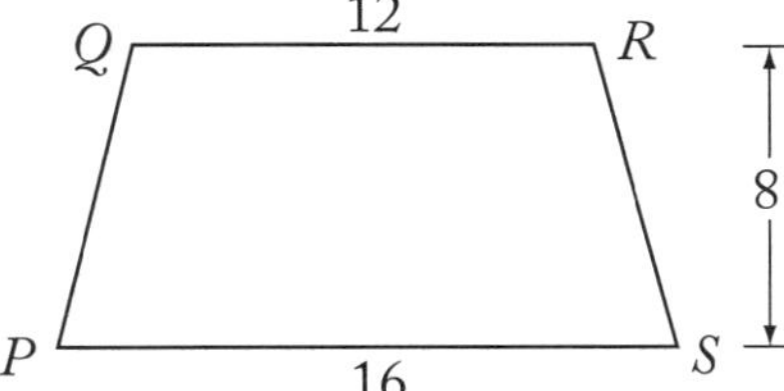

A quadrilateral with two sides that are parallel, as shown above, is a *trapezoid.* The area of trapezoid $PQRS$ may be calculated as follows:

$$\frac{1}{2}(\text{the sum of the lengths of the bases})(\text{the height}) = \frac{1}{2}(QR + PS)(8) = \frac{1}{2}(28 \times 8) = 112.$$

8. Circles

A *circle* is a set of points in a plane that are all located the same distance from a fixed point (the *center* of the circle).

A *chord* of a circle is a line segment that has its endpoints on the circle. A chord that passes through the center of the circle is a *diameter* of the circle. A *radius* of a circle is a segment from the center of the circle to a point on the circle. The words "diameter" and "radius" are also used to refer to the lengths of these segments.

The *circumference* of a circle is the distance around the circle. If r is the radius of the circle, then the circumference is equal to $2\pi r$, where π is approximately $\frac{22}{7}$ or 3.14. The *area* of a circle of radius r is equal to πr^2.

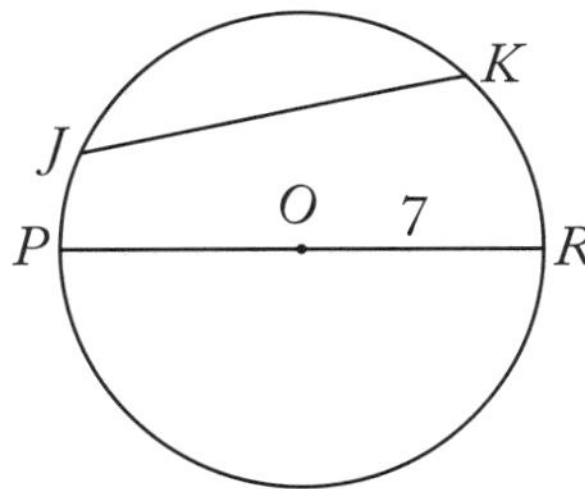

In the circle above, O is the center of the circle and $\overline{JK}$ and $\overline{PR}$ are chords. $\overline{PR}$ is a diameter and $\overline{OR}$ is a radius. If $OR = 7$, then the circumference of the circle is $2\pi(7) = 14\pi$ and the area of the circle is $\pi(7)^2 = 49\pi$.

The number of degrees of arc in a circle (or the number of degrees in a complete revolution) is 360.

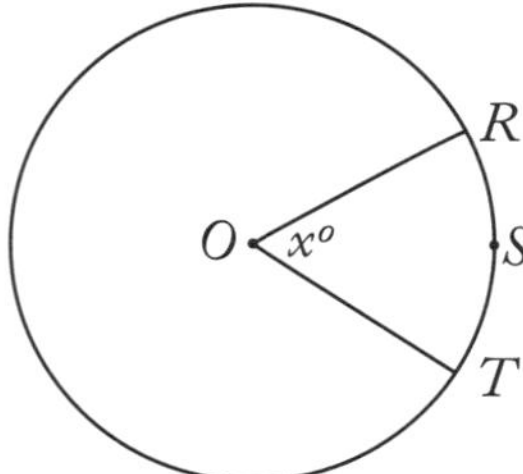

In the circle with center O above, the length of arc RST is $\frac{x}{360}$ of the circumference of the circle; for example, if $x = 60$, then arc RST has length $\frac{1}{6}$ of the circumference of the circle.

A line that has exactly one point in common with a circle is said to be *tangent* to the circle, and that common point is called the *point of tangency.* A radius or diameter with an endpoint at the point of tangency is perpendicular to the tangent line, and, conversely, a line that is perpendicular to a radius or diameter at one of its endpoints is tangent to the circle at that endpoint.

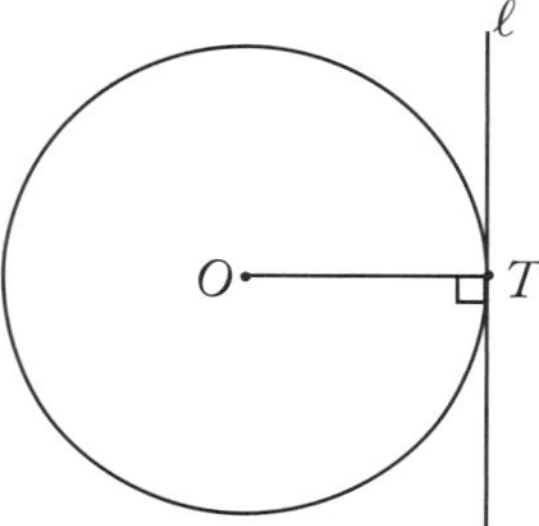

The line ℓ above is tangent to the circle and radius $\overline{OT}$ is perpendicular to ℓ.

If each vertex of a polygon lies on a circle, then the polygon is *inscribed* in the circle and the circle is *circumscribed* about the polygon. If each side of a polygon is tangent to a circle, then the polygon is *circumscribed* about the circle and the circle is *inscribed* in the polygon.

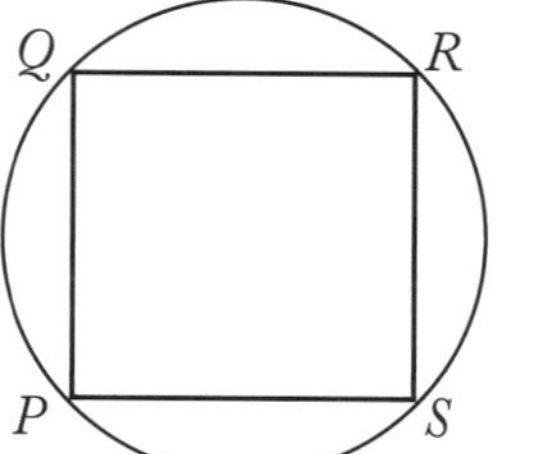

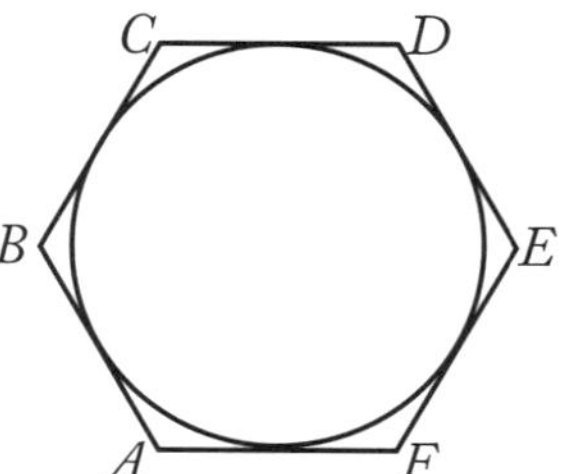

In the figure above, quadrilateral $PQRS$ is inscribed in a circle and hexagon $ABCDEF$ is circumscribed about a circle.

If a triangle is inscribed in a circle so that one of its sides is a diameter of the circle, then the triangle is a right triangle.

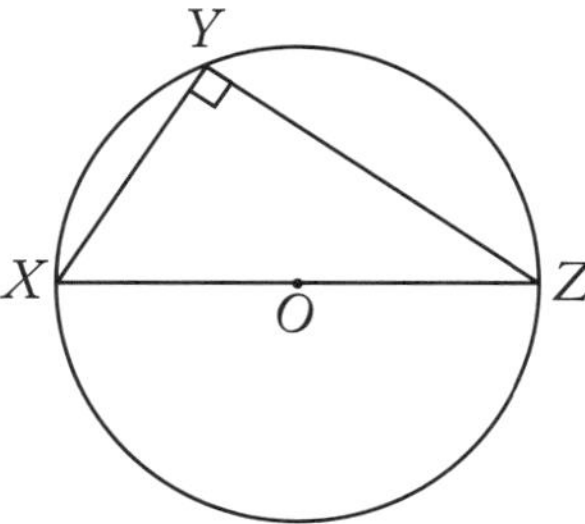

In the circle above, $\overline{XZ}$ is a diameter and the measure of $\angle XYZ$ is 90°.

9. Rectangular Solids and Cylinders

A *rectangular solid* is a three-dimensional figure formed by 6 rectangular surfaces, as shown below. Each rectangular surface is a *face*. Each solid or dotted line segment is an *edge,* and each point at which the edges meet is a *vertex.* A rectangular solid has 6 faces, 12 edges, and 8 vertices. Opposite faces are parallel rectangles that have the same dimensions. A rectangular solid in which all edges are of equal length is a *cube.*

The *surface area* of a rectangular solid is equal to the sum of the areas of all the faces. The *volume* is equal to

$$(\text{length}) \times (\text{width}) \times (\text{height});$$

$$\text{in other words, } (\text{area of base}) \times (\text{height}).$$

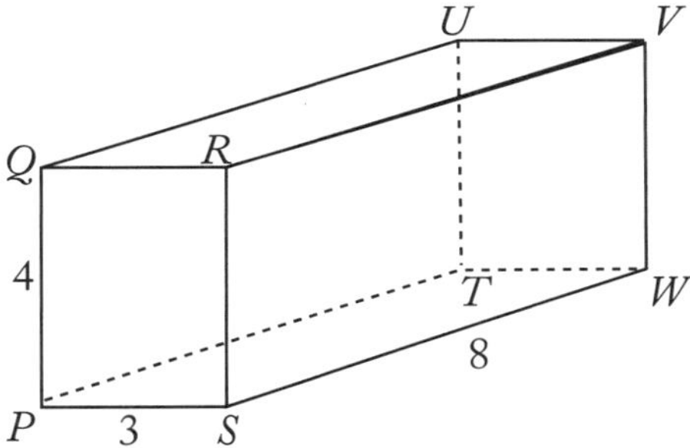

In the rectangular solid above, the dimensions are 3, 4, and 8. The surface area is equal to $2(3 \times 4) + 2(3 \times 8) + 2(4 \times 8) = 136$. The volume is equal to $3 \times 4 \times 8 = 96$.

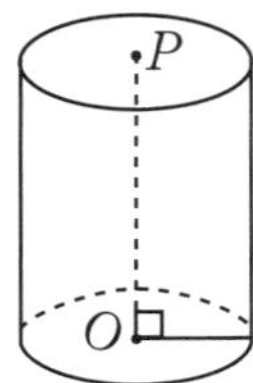

The figure above is a right circular *cylinder*. The two bases are circles of the same size with centers O and P, respectively, and altitude (height) $\overline{OP}$ is perpendicular to the bases. The surface area of a right circular cylinder with a base of radius r and height h is equal to $2(\pi r^2) + 2\pi rh$ (the sum of the areas of the two bases plus the area of the curved surface).

The volume of a cylinder is equal to $\pi r^2 h$, that is,

$$\text{(area of base)} \times \text{(height)}.$$

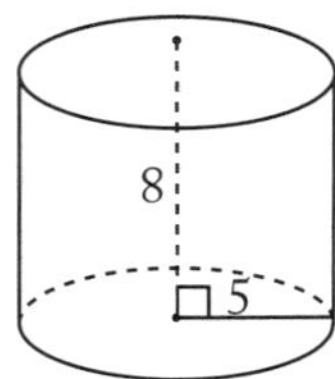

In the cylinder above, the surface area is equal to

$$2(25\pi) + 2\pi(5)(8) = 130\pi,$$

and the volume is equal to

$$25\pi(8) = 200\pi.$$

10. Coordinate Geometry

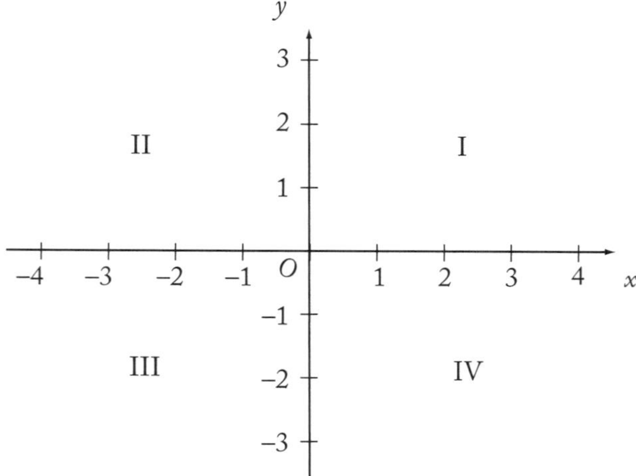

The figure above shows the (rectangular) *coordinate plane*. The horizontal line is called the *x-axis* and the perpendicular vertical line is called the *y-axis*. The point at which these two axes intersect, designated O, is called the *origin*. The axes divide the plane into four quadrants, I, II, III, and IV, as shown.

Each point in the plane has an *x-coordinate* and a *y-coordinate.* A point is identified by an ordered pair (x,y) of numbers in which the x-coordinate is the first number and the y-coordinate is the second number.

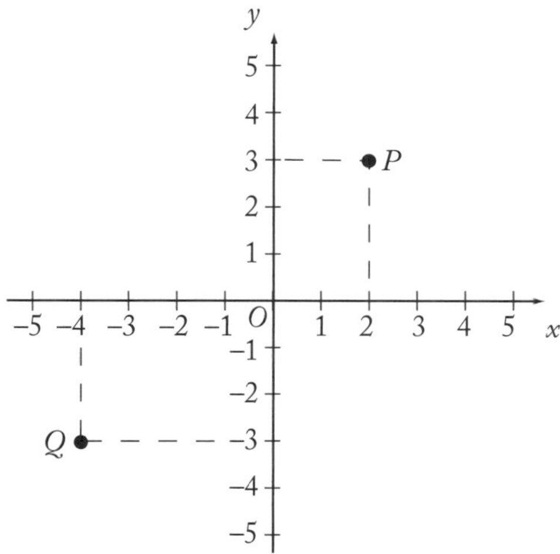

In the graph above, the (x,y) coordinates of point P are (2,3) since P is 2 units to the right of the y-axis (that is, $x = 2$) and 3 units above the x-axis (that is, $y = 3$). Similarly, the (x,y) coordinates of point Q are (−4,−3). The origin O has coordinates (0,0).

One way to find the distance between two points in the coordinate plane is to use the Pythagorean theorem.

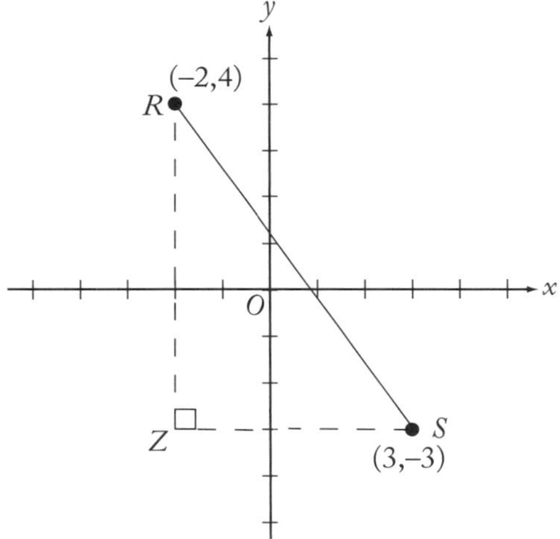

To find the distance between points R and S using the Pythagorean theorem, draw the triangle as shown. Note that Z has (x,y) coordinates (−2,−3), $RZ = 7$, and $ZS = 5$. Therefore, the distance between R and S is equal to

$$\sqrt{7^2 + 5^2} = \sqrt{74}.$$

For a line in the coordinate plane, the coordinates of each point on the line satisfy a linear equation of the form $y = mx + b$ (or the form $x = a$ if the line is vertical). For example, each point on the line on the next page satisfies the equation $y = -\frac{1}{2}x + 1$. One can verify this for the points (−2,2), (2,0), and (0,1) by substituting the respective coordinates for x and y in the equation.

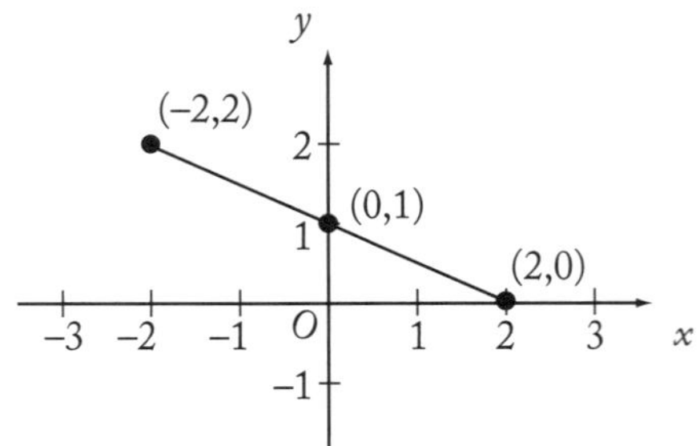

In the equation $y = mx + b$ of a line, the coefficient m is the *slope* of the line and the constant term b is the y-intercept of the line. For any two points on the line, the slope is defined to be the ratio of the difference in the y-coordinates to the difference in the x-coordinates. Using (–2, 2) and (2, 0) above, the slope is

$$\frac{\text{The difference in the } y\text{-coordinates}}{\text{The difference in the } x\text{-coordinates}} = \frac{0-2}{2-(-2)} = \frac{-2}{4} = -\frac{1}{2}.$$

The y-intercept is the y-coordinate of the point at which the line intersects the y-axis. For the line above, the y-intercept is 1, and this is the resulting value of y when x is set equal to 0 in the equation $y = -\frac{1}{2}x + 1$. The x-intercept is the x-coordinate of the point at which the line intersects the x-axis. The x-intercept can be found by setting $y = 0$ and solving for x. For the line $y = -\frac{1}{2}x + 1$, this gives

$$-\frac{1}{2}x + 1 = 0$$
$$-\frac{1}{2}x = -1$$
$$x = 2.$$

Thus, the x-intercept is 2.

Given any two points (x_1, y_1) and (x_2, y_2) with $x_1 \neq x_2$, the equation of the line passing through these points can be found by applying the definition of slope. Since the slope is $m = \frac{y_2 - y_1}{x_2 - x_1}$, then using a point known to be on the line, say (x_1, y_1), any point (x, y) on the line must satisfy $\frac{y - y_1}{x - x_1} = m$, or $y - y_1 = m(x - x_1)$. (Using (x_2, y_2) as the known point would yield an equivalent equation.) For example, consider the points (–2,4) and (3,–3) on the line below.

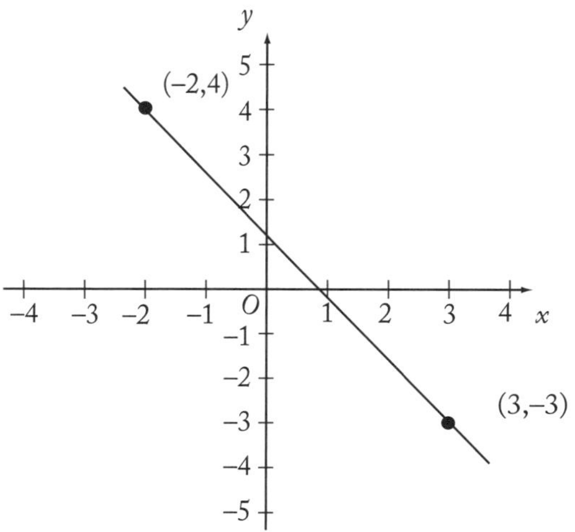

The slope of this line is $\frac{-3-4}{3-(-2)} = \frac{-7}{5}$, so an equation of this line can be found using the point (3,–3) as follows:

$$y-(-3) = -\frac{7}{5}(x-3)$$
$$y+3 = -\frac{7}{5}x + \frac{21}{5}$$
$$y = -\frac{7}{5}x + \frac{6}{5}$$

The y-intercept is $\frac{6}{5}$. The x-intercept can be found as follows:

$$0 = -\frac{7}{5}x + \frac{6}{5}$$
$$\frac{7}{5}x = \frac{6}{5}$$
$$x = \frac{6}{7}$$

Both of these intercepts can be seen on the graph.

If the slope of a line is negative, the line slants downward from left to right; if the slope is positive, the line slants upward. If the slope is 0, the line is horizontal; the equation of such a line is of the form $y = b$ since $m = 0$. For a vertical line, slope is not defined, and the equation is of the form $x = a$, where a is the x-intercept.

There is a connection between graphs of lines in the coordinate plane and solutions of two linear equations with two unknowns. If two linear equations with unknowns x and y have a unique solution, then the graphs of the equations are two lines that intersect in one point, which is the solution. If the equations are equivalent, then they represent the same line with infinitely many points or solutions. If the equations have no solution, then they represent parallel lines, which do not intersect.

There is also a connection between functions (see section 3.2.10) and the coordinate plane. If a function is graphed in the coordinate plane, the function can be understood in different and useful ways. Consider the function defined by

$$f(x) = -\frac{7}{5}x + \frac{6}{5}.$$

If the value of the function, $f(x)$, is equated with the variable y, then the graph of the function in the xy-coordinate plane is simply the graph of the equation

$$y = -\frac{7}{5}x + \frac{6}{5}$$

shown above. Similarly, any function $f(x)$ can be graphed by equating y with the value of the function:

$$y = f(x).$$

So for any x in the domain of the function f, the point with coordinates $(x, f(x))$ is on the graph of f, and the graph consists entirely of these points.

As another example, consider a quadratic polynomial function defined by $f(x) = x^2 - 1$. One can plot several points $(x, f(x))$ on the graph to understand the connection between a function and its graph:

x	$f(x)$
–2	3
–1	0
0	–1
1	0
2	3

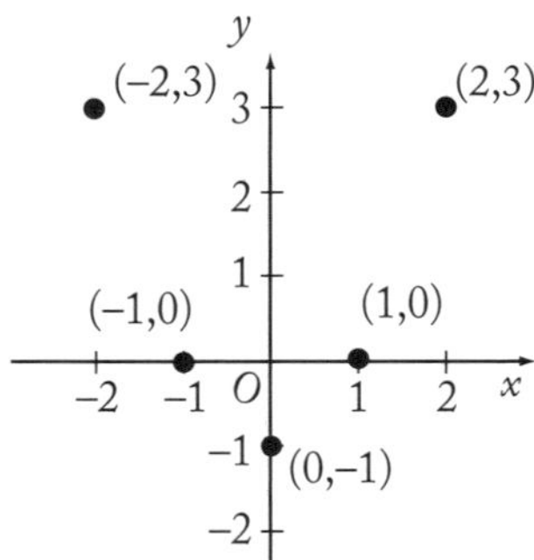

If all the points were graphed for $-2 \leq x \leq 2$, then the graph would appear as follows.

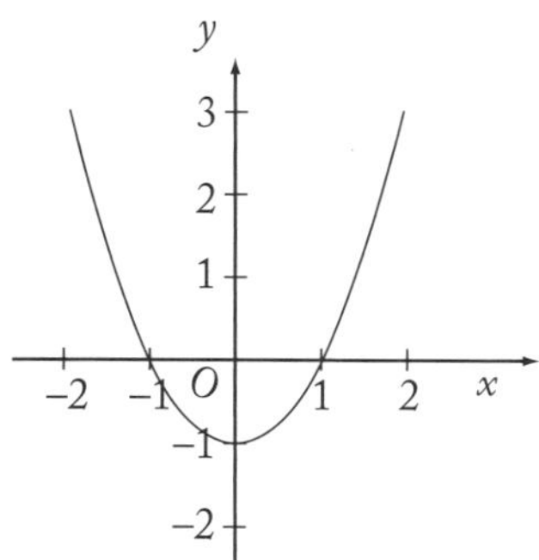

The graph of a quadratic function is called a *parabola* and always has the shape of the curve above, although it may be upside down or have a greater or lesser width. Note that the roots of the equation $f(x) = x^2 - 1 = 0$ are $x = 1$ and $x = -1$; these coincide with the x-intercepts since x-intercepts are found by setting $y = 0$ and solving for x. Also, the y-intercept is $f(0) = -1$ because this is the value of y corresponding to $x = 0$. For any function f, the x-intercepts are the solutions of the equation $f(x) = 0$ and the y-intercept is the value $f(0)$.

3.4 Word Problems

Many of the principles discussed in this chapter are used to solve word problems. The following discussion of word problems illustrates some of the techniques and concepts used in solving such problems.

1. Rate Problems

The distance that an object travels is equal to the product of the average speed at which it travels and the amount of time it takes to travel that distance, that is,

$$\text{Rate} \times \text{Time} = \text{Distance}.$$

Example 1: If a car travels at an average speed of 70 kilometers per hour for 4 hours, how many kilometers does it travel?

Solution: Since rate × time = distance, simply multiply 70 km/hour × 4 hours. Thus, the car travels 280 kilometers in 4 hours.

To determine the average rate at which an object travels, divide the total distance traveled by the total amount of traveling time.

Example 2: On a 400-mile trip, Car X traveled half the distance at 40 miles per hour (mph) and the other half at 50 mph. What was the average speed of Car X ?

Solution: First it is necessary to determine the amount of traveling time. During the first 200 miles, the car traveled at 40 mph; therefore, it took $\frac{200}{40} = 5$ hours to travel the first 200 miles. During the second 200 miles, the car traveled at 50 mph; therefore, it took $\frac{200}{50} = 4$ hours to travel the second 200 miles. Thus, the average speed of Car X was $\frac{400}{9} = 44\frac{4}{9}$ mph. Note that the average speed is *not* $\frac{40+50}{2} = 45$.

Some rate problems can be solved by using ratios.

Example 3: If 5 shirts cost \$44, then, at this rate, what is the cost of 8 shirts?

Solution: If c is the cost of the 8 shirts, then $\frac{5}{44}=\frac{8}{c}$. Cross multiplication results in the equation

$$5c = 8 \times 44 = 352$$

$$c = \frac{352}{5} = 70.40$$

The 8 shirts cost \$70.40.

2. Work Problems

In a work problem, the rates at which certain persons or machines work alone are usually given, and it is necessary to compute the rate at which they work together (or vice versa).

The basic formula for solving work problems is $\frac{1}{r}+\frac{1}{s}=\frac{1}{h}$, where r and s are, for example, the number of hours it takes Rae and Sam, respectively, to complete a job when working alone, and h is the number of hours it takes Rae and Sam to do the job when working together. The reasoning is that in 1 hour Rae does $\frac{1}{r}$ of the job, Sam does $\frac{1}{s}$ of the job, and Rae and Sam together do $\frac{1}{h}$ of the job.

Example 1: If Machine X can produce 1,000 bolts in 4 hours and Machine Y can produce 1,000 bolts in 5 hours, in how many hours can Machines X and Y, working together at these constant rates, produce 1,000 bolts?

Solution:

$$\frac{1}{4}+\frac{1}{5}=\frac{1}{h}$$

$$\frac{5}{20}+\frac{4}{20}=\frac{1}{h}$$

$$\frac{9}{20}=\frac{1}{h}$$

$$9h = 20$$

$$h=\frac{20}{9}=2\frac{2}{9}$$

Working together, Machines X and Y can produce 1,000 bolts in $2\frac{2}{9}$ hours.

Example 2: If Art and Rita can do a job in 4 hours when working together at their respective constant rates and Art can do the job alone in 6 hours, in how many hours can Rita do the job alone?

Solution:

$$
\begin{aligned}
\frac{1}{6}+\frac{1}{R}&=\frac{1}{4}\\
\frac{R+6}{6R}&=\frac{1}{4}\\
4R+24&=6R\\
24&=2R\\
12&=R
\end{aligned}
$$

Working alone, Rita can do the job in 12 hours.

3. Mixture Problems

In mixture problems, substances with different characteristics are combined, and it is necessary to determine the characteristics of the resulting mixture.

Example 1: If 6 pounds of nuts that cost \$1.20 per pound are mixed with 2 pounds of nuts that cost \$1.60 per pound, what is the cost per pound of the mixture?

Solution: The total cost of the 8 pounds of nuts is

$$6(\$1.20)+2(\$1.60)=\$10.40.$$

The cost per pound is

$$\frac{\$10.40}{8}=\$1.30.$$

Example 2: How many liters of a solution that is 15 percent salt must be added to 5 liters of a solution that is 8 percent salt so that the resulting solution is 10 percent salt?

Solution: Let n represent the number of liters of the 15% solution. The amount of salt in the 15% solution $[0.15n]$ plus the amount of salt in the 8% solution $[(0.08)(5)]$ must be equal to the amount of salt in the 10% mixture $[0.10(n + 5)]$. Therefore,

$$
\begin{aligned}
0.15n+0.08(5)&=0.10(n+5)\\
15n+40&=10n+50\\
5n&=10\\
n&=2\text{ liters}
\end{aligned}
$$

Two liters of the 15% salt solution must be added to the 8% solution to obtain the 10% solution.

4. Interest Problems

Interest can be computed in two basic ways. With simple annual interest, the interest is computed on the principal only and is equal to (principal) × (interest rate) × (time). If interest is compounded, then interest is computed on the principal as well as on any interest already earned.

Example 1: If \$8,000 is invested at 6 percent simple annual interest, how much interest is earned after 3 months?

Solution: Since the annual interest rate is 6%, the interest for 1 year is

$$(0.06)(\$8,000) = \$480.$$

The interest earned in 3 months is $\frac{3}{12}(\$480) = \$120.$

Example 2: If \$10,000 is invested at 10 percent annual interest, compounded semiannually, what is the balance after 1 year?

Solution: The balance after the first 6 months would be

$$10,000 + (10,000)(0.05) = \$10,500.$$

The balance after one year would be $10,500 + (10,500)(0.05) = \$11,025.$

Note that the interest rate for each 6-month period is 5%, which is half of the 10% annual rate. The balance after one year can also be expressed as

$$10,000\left(1 + \frac{0.10}{2}\right)^2 \text{ dollars.}$$

5. Discount

If a price is discounted by n percent, then the price becomes $(100 - n)$ percent of the original price.

Example 1: A certain customer paid \$24 for a dress. If that price represented a 25 percent discount on the original price of the dress, what was the original price of the dress?

Solution: If p is the original price of the dress, then $0.75p$ is the discounted price and $0.75p = \$24$, or $p = \$32$. The original price of the dress was \$32.

Example 2: The price of an item is discounted by 20 percent and then this reduced price is discounted by an additional 30 percent. These two discounts are equal to an overall discount of what percent?

Solution: If p is the original price of the item, then $0.8p$ is the price after the first discount. The price after the second discount is $(0.7)(0.8)\,p = 0.56p$. This represents an overall discount of 44 percent (100% – 56%).

6. Profit

Gross profit is equal to revenues minus expenses, or selling price minus cost.

Example: A certain appliance costs a merchant \$30. At what price should the merchant sell the appliance in order to make a gross profit of 50 percent of the cost of the appliance?

Solution: If s is the selling price of the appliance, then $s - 30 = (0.5)(30)$, or $s = \$45$. The merchant should sell the appliance for \$45.

7. Sets

If S is the set of numbers 1, 2, 3, and 4, you can write $S = \{1, 2, 3, 4\}$. Sets can also be represented by Venn diagrams. That is, the relationship among the members of sets can be represented by circles.

Example 1: Each of 25 people is enrolled in history, mathematics, or both. If 20 are enrolled in history and 18 are enrolled in mathematics, how many are enrolled in both history and mathematics?

Solution: The 25 people can be divided into three sets: those who study history only, those who study mathematics only, and those who study history and mathematics. Thus a Venn diagram may be drawn as follows, where n is the number of people enrolled in both courses, $20 - n$ is the number enrolled in history only, and $18 - n$ is the number enrolled in mathematics only.

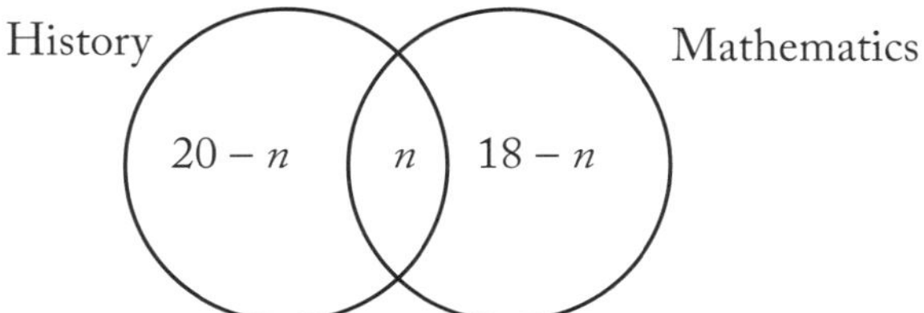

Since there is a total of 25 people, $(20 - n) + n + (18 - n) = 25$, or $n = 13$. Thirteen people are enrolled in both history and mathematics. Note that $20 + 18 - 13 = 25$, which is the general addition rule for two sets (see section 3.1.9).

Example 2: In a certain production lot, 40 percent of the toys are red and the remaining toys are green. Half of the toys are small and half are large. If 10 percent of the toys are red and small, and 40 toys are green and large, how many of the toys are red and large?

Solution: For this kind of problem, it is helpful to organize the information in a table:

	Red	Green	Total
Small	10%		50%
Large			50%
Total	40%	60%	100%

The numbers in the table are the percentages given. The following percentages can be computed on the basis of what is given:

	Red	Green	Total
Small	10%	40%	50%
Large	30%	20%	50%
Total	40%	60%	100%

Since 20% of the number of toys (n) are green and large, $0.20n = 40$ (40 toys are green and large), or $n = 200$. Therefore, 30% of the 200 toys, or $(0.3)(200) = 60$, are red and large.

8. Geometry Problems

The following is an example of a word problem involving geometry.

Example:

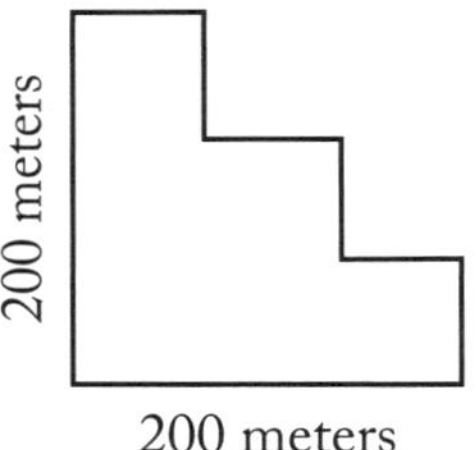

The figure above shows an aerial view of a piece of land. If all angles shown are right angles, what is the perimeter of the piece of land?

Solution: For reference, label the figure as

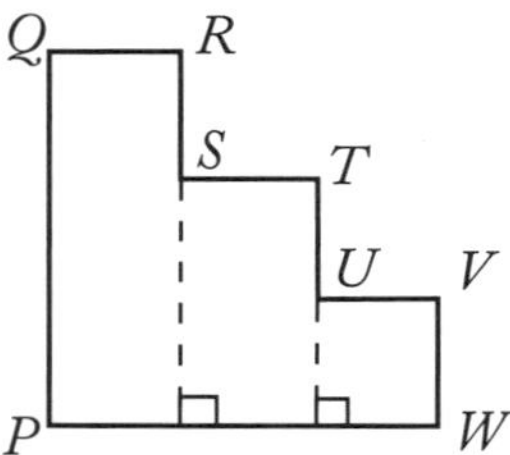

If all the angles are right angles, then $QR + ST + UV = PW$, and $RS + TU + VW = PQ$. Hence, the perimeter of the land is $2PW + 2PQ = 2 \times 200 + 2 \times 200 = 800$ meters.

9. Measurement Problems

Some questions on the GMAT involve metric units of measure, whereas others involve English units of measure. However, except for units of time, if a question requires conversion from one unit of measure to another, the relationship between those units will be given.

Example: A train travels at a constant rate of 25 meters per second. How many kilometers does it travel in 5 minutes? (1 kilometer = 1,000 meters)

Solution: In 1 minute the train travels (25)(60) = 1,500 meters, so in 5 minutes it travels 7,500 meters. Since 1 kilometer = 1,000 meters, it follows that 7,500 meters equals $\frac{7,500}{1,000}$, or 7.5 kilometers.

10. Data Interpretation

Occasionally a question or set of questions will be based on data provided in a table or graph. Some examples of tables and graphs are given below.

Example 1:

Population by Age Group (in thousands)	
Age	Population
17 years and under	63,376
18–44 years	86,738
45–64 years	43,845
65 years and over	24,054

How many people are 44 years old or younger?

Solution: The figures in the table are given in thousands. The answer in thousands can be obtained by adding 63,376 thousand and 86,738 thousand. The result is 150,114 thousand, which is 150,114,000.

Example 2:

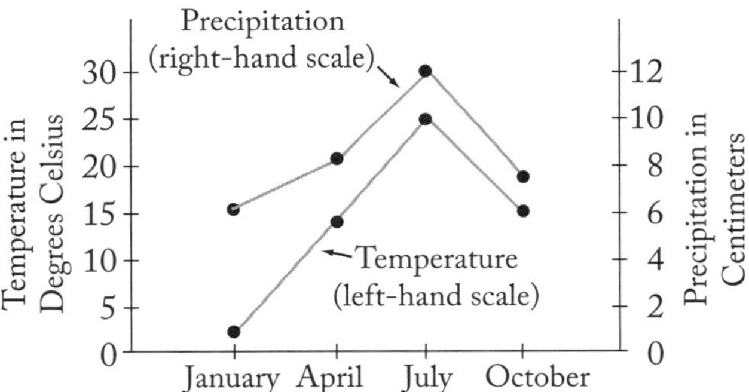

What are the average temperature and precipitation in City X during April?

Solution: Note that the scale on the left applies to the temperature line graph and the one on the right applies to the precipitation line graph. According to the graph, during April the average temperature is approximately 14° Celsius and the average precipitation is approximately 8 centimeters.

Example 3:

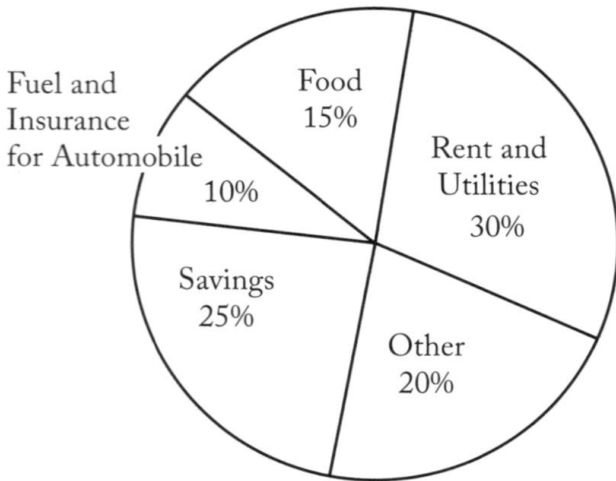

Al's weekly net salary is \$350. To how many of the categories listed was at least \$80 of Al's weekly net salary allocated?

Solution: In the circle graph, the relative sizes of the sectors are proportional to their corresponding values and the sum of the percents given is 100%. Note that $\frac{80}{350}$ is approximately 23%, so at least \$80 was allocated to each of 2 categories—Rent and Utilities, and Savings—since their allocations are each greater than 23%.

4.0 Problem Solving

4.0 Problem Solving

The Quantitative section of the GMAT® exam uses problem solving and data sufficiency questions to gauge your skill level. This chapter focuses on problem solving questions. Remember that quantitative questions require knowledge of the following:

- Arithmetic
- Elementary algebra
- Commonly known concepts of geometry

Problem solving questions are designed to test your basic mathematical skills and understanding of elementary mathematical concepts, as well as your ability to reason quantitatively, solve quantitative problems, and interpret graphic data. The mathematics knowledge required to answer the questions is no more advanced than what is generally taught in secondary school (or high school) mathematics classes.

In these questions, you are asked to solve each problem and select the best of the five answer choices given. Begin by reading the question thoroughly to determine exactly what information is given and to make sure you understand what is being asked. Scan the answer choices to understand your options. If the problem seems simple, take a few moments to see whether you can determine the answer. Then, check your answer against the choices provided.

If you do not see your answer among the choices, or if the problem is complicated, take a closer look at the answer choices and think again about what the problem is asking. See whether you can eliminate some of the answer choices and narrow down your options. If you are still unable to narrow the answer down to a single choice, reread the question. Keep in mind that the answer will be based solely on the information provided in the question—don't allow your own experience and assumptions to interfere with your ability to find the correct answer to the question.

If you find yourself stuck on a question or unable to select the single correct answer, keep in mind that you have about two minutes to answer each quantitative question. You may run out of time if you take too long to answer any one question; you may simply need to pick the answer that seems to make the most sense. Although guessing is generally not the best way to achieve a high GMAT score, making an educated guess is a good strategy for answering questions you are unsure of. Even if your answer to a particular question is incorrect, your answers to other questions will allow the test to accurately gauge your ability level.

The following pages include test-taking strategies, directions that will apply to questions of this type, sample questions, an answer key, and explanations for all the problems. These explanations present problem solving strategies that could be helpful in answering the questions.

4.1 Test-Taking Strategies

1. **Pace yourself.**

   Consult the on-screen timer periodically. Work as carefully as possible, but do not spend valuable time checking answers or pondering problems that you find difficult.

2. **Use the erasable notepad provided.**

   Working a problem out may help you avoid errors in solving the problem. If diagrams or figures are not presented, it may help to draw your own.

3. **Read each question carefully to determine what is being asked.**

   For word problems, take one step at a time, reading each sentence carefully and translating the information into equations or other useful mathematical representations.

4. **Scan the answer choices before attempting to answer a question.**

   Scanning the answers can prevent you from putting answers in a form that is not given (e.g., finding the answer in decimal form, such as 0.25, when the choices are given in fractional form, such as $\frac{1}{4}$). Also, if the question requires approximations, a shortcut could serve well (e.g., you may be able to approximate 48 percent of a number by using half).

5. **Don't waste time trying to solve a problem that is too difficult for you.**

   Make your best guess and then move on to the next question.

4.2 The Directions

These directions are very similar to those you will see for problem solving questions when you take the GMAT exam. If you read them carefully and understand them clearly before sitting for the GMAT exam, you will not need to spend too much time reviewing them once the test begins.

Solve the problem and indicate the best of the answer choices given.

Numbers: All numbers used are real numbers.

Figures: A figure accompanying a problem solving question is intended to provide information useful in solving the problem. Figures are drawn as accurately as possible. Exceptions will be clearly noted. Lines shown as straight are straight, and lines that appear jagged are also straight. The positions of points, angles, regions, etc., exist in the order shown, and angle measures are greater than zero. All figures lie in a plane unless otherwise indicated.

4.3 Sample Questions

Solve the problem and indicate the best of the answer choices given.

Numbers: All numbers used are real numbers.

Figures: A figure accompanying a problem solving question is intended to provide information useful in solving the problem. Figures are drawn as accurately as possible. Exceptions will be clearly noted. Lines shown as straight are straight, and lines that appear jagged are also straight. The positions of points, angles, regions, etc., exist in the order shown, and angle measures are greater than zero. All figures lie in a plane unless otherwise indicated.

1. If $x + y = 2$ and $x^2 + y^2 = 2$, what is the value of xy ?

(A) −2
(B) −1
(C) 0
(D) 1
(E) 2

2. Points *A*, *B*, *C*, and *D*, in that order, lie on a line. If $AB = 3$ cm, $AC = 4$ cm, and $BD = 6$ cm, what is *CD*, in centimeters?

(A) 1
(B) 2
(C) 3
(D) 4
(E) 5

3. What is the value of $x^2yz - xyz^2$, if $x = -2$, $y = 1$, and $z = 3$?

(A) 20
(B) 24
(C) 30
(D) 32
(E) 48

4. If $x > y$ and $y > z$, which of the following represents the greatest number?

(A) $x - z$
(B) $x - y$
(C) $y - x$
(D) $z - y$
(E) $z - x$

5. To order certain plants from a catalog, it costs $3.00 per plant, plus a 5 percent sales tax, plus $6.95 for shipping and handling regardless of the number of plants ordered. If Company C ordered these plants from the catalog at the total cost of $69.95, how many plants did Company C order?

(A) 22
(B) 21
(C) 20
(D) 19
(E) 18

6. Company C produces toy trucks at a cost of $5.00 each for the first 100 trucks and $3.50 for each additional truck. If 500 toy trucks were produced by Company C and sold for $10.00 each, what was Company C's gross profit?

(A) $2,250
(B) $2,500
(C) $3,100
(D) $3,250
(E) $3,500

7. A group of store managers must assemble 280 displays for an upcoming sale. If they assemble 25 percent of the displays during the first hour and 40 percent of the remaining displays during the second hour, how many of the displays will <u>not</u> have been assembled by the end of the second hour?

(A) 70
(B) 98
(C) 126
(D) 168
(E) 182

8. Of the following, which is least?

(A) $\frac{0.03}{0.00071}$

(B) $\frac{0.03}{0.0071}$

(C) $\frac{0.03}{0.071}$

(D) $\frac{0.03}{0.71}$

(E) $\frac{0.03}{7.1}$

9. The maximum recommended pulse rate R, when exercising, for a person who is x years of age is given by the equation $R = 176 - 0.8x$. What is the age, in years, of a person whose maximum recommended pulse rate when exercising is 140 ?

(A) 40
(B) 45
(C) 50
(D) 55
(E) 60

10. If the average (arithmetic mean) of 5 numbers j, $j + 5$, $2j - 1$, $4j - 2$, and $5j - 1$ is 8, what is the value of j ?

(A) $\frac{1}{3}$

(B) $\frac{7}{13}$

(C) 1
(D) 3
(E) 8

11. Guadalupe owns 2 rectangular tracts of land. One is 300 m by 500 m and the other is 250 m by 630 m. The combined area of these 2 tracts is how many square meters?

(A) 3,360
(B) 307,500
(C) 621,500
(D) 704,000
(E) 2,816,000

12. There are five sales agents in a certain real estate office. One month Andy sold twice as many properties as Ellen, Bob sold 3 more than Ellen, Cary sold twice as many as Bob, and Dora sold as many as Bob and Ellen together. Who sold the most properties that month?

(A) Andy
(B) Bob
(C) Cary
(D) Dora
(E) Ellen

13. In a field day at a school, each child who competed in n events and scored a total of p points was given an overall score of $\frac{p}{n} + n$. Andrew competed in 1 event and scored 9 points. Jason competed in 3 events and scored 5, 6, and 7 points, respectively. What was the ratio of Andrew's overall score to Jason's overall score?

(A) $\frac{10}{23}$

(B) $\frac{7}{10}$

(C) $\frac{4}{5}$

(D) $\frac{10}{9}$

(E) $\frac{12}{7}$

14. Which of the following represent positive numbers?

I. $-3 - (-5)$
II. $(-3)(-5)$
III. $-5 - (-3)$

(A) I only
(B) II only
(C) III only
(D) I and II
(E) II and III

15. If $\frac{x}{4}$ is 2 more than $\frac{x}{8}$, then $x =$

(A) 4
(B) 8
(C) 16
(D) 32
(E) 64

16. If Mario was 32 years old 8 years ago, how old was he x years ago?

(A) $x - 40$
(B) $x - 24$
(C) $40 - x$
(D) $24 - x$
(E) $24 + x$

17. A grocer has 400 pounds of coffee in stock, 20 percent of which is decaffeinated. If the grocer buys another 100 pounds of coffee of which 60 percent is decaffeinated, what percent, by weight, of the grocer's stock of coffee is decaffeinated?

(A) 28%
(B) 30%
(C) 32%
(D) 34%
(E) 40%

18. The toll T, in dollars, for a truck using a certain bridge is given by the formula $T = 1.50 + 0.50(x - 2)$, where x is the number of axles on the truck. What is the toll for an 18-wheel truck that has 2 wheels on its front axle and 4 wheels on each of its other axles?

(A) \$2.50
(B) \$3.00
(C) \$3.50
(D) \$4.00
(E) \$5.00

19. For what value of x between –4 and 4, inclusive, is the value of $x^2 - 10x + 16$ the greatest?

(A) –4
(B) –2
(C) 0
(D) 2
(E) 4

20. If $x = -\frac{5}{8}$ and $y = -\frac{1}{2}$, what is the value of the expression $-2x - y^2$?

(A) $-\frac{3}{2}$
(B) -1
(C) 1
(D) $\frac{3}{2}$
(E) $\frac{7}{4}$

21. The number $2 - 0.5$ is how many times the number $1 - 0.5$?

(A) 2
(B) 2.5
(C) 3
(D) 3.5
(E) 4

22. If $x - y = R$ and $xy = S$, then $(x - 2)(y + 2) =$

(A) $R + S - 4$
(B) $R + 2S - 4$
(C) $2R - S - 4$
(D) $2R + S - 4$
(E) $2R + S$

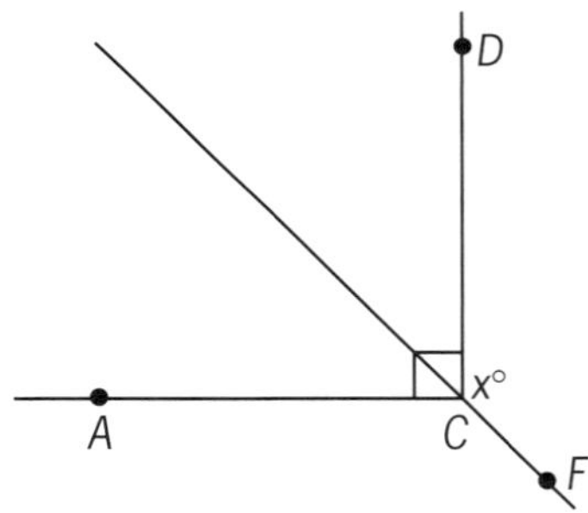

23. In the figure above, if F is a point on the line that bisects angle ACD and the measure of angle DCF is $x°$, which of the following is true of x ?

(A) $90 \le x < 100$
(B) $100 \le x < 110$
(C) $110 \le x < 120$
(D) $120 \le x < 130$
(E) $130 \le x < 140$

24. In which of the following pairs are the two numbers reciprocals of each other?

    I. 3 and $\frac{1}{3}$

    II. $\frac{1}{17}$ and $\frac{-1}{17}$

    III. $\sqrt{3}$ and $\frac{\sqrt{3}}{3}$

    (A) I only
    (B) II only
    (C) I and II
    (D) I and III
    (E) II and III

25. A rope 20.6 meters long is cut into two pieces. If the length of one piece of rope is 2.8 meters shorter than the length of the other, what is the length, in meters, of the longer piece of rope?

    (A) 7.5
    (B) 8.9
    (C) 9.9
    (D) 10.3
    (E) 11.7

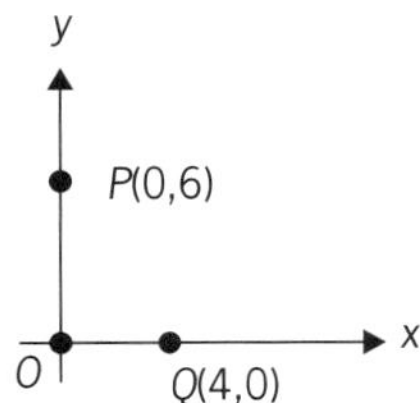

26. In the rectangular coordinate system shown above, points *O*, *P*, and *Q* represent the sites of three proposed housing developments. If a fire station can be built at any point in the coordinate system, at which point would it be equidistant from all three developments?

    (A) (3,1)
    (B) (1,3)
    (C) (3,2)
    (D) (2,2)
    (E) (2,3)

27. What is the perimeter, in meters, of a rectangular garden 6 meters wide that has the same area as a rectangular playground 16 meters long and 12 meters wide?

    (A) 48
    (B) 56
    (C) 60
    (D) 76
    (E) 192

28. Of the total amount that Jill spent on a shopping trip, excluding taxes, she spent 50 percent on clothing, 20 percent on food, and 30 percent on other items. If Jill paid a 4 percent tax on the clothing, no tax on the food, and an 8 percent tax on all other items, then the total tax that she paid was what percent of the total amount that she spent, excluding taxes?

    (A) 2.8%
    (B) 3.6%
    (C) 4.4%
    (D) 5.2%
    (E) 6.0%

29. How many integers x satisfy both $2 < x \leq 4$ and $0 \leq x \leq 3$?

    (A) 5
    (B) 4
    (C) 3
    (D) 2
    (E) 1

30. At the opening of a trading day at a certain stock exchange, the price per share of stock K was \$8. If the price per share of stock K was \$9 at the closing of the day, what was the percent increase in the price per share of stock K for that day?

    (A) 1.4%
    (B) 5.9%
    (C) 11.1%
    (D) 12.5%
    (E) 23.6%

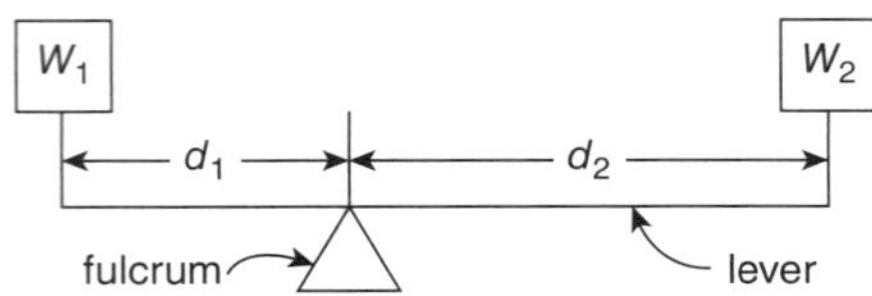

31. As shown in the diagram above, a lever resting on a fulcrum has weights of w_1 pounds and w_2 pounds, located d_1 feet and d_2 feet from the fulcrum. The lever is balanced and $w_1d_1 = w_2d_2$. Suppose w_1 is 50 pounds and w_2 is 30 pounds. If d_1 is 4 feet less than d_2, what is d_2, in feet?

    (A) 1.5
    (B) 2.5
    (C) 6
    (D) 10
    (E) 20

32. The number of rooms at Hotel G is 10 less than twice the number of rooms at Hotel H. If the total number of rooms at Hotel G and Hotel H is 425, what is the number of rooms at Hotel G ?

    (A) 140
    (B) 180
    (C) 200
    (D) 240
    (E) 280

33. $\left(1+\sqrt{5}\right)\left(1-\sqrt{5}\right)=$

    (A) -4
    (B) 2
    (C) 6
    (D) $-4-2\sqrt{5}$
    (E) $6-2\sqrt{5}$

34. A certain population of bacteria doubles every 10 minutes. If the number of bacteria in the population initially was 10^4, what was the number in the population 1 hour later?

    (A) $2(10^4)$
    (B) $6(10^4)$
    (C) $(2^6)(10^4)$
    (D) $(10^6)(10^4)$
    (E) $(10^4)^6$

35. $\frac{3}{100}+\frac{5}{1{,}000}+\frac{7}{100{,}000}=$

    (A) 0.357
    (B) 0.3507
    (C) 0.35007
    (D) 0.0357
    (E) 0.03507

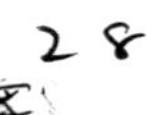

36. If r and s are positive integers such that $(2^r)(4^s) = 16$, then $2r + s =$

    (A) 2
    (B) 3
    (C) 4
    (D) 5
    (E) 6

37. The annual budget of a certain college is to be shown on a circle graph. If the size of each sector of the graph is to be proportional to the amount of the budget it represents, how many degrees of the circle should be used to represent an item that is 15 percent of the budget?

    (A) 15°
    (B) 36°
    (C) 54°
    (D) 90°
    (E) 150°

38. $\sqrt{16+16}=$

    (A) $4\sqrt{2}$
    (B) $8\sqrt{2}$
    (C) $16\sqrt{2}$
    (D) 8
    (E) 16

39. Three people each contributed x dollars toward the purchase of a car. They then bought the car for y dollars, an amount less than the total number of dollars contributed. If the excess amount is to be refunded to the three people in equal amounts, each person should receive a refund of how many dollars?

(A) $\frac{3x-y}{3}$

(B) $\frac{x-y}{3}$

(C) $\frac{x-3y}{3}$

(D) $\frac{y-3x}{3}$

(E) $3(x-y)$

40. What is the ratio of $\frac{3}{4}$ to the product $4\left(\frac{3}{4}\right)$?

(A) $\frac{1}{4}$

(B) $\frac{1}{3}$

(C) $\frac{4}{9}$

(D) $\frac{9}{4}$

(E) 4

$$2x+2y=-4$$
$$4x+y=1$$

41. In the system of equations above, what is the value of x?

(A) -3

(B) -1

(C) $\frac{2}{5}$

(D) 1

(E) $1\frac{3}{4}$

42. Last week Jack worked 70 hours and earned \$1,260. If he earned his regular hourly wage for the first 40 hours worked, $1\frac{1}{2}$ times his regular hourly wage for the next 20 hours worked, and 2 times his regular hourly wage for the remaining 10 hours worked, what was his regular hourly wage?

(A) \$7.00

(B) \$14.00

(C) \$18.00

(D) \$22.00

(E) \$31.50

43. $\frac{2+2\sqrt{6}}{2}=$

(A) $\sqrt{6}$

(B) $2\sqrt{6}$

(C) $1+\sqrt{6}$

(D) $1+2\sqrt{6}$

(E) $2+\sqrt{6}$

44. A certain fishing boat is chartered by 6 people who are to contribute equally to the total charter cost of \$480. If each person contributes equally to a \$150 down payment, how much of the charter cost will each person still owe?

(A) \$80

(B) \$66

(C) \$55

(D) \$50

(E) \$45

45. Which of the following must be equal to zero for all real numbers x?

I. $-\frac{1}{x}$

II. $x+(-x)$

III. x^0

(A) I only

(B) II only

(C) I and III only

(D) II and III only

(E) I, II, and III

46. $\frac{31}{125} =$

(A) 0.248
(B) 0.252
(C) 0.284
(D) 0.312
(E) 0.320

47. If Mel saved more than \$10 by purchasing a sweater at a 15 percent discount, what is the smallest amount the original price of the sweater could be, to the nearest dollar?

(A) 45
(B) 67
(C) 75
(D) 83
(E) 150

48. If a and b are positive integers and $(2^a)^b = 2^3$, what is the value of $2^a 2^b$?

(A) 6
(B) 8
(C) 16
(D) 32
(E) 64

49. $\frac{1}{3-\frac{1}{3-\frac{1}{3-1}}} =$

(A) $\frac{7}{23}$
(B) $\frac{5}{13}$
(C) $\frac{2}{3}$
(D) $\frac{23}{7}$
(E) $\frac{13}{5}$

50. After 4,000 gallons of water were added to a large water tank that was already filled to $\frac{3}{4}$ of its capacity, the tank was then at $\frac{4}{5}$ of its capacity. How many gallons of water does the tank hold when filled to capacity?

(A) 5,000
(B) 6,200
(C) 20,000
(D) 40,000
(E) 80,000

51. Five machines at a certain factory operate at the same constant rate. If four of these machines, operating simultaneously, take 30 hours to fill a certain production order, how many <u>fewer</u> hours does it take all five machines, operating simultaneously, to fill the same production order?

(A) 3
(B) 5
(C) 6
(D) 16
(E) 24

52. How many integers between 1 and 16, inclusive, have exactly 3 different positive integer factors? (Note: 6 is NOT such an integer because 6 has 4 different positive integer factors: 1, 2, 3, and 6.)

(A) 1
(B) 2
(C) 3
(D) 4
(E) 6

53. If $d = 2.0453$ and d^* is the decimal obtained by rounding d to the nearest hundredth, what is the value of $d^* - d$?

(A) –0.0053
(B) –0.0003
(C) 0.0007
(D) 0.0047
(E) 0.0153

54. Stephanie has $2\frac{1}{4}$ cups of milk on hand and makes 2 batches of cookies, using $\frac{2}{3}$ cup of milk for each batch of cookies. Which of the following describes the amount of milk remaining after she makes the cookies?

(A) Less than $\frac{1}{2}$ cup

(B) Between $\frac{1}{2}$ cup and $\frac{3}{4}$ cup

(C) Between $\frac{3}{4}$ cup and 1 cup

(D) Between 1 cup and $1\frac{1}{2}$ cups

(E) More than $1\frac{1}{2}$ cups

55. A school club plans to package and sell dried fruit to raise money. The club purchased 12 containers of dried fruit, each containing $16\frac{3}{4}$ pounds. What is the maximum number of individual bags of dried fruit, each containing $\frac{1}{4}$ pounds, that can be sold from the dried fruit the club purchased?

(A) 50
(B) 64
(C) 67
(D) 768
(E) 804

56. The sequence a_1, a_2, a_3, a_4, a_5 is such that $a_n = a_{n-1} + 5$ for $2 \le n \le 5$. If $a_5 = 31$, what is the value of a_1 ?

(A) 1
(B) 6
(C) 11
(D) 16
(E) 21

57. A certain bridge is 4,024 feet long. Approximately how many minutes does it take to cross this bridge at a constant speed of 20 miles per hour? (1 mile = 5,280 feet)

(A) 1
(B) 2
(C) 4
(D) 6
(E) 7

58. If $S = \{0, 4, 5, 2, 11, 8\}$, how much greater than the median of the numbers in S is the mean of the numbers in S ?

(A) 0.5
(B) 1.0
(C) 1.5
(D) 2.0
(E) 2.5

59. The annual interest rate earned by an investment increased by 10 percent from last year to this year. If the annual interest rate earned by the investment this year was 11 percent, what was the annual interest rate last year?

(A) 1%
(B) 1.1%
(C) 9.1%
(D) 10%
(E) 10.8%

60. A total of 5 liters of gasoline is to be poured into two empty containers with capacities of 2 liters and 6 liters, respectively, such that both containers will be filled to the same percent of their respective capacities. What amount of gasoline, in liters, must be poured into the 6-liter container?

(A) $4\frac{1}{2}$

(B) 4

(C) $3\frac{3}{4}$

(D) 3

(E) $1\frac{1}{4}$

61. List S consists of 10 consecutive odd integers, and list T consists of 5 consecutive even integers. If the least integer in S is 7 more than the least integer in T, how much greater is the average (arithmetic mean) of the integers in S than the average of the integers in T ?

(A) 2
(B) 7
(C) 8
(D) 12
(E) 22

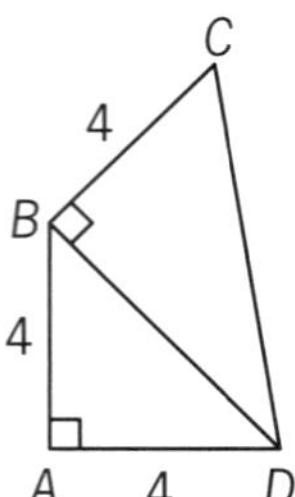

62. In the figure above, what is the area of triangular region *BCD* ?

(A) $4\sqrt{2}$
(B) 8
(C) $8\sqrt{2}$
(D) 16
(E) $16\sqrt{2}$

63. What is the larger of the 2 solutions of the equation $x^2 - 4x = 96$?

(A) 8
(B) 12
(C) 16
(D) 32
(E) 100

64. Of the goose eggs laid at a certain pond, $\frac{2}{3}$ hatched, and $\frac{3}{4}$ of the geese that hatched from those eggs survived the first month. Of the geese that survived the first month, $\frac{3}{5}$ did not survive the first year. If 120 geese survived the first year and if no more than one goose hatched from each egg, how many goose eggs were laid at the pond?

(A) 280
(B) 400
(C) 540
(D) 600
(E) 840

65. Judy bought a quantity of pens in packages of 5 for \$0.80 per package. She sold all of the pens in packages of 3 for \$0.60 per package. If Judy's profit from the pens was \$8.00, how many pens did she buy and sell?

(A) 40
(B) 80
(C) 100
(D) 200
(E) 400

66. If $x^2 - 2x - 15 = 0$ and $x > 0$ which of the following must be equal to 0 ?

I. $x^2 - 6x + 9$
II. $x^2 - 7x + 10$
III. $x^2 - 10x + 25$

(A) I only
(B) II only
(C) III only
(D) II and III only
(E) I, II, and III

67. $\frac{(39{,}897)(0.0096)}{198.76}$ is approximately

(A) 0.02
(B) 0.2
(C) 2
(D) 20
(E) 200

68. If a square region has area *n*, what is the length of the diagonal of the square in terms of *n* ?

(A) $\sqrt{2n}$
(B) $\sqrt{n}$
(C) $2\sqrt{n}$
(D) $2n$
(E) $2n^2$

69. The "prime sum" of an integer n greater than 1 is the sum of all the prime factors of n, including repetitions. For example, the prime sum of 12 is 7, since $12 = 2 \times 2 \times 3$ and $2 + 2 + 3 = 7$. For which of the following integers is the prime sum greater than 35 ?

(A) 440
(B) 512
(C) 620
(D) 700
(E) 750

70. Each machine at a toy factory assembles a certain kind of toy at a constant rate of one toy every 3 minutes. If 40 percent of the machines at the factory are to be replaced by new machines that assemble this kind of toy at a constant rate of one toy every 2 minutes, what will be the percent increase in the number of toys assembled in one hour by all the machines at the factory, working at their constant rates?

(A) 20%
(B) 25%
(C) 30%
(D) 40%
(E) 50%

71. When a subscription to a new magazine was purchased for m months, the publisher offered a discount of 75 percent off the regular monthly price of the magazine. If the total value of the discount was equivalent to buying the magazine at its regular monthly price for 27 months, what was the value of m ?

(A) 18
(B) 24
(C) 30
(D) 36
(E) 48

72. At a garage sale, all of the prices of the items sold were different. If the price of a radio sold at the garage sale was both the 15th highest price and the 20th lowest price among the prices of the items sold, how many items were sold at the garage sale?

(A) 33
(B) 34
(C) 35
(D) 36
(E) 37

73. Half of a large pizza is cut into 4 equal-sized pieces, and the other half is cut into 6 equal-sized pieces. If a person were to eat 1 of the larger pieces and 2 of the smaller pieces, what fraction of the pizza would remain <u>uneaten</u>?

(A) $\frac{5}{12}$
(B) $\frac{13}{24}$
(C) $\frac{7}{12}$
(D) $\frac{2}{3}$
(E) $\frac{17}{24}$

74. If $a = 1 + \frac{1}{4} + \frac{1}{16} + \frac{1}{64}$ and $b = 1 + \frac{1}{4}a$, then what is the value of $a - b$?

(A) $-\frac{85}{256}$
(B) $-\frac{1}{256}$
(C) $-\frac{1}{4}$
(D) $\frac{125}{256}$
(E) $\frac{169}{256}$

75. In a certain learning experiment, each participant had three trials and was assigned, for each trial, a score of either –2, –1, 0, 1, or 2. The participant's final score consisted of the sum of the first trial score, 2 times the second trial score, and 3 times the third trial score. If Anne received scores of 1 and –1 for her first two trials, not necessarily in that order, which of the following could NOT be her final score?

(A) –4
(B) –2
(C) 1
(D) 5
(E) 6

76. For all positive integers m and v, the expression $m \Theta v$ represents the remainder when m is divided by v. What is the value of $((98 \Theta 33) \Theta 17) - (98 \Theta (33 \Theta 17))$?

(A) −10
(B) −2
(C) 8
(D) 13
(E) 17

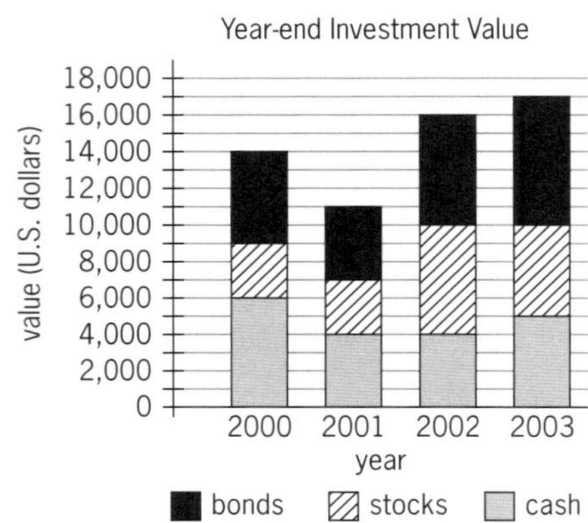

77. The chart above shows year-end values for Darnella's investments. For just the stocks, what was the increase in value from year-end 2000 to year-end 2003 ?

(A) $1,000
(B) $2,000
(C) $3,000
(D) $4,000
(E) $5,000

78. If the sum of the reciprocals of two consecutive odd integers is $\frac{12}{35}$, then the greater of the two integers is

(A) 3
(B) 5
(C) 7
(D) 9
(E) 11

79. What is the sum of the odd integers from 35 to 85, inclusive?

(A) 1,560
(B) 1,500
(C) 1,240
(D) 1,120
(E) 1,100

80. In a certain sequence, each term after the first term is one-half the previous term. If the tenth term of the sequence is between 0.0001 and 0.001, then the twelfth term of the sequence is between

(A) 0.0025 and 0.025
(B) 0.00025 and 0.0025
(C) 0.000025 and 0.00025
(D) 0.0000025 and 0.000025
(E) 0.00000025 and 0.0000025

81. A certain drive-in movie theater has a total of 17 rows of parking spaces. There are 20 parking spaces in the first row and 21 parking spaces in the second row. In each subsequent row there are 2 more parking spaces than in the previous row. What is the total number of parking spaces in the movie theater?

(A) 412
(B) 544
(C) 596
(D) 632
(E) 692

82. Ada and Paul received their scores on three tests. On the first test, Ada's score was 10 points higher than Paul's score. On the second test, Ada's score was 4 points higher than Paul's score. If Paul's average (arithmetic mean) score on the three tests was 3 points higher than Ada's average score on the three tests, then Paul's score on the third test was how many points higher than Ada's score?

(A) 9
(B) 14
(C) 17
(D) 23
(E) 25

83. The price of a certain stock increased by 0.25 of 1 percent on a certain day. By what fraction did the price of the stock increase that day?

(A) $\frac{1}{2,500}$
(B) $\frac{1}{400}$
(C) $\frac{1}{40}$
(D) $\frac{1}{25}$
(E) $\frac{1}{4}$

84. Three business partners, Q, R, and S, agree to divide their total profit for a certain year in the ratios 2:5:8, respectively. If Q's share was $4,000, what was the total profit of the business partners for the year?

(A) $26,000
(B) $30,000
(C) $52,000
(D) $60,000
(E) $300,000

85. For each trip, a taxicab company charges $4.25 for the first mile and $2.65 for each additional mile or fraction thereof. If the total charge for a certain trip was $62.55, how many miles at most was the trip?

(A) 21
(B) 22
(C) 23
(D) 24
(E) 25

86. When 24 is divided by the positive integer *n*, the remainder is 4. Which of the following statements about *n* must be true?

I. *n* is even.
II. *n* is a multiple of 5.
III. *n* is a factor of 20.

(A) III only
(B) I and II only
(C) I and III only
(D) II and III only
(E) I, II, and III

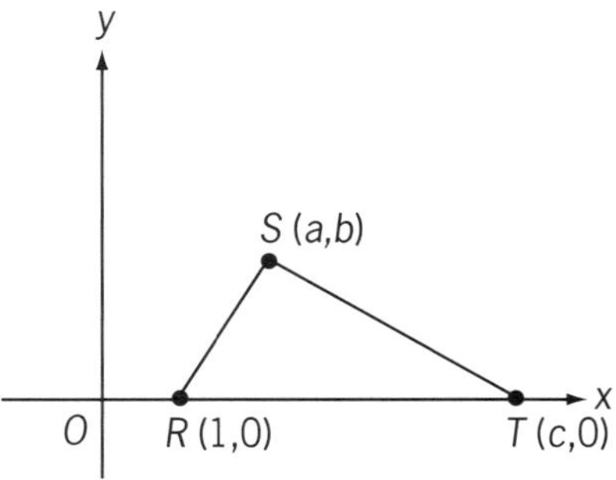

87. In the rectangular coordinate system above, the area of ΔRST is

(A) $\frac{bc}{2}$
(B) $\frac{b(c-1)}{2}$
(C) $\frac{c(b-1)}{2}$
(D) $\frac{a(c-1)}{2}$
(E) $\frac{c(a-1)}{2}$

88. What is the thousandths digit in the decimal equivalent of $\frac{53}{5,000}$?

(A) 0
(B) 1
(C) 3
(D) 5
(E) 6

89. The product of 3,305 and the 1-digit integer x is a 5-digit integer. The units (ones) digit of the product is 5 and the hundreds digit is y. If A is the set of all possible values of x and B is the set of all possible values of y, then which of the following gives the members of A and B?

	$\underline{A}$	$\underline{B}$
(A)	{1, 3, 5, 7, 9}	{0, 1, 2, 3, 4, 5, 6, 7, 8, 9}
(B)	{1, 3, 5, 7, 9}	{1, 3, 5, 7, 9}
(C)	{3, 5, 7, 9}	{1, 5, 7, 9}
(D)	{5, 7, 9}	{1, 5, 7}
(E)	{5, 7, 9}	{1, 5, 9}

90. What is the largest integer n such that $\frac{1}{2^n} > 0.01$?

(A) 5
(B) 6
(C) 7
(D) 10
(E) 51

91. If x and y are integers such that $2 < x \le 8$ and $2 < y \le 9$, what is the maximum value of $\frac{1}{x} - \frac{x}{y}$?

(A) $-3\frac{1}{8}$
(B) 0
(C) $\frac{1}{4}$
(D) $\frac{5}{18}$
(E) 2

92. Items that are purchased together at a certain discount store are priced at \$3 for the first item purchased and \$1 for each additional item purchased. What is the maximum number of items that could be purchased together for a total price that is less than \$30?

(A) 25
(B) 26
(C) 27
(D) 28
(E) 29

93. The average (arithmetic mean) length per film for a group of 21 films is t minutes. If a film that runs for 66 minutes is removed from the group and replaced by one that runs for 52 minutes, what is the average length per film, in minutes, for the new group of films, in terms of t?

(A) $t + \frac{2}{3}$
(B) $t - \frac{2}{3}$
(C) $21t + 14$
(D) $t + \frac{3}{2}$
(E) $t - \frac{3}{2}$

94. A garden center sells a certain grass seed in 5-pound bags at \$13.85 per bag, 10-pound bags at \$20.43 per bag, and 25-pound bags at \$32.25 per bag. If a customer is to buy at least 65 pounds of the grass seed, but no more than 80 pounds, what is the least possible cost of the grass seed that the customer will buy?

(A) \$94.03
(B) \$96.75
(C) \$98.78
(D) \$102.07
(E) \$105.36

95. If $x = -|w|$, which of the following must be true?

(A) $x = -w$
(B) $x = w$
(C) $x^2 = w$
(D) $x^2 = w^2$
(E) $x^3 = w^3$

96. Which of the following lines in the xy-plane does <u>not</u> contain any point with integers as both coordinates?

(A) $y = x$
(B) $y = x + \frac{1}{2}$
(C) $y = x + 5$
(D) $y = \frac{1}{2}x$
(E) $y = \frac{1}{2}x + 5$

97. One inlet pipe fills an empty tank in 5 hours. A second inlet pipe fills the same tank in 3 hours. If both pipes are used together, how long will it take to fill $\frac{2}{3}$ of the tank?

(A) $\frac{8}{15}$ hr

(B) $\frac{3}{4}$ hr

(C) $\frac{5}{4}$ hr

(D) $\frac{15}{8}$ hr

(E) $\frac{8}{3}$ hr

98. For a light that has an intensity of 60 candles at its source, the intensity in candles, S, of the light at a point d feet from the source is given by the formula $S = \frac{60k}{d^2}$, where k is a constant. If the intensity of the light is 30 candles at a distance of 2 feet from the source, what is the intensity of the light at a distance of 20 feet from the source?

(A) $\frac{3}{10}$ candle

(B) $\frac{1}{2}$ candle

(C) 1 candle

(D) 2 candles

(E) 3 candles

99. A certain financial institution reported that its assets totaled $2,377,366.30 on a certain day. Of this amount, $31,724.54 was held in cash. Approximately what percent of the reported assets was held in cash on that day?

(A) 0.00013%

(B) 0.0013%

(C) 0.013%

(D) 0.13%

(E) 1.3%

$$\begin{array}{r} AB \\ +\ BA \\ \hline AAC \end{array}$$

100. In the correctly worked addition problem shown, where the sum of the two-digit positive integers AB and BA is the three-digit integer AAC, and A, B, and C are different digits, what is the units digit of the integer AAC ?

(A) 9

(B) 6

(C) 3

(D) 2

(E) 0

$$3r \le 4s + 5$$
$$|s| \le 5$$

101. Given the inequalities above, which of the following CANNOT be the value of r ?

(A) –20

(B) –5

(C) 0

(D) 5

(E) 20

102. If m is an even integer, v is an odd integer, and $m > v > 0$, which of the following represents the number of even integers less than m and greater than v ?

(A) $\frac{m-v}{2} - 1$

(B) $\frac{m-v-1}{2}$

(C) $\frac{m-v}{2}$

(D) $m - v - 1$

(E) $m - v$

103. A positive integer is divisible by 9 if and only if the sum of its digits is divisible by 9. If n is a positive integer, for which of the following values of k is $25 \times 10^n + k \times 10^{2n}$ divisible by 9 ?

(A) 9
(B) 16
(C) 23
(D) 35
(E) 47

104. The perimeter of rectangle A is 200 meters. The length of rectangle B is 10 meters less than the length of rectangle A and the width of rectangle B is 10 meters more than the width of rectangle A. If rectangle B is a square, what is the width, in meters, of rectangle A ?

(A) 10
(B) 20
(C) 40
(D) 50
(E) 60

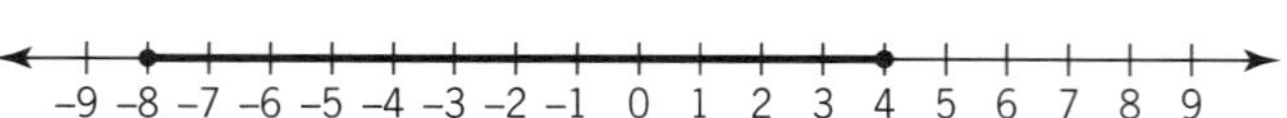

105. On the number line, the shaded interval is the graph of which of the following inequalities?

(A) $|x| \le 4$
(B) $|x| \le 8$
(C) $|x - 2| \le 4$
(D) $|x - 2| \le 6$
(E) $|x + 2| \le 6$

106. Of all the students in a certain dormitory, $\frac{1}{2}$ are first-year students and the rest are second-year students. If $\frac{4}{5}$ of the first-year students have not declared a major and if the fraction of second-year students who have declared a major is 3 times the fraction of first-year students who have declared a major, what fraction of all the students in the dormitory are second-year students who have not declared a major?

(A) $\frac{1}{15}$
(B) $\frac{1}{5}$
(C) $\frac{4}{15}$
(D) $\frac{1}{3}$
(E) $\frac{2}{5}$

107. If the average (arithmetic mean) of x, y, and z is $7x$ and $x \ne 0$, what is the ratio of x to the sum of y and z ?

(A) 1:21
(B) 1:20
(C) 1:6
(D) 6:1
(E) 20:1

108. $\frac{(-1.5)(1.2)-(4.5)(0.4)}{30} =$

(A) −1.2
(B) −0.12
(C) 0
(D) 0.12
(E) 1.2

109. In the coordinate plane, line k passes through the origin and has slope 2. If points $(3,y)$ and $(x,4)$ are on line k, then $x + y =$

(A) 3.5
(B) 7
(C) 8
(D) 10
(E) 14

110. If a, b, and c are constants, $a > b > c$, and $x^3 - x = (x - a)(x - b)(x - c)$ for all numbers x, what is the value of b ?

(A) -3
(B) -1
(C) 0
(D) 1
(E) 3

111. Company K's earnings were $12 million last year. If this year's earnings are projected to be 150 percent greater than last year's earnings, what are Company K's projected earnings this year?

(A) $13.5 million
(B) $15 million
(C) $18 million
(D) $27 million
(E) $30 million

112. $17^3 + 17^4 =$

(A) 17^7
(B) $17^3(18)$
(C) $17^6(18)$
(D) $2(17^3) + 17$
(E) $2(17^3) - 17$

113. Jonah drove the first half of a 100-mile trip in x hours and the second half in y hours. Which of the following is equal to Jonah's average speed, in miles per hour, for the entire trip?

(A) $\frac{50}{x+y}$
(B) $\frac{100}{x+y}$
(C) $\frac{25}{x}+\frac{25}{y}$
(D) $\frac{50}{x}+\frac{50}{y}$
(E) $\frac{100}{x}+\frac{100}{y}$

114. What is the greatest number of identical bouquets that can be made out of 21 white and 91 red tulips if no flowers are to be left out? (Two bouquets are identical whenever the number of red tulips in the two bouquets is equal and the number of white tulips in the two bouquets is equal.)

(A) 3
(B) 4
(C) 5
(D) 6
(E) 7

115. In the xy-plane, the points (c,d), $(c,-d)$, and $(-c,-d)$ are three vertices of a certain square. If $c < 0$ and $d > 0$, which of the following points is in the same quadrant as the fourth vertex of the square?

(A) $(-5,-3)$
(B) $(-5,3)$
(C) $(5,-3)$
(D) $(3,-5)$
(E) $(3,5)$

116. For all numbers s and t, the operation $\star$ is defined by $s \star t = (s - 1)(t + 1)$. If $(-2) \star x = -12$, then $x =$

(A) 2
(B) 3
(C) 5
(D) 6
(E) 11

117. If the amount of federal estate tax due on an estate valued at $1.35 million is $437,000 plus 43 percent of the value of the estate in excess of $1.25 million, then the federal tax due is approximately what percent of the value of the estate?

A. 30%
B. 35%
C. 40%
D. 45%
E. 50%

118. If $\frac{3}{10^4} = x\%$, then $x =$

(A) 0.3
(B) 0.03
(C) 0.003
(D) 0.0003
(E) 0.00003

119. If a basketball team scores an average (arithmetic mean) of x points per game for n games and then scores y points in its next game, what is the team's average score for the $n + 1$ games?

(A) $\frac{nx+y}{n+1}$
(B) $x+\frac{y}{n+1}$
(C) $x+\frac{y}{n}$
(D) $\frac{n(x+y)}{n+1}$
(E) $\frac{x+ny}{n+1}$

120. At a certain pizzeria, $\frac{1}{8}$ of the pizzas sold in one week were mushroom and $\frac{1}{3}$ of the remaining pizzas sold were pepperoni. If n of the pizzas sold were pepperoni, how many were mushroom?

(A) $\frac{3}{8}n$
(B) $\frac{3}{7}n$
(C) $\frac{7}{16}n$
(D) $\frac{7}{8}n$
(E) $3n$

121. What is the value of $2x^2 - 2.4x - 1.7$ for $x = 0.7$?

(A) −0.72
(B) −1.42
(C) −1.98
(D) −2.40
(E) −2.89

122. What is the remainder when 3^{24} is divided by 5 ?

(A) 0
(B) 1
(C) 2
(D) 3
(E) 4

123. If the volume of a ball is 32,490 cubic millimeters, what is the volume of the ball in cubic centimeters? (1 millimeter = 0.1 centimeter)

(A) 0.3249
(B) 3.249
(C) 32.49
(D) 324.9
(E) 3,249

124. David used part of $100,000 to purchase a house. Of the remaining portion, he invested $\frac{1}{3}$ of it at 4 percent simple annual interest and $\frac{2}{3}$ of it at 6 percent simple annual interest. If after a year the income from the two investments totaled $320, what was the purchase price of the house?

(A) $96,000
(B) $94,000
(C) $88,000
(D) $75,000
(E) $40,000

125. The cost to rent a small bus for a trip is x dollars, which is to be shared equally among the people taking the trip. If 10 people take the trip rather than 16, how many more dollars, in terms of x, will it cost per person?

(A) $\frac{x}{6}$
(B) $\frac{x}{10}$
(C) $\frac{x}{16}$
(D) $\frac{3x}{40}$
(E) $\frac{3x}{80}$

126. Last year Department Store X had a sales total for December that was 4 times the average (arithmetic mean) of the monthly sales totals for January through November. The sales total for December was what fraction of the sales total for the year?

(A) $\frac{1}{4}$

(B) $\frac{4}{15}$

(C) $\frac{1}{3}$

(D) $\frac{4}{11}$

(E) $\frac{4}{5}$

127. In the sequence $x_0, x_1, x_2, \ldots, x_n$, each term from x_1 to x_k is 3 greater than the previous term, and each term from x_{k+1} to x_n is 3 less than the previous term, where n and k are positive integers and $k < n$. If $x_0 = x_n = 0$ and if $x_k = 15$, what is the value of n?

(A) 5
(B) 6
(C) 9
(D) 10
(E) 15

128. If $x \neq 2$, then $\frac{3x^2(x-2)-x+2}{x-2} =$

(A) $3x^2 - x + 2$
(B) $3x^2 + 1$
(C) $3x^2$
(D) $3x^2 - 1$
(E) $3x^2 - 2$

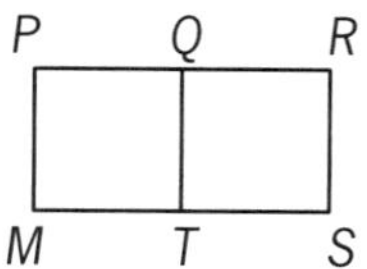

Note: Not drawn to scale.

129. In the figure shown above, line segment QR has length 12, and rectangle $MPQT$ is a square. If the area of rectangular region $MPRS$ is 540, what is the area of rectangular region $TQRS$?

(A) 144
(B) 216
(C) 324
(D) 360
(E) 396

130. Machines A and B always operate independently and at their respective constant rates. When working alone, Machine A can fill a production lot in 5 hours, and Machine B can fill the same lot in x hours. When the two machines operate simultaneously to fill the production lot, it takes them 2 hours to complete the job. What is the value of x?

(A) $3\frac{1}{3}$

(B) 3

(C) $2\frac{1}{2}$

(D) $2\frac{1}{3}$

(E) $1\frac{1}{2}$

131. A certain manufacturer sells its product to stores in 113 different regions worldwide, with an average (arithmetic mean) of 181 stores per region. If last year these stores sold an average of 51,752 units of the manufacturer's product per store, which of the following is closest to the total number of units of the manufacturer's product sold worldwide last year?

(A) 10^6
(B) 10^7
(C) 10^8
(D) 10^9
(E) 10^{10}

132. Andrew started saving at the beginning of the year and had saved $240 by the end of the year. He continued to save and by the end of 2 years had saved a total of $540. Which of the following is closest to the percent increase in the amount Andrew saved during the second year compared to the amount he saved during the first year?

(A) 11%
(B) 25%
(C) 44%
(D) 56%
(E) 125%

133. Two numbers differ by 2 and sum to S. Which of the following is the greater of the numbers in terms of S?

(A) $\frac{S}{2} - 1$
(B) $\frac{S}{2}$
(C) $\frac{S}{2} + \frac{1}{2}$
(D) $\frac{S}{2} + 1$
(E) $\frac{S}{2} + 2$

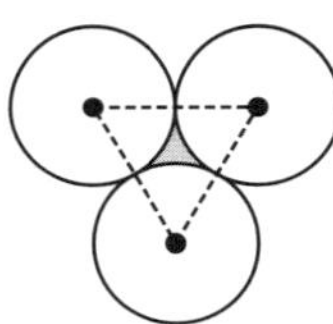

134. The figure shown above consists of three identical circles that are tangent to each other. If the area of the shaded region is $64\sqrt{3} - 32\pi$, what is the radius of each circle?

(A) 4
(B) 8
(C) 16
(D) 24
(E) 32

135. In a numerical table with 10 rows and 10 columns, each entry is either a 9 or a 10. If the number of 9s in the nth row is $n - 1$ for each n from 1 to 10, what is the average (arithmetic mean) of all the numbers in the table?

(A) 9.45
(B) 9.50
(C) 9.55
(D) 9.65
(E) 9.70

136. A positive integer n is a perfect number provided that the sum of all the positive factors of n, including 1 and n, is equal to $2n$. What is the sum of the reciprocals of all the positive factors of the perfect number 28?

(A) $\frac{1}{4}$
(B) $\frac{56}{27}$
(C) 2
(D) 3
(E) 4

137. The infinite sequence $a_1, a_2, \ldots, a_n, \ldots$ is such that $a_1 = 2$, $a_2 = -3$, $a_3 = 5$, $a_4 = -1$, and $a_n = a_{n-4}$ for $n > 4$. What is the sum of the first 97 terms of the sequence?

(A) 72
(B) 74
(C) 75
(D) 78
(E) 80

138. The sequence $a_1, a_2, \ldots a_n, \ldots$ is such that $a_n = 2a_{n-1} - x$ for all positive integers $n \geq 2$ and for a certain number x. If $a_5 = 99$ and $a_3 = 27$, what is the value of x?

(A) 3
(B) 9
(C) 18
(D) 36
(E) 45

139. A window is in the shape of a regular hexagon with each side of length 80 centimeters. If a diagonal through the center of the hexagon is *w* centimeters long, then *w* =

(A) 80
(B) 120
(C) 150
(D) 160
(E) 240

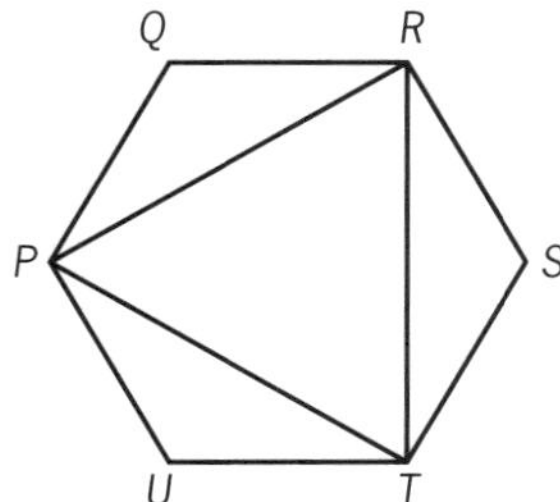

140. In the figure shown, *PQRSTU* is a regular polygon with sides of length x. What is the perimeter of triangle *PRT* in terms of *x* ?

(A) $\frac{x\sqrt{3}}{2}$
(B) $x\sqrt{3}$
(C) $\frac{3x\sqrt{3}}{2}$
(D) $3x\sqrt{3}$
(E) $4x\sqrt{3}$

141. In a certain medical survey, 45 percent of the people surveyed had the type A antigen in their blood and 3 percent had both the type A antigen and the type B antigen. Which of the following is closest to the percent of those with the type A antigen who also had the type B antigen?

(A) 1.35%
(B) 6.67%
(C) 13.50%
(D) 15.00%
(E) 42.00%

142. On a certain transatlantic crossing, 20 percent of a ship's passengers held round-trip tickets and also took their cars aboard the ship. If 60 percent of the passengers with round-trip tickets did not take their cars aboard the ship, what percent of the ship's passengers held round-trip tickets?

(A) $33\frac{1}{3}\%$
(B) 40%
(C) 50%
(D) 60%
(E) $66\frac{2}{3}\%$

143. If *x* and *k* are integers and $(12^x)(4^{2x+1}) = (2^k)(3^2)$, what is the value of *k* ?

(A) 5
(B) 7
(C) 10
(D) 12
(E) 14

144. If *S* is the sum of the reciprocals of the 10 consecutive integers from 21 to 30, then *S* is between which of the following two fractions?

(A) $\frac{1}{3}$ and $\frac{1}{2}$
(B) $\frac{1}{4}$ and $\frac{1}{3}$
(C) $\frac{1}{5}$ and $\frac{1}{4}$
(D) $\frac{1}{6}$ and $\frac{1}{5}$
(E) $\frac{1}{7}$ and $\frac{1}{6}$

145. For every even positive integer m, $f(m)$ represents the product of all even integers from 2 to m, inclusive. For example, $f(12) = 2 \times 4 \times 6 \times 8 \times 10 \times 12$. What is the greatest prime factor of $f(24)$?

(A) 23
(B) 19
(C) 17
(D) 13
(E) 11

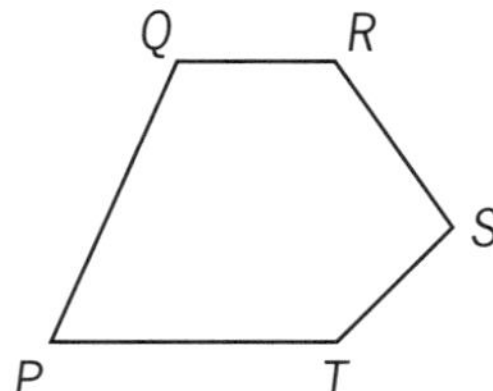

Note: Not drawn to scale.

146. In pentagon $PQRST$, $PQ = 3$, $QR = 2$, $RS = 4$, and $ST = 5$. Which of the lengths 5, 10, and 15 could be the value of PT ?

(A) 5 only
(B) 15 only
(C) 5 and 10 only
(D) 10 and 15 only
(E) 5, 10, and 15

3, k, 2, 8, m, 3

147. The arithmetic mean of the list of numbers above is 4. If k and m are integers and $k \neq m$, what is the median of the list?

(A) 2
(B) 2.5
(C) 3
(D) 3.5
(E) 4

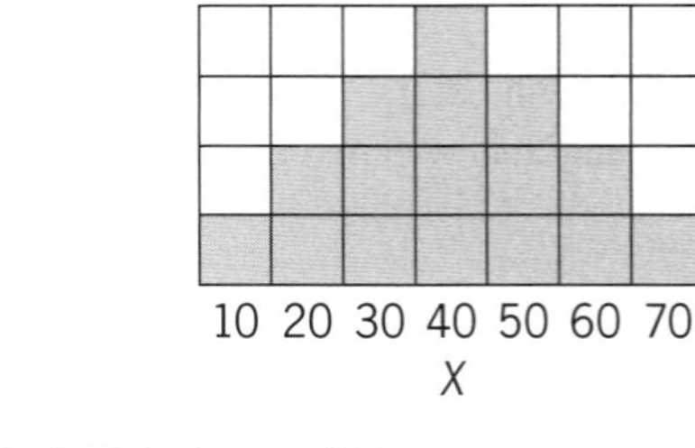

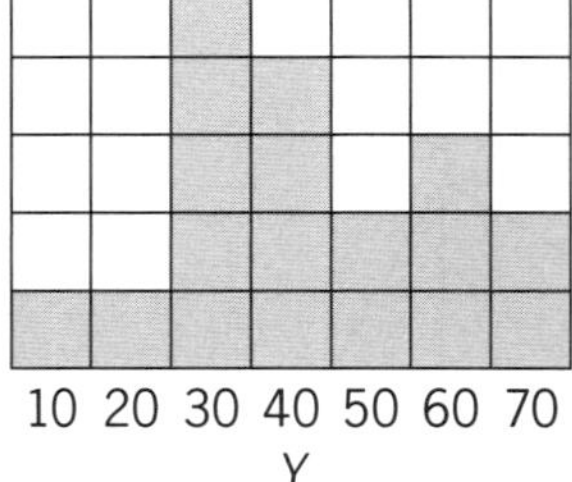

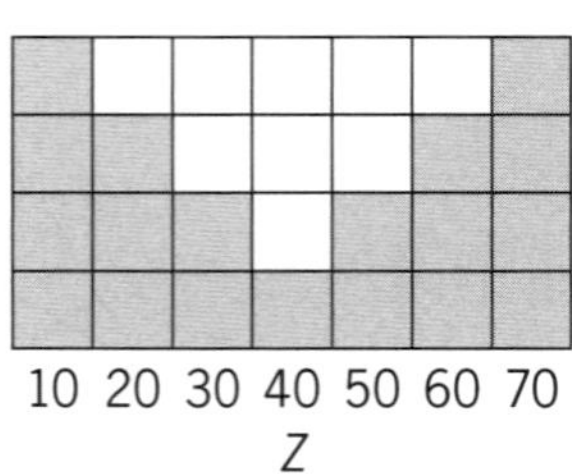

148. If the variables, X, Y, and Z take on only the values 10, 20, 30, 40, 50, 60, or 70 with frequencies indicated by the shaded regions above, for which of the frequency distributions is the mean equal to the median?

(A) X only
(B) Y only
(C) Z only
(D) X and Y
(E) X and Z

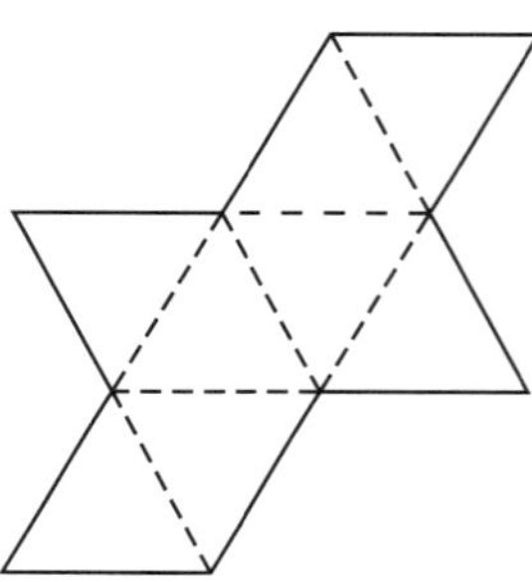

149. When the figure above is cut along the solid lines, folded along the dashed lines, and taped along the solid lines, the result is a model of a geometric solid. This geometric solid consists of 2 pyramids, each with a square base that they share. What is the sum of the number of edges and the number of faces of this geometric solid?

(A) 10
(B) 18
(C) 20
(D) 24
(E) 25

$$2x + y = 12$$
$$|y| \le 12$$

150. For how many ordered pairs (x,y) that are solutions of the system above are x and y both integers?

(A) 7
(B) 10
(C) 12
(D) 13
(E) 14

151. The points R, T, and U lie on a circle that has radius 4. If the length of arc RTU is $\frac{4\pi}{3}$, what is the length of line segment RU?

(A) $\frac{4}{3}$
(B) $\frac{8}{3}$
(C) 3
(D) 4
(E) 6

152. A certain university will select 1 of 7 candidates eligible to fill a position in the mathematics department and 2 of 10 candidates eligible to fill 2 identical positions in the computer science department. If none of the candidates is eligible for a position in both departments, how many different sets of 3 candidates are there to fill the 3 positions?

(A) 42
(B) 70
(C) 140
(D) 165
(E) 315

153. A survey of employers found that during 1993 employment costs rose 3.5 percent, where employment costs consist of salary costs and fringe-benefit costs. If salary costs rose 3 percent and fringe-benefit costs rose 5.5 percent during 1993, then fringe-benefit costs represented what percent of employment costs at the beginning of 1993?

(A) 16.5%
(B) 20%
(C) 35%
(D) 55%
(E) 65%

154. The subsets of the set $\{w, x, y\}$ are $\{w\}$, $\{x\}$, $\{y\}$, $\{w, x\}$, $\{w, y\}$, $\{x, y\}$, $\{w, x, y\}$, and $\{\ \}$ (the empty subset). How many subsets of the set $\{w, x, y, z\}$ contain w?

(A) Four
(B) Five
(C) Seven
(D) Eight
(E) Sixteen

155. There are 5 cars to be displayed in 5 parking spaces, with all the cars facing the same direction. Of the 5 cars, 3 are red, 1 is blue, and 1 is yellow. If the cars are identical except for color, how many different display arrangements of the 5 cars are possible?

(A) 20
(B) 25
(C) 40
(D) 60
(E) 125

156. The number $\sqrt{63 - 36\sqrt{3}}$ can be expressed as $x + y\sqrt{3}$ for some integers x and y. What is the value of xy?

(A) −18
(B) −6
(C) 6
(D) 18
(E) 27

157. There are 10 books on a shelf, of which 4 are paperbacks and 6 are hardbacks. How many possible selections of 5 books from the shelf contain at least one paperback and at least one hardback?

(A) 75
(B) 120
(C) 210
(D) 246
(E) 252

158. If x is to be chosen at random from the set {1, 2, 3, 4} and y is to be chosen at random from the set {5, 6, 7}, what is the probability that xy will be even?

(A) $\frac{1}{6}$

(B) $\frac{1}{3}$

(C) $\frac{1}{2}$

(D) $\frac{2}{3}$

(E) $\frac{5}{6}$

159. The function f is defined for each positive three-digit integer n by $f(n) = 2^x 3^y 5^z$, where x, y, and z are the hundreds, tens, and units digits of n, respectively. If m and v are three-digit positive integers such that $f(m) = 9f(v)$, then $m - v =$

(A) 8

(B) 9

(C) 18

(C) 20

(E) 80

160. If $10^{50} - 74$ is written as an integer in base 10 notation, what is the sum of the digits in that integer?

(A) 424

(B) 433

(C) 440

(D) 449

(E) 467

161. A certain company that sells only cars and trucks reported that revenues from car sales in 1997 were down 11 percent from 1996 and revenues from truck sales in 1997 were up 7 percent from 1996. If total revenues from car sales and truck sales in 1997 were up 1 percent from 1996, what is the ratio of revenue from car sales in 1996 to revenue from truck sales in 1996 ?

(A) 1:2

(B) 4:5

(C) 1:1

(D) 3:2

(E) 5:3

162. Becky rented a power tool from a rental shop. The rent for the tool was $12 for the first hour and $3 for each additional hour. If Becky paid a total of $27, excluding sales tax, to rent the tool, for how many hours did she rent it?

(A) 5

(B) 6

(C) 9

(D) 10

(E) 12

163. If $4 < \frac{7-x}{3}$, which of the following must be true?

I. $5 < x$

II. $|x + 3| > 2$

III. $-(x + 5)$ is positive.

(A) II only

(B) III only

(C) I and II only

(D) II and III only

(E) I, II, and III

164. A certain right triangle has sides of length x, y, and z, where $x < y < z$. If the area of this triangular region is 1, which of the following indicates all of the possible values of y ?

(A) $y > \sqrt{2}$

(B) $\frac{\sqrt{3}}{2} < y < \sqrt{2}$

(C) $\frac{\sqrt{2}}{3} < y < \frac{\sqrt{3}}{2}$

(D) $\frac{\sqrt{3}}{4} < y < \frac{\sqrt{2}}{3}$

(E) $y < \frac{\sqrt{3}}{4}$

165. On a certain day, a bakery produced a batch of rolls at a total production cost of \$300. On that day, $\frac{4}{5}$ of the rolls in the batch were sold, each at a price that was 50 percent greater than the average (arithmetic mean) production cost per roll. The remaining rolls in the batch were sold the next day, each at a price that was 20 percent less than the price of the day before. What was the bakery's profit on this batch of rolls?

(A) \$150
(B) \$144
(C) \$132
(D) \$108
(E) \$90

166. A set of numbers has the property that for any number t in the set, $t + 2$ is in the set. If -1 is in the set, which of the following must also be in the set?

I. -3
II. 1
III. 5

(A) I only
(B) II only
(C) I and II only
(D) II and III only
(E) I, II, and III

167. A couple decides to have 4 children. If they succeed in having 4 children and each child is equally likely to be a boy or a girl, what is the probability that they will have exactly 2 girls and 2 boys?

(A) $\frac{3}{8}$
(B) $\frac{1}{4}$
(C) $\frac{3}{16}$
(D) $\frac{1}{8}$
(E) $\frac{1}{16}$

168. The closing price of Stock X changed on each trading day last month. The percent change in the closing price of Stock X from the first trading day last month to each of the other trading days last month was less than 50 percent. If the closing price on the second trading day last month was \$10.00, which of the following CANNOT be the closing price on the last trading day last month?

(A) \$3.00
(B) \$9.00
(C) \$19.00
(D) \$24.00
(E) \$29.00

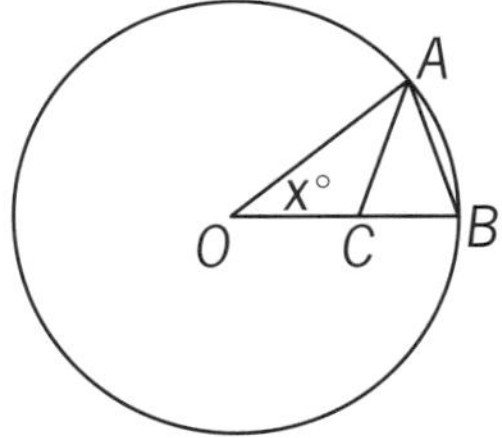

169. In the figure above, point O is the center of the circle and $OC = AC = AB$. What is the value of x?

(A) 40
(B) 36
(C) 34
(D) 32
(E) 30

170. An airline passenger is planning a trip that involves three connecting flights that leave from Airports A, B, and C, respectively. The first flight leaves Airport A every hour, beginning at 8:00 a.m., and arrives at Airport B $2\frac{1}{2}$ hours later. The second flight leaves Airport B every 20 minutes, beginning at 8:00 a.m., and arrives at Airport C $1\frac{1}{6}$ hours later. The third flight leaves Airport C every hour, beginning at 8:45 a.m. What is the <u>least</u> total amount of time the passenger must spend between flights if all flights keep to their schedules?

(A) 25 min
(B) 1 hr 5 min
(C) 1 hr 15 min
(D) 2 hr 20 min
(E) 3 hr 40 min

171. If n is a positive integer and n^2 is divisible by 72, then the largest positive integer that must divide n is

(A) 6
(B) 12
(C) 24
(D) 36
(E) 48

172. A certain grocery purchased x pounds of produce for p dollars per pound. If y pounds of the produce had to be discarded due to spoilage and the grocery sold the rest for s dollars per pound, which of the following represents the gross profit on the sale of the produce?

(A) $(x - y)s - xp$
(B) $(x - y)p - ys$
(C) $(s - p)y - xp$
(D) $xp - ys$
(E) $(x - y)(s - p)$

173. If x, y, and z are positive integers such that x is a factor of y, and x is a multiple of z, which of the following is NOT necessarily an integer?

(A) $\frac{x+z}{z}$
(B) $\frac{y+z}{x}$
(C) $\frac{x+y}{z}$
(D) $\frac{xy}{z}$
(E) $\frac{yz}{x}$

174. Running at their respective constant rates, Machine X takes 2 days longer to produce w widgets than Machine Y. At these rates, if the two machines together produce $\frac{5}{4}w$ widgets in 3 days, how many days would it take Machine X alone to produce $2w$ widgets?

(A) 4
(B) 6
(C) 8
(D) 10
(E) 12

175. A square wooden plaque has a square brass inlay in the center, leaving a wooden strip of uniform width around the brass square. If the ratio of the brass area to the wooden area is 25 to 39, which of the following could be the width, in inches, of the wooden strip?

I. 1
II. 3
III. 4

(A) I only
(B) II only
(C) I and II only
(D) I and III only
(E) I, II, and III

176. $\dfrac{2\frac{3}{5}-1\frac{2}{3}}{\frac{2}{3}-\frac{3}{5}}=$

(A) 16
(B) 14
(C) 3
(D) 1
(E) -1

4.4 Answer Key

1.	D	33.	A	65.	D	97.	C
2.	E	34.	C	66.	D	98.	A
3.	C	35.	E	67.	C	99.	E
4.	A	36.	D	68.	A	100.	E
5.	C	37.	C	69.	C	101.	E
6.	C	38.	A	70.	A	102.	B
7.	C	39.	A	71.	D	103.	E
8.	E	40.	A	72.	B	104.	C
9.	B	41.	D	73.	E	105.	E
10.	D	42.	B	74.	B	106.	B
11.	B	43.	C	75.	E	107.	B
12.	C	44.	C	76.	D	108.	B
13.	D	45.	B	77.	B	109.	C
14.	D	46.	A	78.	C	110.	C
15.	C	47.	B	79.	A	111.	E
16.	C	48.	C	80.	C	112.	B
17.	A	49.	B	81.	C	113.	B
18.	B	50.	E	82.	D	114.	E
19.	A	51.	C	83.	B	115.	E
20.	C	52.	B	84.	B	116.	B
21.	C	53.	D	85.	C	117.	B
22.	D	54.	C	86.	D	118.	B
23.	E	55.	E	87.	B	119.	A
24.	D	56.	C	88.	A	120.	B
25.	E	57.	B	89.	D	121.	D
26.	E	58.	A	90.	B	122.	B
27.	D	59.	D	91.	B	123.	C
28.	C	60.	C	92.	C	124.	B
29.	E	61.	D	93.	B	125.	E
30.	D	62.	C	94.	B	126.	B
31.	D	63.	B	95.	D	127.	D
32.	E	64.	D	96.	B	128.	D

129. B
130. A
131. D
132. B
133. D
134. B
135. C
136. C
137. B
138. A
139. D
140. D
141. B
142. C
143. E
144. A
145. E
146. C
147. C
148. E
149. C
150. D
151. D
152. E
153. B
154. D
155. A
156. A
157. D
158. D
159. D
160. C
161. A
162. B
163. D
164. A
165. C
166. D
167. A
168. A
169. B
170. B
171. B
172. A
173. B
174. E
175. E
176. B

4.5 Answer Explanations

The following discussion is intended to familiarize you with the most efficient and effective approaches to the kinds of problems common to problem solving questions. The particular questions in this chapter are generally representative of the kinds of problem solving questions you will encounter on the GMAT. Remember that it is the problem solving strategy that is important, not the specific details of a particular question.

1. If $x + y = 2$ and $x^2 + y^2 = 2$, what is the value of xy ?

(A) −2
(B) −1
(C) 0
(D) 1
(E) 2

Algebra Second-degree equations

$x + y = 2$	given
$y = 2 - x$	subtract x from both sides
$x^2 + (2 - x)^2 = 2$	substitute $y = 2 - x$ into $x^2 + y^2 = 2$
$2x^2 - 4x + 4 = 2$	expand and combine like terms
$2x^2 - 4x + 2 = 0$	subtract 2 from both sides
$x^2 - 2x + 1 = 0$	divide both sides by 2
$(x - 1)(x - 1) = 0$	factor
$x = 1$	set each factor equal to 0
$y = 1$	use $x = 1$ and $y = 2 - x$
$xy = 1$	multiply 1 and 1

Alternatively, the value of xy can be found by first squaring both sides of the equation $x + y = 2$.

$x + y = 2$	given
$(x + y)^2 = 4$	square both sides
$x^2 + 2xy + y^2 = 4$	expand and combine like terms
$2 + 2xy = 4$	replace $x^2 + y^2$ with 2
$2xy = 2$	subtract 2 from both sides
$xy = 1$	divide both sides by 2

The correct answer is D.

2. Points A, B, C, and D, in that order, lie on a line. If $AB = 3$ cm, $AC = 4$ cm, and $BD = 6$ cm, what is CD, in centimeters?

(A) 1
(B) 2
(C) 3
(D) 4
(E) 5

Geometry Lines and segments

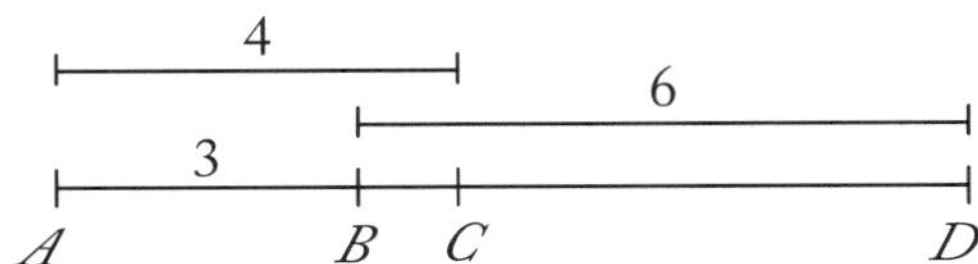

The figure shows points A, B, C, and D as well as the given measurements. Since $AC = AB + BC$, it follows that $4 = 3 + BC$, and so $BC = 1$. Then, since $BD = BC + CD$, it follows that $6 = 1 + CD$, and so $CD = 5$.

Alternately, $AD = AB + BD = 3 + 6 = 9$. Also, $AD = AC + CD$, so $9 = 4 + CD$ and $CD = 5$.

The correct answer is E.

3. What is the value of $x^2yz - xyz^2$, if $x = -2$, $y = 1$, and $z = 3$?

(A) 20
(B) 24
(C) 30
(D) 32
(E) 48

Algebra Operations on integers

Given that $x = -2$, $y = 1$, and $z = 3$, it follows by substitution that

$$\begin{aligned} x^2yz - xyz^2 &= (-2)^2(1)(3) - (-2)(1)(3^2) \\ &= (4)(1)(3) - (-2)(1)(9) \\ &= 12 - (-18) \\ &= 12 + 18 \\ &= 30 \end{aligned}$$

The correct answer is C.

4. If $x > y$ and $y > z$, which of the following represents the greatest number?

(A) $x - z$
(B) $x - y$
(C) $y - x$
(D) $z - y$
(E) $z - x$

Algebra Inequalities

From $x > y$ and $y > z$, it follows that $x > z$. These inequalities imply the following about the differences that are given in the answer choices:

Answer choice	Difference	Algebraic sign	Reason
(A)	$x - z$	positive	$x > z$ implies $x - z > 0$
(B)	$x - y$	positive	$x > y$ implies $x - y > 0$
(C)	$y - x$	negative	$x - y > 0$ implies $y - x < 0$
(D)	$z - y$	negative	$y > z$ implies $0 > z - y$
(E)	$z - x$	negative	$x - z > 0$ implies $z - x < 0$

Since the expressions in A and B represent positive numbers and the expressions in C, D, and E represent negative numbers, the latter can be eliminated because every negative number is less than every positive number. To determine which of $x - z$ and $x - y$ is greater, consider the placement of points with coordinates x, y, and z on the number line.

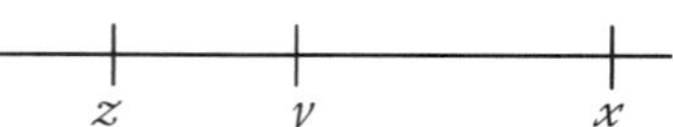

The distance between x and z (that is, $x - z$) is the sum of the distance between x and y (that is, $x - y$) and the distance between y and z (that is, $y - z$). Therefore, $(x - z) > (x - y)$, which means that $x - z$ represents the greater of the numbers represented by $(x - z)$ and $(x - y)$. Thus, $x - z$ represents the greatest of the numbers represented by the answer choices.

Alternatively,

$y > z$	given
$-y < -z$	multiply both sides by -1
$x - y < x - z$	add x to both sides

Thus, $x - z$ represents the greater of the numbers represented by $(x - z)$ and $(x - y)$. Therefore, $x - z$ represents the greatest of the numbers represented by the answer choices.

The correct answer is A.

5. To order certain plants from a catalog, it costs \$3.00 per plant, plus a 5 percent sales tax, plus \$6.95 for shipping and handling regardless of the number of plants ordered. If Company C ordered these plants from the catalog at the total cost of \$69.95, how many plants did Company C order?

(A) 22
(B) 21
(C) 20
(D) 19
(E) 18

Algebra First-degree equations

Letting x represent the number of plants Company C bought from the catalog, then, in dollars, $3.00x$ is the cost of the plants, $(0.05)(3.00x)$ is the sales tax, and 6.95 is the shipping and handling fee. It follows that

$3.00x + (0.05)(3.00x) + 6.95 = 69.95$	plants + tax + shipping = total
$(3.00x)(1.05) + 6.95 = 69.95$	add like terms
$(3.00x)(1.05) = 63.00$	subtract 6.95 from both sides
$x = 20$	divide both sides by (3.00)(1.05)

Therefore, Company C bought 20 plants from the catalog.

The correct answer is C.

6. Company C produces toy trucks at a cost of \$5.00 each for the first 100 trucks and \$3.50 for each additional truck. If 500 toy trucks were produced by Company C and sold for \$10.00 each, what was Company C's gross profit?

(A) \$2,250
(B) \$2,500
(C) \$3,100
(D) \$3,250
(E) \$3,500

Arithmetic Applied problems

The company's gross profit on the 500 toy trucks is the company's revenue from selling the trucks minus the company's cost of producing the trucks. The revenue is (500)(\$10.00) = \$5,000. The cost for the first 100 trucks is (100)(\$5.00) = \$500, and the cost for the other 400 trucks is (400)(\$3.50) = \$1,400 for a total cost of \$500 + \$1,400 = \$1,900. Thus, the company's gross profit is \$5,000 – \$1,900 = \$3,100.

The correct answer is C.

7. A group of store managers must assemble 280 displays for an upcoming sale. If they assemble 25 percent of the displays during the first hour and 40 percent of the remaining displays during the second hour, how many of the displays will <u>not</u> have been assembled by the end of the second hour?

(A) 70
(B) 98
(C) 126
(D) 168
(E) 182

Arithmetic Percents

If, during the first hour, 25 percent of the total displays were assembled, then 280(0.25) = 70 displays were assembled, leaving 280 – 70 = 210 displays remaining to be assembled. Since 40 percent of the remaining displays were assembled during the second hour, 0.40(210) = 84 displays were assembled during the second hour. Thus, 70 + 84 = 154 displays were assembled during the first two hours and 280 – 154 = 126 displays had not been assembled by the end of the second hour.

The correct answer is C.

8. Of the following, which is least?

(A) $\frac{0.03}{0.00071}$
(B) $\frac{0.03}{0.0071}$
(C) $\frac{0.03}{0.071}$
(D) $\frac{0.03}{0.71}$
(E) $\frac{0.03}{7.1}$

Arithmetic Operations on rational numbers

Since the numerator of all of the fractions in the answer choices is 0.03, the least of the fractions will be the fraction with the greatest denominator. The greatest denominator is 7.1, and so the least of the fractions is $\frac{0.03}{7.1}$.

The correct answer is E.

9. The maximum recommended pulse rate R, when exercising, for a person who is x years of age is given by the equation $R = 176 - 0.8x$. What is the age, in years, of a person whose maximum recommended pulse rate when exercising is 140 ?

(A) 40
(B) 45
(C) 50
(D) 55
(E) 60

Algebra Substitution; Operations with rational numbers

Substitute 140 for R in the given equation and solve for x.

$$140 = 176 - 0.8x$$
$$-36 = -0.8x$$
$$\frac{-36}{-0.8} = x$$
$$45 = x$$

The correct answer is B.

10. If the average (arithmetic mean) of 5 numbers j, $j + 5$, $2j - 1$, $4j - 2$, and $5j - 1$ is 8, what is the value of j?

(A) $\frac{1}{3}$
(B) $\frac{7}{13}$
(C) 1
(D) 3
(E) 8

Algebra First-degree equations

$\frac{j+(j+5)+(2j-1)+(4j-2)+(5j-1)}{5} = 8$	given
$j+(j+5)+(2j-1)+(4j-2)+(5j-1) = 40$	multiply both sides by 5
$13j + 1 = 40$	combine like terms
$13j = 39$	subtract 1 from both sides
$j = 3$	divide both sides by 13

The correct answer is D.

11. Guadalupe owns 2 rectangular tracts of land. One is 300 m by 500 m and the other is 250 m by 630 m. The combined area of these 2 tracts is how many square meters?

(A) 3,360
(B) 307,500
(C) 621,500
(D) 704,000
(E) 2,816,000

Geometry Area

The area of a rectangle can be found by multiplying the length and width of the rectangle. Therefore, the combined area, in square meters, of the 2 rectangular tracts of land is $(300)(500) + (250)(630) = 150{,}000 + 157{,}500 = 307{,}500$.

The correct answer is B.

12. There are five sales agents in a certain real estate office. One month Andy sold twice as many properties as Ellen, Bob sold 3 more than Ellen, Cary sold twice as many as Bob, and Dora sold as many as Bob and Ellen together. Who sold the most properties that month?

(A) Andy
(B) Bob
(C) Cary
(D) Dora
(E) Ellen

Algebra Order

Let x represent the number of properties that Ellen sold, where $x \geq 0$. Then, since Andy sold twice as many properties as Ellen, $2x$ represents the number of properties that Andy sold. Bob sold 3 more properties than Ellen, so $(x + 3)$ represents the number of properties that Bob sold. Cary sold twice as many properties as Bob, so $2(x + 3) = (2x + 6)$ represents the number of properties that Cary sold. Finally, Dora sold as many properties as Bob and Ellen combined, so $[(x + 3) + x] = (2x + 3)$ represents the number of properties that Dora sold. The following table summarizes these results.

Agent	Properties sold
Andy	$2x$
Bob	$x + 3$
Cary	$2x + 6$
Dora	$2x + 3$
Ellen	x

Since $x \geq 0$, clearly $2x + 6$ exceeds x, $x + 3$, $2x$, and $2x + 3$. Therefore, Cary sold the most properties.

The correct answer is C.

13. In a field day at a school, each child who competed in n events and scored a total of p points was given an overall score of $\frac{p}{n}+n$. Andrew competed in 1 event and scored 9 points. Jason competed in 3 events and scored 5, 6, and 7 points, respectively. What was the ratio of Andrew's overall score to Jason's overall score?

(A) $\frac{10}{23}$

(B) $\frac{7}{10}$

(C) $\frac{4}{5}$

(D) $\frac{10}{9}$

(E) $\frac{12}{7}$

Algebra Applied problems; Substitution

Andrew participated in 1 event and scored 9 points, so his overall score was $\frac{9}{1}+1=10$. Jason participated in 3 events and scored $5+6+7=18$ points, so his overall score was $\frac{18}{3}+3=9$. The ratio of Andrew's overall score to Jason's overall score was $\frac{10}{9}$.

The correct answer is D.

14. Which of the following represent positive numbers?

I. $-3-(-5)$

II. $(-3)(-5)$

III. $-5-(-3)$

(A) I only

(B) II only

(C) III only

(D) I and II

(E) II and III

Arithmetic Operations on integers

Find the value of each expression to determine if it is positive.

I. $-3-(-5)=-3+5=2$, which is positive.

II. $(-3)(-5)=15$, which is positive.

III. $-5-(-3)=-5+3=-2$, which is not positive.

The correct answer is D.

15. If $\frac{x}{4}$ is 2 more than $\frac{x}{8}$, then $x=$

(A) 4

(B) 8

(C) 16

(D) 32

(E) 64

Algebra First-degree equations

Write an equation for the given information and solve for x.

$$\frac{x}{4}=2+\frac{x}{8}$$

$$(8)\left(\frac{x}{4}\right)=(8)\left(2+\frac{x}{8}\right)$$

$$2x=16+x$$

$$x=16$$

The correct answer is C.

16. If Mario was 32 years old 8 years ago, how old was he x years ago?

(A) $x-40$

(B) $x-24$

(C) $40-x$

(D) $24-x$

(E) $24+x$

Arithmetic Operations on rational numbers

Since Mario was 32 years old 8 years ago, his age now is $32+8=40$ years old. Therefore, x years ago Mario was $40-x$ years old.

The correct answer is C.

17. A grocer has 400 pounds of coffee in stock, 20 percent of which is decaffeinated. If the grocer buys another 100 pounds of coffee of which 60 percent is decaffeinated, what percent, by weight, of the grocer's stock of coffee is decaffeinated?

(A) 28%
(B) 30%
(C) 32%
(D) 34%
(E) 40%

Arithmetic Percents

The grocer has 400 pounds of coffee in stock, of which (400)(20%) = 80 pounds is decaffeinated coffee. Therefore, if the grocer buys 100 pounds of coffee, of which (100)(60%) = 60 pounds is decaffeinated coffee, then the percent of the grocer's stock of coffee that is decaffeinated would be $\frac{80+60}{400+100}=\frac{140}{500}=\frac{28}{100}=28\%$.

The correct answer is A.

18. The toll T, in dollars, for a truck using a certain bridge is given by the formula $T = 1.50 + 0.50(x - 2)$, where x is the number of axles on the truck. What is the toll for an 18-wheel truck that has 2 wheels on its front axle and 4 wheels on each of its other axles?

(A) \$2.50
(B) \$3.00
(C) \$3.50
(D) \$4.00
(E) \$5.00

Algebra Operations on rational numbers

The 18-wheel truck has 2 wheels on its front axle and 4 wheels on each of its other axles, and so if A represents the number of axles on the truck in addition to the front axle, then $2 + 4A = 18$, from which it follows that $4A = 16$ and $A = 4$. Therefore, the total number of axles on the truck is $1 + A = 1 + 4 = 5$. Then, using $T = 1.50 + 0.50(x - 2)$, where x is the number of axles on the truck and $x = 5$, it follows that $T = 1.50 + 0.50(5 - 2) = 1.50 + 1.50 = 3.00$. Therefore, the toll for the truck is \$3.00.

The correct answer is B.

19. For what value of x between –4 and 4, inclusive, is the value of $x^2 - 10x + 16$ the greatest?

(A) –4
(B) –2
(C) 0
(D) 2
(E) 4

Algebra Second-degree equations

Given the expression $x^2 - 10x + 16$, a table of values can be created for the corresponding function $f(x) = x^2 - 10x + 16$ and the graph in the standard (x,y) coordinate plane can be sketched by plotting selected points:

x	$f(x)$
–4	72
–3	55
–2	40
–1	27
0	16
1	7
2	0
3	–5
4	–8
5	–9
6	–8
7	–5
8	0
9	7

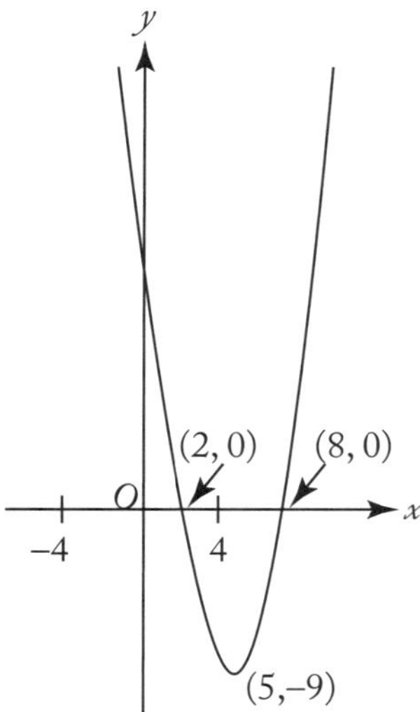

It is clear from both the table of values and the sketch of the graph that as the value of x increases from –4 to 4, the values of $x^2 - 10x + 16$ decrease. Therefore, the value of $x^2 - 10x + 16$ is greatest when $x = -4$.

Alternatively, the given expression, $x^2 - 10x + 16$, has the form $ax^2 + bx + c$, where $a = 1$, $b = -10$, and $c = 16$. The graph in the standard (x,y) coordinate plane of the corresponding function $f(x) = ax^2 + bx + c$ is a parabola with vertex at $x = -\frac{b}{2a}$, and so the vertex of the graph of $f(x) = x^2 - 10x + 16$ is at

$$x = -\left(\frac{-10}{2(1)}\right) = 5.$$

Because $a = 1$ and 1 is positive, this parabola opens upward and values of $x^2 - 10x + 16$ decrease as x increases from –4 to 4. Therefore, the greatest value of $x^2 - 10x + 16$ for all values of x between –4 and 4, inclusive, is at $x = -4$.

The correct answer is A.

20. If $x = -\frac{5}{8}$ and $y = -\frac{1}{2}$, what is the value of the expression $-2x - y^2$?

(A) $-\frac{3}{2}$

(B) –1

(C) 1

(D) $\frac{3}{2}$

(E) $\frac{7}{4}$

Algebra Fractions

If $x = -\frac{5}{8}$ and $y = -\frac{1}{2}$, then

$$-2x - y^2 = -2\left(-\frac{5}{8}\right) - \left(-\frac{1}{2}\right)^2 = \frac{5}{4} - \frac{1}{4} = \frac{4}{4} = 1.$$

The correct answer is C.

21. The number 2 – 0.5 is how many times the number 1 – 0.5 ?

(A) 2

(B) 2.5

(C) 3

(D) 3.5

(E) 4

Arithmetic Operations on rational numbers

Set up an equation in the order given in the problem, and solve for x.

$$(2 - 0.5) = (1 - 0.5)x$$
$$1.5 = 0.5x$$
$$3 = x$$

The correct answer is C.

22. If $x - y = R$ and $xy = S$, then $(x - 2)(y + 2) =$

(A) $R + S - 4$

(B) $R + 2S - 4$

(C) $2R - S - 4$

(D) $2R + S - 4$

(E) $2R + S$

Algebra Simplifying algebraic expressions; Substitution

$$\begin{aligned}(x-2)(y+2) &= xy + 2x - 2y - 4 && \text{multiply binomials}\\ &= xy + 2(x - y) - 4 && \text{distributive principle}\\ &= S + 2R - 4 && \text{substitution}\\ &= 2R + S - 4 && \text{commutative principle}\end{aligned}$$

The correct answer is D.

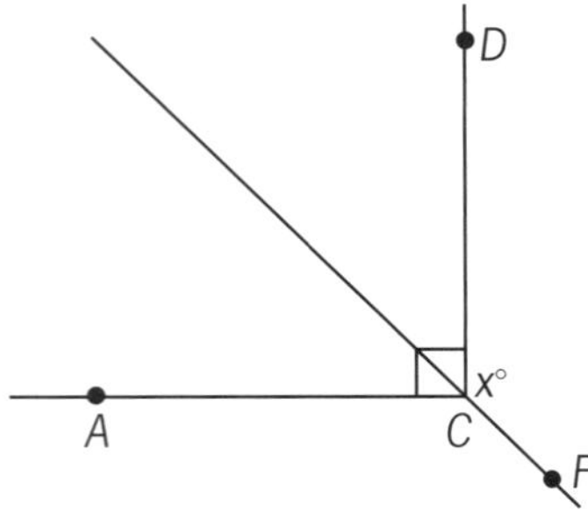

23. In the figure above, if *F* is a point on the line that bisects angle *ACD* and the measure of angle *DCF* is $x°$, which of the following is true of x ?

(A) $90 \le x < 100$
(B) $100 \le x < 110$
(C) $110 \le x < 120$
(D) $120 \le x < 130$
(E) $130 \le x < 140$

Geometry Angles

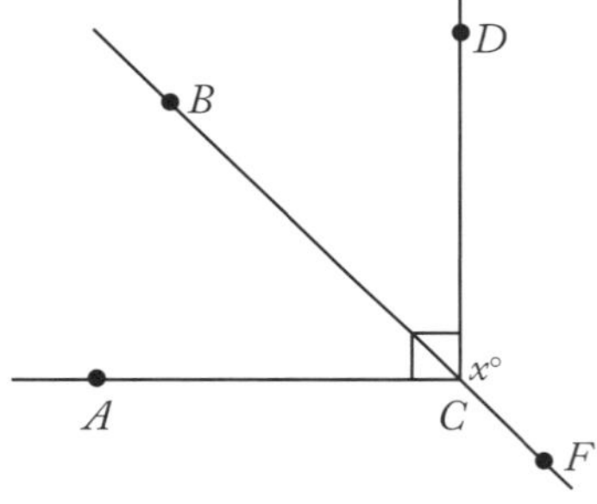

As shown in the figure above, if B is on the line that bisects $\angle ACD$ then the degree measure of $\angle DCB$ is $\frac{90}{2} = 45$. Then because B, C, and F are collinear, the sum of the degree measures of $\angle BCD$ and $\angle DCF$ is 180. Therefore, $x = 180 - 45 = 135$ and $130 \le 135 < 140$.

The correct answer is E.

24. In which of the following pairs are the two numbers reciprocals of each other?

I. 3 and $\frac{1}{3}$
II. $\frac{1}{17}$ and $\frac{-1}{17}$
III. $\sqrt{3}$ and $\frac{\sqrt{3}}{3}$

(A) I only
(B) II only
(C) I and II
(D) I and III
(E) II and III

Arithmetic Properties of numbers (reciprocals)

Two numbers are reciprocals of each other if and only if their product is 1.

I. $3\left(\frac{1}{3}\right) = 1$ reciprocals

II. $\left(\frac{1}{17}\right)\left(-\frac{1}{17}\right) = -\frac{1}{(17)(17)}$ not reciprocals

III. $\left(\sqrt{3}\right)\left(\frac{\sqrt{3}}{3}\right) = \frac{3}{3} = 1$ reciprocals

The correct answer is D.

25. A rope 20.6 meters long is cut into two pieces. If the length of one piece of rope is 2.8 meters shorter than the length of the other, what is the length, in meters, of the longer piece of rope?

(A) 7.5
(B) 8.9
(C) 9.9
(D) 10.3
(E) 11.7

Algebra First-degree equations

If x represents the length of the longer piece of rope, then $x - 2.8$ represents the length of the shorter piece, where both lengths are in meters. The total length of the two pieces of rope is 20.6 meters so,

$x + (x - 2.8) = 20.6$	given
$2x - 2.8 = 20.6$	add like terms
$2x = 23.4$	add 2.8 to both sides
$x = 11.7$	divide both sides by 2

Thus, the length of the longer piece of rope is 11.7 meters.

The correct answer is E.

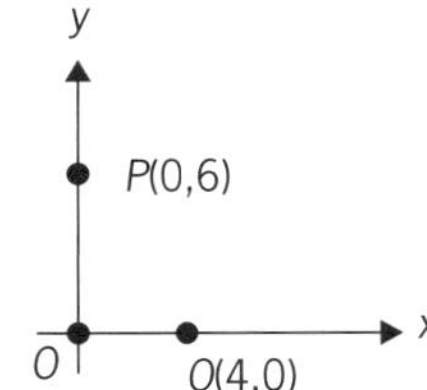

26. In the rectangular coordinate system shown above, points O, P, and Q represent the sites of three proposed housing developments. If a fire station can be built at any point in the coordinate system, at which point would it be equidistant from all three developments?

(A) (3,1)
(B) (1,3)
(C) (3,2)
(D) (2,2)
(E) (2,3)

Geometry Coordinate geometry

Any point equidistant from the points (0,0) and (4,0) must lie on the perpendicular bisector of the segment with endpoints (0,0) and (4,0), which is the line with equation $x = 2$. Any point equidistant from the points (0,0) and (0,6) must lie on the perpendicular bisector of the segment with endpoints (0,0) and (0,6), which is the line with equation $y = 3$. Therefore, the point that is equidistant from (0,0), (4,0), and (0,6) must lie on both of the lines $x = 2$ and $y = 3$, which is the point (2,3).

Alternatively, let (x,y) be the point equidistant from (0,0), (4,0), and (0,6). Since the distance between (x,y) and (0,0) is equal to the distance between (x,y) and (4,0), it follows from the distance formula that $\sqrt{x^2 + y^2} = \sqrt{(x-4)^2 + y^2}$. Squaring both sides gives $x^2 + y^2 = (x - 4)^2 + y^2$. Subtracting y^2 from both sides of the last equation and then expanding the right side gives $x^2 = x^2 - 8x + 16$, or $0 = -8x + 16$, or $x = 2$. Also, since the distance between (x,y) and (0,0) is equal to the distance between (x,y) and (0,6), it follows from the distance formula that $\sqrt{x^2 + y^2} = \sqrt{x^2 + (y-6)^2}$. Squaring both sides of the last equation gives $x^2 + y^2 = x^2 + (y - 6)^2$. Subtracting x^2 from both sides and then expanding the right side gives $y^2 = y^2 - 12y + 36$, or $0 = -12y + 36$, or $y = 3$.

The correct answer is E.

27. What is the perimeter, in meters, of a rectangular garden 6 meters wide that has the same area as a rectangular playground 16 meters long and 12 meters wide?

(A) 48
(B) 56
(C) 60
(D) 76
(E) 192

Geometry Perimeter and area

Let L represent the length, in meters, of the rectangular garden. It is given that the width of the garden is 6 meters and the area of the garden is the same as the area of a rectangular playground that is 16 meters long and 12 meters wide. It follows that $6L = (16)(12)$, and so $L = 32$. The perimeter of the garden is, then, $2(32 + 6) = 2(38) = 76$ meters.

The correct answer is D.

28. Of the total amount that Jill spent on a shopping trip, excluding taxes, she spent 50 percent on clothing, 20 percent on food, and 30 percent on other items. If Jill paid a 4 percent tax on the clothing, no tax on the food, and an 8 percent tax on all other items, then the total tax that she paid was what percent of the total amount that she spent, excluding taxes?

(A) 2.8%
(B) 3.6%
(C) 4.4%
(D) 5.2%
(E) 6.0%

Arithmetic Applied problems

Let T represent the total amount Jill spent, excluding taxes. Jill paid a 4% tax on the clothing she bought, which accounted for 50% of the total amount she spent, and so the tax she paid on the clothing was $(0.04)(0.5T)$. Jill paid an 8% tax on the other items she bought, which accounted for 30% of the total amount she spent, and so the tax she paid on the other items was $(0.08)(0.3T)$. Therefore, the total amount of tax Jill paid was $(0.04)(0.5T) + (0.08)(0.3T) = 0.02T + 0.024T = 0.044T$. The tax as a percent of the total amount Jill spent, excluding taxes, was $\left(\frac{0.044T}{T} \times 100\right)\% = 4.4\%$.

The correct answer is C.

29. How many integers x satisfy both $2 < x \leq 4$ and $0 \leq x \leq 3$?

(A) 5
(B) 4
(C) 3
(D) 2
(E) 1

Arithmetic Inequalities

The integers that satisfy $2 < x \leq 4$ are 3 and 4. The integers that satisfy $0 \leq x \leq 3$ are 0, 1, 2, and 3. The only integer that satisfies both $2 < x \leq 4$ and $0 \leq x \leq 3$ is 3, and so there is only one integer that satisfies both $2 < x \leq 4$ and $0 \leq x \leq 3$.

The correct answer is E.

30. At the opening of a trading day at a certain stock exchange, the price per share of stock K was $8. If the price per share of stock K was $9 at the closing of the day, what was the percent increase in the price per share of stock K for that day?

(A) 1.4%
(B) 5.9%
(C) 11.1%
(D) 12.5%
(E) 23.6%

Arithmetic Percents

An increase from \$8 to \$9 represents an increase of $\left(\frac{9-8}{8} \times 100\right)\% = \frac{100}{8}\% = 12.5\%$.

The correct answer is D.

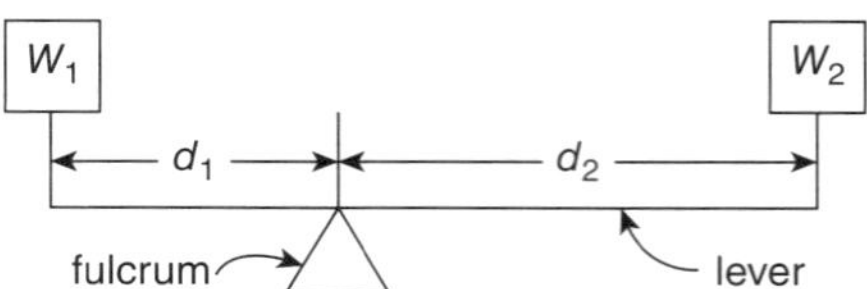

31. As shown in the diagram above, a lever resting on a fulcrum has weights of w_1 pounds and w_2 pounds, located d_1 feet and d_2 feet from the fulcrum. The lever is balanced and $w_1d_1 = w_2d_2$. Suppose w_1 is 50 pounds and w_2 is 30 pounds. If d_1 is 4 feet less than d_2, what is d_2, in feet?

(A) 1.5
(B) 2.5
(C) 6
(D) 10
(E) 20

Algebra First-degree equations; Substitution

Given $w_1d_1 = w_2d_2$, $w_1 = 50$, $w_2 = 30$, and $d_1 = d_2 - 4$, it follows that $50(d_2 - 4) = 30d_2$, and so

$$\begin{aligned} 50(d_2 - 4) &= 30d_2 && \text{given} \\ 50d_2 - 200 &= 30d_2 && \text{distributive principle} \\ 20d_2 &= 200 && \text{add } 200 - 30d_2 \text{ to both sides} \\ d_2 &= 10 && \text{divide both sides by 20} \end{aligned}$$

The correct answer is D.

32. The number of rooms at Hotel G is 10 less than twice the number of rooms at Hotel H. If the total number of rooms at Hotel G and Hotel H is 425, what is the number of rooms at Hotel G?

(A) 140
(B) 180
(C) 200
(D) 240
(E) 280

Algebra Simultaneous equations

Let G be the number of rooms in Hotel G and let H be the number of rooms in Hotel H. Expressed in symbols, the given information is the following system of equations

$$\begin{cases} G = 2H - 10 \\ 425 = G + H \end{cases}$$

Solving the second equation for H gives $H = 425 - G$. Then, substituting $425 - G$ for H in the first equation gives

$$\begin{aligned} G &= 2(425 - G) - 10 \\ G &= 850 - 2G - 10 \\ G &= 840 - 2G \\ 3G &= 840 \\ G &= 280 \end{aligned}$$

The correct answer is E.

33. $(1+\sqrt{5})(1-\sqrt{5}) =$

(A) -4
(B) 2
(C) 6
(D) $-4 - 2\sqrt{5}$
(E) $6 - 2\sqrt{5}$

Arithmetic Operations on radical expressions

Work the problem.

$$(1+\sqrt{5})(1-\sqrt{5}) = 1^2 + \sqrt{5} - \sqrt{5} - (\sqrt{5})^2 = 1 - (\sqrt{5})^2 = 1 - 5 = -4$$

The correct answer is A.

34. A certain population of bacteria doubles every 10 minutes. If the number of bacteria in the population initially was 10^4, what was the number in the population 1 hour later?

(A) $2(10^4)$
(B) $6(10^4)$
(C) $(2^6)(10^4)$
(D) $(10^6)(10^4)$
(E) $(10^4)^6$

Arithmetic Operations on rational numbers

If the population of bacteria doubles every 10 minutes, it doubles 6 times in one hour. This doubling action can be expressed as (2)(2)(2)(2)(2)(2) or 2^6. Thus, if the initial population is 10^4, the population will be $(2^6)(10^4)$ after one hour.

The correct answer is C.

35. $\frac{3}{100} + \frac{5}{1{,}000} + \frac{7}{100{,}000} =$

(A) 0.357
(B) 0.3507
(C) 0.35007
(D) 0.0357
(E) 0.03507

Arithmetic Operations on rational numbers

If each fraction is written in decimal form, the sum to be found is

$$\begin{array}{r} 0.03 \\ 0.005 \\ +0.00007 \\ \hline 0.03507 \end{array}$$

The correct answer is E.

36. If r and s are positive integers such that $(2^r)(4^s) = 16$, then $2r + s =$

(A) 2
(B) 3
(C) 4
(D) 5
(E) 6

Algebra Exponents

Using the rules of exponents,

$(2^r)(4^s)$	$= 16$	given
$(2^r)(2^{2s})$	$= 2^4$	$4^s = (2^2)^s = 2^{2s}$, $16 = 2^4$
2^{r+2s}	$= 2^4$	addition property of exponents

Thus, $r + 2s = 4$. However, the problem asks for the value of $2r + s$. Since r and s are positive integers, $s < 2$; otherwise, r would not be positive. Therefore, $s = 1$, and it follows that $r + (2)(1) = 4$, or $r = 2$. The value of $2r + s$ is $(2)(2) + 1 = 5$.

Alternatively, since $(2^r)(4^s) = 16$ and both r and s are positive, it follows that $s < 2$; otherwise, $4^s \geq 16$ and r would not be positive. Therefore, $s = 1$ and $(2^r)(4) = 16$. It follows that $2^r = 4$ and $r = 2$. The value of $2r + s$ is $(2)(2) + 1 = 5$.

The correct answer is D.

37. The annual budget of a certain college is to be shown on a circle graph. If the size of each sector of the graph is to be proportional to the amount of the budget it represents, how many degrees of the circle should be used to represent an item that is 15 percent of the budget?

(A) 15°
(B) 36°
(C) 54°
(D) 90°
(E) 150°

Arithmetic Percents; Interpretation of graphs

Since there are 360 degrees in a circle, the measure of the central angle in the circle should be $0.15(360°) = 54°$.

The correct answer is C.

38. $\sqrt{16+16} =$

(A) $4\sqrt{2}$
(B) $8\sqrt{2}$
(C) $16\sqrt{2}$
(D) 8
(E) 16

Arithmetic Operations on radical expressions

Working this problem gives

$$\sqrt{16+16} = \sqrt{(16)(2)} = \left(\sqrt{16}\right)\left(\sqrt{2}\right) = 4\sqrt{2}$$

The correct answer is A.

39. Three people each contributed x dollars toward the purchase of a car. They then bought the car for y dollars, an amount less than the total number of dollars contributed. If the excess amount is to be refunded to the three people in equal amounts, each person should receive a refund of how many dollars?

(A) $\frac{3x-y}{3}$
(B) $\frac{x-y}{3}$
(C) $\frac{x-3y}{3}$
(D) $\frac{y-3x}{3}$
(E) $3(x-y)$

Algebra Applied problems

The total to be refunded is equal to the total contributed minus the amount paid, or $3x - y$. If $3x - y$ is divided into three equal amounts, then each amount will be $\frac{3x-y}{3}$.

The correct answer is A.

40. What is the ratio of $\frac{3}{4}$ to the product $4\left(\frac{3}{4}\right)$?

(A) $\frac{1}{4}$
(B) $\frac{1}{3}$
(C) $\frac{4}{9}$
(D) $\frac{9}{4}$
(E) 4

Arithmetic Operations on rational numbers

Work the problem.

$$\frac{\frac{3}{4}}{4\left(\frac{3}{4}\right)} = \frac{\frac{3}{4}}{\frac{12}{4}} = \frac{\frac{3}{4}}{3} = \frac{3}{4} \times \frac{1}{3} = \frac{1}{4}$$

The correct answer is A.

$$2x + 2y = -4$$
$$4x + y = 1$$

41. In the system of equations above, what is the value of x ?

(A) −3
(B) −1
(C) $\frac{2}{5}$
(D) 1
(E) $1\frac{3}{4}$

Algebra Simultaneous equations

Solving the second equation for y gives $y = 1 - 4x$. Then, substituting $1 - 4x$ for y in the first equation gives

$$
\begin{aligned}
2x + 2(1 - 4x) &= -4 \\
2x + 2 - 8x &= -4 \\
-6x + 2 &= -4 \\
-6x &= -6 \\
x &= 1
\end{aligned}
$$

The correct answer is D.

42. Last week Jack worked 70 hours and earned \$1,260. If he earned his regular hourly wage for the first 40 hours worked, $1\frac{1}{2}$ times his regular hourly wage for the next 20 hours worked, and 2 times his regular hourly wage for the remaining 10 hours worked, what was his regular hourly wage?

(A) \$7.00
(B) \$14.00
(C) \$18.00
(D) \$22.00
(E) \$31.50

Algebra First-degree equations

If w represents Jack's regular hourly wage, then Jack's earnings for the week can be represented by the sum of the following amounts, in dollars: $40w$ (his earnings for the first 40 hours he worked), $(20)(1.5w)$ (his earnings for the next 20 hours he worked), and $(10)(2w)$ (his earnings for the last 10 hours he worked). Therefore,

$40w + (20)(1.5w) + (10)(2w) = 1{,}260$	given
$90w = 1{,}260$	add like terms
$w = 14$	divide both sides by 90

Jack's regular hourly wage was \$14.00.

The correct answer is B.

43. $\frac{2+2\sqrt{6}}{2} =$

(A) $\sqrt{6}$
(B) $2\sqrt{6}$
(C) $1+\sqrt{6}$
(D) $1+2\sqrt{6}$
(E) $2+\sqrt{6}$

Arithmetic Operations on radical expressions

Rewrite the expression to eliminate the denominator.

$$\frac{2+2\sqrt{6}}{2} = \frac{2\left(1+\sqrt{6}\right)}{2} = 1+\sqrt{6}$$

or

$$\frac{2+2\sqrt{6}}{2} = \frac{2}{2} + \frac{2\sqrt{6}}{2} = 1+\sqrt{6}$$

The correct answer is C.

44. A certain fishing boat is chartered by 6 people who are to contribute equally to the total charter cost of \$480. If each person contributes equally to a \$150 down payment, how much of the charter cost will each person still owe?

(A) \$80
(B) \$66
(C) \$55
(D) \$50
(E) \$45

Arithmetic Operations on rational numbers

Since each of the 6 individuals contributes equally to the \$150 down payment, and since it is given that the total cost of the chartered boat is \$480, each person still owes $\frac{\$480 - \$150}{6} = \$55$.

The correct answer is C.

45. Which of the following must be equal to zero for all real numbers x?

I. $-\frac{1}{x}$

II. $x + (-x)$

III. x^0

(A) I only
(B) II only
(C) I and III only
(D) II and III only
(E) I, II, and III

Arithmetic Properties of numbers

Consider the numeric properties of each answer choice.

I. $-\frac{1}{x} \neq 0$ for all real numbers x.

II. $x + (-x) = 0$ for all real numbers x.

III. $x^0 = 1 \neq 0$ for all nonzero real numbers x.

Thus, only the expression in II must be equal to zero for all real numbers x.

The correct answer is B.

46. $\frac{31}{125} =$

(A) 0.248
(B) 0.252
(C) 0.284
(D) 0.312
(E) 0.320

Arithmetic Operations on rational numbers

To avoid long division, multiply the given fraction by 1 using a form for 1 that will result in a power of 10 in the denominator.

$$\frac{31}{125} = \frac{31}{5^3} = \frac{31}{5^3} \times \frac{2^3}{2^3} = \frac{(31)(8)}{10^3} = \frac{248}{1,000} = 0.248$$

The correct answer is A.

47. If Mel saved more than \$10 by purchasing a sweater at a 15 percent discount, what is the smallest amount the original price of the sweater could be, to the nearest dollar?

(A) 45
(B) 67
(C) 75
(D) 83
(E) 150

Arithmetic; Algebra Percents; Inequalities; Applied problems

Letting P be the original price of the sweater in dollars, the given information can be expressed as $(0.15)P > 10$. Solving for P gives

$$(0.15)P > 10$$

$$P > \frac{10}{0.15} = \frac{1,000}{15} = \frac{200}{3}$$

$$P > 66\frac{2}{3}$$

Thus, to the nearest dollar, the smallest amount P could have been is \$67.

The correct answer is B.

48. If a and b are positive integers and $(2^a)^b = 2^3$, what is the value of $2^a 2^b$?

(A) 6
(B) 8
(C) 16
(D) 32
(E) 64

Algebra Exponents

It is given that $(2^a)^b = 2^3$, or $2^{ab} = 2^3$. Therefore, $ab = 3$. Since a and b are positive integers, it follows that either $a = 1$ and $b = 3$, or $a = 3$ and $b = 1$. In either case $a + b = 4$, and so $2^a 2^b = 2^{a+b} = 2^4 = 16$.

The correct answer is C.

49. $\dfrac{1}{3-\dfrac{1}{3-\dfrac{1}{3-1}}} =$

(A) $\frac{7}{23}$

(B) $\frac{5}{13}$

(C) $\frac{2}{3}$

(D) $\frac{23}{7}$

(E) $\frac{13}{5}$

Arithmetic Operations with rational numbers

Perform each subtraction beginning at the lowest level in the fraction and proceeding upward.

$$\begin{aligned}
\frac{1}{3-\dfrac{1}{3-\dfrac{1}{3-1}}} &= \frac{1}{3-\dfrac{1}{3-\dfrac{1}{2}}} \\
&= \frac{1}{3-\dfrac{1}{\dfrac{6}{2}-\dfrac{1}{2}}} \\
&= \frac{1}{3-\dfrac{1}{\dfrac{5}{2}}} \\
&= \frac{1}{3-\dfrac{2}{5}} \\
&= \frac{1}{\dfrac{15}{5}-\dfrac{2}{5}} \\
&= \frac{1}{\dfrac{13}{5}} \\
&= \frac{5}{13}
\end{aligned}$$

The correct answer is B.

50. After 4,000 gallons of water were added to a large water tank that was already filled to $\frac{3}{4}$ of its capacity, the tank was then at $\frac{4}{5}$ of its capacity. How many gallons of water does the tank hold when filled to capacity?

(A) 5,000
(B) 6,200
(C) 20,000
(D) 40,000
(E) 80,000

Algebra First-degree equations

Let C be the capacity of the tank. In symbols, the given information is $4,000+\frac{3}{4}C=\frac{4}{5}C$. Solve for C.

$$\begin{aligned}
4,000+\frac{3}{4}C &= \frac{4}{5}C \\
4,000 &= \left(\frac{4}{5}-\frac{3}{4}\right)C \\
4,000 &= \frac{16-15}{20}C \\
4,000 &= \frac{1}{20}C \\
20(4,000) &= C \\
80,000 &= C
\end{aligned}$$

The correct answer is E.

51. Five machines at a certain factory operate at the same constant rate. If four of these machines, operating simultaneously, take 30 hours to fill a certain production order, how many fewer hours does it take all five machines, operating simultaneously, to fill the same production order?

(A) 3
(B) 5
(C) 6
(D) 16
(E) 24

Arithmetic Applied problems

If 4 machines, working simultaneously, each work for 30 hours to fill a production order, it takes (4)(30) machine hours to fill the order.
If 5 machines are working simultaneously, it will take $\frac{(4)(30)}{5} = 24$ hours. Thus, 5 machines working simultaneously will take $30 - 24 = 6$ fewer hours to fill the production order than 4 machines working simultaneously.

The correct answer is C.

52. How many integers between 1 and 16, inclusive, have exactly 3 different positive integer factors? (Note: 6 is NOT such an integer because 6 has 4 different positive integer factors: 1, 2, 3, and 6.)

(A) 1
(B) 2
(C) 3
(D) 4
(E) 6

Arithmetic Properties of numbers

Using the process of elimination to eliminate integers that do NOT have exactly 3 different positive integer factors, the integer 1 can be eliminated since 1 has only 1 positive integer factor, namely 1 itself. Because each prime number has exactly 2 positive factors, each prime number between 1 and 16, inclusive, (namely, 2, 3, 5, 7, 11, and 13) can be eliminated. The integer 6 can also be eliminated since it was used as an example of an integer with exactly 4 positive integer factors. Check the positive integer factors of each of the remaining integers.

Integer	Positive integer factors	Number of factors
4	1, 2, 4	3
8	1, 2, 4, 8	4
9	1, 3, 9	3
10	1, 2, 5, 10	4
12	1, 2, 3, 4, 6, 12	6
14	1, 2, 7, 14	4
15	1, 3, 5, 15	4
16	1, 2, 4, 8, 16	5

Just the integers 4 and 9 have exactly 3 positive integer factors.

Alternatively, if the integer n, where $n > 1$, has exactly 3 positive integer factors, which include 1 and n, then n has exactly one other positive integer factor, say p. Since any factor of p would also be a factor of n, then p is prime, and so p is the only prime factor of n. It follows that $n = p^k$ for some integer $k > 1$. But if $k \geq 3$, then p^2 is a factor of n in addition to 1, p, and n, which contradicts the fact that n has exactly 3 positive integer factors. Therefore, $k = 2$ and $n = p^2$, which means that n is the square of a prime number. Of the integers between 1 and 16, inclusive, only 4 and 9 are the squares of prime numbers.

The correct answer is B.

53. If $d = 2.0453$ and d^* is the decimal obtained by rounding d to the nearest hundredth, what is the value of $d^* - d$?

(A) −0.0053
(B) −0.0003
(C) 0.0007
(D) 0.0047
(E) 0.0153

Arithmetic Operations on rational numbers

Since $d = 2.0453$ rounded to the nearest hundredth is 2.05, $d^* = 2.05$; therefore, $d^* - d = 2.05 - 2.0453 = 0.0047$.

The correct answer is D.

54. Stephanie has $2\frac{1}{4}$ cups of milk on hand and makes 2 batches of cookies, using $\frac{2}{3}$ cup of milk for each batch of cookies. Which of the following describes the amount of milk remaining after she makes the cookies?

(A) Less than $\frac{1}{2}$ cup
(B) Between $\frac{1}{2}$ cup and $\frac{3}{4}$ cup
(C) Between $\frac{3}{4}$ cup and 1 cup
(D) Between 1 cup and $1\frac{1}{2}$ cups
(E) More than $1\frac{1}{2}$ cups

Arithmetic Applied problems

In cups, the amount of milk remaining is

$2\frac{1}{4}-2\left(\frac{2}{3}\right)=\frac{9}{4}-\frac{4}{3}=\frac{27-16}{12}=\frac{11}{12}$, which is greater than $\frac{3}{4}=\frac{9}{12}$ and less than 1.

The correct answer is C.

55. A school club plans to package and sell dried fruit to raise money. The club purchased 12 containers of dried fruit, each containing $16\frac{3}{4}$ pounds. What is the maximum number of individual bags of dried fruit, each containing $\frac{1}{4}$ pounds, that can be sold from the dried fruit the club purchased?

(A) 50
(B) 64
(C) 67
(D) 768
(E) 804

Arithmetic Applied problems; Operations with fractions

The 12 containers, each containing $16\frac{3}{4}$ pounds of dried fruit, contain a total of $(12)\left(16\frac{3}{4}\right)=(12)\left(\frac{67}{4}\right)=(3)(67)=201$ pounds of dried fruit, which will make $\frac{201}{\frac{1}{4}}=(201)(4)=804$ individual bags that can be sold.

The correct answer is E.

56. The sequence a_1, a_2, a_3, a_4, a_5 is such that $a_n=a_{n-1}+5$ for $2\le n\le 5$. If $a_5=31$, what is the value of a_1 ?

(A) 1
(B) 6
(C) 11
(D) 16
(E) 21

Algebra Sequences

Since $a_n=a_{n-1}+5$, then $a_n-a_{n-1}=5$. So,

$$a_5-a_4=5$$
$$a_4-a_3=5$$
$$a_3-a_2=5$$
$$a_2-a_1=5$$

Adding the equations gives

$$a_5-a_4+a_4-a_3+a_3-a_2+a_2-a_1=5+5+5+5$$
$$a_5-a_1=20$$

and substituting 31 for a_5 gives

$$31-a_1=20$$
$$a_1=11.$$

The correct answer is C.

57. A certain bridge is 4,024 feet long. Approximately how many minutes does it take to cross this bridge at a constant speed of 20 miles per hour? (1 mile = 5,280 feet)

(A) 1
(B) 2
(C) 4
(D) 6
(E) 7

Arithmetic Applied problems

First, convert 4,024 feet to miles since the speed is given in miles per hour:

$4{,}024\ \cancel{\text{ft}}\times\frac{1\text{ mi}}{5{,}280\ \cancel{\text{ft}}}=\frac{4{,}024}{5{,}280}\text{ mi.}$

Now, divide by 20 mph: $\frac{4{,}024}{5{,}280}\text{ mi}\div\frac{20\text{ mi}}{1\text{ hr}}$

$=\frac{4{,}024\ \cancel{\text{mi}}}{5{,}280}\times\frac{1\text{ hr}}{20\ \cancel{\text{mi}}}=\frac{4{,}024\text{ hr}}{(5{,}280)(20)}.$

Last, convert $\frac{4{,}024\text{ hr}}{(5{,}280)(20)}$ to minutes:

$\frac{4{,}024\ \cancel{\text{hr}}}{(5{,}280)(20)}\times\frac{60\text{ min}}{1\ \cancel{\text{hr}}}=\frac{(4{,}024)(60)\text{ min}}{(5{,}280)(20)}\approx\frac{4{,}000}{5{,}000}\times\frac{60}{20}\text{ min}$. Then, $\frac{4{,}000}{5{,}000}\times\frac{60}{20}\text{ min}=$ $=0.8\times 3\text{ min}\approx 2\text{ min}$. Thus, at a constant speed of 20 miles per hour, it takes approximately 2 minutes to cross the bridge.

The correct answer is B.

58. If $S = \{0, 4, 5, 2, 11, 8\}$, how much greater than the median of the numbers in S is the mean of the numbers in S?

(A) 0.5
(B) 1.0
(C) 1.5
(D) 2.0
(E) 2.5

Arithmetic; Algebra Statistics; Concepts of sets

The median of S is found by ordering the values according to size (0, 2, 4, 5, 8, 11) and taking the average of the two middle numbers: $\frac{4+5}{2} = 4.5$.

The mean is $\frac{\text{sum of } n \text{ values}}{n} =$

$\frac{0+4+5+2+11+8}{6} = 5$.

The difference between the mean and the median is $5 - 4.5 = 0.5$.

The correct answer is A.

59. The annual interest rate earned by an investment increased by 10 percent from last year to this year. If the annual interest rate earned by the investment this year was 11 percent, what was the annual interest rate last year?

(A) 1%
(B) 1.1%
(C) 9.1%
(D) 10%
(E) 10.8%

Arithmetic Percents

If L is the annual interest rate last year, then the annual interest rate this year is 10% greater than L, or $1.1L$. It is given that $1.1L = 11\%$. Therefore, $L = \frac{11\%}{1.1} = 10\%$. (Note that if the given information had been that the investment increased by *10 percentage points*, then the equation would have been $L + 10\% = 11\%$.)

The correct answer is D.

60. A total of 5 liters of gasoline is to be poured into two empty containers with capacities of 2 liters and 6 liters, respectively, such that both containers will be filled to the same percent of their respective capacities. What amount of gasoline, in liters, must be poured into the 6-liter container?

(A) $4\frac{1}{2}$
(B) 4
(C) $3\frac{3}{4}$
(D) 3
(E) $1\frac{1}{4}$

Algebra Ratio and proportion

If x represents the amount, in liters, of gasoline poured into the 6-liter container, then $5 - x$ represents the amount, in liters, of gasoline poured into the 2-liter container. After the gasoline is poured into the containers, the 6-liter container will be filled to $\left(\frac{x}{6} \times 100\right)\%$ of its capacity and the 2-liter container will be filled to $\left(\frac{5-x}{2} \times 100\right)\%$ of its capacity. Because these two percents are equal,

$\frac{x}{6} = \frac{5-x}{2}$	given
$2x = 6(5-x)$	multiply both sides by 12
$2x = 30 - 6x$	use distributive property
$8x = 30$	add $6x$ to both sides
$x = 3\frac{3}{4}$	divide both sides by 8

Therefore, $3\frac{3}{4}$ liters of gasoline must be poured into the 6-liter container.

The correct answer is C.

61. List S consists of 10 consecutive odd integers, and list T consists of 5 consecutive even integers. If the least integer in S is 7 more than the least integer in T, how much greater is the average (arithmetic mean) of the integers in S than the average of the integers in T?

(A) 2
(B) 7
(C) 8
(D) 12
(E) 22

Arithmetic Statistics

Let the integers in S be $s, s + 2, s + 4, \ldots, s + 18$, where s is odd. Let the integers in T be $t, t + 2, t + 4, t + 6, t + 8$, where t is even. Given that $s = t + 7$, it follows that $s - t = 7$. The average of the integers in S is $\frac{10s + 90}{10} = s + 9$, and, similarly, the average of the integers in T is $\frac{5t + 20}{5} = t + 4$. The difference in these averages is $(s + 9) - (t + 4) = (s - t) + (9 - 4) = 7 + 5 = 12$. Thus, the average of the integers in S is 12 greater than the average of the integers in T.

The correct answer is D.

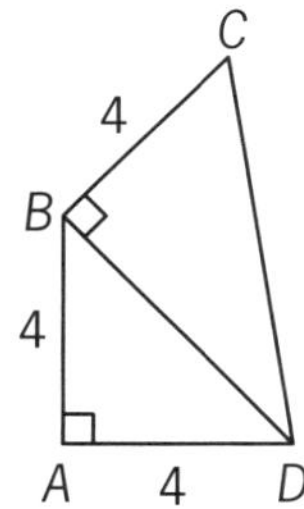

62. In the figure above, what is the area of triangular region BCD?

(A) $4\sqrt{2}$
(B) 8
(C) $8\sqrt{2}$
(D) 16
(E) $16\sqrt{2}$

Geometry Triangles; Area

By the Pythagorean theorem, $BD = \sqrt{4^2 + 4^2} = 4\sqrt{2}$. Then the area of ΔBCD is $\frac{1}{2}\left(4\sqrt{2}\right)(4) = 8\sqrt{2}$.

The correct answer is C.

63. What is the larger of the 2 solutions of the equation $x^2 - 4x = 96$?

(A) 8
(B) 12
(C) 16
(D) 32
(E) 100

Algebra Second-degree equations

It is given that $x^2 - 4x = 96$, or $x^2 - 4x - 96 = 0$, or $(x - 12)(x + 8) = 0$. Therefore, $x = 12$ or $x = -8$, and the larger of these two numbers is 12.

Alternatively, from $x^2 - 4x = 96$ it follows that $x(x - 4) = 96$. By inspection, the left side is either the product of 12 and 8, where the value of x is 12, or the product of -8 and -12, where the value of x is -8, and the larger of these two values of x is 12.

The correct answer is B.

64. Of the goose eggs laid at a certain pond, $\frac{2}{3}$ hatched, and $\frac{3}{4}$ of the geese that hatched from those eggs survived the first month. Of the geese that survived the first month, $\frac{3}{5}$ did not survive the first year. If 120 geese survived the first year and if no more than one goose hatched from each egg, how many goose eggs were laid at the pond?

(A) 280
(B) 400
(C) 540
(D) 600
(E) 840

Arithmetic Operations with rational numbers

Let N represent the number of eggs laid at the pond. Then $\frac{2}{3}N$ eggs hatched and $\frac{3}{4}\left(\frac{2}{3}N\right)$ goslings (baby geese) survived the first month. Since $\frac{3}{5}$ of these goslings did not survive the first year, then $\frac{2}{5}$ did survive the first year. This means that $\frac{2}{5}\left(\frac{3}{4}\left(\frac{2}{3}N\right)\right)$ goslings survived the first year. But this number is 120 and so, $\frac{2}{5}\left(\frac{3}{4}\left(\frac{2}{3}N\right)\right)=120$, $\frac{1}{5}N=120$ and $N=5(120)=600$.

The correct answer is D.

65. Judy bought a quantity of pens in packages of 5 for \$0.80 per package. She sold all of the pens in packages of 3 for \$0.60 per package. If Judy's profit from the pens was \$8.00, how many pens did she buy and sell?

(A) 40
(B) 80
(C) 100
(D) 200
(E) 400

Arithmetic Applied problems; Operations with decimals

Judy purchased the pens for $\frac{\$0.80}{5}=\$0.16$ each and sold them for $\frac{\$0.60}{3}=\$0.20$ each. Therefore, her profit on each pen was \$0.20 – \$0.16 = \$0.04. If her total profit was \$8.00, then she bought and sold $\frac{\$8.00}{\$0.04}=200$ pens.

The correct answer is D.

66. If $x^2-2x-15=0$ and $x>0$, which of the following must be equal to 0 ?

I. x^2-6x+9
II. $x^2-7x+10$
III. $x^2-10x+25$

(A) I only
(B) II only
(C) III only
(D) II and III only
(E) I, II, and III

Algebra Second-degree equations

Since $x^2-2x-15=0$, then $(x-5)(x+3)=0$, so $x=5$ or $x=-3$. Since $x>0$, then $x=5$.

I. $5^2-6(5)+9=25-30+9=4\neq0$
II. $5^2-7(5)+10=25-35+10=0$
III. $5^2-10(5)+25=25-50+25=0$

The correct answer is D.

67. $\frac{(39{,}897)(0.0096)}{198.76}$ is approximately

(A) 0.02
(B) 0.2
(C) 2
(D) 20
(E) 200

Arithmetic Estimation

$$\frac{(39{,}897)(0.0096)}{198.76}\approx\frac{(40{,}000)(0.01)}{200}=(200)(0.01)=2$$

The correct answer is C.

68. If a square region has area n, what is the length of the diagonal of the square in terms of n ?

(A) $\sqrt{2n}$
(B) $\sqrt{n}$
(C) $2\sqrt{n}$
(D) $2n$
(E) $2n^2$

Geometry Area; Pythagorean theorem

If s represents the side length of the square, then $n = s^2$. By the Pythagorean theorem, the length of the diagonal of the square is $\sqrt{s^2 + s^2} = \sqrt{n + n} = \sqrt{2n}$.

The correct answer is A.

69. The "prime sum" of an integer n greater than 1 is the sum of all the prime factors of n, including repetitions. For example, the prime sum of 12 is 7, since $12 = 2 \times 2 \times 3$ and $2 + 2 + 3 = 7$. For which of the following integers is the prime sum greater than 35 ?

(A) 440
(B) 512
(C) 620
(D) 700
(E) 750

Arithmetic Properties of numbers

A Since $440 = 2 \times 2 \times 2 \times 5 \times 11$, the prime sum of 440 is $2 + 2 + 2 + 5 + 11 = 22$, which is not greater than 35.

B Since $512 = 2^9$, the prime sum of 512 is $9(2) = 18$, which is not greater than 35.

C Since $620 = 2 \times 2 \times 5 \times 31$, the prime sum of 620 is $2 + 2 + 5 + 31 = 40$, which is greater than 35.

Because there can be only one correct answer, D and E need not be checked. However, for completeness,

D Since $700 = 2 \times 2 \times 5 \times 5 \times 7$, the prime sum of 700 is $2 + 2 + 5 + 5 + 7 = 21$, which is not greater than 35.

E Since $750 = 2 \times 3 \times 5 \times 5 \times 5$, the prime sum of 750 is $2 + 3 + 5 + 5 + 5 = 20$, which is not greater than 35.

The correct answer is C.

70. Each machine at a toy factory assembles a certain kind of toy at a constant rate of one toy every 3 minutes. If 40 percent of the machines at the factory are to be replaced by new machines that assemble this kind of toy at a constant rate of one toy every 2 minutes, what will be the percent increase in the number of toys assembled in one hour by all the machines at the factory, working at their constant rates?

(A) 20%
(B) 25%
(C) 30%
(D) 40%
(E) 50%

Arithmetic Applied problems; Percents

Let n be the total number of machines working. Currently, it takes each machine 3 minutes to assemble 1 toy, so each machine assembles 20 toys in 1 hour and the total number of toys assembled in 1 hour by all the current machines is $20n$. It takes each new machine 2 minutes to assemble 1 toy, so each new machine assembles 30 toys in 1 hour. If 60% of the machines assemble 20 toys each hour and 40% assemble 30 toys each hour, then the total number of toys produced by the machines each hour is $(0.60n)(20) + (0.40n)(30) = 24n$. The percent increase in hourly production is $\frac{24n - 20n}{20n} = \frac{1}{5}$ or 20%.

The correct answer is A.

71. When a subscription to a new magazine was purchased for m months, the publisher offered a discount of 75 percent off the regular monthly price of the magazine. If the total value of the discount was equivalent to buying the magazine at its regular monthly price for 27 months, what was the value of m ?

(A) 18
(B) 24
(C) 30
(D) 36
(E) 48

Algebra Percents

Let P represent the regular monthly price of the magazine. The discounted monthly price is then $0.75P$. Paying this price for m months is equivalent to paying the regular price for 27 months. Therefore, $0.75mP = 27P$, and so $0.75m = 27$. It follows that $m = \frac{27}{0.75} = 36$.

The correct answer is D.

72. At a garage sale, all of the prices of the items sold were different. If the price of a radio sold at the garage sale was both the 15th highest price and the 20th lowest price among the prices of the items sold, how many items were sold at the garage sale?

(A) 33
(B) 34
(C) 35
(D) 36
(E) 37

Arithmetic Operations with integers

If the price of the radio was the 15th highest price, there were 14 items that sold for prices higher than the price of the radio. If the price of the radio was the 20th lowest price, there were 19 items that sold for prices lower than the price of the radio. Therefore, the total number of items sold is $14 + 1 + 19 = 34$.

The correct answer is B.

73. Half of a large pizza is cut into 4 equal-sized pieces, and the other half is cut into 6 equal-sized pieces. If a person were to eat 1 of the larger pieces and 2 of the smaller pieces, what fraction of the pizza would remain <u>uneaten</u>?

(A) $\frac{5}{12}$

(B) $\frac{13}{24}$

(C) $\frac{7}{12}$

(D) $\frac{2}{3}$

(E) $\frac{17}{24}$

Arithmetic Operations with fractions

Each of the 4 equal-sized pieces represents $\frac{1}{8}$ of the whole pizza since each slice is $\frac{1}{4}$ of $\frac{1}{2}$ of the pizza. Each of the 6 equal-sized pieces represents $\frac{1}{12}$ of the whole pizza since each slice is $\frac{1}{6}$ of $\frac{1}{2}$ of the pizza. The fraction of the pizza remaining after a person eats one of the larger pieces and 2 of the smaller pieces is $1 - \left[\frac{1}{8} + 2\left(\frac{1}{12}\right)\right] = 1 - \left(\frac{1}{8} + \frac{1}{6}\right) = 1 - \frac{6+8}{48} = 1 - \frac{7}{24} = \frac{17}{24}$.

The correct answer is E.

74. If $a = 1 + \frac{1}{4} + \frac{1}{16} + \frac{1}{64}$ and $b = 1 + \frac{1}{4}a$, then what is the value of $a - b$?

(A) $-\frac{85}{256}$

(B) $-\frac{1}{256}$

(C) $-\frac{1}{4}$

(D) $\frac{125}{256}$

(E) $\frac{169}{256}$

Arithmetic Operations with fractions

Given that $a = 1 + \frac{1}{4} + \frac{1}{16} + \frac{1}{64}$, it follows that $\frac{1}{4}a = \frac{1}{4} + \frac{1}{16} + \frac{1}{64} + \frac{1}{256}$ and so $b = 1 + \frac{1}{4} + \frac{1}{16} + \frac{1}{64} + \frac{1}{256}$. Then $a - b = \left(1+\frac{1}{4}+\frac{1}{16}+\frac{1}{64}\right) - \left(1+\frac{1}{4}+\frac{1}{16}+\frac{1}{64}+\frac{1}{256}\right) = -\frac{1}{256}$.

The correct answer is B.

75. In a certain learning experiment, each participant had three trials and was assigned, for each trial, a score of either −2, −1, 0, 1, or 2. The participant's final score consisted of the sum of the first trial score, 2 times the second trial score, and 3 times the third trial score. If Anne received scores of 1 and −1 for her first two trials, not necessarily in that order, which of the following could NOT be her final score?

(A) −4
(B) −2
(C) 1
(D) 5
(E) 6

Arithmetic Applied problems

If x represents Anne's score on the third trial, then Anne's final score is either $1 + 2(-1) + 3x = 3x - 1$ or $-1 + 2(1) + 3x = 3x + 1$, where x can have the value −2, −1, 0, 1, or 2. The following table shows Anne's final score for each possible value of x.

x	$3x - 1$	$3x + 1$
−2	−7	−5
−1	−4	−2
0	−1	1
1	2	4
2	5	7

Among the answer choices, the only one not found in the table is 6.

The correct answer is E.

76. For all positive integers m and v, the expression $m \ominus v$ represents the remainder when m is divided by v. What is the value of $((98 \ominus 33) \ominus 17) - (98 \ominus (33 \ominus 17))$?

(A) −10
(B) −2
(C) 8
(D) 13
(E) 17

Arithmetic Operations with integers

First, for $((98 \ominus 33) \ominus 17)$, determine $98 \ominus 33$, which equals 32, since 32 is the remainder when 98 is divided by 33 $(98 = 2(33) + 32)$. Then, determine $32 \ominus 17$, which equals 15, since 15 is the remainder when 32 is divided by 17 $(32 = 1(17) + 15)$. Thus, $((98 \ominus 33) \ominus 17) = 15$.

Next, for $(98 \ominus (33 \ominus 17))$, determine $33 \ominus 17$, which equals 16, since 16 is the remainder when 33 is divided by 17 $(33 = 1(17) + 16)$. Then, determine $98 \ominus 16$, which equals 2, since 2 is the remainder when 98 is divided by 16 $(98 = 6(16) + 2)$. Thus, $(98 \ominus (33 \ominus 17)) = 2$.

Finally, $((98 \ominus 33) \ominus 17 - (98 \ominus (33 \ominus 17)) = 15 - 2 = 13$.

The correct answer is D.

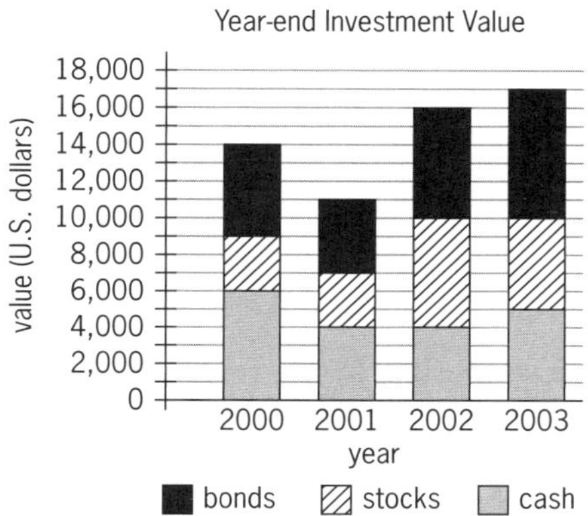

77. The chart above shows year-end values for Darnella's investments. For just the stocks, what was the increase in value from year-end 2000 to year-end 2003 ?

(A) $1,000
(B) $2,000
(C) $3,000
(D) $4,000
(E) $5,000

Arithmetic Interpretation of graphs

From the graph, the year-end 2000 value for stocks is 9,000 – 6,000 = 3,000 and the year-end 2003 value for stocks is 10,000 – 5,000 = 5,000. Therefore, for just the stocks, the increase in value from year-end 2000 to year-end 2003 is 5,000 – 3,000 = 2,000.

The correct answer is B.

78. If the sum of the reciprocals of two consecutive odd integers is $\frac{12}{35}$, then the greater of the two integers is

(A) 3
(B) 5
(C) 7
(D) 9
(E) 11

Arithmetic Operations with fractions

The sum of the reciprocals of 2 integers, a and b, is $\frac{1}{a}+\frac{1}{b}=\frac{a+b}{ab}$. Therefore, since $\frac{12}{35}$ is the sum of the reciprocals of 2 consecutive odd integers, the integers must be such that their sum is a multiple of 12 and their product is the same multiple of 35 so that the fraction reduces to $\frac{12}{35}$. Considering the simplest case where $a + b = 12$ and $ab = 35$, it is easy to see that the integers are 5 and 7 since 5 and 7 are the only factors of 35 that are consecutive odd integers. The larger of these is 7.

Algebraically, if a is the greater of the two integers, then $b = a - 2$ and

$$\frac{a+(a-2)}{a(a-2)}=\frac{12}{35}$$

$$\frac{2a-2}{a(a-2)}=\frac{12}{35}$$

$$35(2a-2)=12a(a-2)$$
$$70a-70=12a^2-24a$$
$$0=12a^2-94a+70$$
$$0=2(6a-5)(a-7)$$

Thus, $6a - 5 = 0$, so $a=\frac{5}{6}$, or $a - 7 = 0$, so $a = 7$. Since a must be an integer, it follows that $a = 7$.

The correct answer is C.

79. What is the sum of the odd integers from 35 to 85, inclusive?

(A) 1,560
(B) 1,500
(C) 1,240
(D) 1,120
(E) 1,100

Arithmetic Operations on integers

The odd integers from 35 through 85 form an arithmetic sequence with first term 35 and each subsequent term 2 more than the preceding term. Thus the sum 35 + 37 + 39 + … + 85 can be found as follows:

1st term	35	= 35		
2nd term	37	= 35	+	1(2)
3rd term	39	= 35	+	2(2)
4th term	41	= 35	+	3(2)
…	…	… …	…	…
26th term	85	= 35	+	25(2)
	Sum	= 35(26)	+	(1 + 2 + 3 + … + 25)(2)
		= 35(26)	+	$\frac{(25)(26)}{2}(2)$ See note below
		= 910	+	650
		= 1,560		

Note that if $s = 1 + 2 + 3 + \ldots + 25$, then $2s = (1 + 2 + 3 + \ldots + 25) + (25 + 24 + 23 + \ldots + 1)$, and so $2s = (1 + 25) + (2 + 24) + (3 + 23) + \ldots + (25 + 1) = (25)(26)$. Therefore, $s=\frac{(25)(26)}{2}$.

Alternatively, to determine the number of odd integers from 35 to 85, inclusive, consider that 3 of them (35, 37, and 39) have tens digit 3. Half of the integers with tens digit 4 are odd, so 5 of the odd integers between 35 and 85, inclusive, have tens digit 4. Similarly, 5 of the odd integers between 35 and 85, inclusive, have tens digit 5; 5 have tens digit 6; and 5 have tens digit 7. Finally, 3 have tens digit 8 (81, 83, and 85), and so the number of odd integers between 35 and 85, inclusive, is 3 + 5 + 5 + 5 + 5 + 3 = 26. Now, let $S = 35 + 37 + 39 + \ldots + 85$. Then, $S = 85 + 83 + 81 + \ldots + 35$, and it follows that $2S = (35 + 85) + (37 + 83) + (39 + 81) + \ldots + (85 + 35) = (120)(26)$. Thus, $S = 35 + 37 + 39 + \ldots + 85 = \frac{(120)(26)}{2} = 1{,}560$.

The correct answer is A.

80. In a certain sequence, each term after the first term is one-half the previous term. If the tenth term of the sequence is between 0.0001 and 0.001, then the twelfth term of the sequence is between

(A) 0.0025 and 0.025
(B) 0.00025 and 0.0025
(C) 0.000025 and 0.00025
(D) 0.0000025 and 0.000025
(E) 0.00000025 and 0.0000025

Arithmetic Sequences

Let a_n represent the nth term of the sequence. It is given that each term after the first term is $\frac{1}{2}$ the previous term and that $0.0001 < a_{10} < 0.001$.

Then for a_{11}, $\frac{0.0001}{2} < a_{11} < \frac{0.001}{2}$, or $0.00005 < a_{11} < 0.0005$. For a_{12}, $\frac{0.00005}{2} < a_{12} < \frac{0.0005}{2}$, or $0.000025 < a_{12} < 0.00025$. Thus, the twelfth term of the sequence is between 0.000025 and 0.00025.

The correct answer is C.

81. A certain drive-in movie theater has a total of 17 rows of parking spaces. There are 20 parking spaces in the first row and 21 parking spaces in the second row. In each subsequent row there are 2 more parking spaces than in the previous row. What is the total number of parking spaces in the movie theater?

(A) 412
(B) 544
(C) 596
(D) 632
(E) 692

Arithmetic Operations on integers

Row	Number of parking spaces
1st row	20
2nd row	21
3rd row	21 + 1(2)
4th row	21 + 2(2)
…	… … …
17th row	21 + 15(2)

Then, letting S represent the total number of parking spaces in the theater,

$$S = 20 + (16)(21) + (1 + 2 + 3 + \ldots + 15)(2)$$
$$= 20 + 336 + \frac{(15)(16)}{2}(2) \quad \text{See note below}$$
$$= 356 + 240$$
$$= 596$$

Note that if $s = 1 + 2 + 3 + \ldots + 15$, then $2s = (1 + 2 + 3 + \ldots + 15) + (15 + 14 + 13 + \ldots + 1)$, and so $2s = (1 + 15) + (2 + 14) + (3 + 13) + \ldots + (15 + 1) = (15)(16)$. Therefore, $s = \frac{(15)(16)}{2}$.

The correct answer is C.

82. Ada and Paul received their scores on three tests. On the first test, Ada's score was 10 points higher than Paul's score. On the second test, Ada's score was 4 points higher than Paul's score. If Paul's average (arithmetic mean) score on the three tests was 3 points higher than Ada's average score on the three tests, then Paul's score on the third test was how many points higher than Ada's score?

(A) 9
(B) 14
(C) 17
(D) 23
(E) 25

Algebra Statistics

Let a_1, a_2, and a_3 be Ada's scores on the first, second, and third tests, respectively, and let p_1, p_2, and p_3 be Paul's scores on the first, second, and third tests, respectively. Then, Ada's average score is $\frac{a_1+a_2+a_3}{3}$ and Paul's average score is $\frac{p_1+p_2+p_3}{3}$. But, Paul's average score is 3 points higher than Ada's average score, so $\frac{p_1+p_2+p_3}{3}=\frac{a_1+a_2+a_3}{3}+3$. Also, it is given that $a_1=p_1+10$ and $a_2=p_2+4$, so by substitution, $\frac{p_1+p_2+p_3}{3}=\frac{(p_1+10)+(p_2+4)+a_3}{3}+3$. Then, $p_1+p_2+p_3=(p_1+10)+(p_2+4)+a_3+9$ and so $p_3=a_3+23$. On the third test, Paul's score was 23 points higher than Ada's score.

The correct answer is D.

83. The price of a certain stock increased by 0.25 of 1 percent on a certain day. By what fraction did the price of the stock increase that day?

(A) $\frac{1}{2{,}500}$

(B) $\frac{1}{400}$

(C) $\frac{1}{40}$

(D) $\frac{1}{25}$

(E) $\frac{1}{4}$

Arithmetic Percents

It is given that the price of a certain stock increased by 0.25 of 1 percent on a certain day. This is equivalent to an increase of $\frac{1}{4}$ of $\frac{1}{100}$, which is $\left(\frac{1}{4}\right)\left(\frac{1}{100}\right)$, and $\left(\frac{1}{4}\right)\left(\frac{1}{100}\right)=\frac{1}{400}$.

The correct answer is B.

84. Three business partners, Q, R, and S, agree to divide their total profit for a certain year in the ratios 2:5:8, respectively. If Q's share was $4,000, what was the total profit of the business partners for the year?

(A) $26,000

(B) $30,000

(C) $52,000

(C) $60,000

(C) $300,000

Algebra Applied problems

Letting T represent the total profit and using the given ratios, Q's share is $\frac{2}{2+5+8}T=\frac{2}{15}T$. Since Q's share is \$4,000, then $\frac{2}{15}T=4{,}000$ and $T=\frac{15}{2}(4{,}000)=30{,}000$.

The correct answer is B.

85. For each trip, a taxicab company charges $4.25 for the first mile and $2.65 for each additional mile or fraction thereof. If the total charge for a certain trip was $62.55, how many miles at most was the trip?

(A) 21

(B) 22

(C) 23

(D) 24

(E) 25

Arithmetic Applied problems

Subtracting the charge for the first mile leaves a charge of $62.55 – $4.25 = $58.30 for the miles after the first mile. Divide this amount by $2.65 to find the number of miles to which $58.30 corresponds: $\frac{58.30}{2.65}=22$ miles. Therefore, the total number of miles is at most 1 (the first mile) added to 22 (the number of miles after the first mile), which equals 23.

The correct answer is C.

86. When 24 is divided by the positive integer n, the remainder is 4. Which of the following statements about n must be true?

I. n is even.
II. n is a multiple of 5.
III. n is a factor of 20.

(A) III only
(B) I and II only
(C) I and III only
(D) II and III only
(E) I, II, and III

Arithmetic Properties of numbers

Since the remainder is 4 when 24 is divided by the positive integer n and the remainder must be less than the divisor, it follows that $24 = qn + 4$ for some positive integer q and $4 < n$, or $qn = 20$ and $n > 4$. It follows that $n = 5$, or $n = 10$, or $n = 20$ since these are the only factors of 20 that exceed 4.

I. n is not necessarily even. For example, n could be 5.
II. n is necessarily a multiple of 5 since the value of n is either 5, 10, or 20.
III. n is a factor of 20 since $20 = qn$ for some positive integer q.

The correct answer is D.

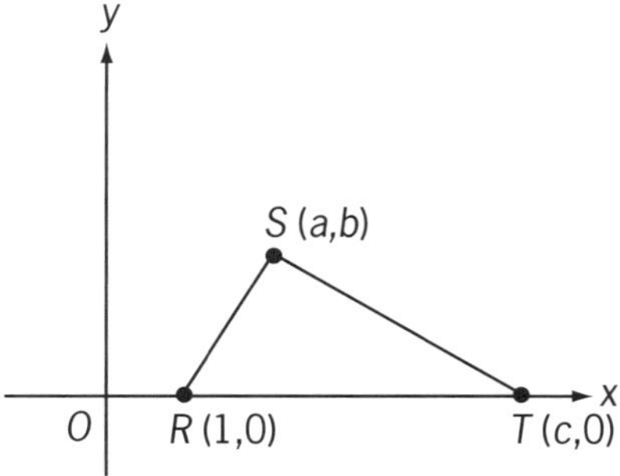

87. In the rectangular coordinate system above, the area of ΔRST is

(A) $\frac{bc}{2}$

(B) $\frac{b(c-1)}{2}$

(C) $\frac{c(b-1)}{2}$

(D) $\frac{a(c-1)}{2}$

(E) $\frac{c(a-1)}{2}$

Geometry Simple coordinate geometry

Letting $\overline{RT}$ be the base of the triangle, since $RT = c - 1$, the length of the base of ΔRST is $c - 1$. The altitude to the base $\overline{RT}$ is a perpendicular dropped from S to the x-axis. The length of this perpendicular is $b - 0 = b$. Using the formula for the area, A, of a triangle, $A = \frac{1}{2}bh$, where b is the length of the base and h is the length of the altitude to that base, the area of ΔRST is $\frac{1}{2}(c-1)(b)$ or $\frac{b(c-1)}{2}$.

The correct answer is B.

88. What is the thousandths digit in the decimal equivalent of $\frac{53}{5{,}000}$?

(A) 0
(B) 1
(C) 3
(D) 5
(E) 6

Arithmetic Place value

$\frac{53}{5,000} = \frac{106}{10,000} = 0.0106$ and the thousandths digit is 0.

The correct answer is A.

89. The product of 3,305 and the 1-digit integer *x* is a 5-digit integer. The units (ones) digit of the product is 5 and the hundreds digit is *y*. If *A* is the set of all possible values of *x* and *B* is the set of all possible values of *y*, then which of the following gives the members of *A* and *B* ?

	A	*B*
(A)	{1, 3, 5, 7, 9}	{0, 1, 2, 3, 4, 5, 6, 7, 8, 9}
(B)	{1, 3, 5, 7, 9}	{1, 3, 5, 7, 9}
(C)	{3, 5, 7, 9}	{1, 5, 7, 9}
(D)	{5, 7, 9}	{1, 5, 7}
(E)	{5, 7, 9}	{1, 5, 9}

Arithmetic Properties of numbers

Since the products of 3,305 and 1, 3,305 and 2, and 3,305 and 3 are the 4-digit integers 3,305, 6,610, and 9,915, respectively, it follows that x must be among the 1-digit integers 4, 5, 6, 7, 8, and 9. Also, since the units digit of the product of 3,305 and x is 5, it follows that x cannot be 4 (product has units digit 0), 6 (product has units digit 0), or 8 (product has units digit 0). Therefore, $A = \{5, 7, 9\}$. The possibilities for y will be the hundreds digits of the products $(3,305)(5) = 16,525$, $(3,305)(7) = 23,135$, and $(3,305)(9) = 29,745$. Thus, y can be 5, 1, or 7, and so $B = \{1, 5, 7\}$.

The correct answer is D.

90. What is the largest integer *n* such that $\frac{1}{2^n} > 0.01$?

(A) 5
(B) 6
(C) 7
(D) 10
(E) 51

Arithmetic Exponents; Operations with rational numbers

Since $\frac{1}{2^n} > 0.01$ is equivalent to $2^n < 100$, find the largest integer n such that $2^n < 100$. Using trial and error, $2^6 = 64$ and $64 < 100$, but $2^7 = 128$ and $128 > 100$. Therefore, 6 is the largest integer such that $\frac{1}{2^n} > 0.01$.

The correct answer is B.

91. If *x* and *y* are integers such that $2 < x \leq 8$ and $2 < y \leq 9$, what is the maximum value of $\frac{1}{x} - \frac{x}{y}$?

(A) $-3\frac{1}{8}$
(B) 0
(C) $\frac{1}{4}$
(D) $\frac{5}{18}$
(E) 2

Algebra Inequalities

Because x and y are both positive, the maximum value of $\frac{1}{x} - \frac{x}{y}$ will occur when the value of $\frac{1}{x}$ is maximum and the value of $\frac{x}{y}$ is minimum. The value of $\frac{1}{x}$ is maximum when the value of x is minimum or when $x = 3$. The value of $\frac{x}{y}$ is minimum when the value of x is minimum (or when $x = 3$) and the value of y is maximum (or when $y = 9$). Thus, the maximum value of $\frac{1}{x} - \frac{x}{y}$ is $\frac{1}{3} - \frac{3}{9} = 0$.

The correct answer is B.

92. Items that are purchased together at a certain discount store are priced at \$3 for the first item purchased and \$1 for each additional item purchased. What is the maximum number of items that could be purchased together for a total price that is less than \$30 ?

(A) 25
(B) 26
(C) 27
(D) 28
(E) 29

Arithmetic Applied problems

After the first item is purchased, \$29.99 – \$3.00 = \$26.99 remains to purchase the additional items. Since the price for each of the additional items is \$1.00, a maximum of 26 additional items could be purchased. Therefore, a maximum of 1 + 26 = 27 items could be purchased for less than \$30.00.

The correct answer is C.

93. The average (arithmetic mean) length per film for a group of 21 films is t minutes. If a film that runs for 66 minutes is removed from the group and replaced by one that runs for 52 minutes, what is the average length per film, in minutes, for the new group of films, in terms of t?

(A) $t+\frac{2}{3}$

(B) $t-\frac{2}{3}$

(C) $21t+14$

(D) $t+\frac{3}{2}$

(E) $t-\frac{3}{2}$

Arithmetic Statistics

Let S denote the sum of the lengths, in minutes, of the 21 films in the original group. Since the average length is t minutes, it follows that $\frac{S}{21}=t$.

If a 66-minute film is replaced by a 52-minute film, then the sum of the lengths of the 21 films in the resulting group is $S - 66 + 52 = S - 14$. Therefore, the average length of the resulting 21 films is $\frac{S-14}{21}=\frac{S}{21}-\frac{14}{21}=t-\frac{2}{3}$.

The correct answer is B.

94. A garden center sells a certain grass seed in 5-pound bags at \$13.85 per bag, 10-pound bags at \$20.43 per bag, and 25-pound bags at \$32.25 per bag. If a customer is to buy at least 65 pounds of the grass seed, but no more than 80 pounds, what is the least possible cost of the grass seed that the customer will buy?

(A) \$94.03

(B) \$96.75

(C) \$98.78

(D) \$102.07

(E) \$105.36

Arithmetic Applied problems

Let x represent the amount of grass seed, in pounds, the customer is to buy. It follows that $65 \le x \le 80$. Since the grass seed is available in only 5-pound, 10-pound, and 25-pound bags, then the customer must buy either 65, 70, 75, or 80 pounds of grass seed. Because the seed is more expensive per pound for smaller bags, the customer should minimize the number of the smaller bags and maximize the number of 25-pound bags to incur the least possible cost for the grass seed. The possible purchases are given in the table below.

x	Number of 25-pound bags	Number of 10-pound bags	Number of 5-pound bags	Total cost
65	2	1	1	\$98.78
70	2	2	0	\$105.36
75	3	0	0	\$96.75
80	3	0	1	\$110.60

The least possible cost is then 3(\$32.25) = \$96.75.

The correct answer is B.

95. If $x = -|w|$, which of the following must be true?

(A) $x = -w$

(B) $x = w$

(C) $x^2 = w$

(D) $x^2 = w^2$

(E) $x^3 = w^3$

Algebra Absolute value

Squaring both sides of $x = -|w|$ gives $x^2 = (-|w|)^2$, or $x^2 = |w|^2 = w^2$.

Alternatively, if (x, w) is equal to either of the pairs $(-1,1)$ or $(-1,-1)$, then $x = -|w|$ is true. However, each of the answer choices except $x^2 = w^2$ is false for at least one of these two pairs.

The correct answer is D.

96. Which of the following lines in the xy-plane does not contain any point with integers as both coordinates?

(A) $y = x$

(B) $y = x + \frac{1}{2}$

(C) $y = x + 5$

(D) $y = \frac{1}{2}x$

(E) $y = \frac{1}{2}x + 5$

Algebra; Arithmetic Substitution; Operations with rational numbers

A If x is an integer, y is an integer since $y = x$ Thus, the line given by $y = x$ contains points with integers as both coordinates.

B If x is an integer, then if y were an integer, then $y - x$ would be an integer. But, $y - x = \frac{1}{2}$ and $\frac{1}{2}$ is NOT an integer. Since assuming that y is an integer leads to a contradiction, then y cannot be an integer and the line given by $y = x + \frac{1}{2}$ does NOT contain any points with integers as both coordinates.

Since there can be only one correct answer, the lines in C, D, and E need not be checked, but for completeness,

C If x is an integer, $x + 5$ is an integer and so y is an integer since $y = x + 5$. Thus, the line given by $y = x + 5$ contains points with integers as both coordinates.

D If x is an even integer, $\frac{1}{2}x$ is an integer and so y is an integer since $y = \frac{1}{2}x$. Thus, the line given by $y = \frac{1}{2}x$ contains points with integers as both coordinates.

E If x is an even integer, $\frac{1}{2}x$ is an integer and $\frac{1}{2}x + 5$ is also an integer so y is an integer since $y = \frac{1}{2}x + 5$. Thus, the line given by $y = \frac{1}{2}x + 5$ contains points with integers as both coordinates.

The correct answer is B.

97. One inlet pipe fills an empty tank in 5 hours. A second inlet pipe fills the same tank in 3 hours. If both pipes are used together, how long will it take to fill $\frac{2}{3}$ of the tank?

(A) $\frac{8}{15}$ hr

(B) $\frac{3}{4}$ hr

(C) $\frac{5}{4}$ hr

(D) $\frac{15}{8}$ hr

(E) $\frac{8}{3}$ hr

Algebra Applied problems

If the first pipe fills the tank in 5 hours, then it fills $\frac{1}{5}$ of the tank in one hour. If the second pipe fills the tank in 3 hours, then it fills $\frac{1}{3}$ of the tank in one hour. Together, the two pipes fill $\frac{1}{5} + \frac{1}{3} = \frac{8}{15}$ of the tank in one hour, which means they fill the whole tank in $\frac{15}{8}$ hours. To fill $\frac{2}{3}$ of the tank at this constant rate would then take $\left(\frac{2}{3}\right)\left(\frac{15}{8}\right) = \frac{5}{4}$ hours.

The correct answer is C.

98. For a light that has an intensity of 60 candles at its source, the intensity in candles, S, of the light at a point d feet from the source is given by the formula $S = \frac{60k}{d^2}$, where k is a constant. If the intensity of the light is 30 candles at a distance of 2 feet from the source, what is the intensity of the light at a distance of 20 feet from the source?

(A) $\frac{3}{10}$ candle
(B) $\frac{1}{2}$ candle
(C) 1 candle
(D) 2 candles
(E) 3 candles

Algebra Applied problems

First, solve the equation for the constant k using the values where both the intensity (S) and distance (d) are known.

$$S = \frac{60k}{d^2}$$

$$30 = \frac{60k}{2^2} \quad \text{substitute } S = 30 \text{ candles and } d = 2 \text{ feet}$$

$$120 = 60k \quad \text{solve for } k$$

$$2 = k$$

Then, with this known value of k, solve the equation for S where only the distance (d) is known.

$$S = \frac{60k}{d^2}$$

$$S = \frac{60(2)}{20^2} \quad \text{substitute } k = 2 \text{ and } d = 20 \text{ feet}$$

$$S = \frac{120}{400} = \frac{3}{10}$$

The correct answer is A.

99. A certain financial institution reported that its assets totaled \$2,377,366.30 on a certain day. Of this amount, \$31,724.54 was held in cash. Approximately what percent of the reported assets was held in cash on that day?

(A) 0.00013%
(B) 0.0013%
(C) 0.013%
(D) 0.13%
(E) 1.3%

Arithmetic Percents; Estimation

The requested percent can be estimated by converting the values into scientific notation.

$$\frac{31{,}724.54}{2{,}377{,}366.30} \quad \text{value as fraction}$$

$$= \frac{3.172454 \times 10^4}{2.37736630 \times 10^6} \quad \text{convert to scientific notation}$$

$$= \frac{3.172454}{2.37736630} \times \frac{10^4}{10^6} \quad \text{arithmetic property of fractions}$$

$$= \frac{3.172454}{2.37736630} \times 10^{-2} \quad \text{subtract exponents}$$

$$\approx \frac{3}{2} \times 10^{-2} \quad \text{approximate}$$

$$= 1.5 \times 10^{-2} \quad \text{convert to decimal fraction}$$

$$= 0.015 \quad \text{multiply}$$

$$= 1.5\% \quad \text{convert to percent}$$

A more detailed computation would show that 1.3% is a better approximation. However, in order to select the best value from the values given as answer choices, the above computation is sufficient.

The correct answer is E.

$$\begin{array}{r} AB \\ +\ BA \\ \hline AAC \end{array}$$

100. In the correctly worked addition problem shown, where the sum of the two-digit positive integers *AB* and *BA* is the three-digit integer *AAC*, and *A*, *B*, and *C* are different digits, what is the units digit of the integer *AAC* ?

(A) 9
(B) 6
(C) 3
(D) 2
(E) 0

Arithmetic Place value

Determine the value of C.

It is given that $(10A + B) + (10B + A) = 100A + 10A + C$ or $11A + 11B = 110A + C$. Thus, $11B - 99A = C$, or $11(B - 9A) = C$. Therefore, C is divisible by 11, and 0 is the only digit that is divisible by 11.

The correct answer is E.

$$3r \le 4s + 5$$
$$|s| \le 5$$

101. Given the inequalities above, which of the following CANNOT be the value of *r* ?

(A) –20
(B) –5
(C) 0
(D) 5
(E) 20

Algebra Inequalities

Since $|s| \le 5$, it follows that $-5 \le s \le 5$. Therefore, $-20 \le 4s \le 20$, and hence $-15 \le 4s + 5 \le 25$. Since $3r \le 4s + 5$ (given) and $4s + 5 \le 25$ (end of previous sentence), it follows that $3r \le 25$. Among the answer choices, $3r \le 25$ is false only for $r = 20$.

The correct answer is E.

102. If *m* is an even integer, *v* is an odd integer, and $m > v > 0$, which of the following represents the number of even integers less than *m* and greater than *v* ?

(A) $\frac{m-v}{2} - 1$
(B) $\frac{m-v-1}{2}$
(C) $\frac{m-v}{2}$
(D) $m - v - 1$
(E) $m - v$

Arithmetic Properties of numbers

Since there is only one correct answer, one method of solving the problem is to choose values for m and v and determine which of the expressions gives the correct number for these values. For example, if $m = 6$ and $v = 1$, then there are 2 even integers less than 6 and greater than 1, namely the even integers 2 and 4. As the table below shows, $\frac{m-v-1}{2}$ is the only expression given that equals 2.

$$\frac{m-v}{2} - 1 = 1.5$$
$$\frac{m-v-1}{2} = 2$$
$$\frac{m-v}{2} = 2.5$$
$$m - v - 1 = 4$$
$$m - v = 5$$

To solve this problem it is not necessary to show that $\frac{m-v-1}{2}$ always gives the correct number of even integers. However, one way this can be done is by the following method, first shown for a specific example and then shown in general. For the specific example, suppose $v = 15$ and $m = 144$. Then a list—call it the first list—of the even integers greater than v and less than m is 16, 18, 20, …, 140, 142. Now subtract 14 (chosen so that the second list will begin with 2) from each of the integers in the first list to form a second list, which has the same number of integers as the first list: 2, 4, 6, …, 128. Finally, divide each of the integers in the second list (all of which are even) by 2 to form a third list, which also has the same number of integers as the first list: 1, 2, 3, …, 64. Since the number of integers in the third list is 64, it follows that the number of integers in the first list is 64. For the general situation, the first list is the following list of even integers: $v + 1$, $v + 3$, $v + 5$, …, $m - 4$, $m - 2$. Now subtract the even integer $v - 1$ from (i.e., add $-v + 1$ to) each of the integers in the first list to obtain the second list: 2, 4, 6, …, $m - v - 3$, $m - v - 1$. (Note, for example, that $m - 4 - (v - 1) = m - v - 3$.) Finally, divide each of the integers (all of which are even) in the second list by 2 to obtain the third list: 1, 2, 3, …, $\frac{m-v-3}{2}$, $\frac{m-v-1}{2}$.

Since the number of integers in the third list is $\frac{m-v-1}{2}$, it follows that the number of integers in the first list is $\frac{m-v-1}{2}$.

The correct answer is B.

103. A positive integer is divisible by 9 if and only if the sum of its digits is divisible by 9. If n is a positive integer, for which of the following values of k is $25 \times 10^n + k \times 10^{2n}$ divisible by 9 ?

(A) 9
(B) 16
(C) 23
(D) 35
(E) 47

Arithmetic Properties of numbers

Since n can be any positive integer, let $n = 2$. Then $25 \times 10^n = 2{,}500$, so its digits consist of the digits 2 and 5 followed by two digits of 0. Also, $k \times 10^{2n} = k \times 10{,}000$, so its digits consist of the digits of k followed by four digits of 0. Therefore, the digits of $(25 \times 10^n) + (k \times 10^{2n})$ consist of the digits of k followed by the digits 2 and 5, followed by two digits of 0. The table below shows this for $n = 2$ and $k = 35$:

$$\begin{aligned} 25 \times 10^n &= 2{,}500 \\ 35 \times 10^{2n} &= 350{,}000 \\ (25 \times 10^n) + (35 \times 10^{2n}) &= 352{,}500 \end{aligned}$$

Thus, when $n = 2$, the sum of the digits of $(25 \times 10^n) + (k \times 10^{2n})$ will be $2 + 5 = 7$ plus the sum of the digits of k. Of the answer choices, this sum of digits is divisible by 9 only for $k = 47$, which gives $2 + 5 + 4 + 7 = 18$. It can also be verified that, for each positive integer n, the only such answer choice is $k = 47$, although this additional verification is not necessary to obtain the correct answer.

The correct answer is E.

104. The perimeter of rectangle A is 200 meters. The length of rectangle B is 10 meters less than the length of rectangle A and the width of rectangle B is 10 meters more than the width of rectangle A. If rectangle B is a square, what is the width, in meters, of rectangle A ?

(A) 10
(B) 20
(C) 40
(D) 50
(E) 60

Geometry Rectangles; Perimeter

Let L meters and W meters be the length and width, respectively, of rectangle A. Then $(L - 10)$ meters and $(W + 10)$ meters are the length and width, respectively, of rectangle B. Since the perimeter of rectangle A is 200 meters, it follows that $2L + 2W = 200$, or $L + W = 100$. Since rectangle B is a square, it follows that $L - 10 = W + 10$, or $L - W = 20$. Adding the equations $L + W = 100$ and $L - W = 20$ gives $2L = 120$, or $L = 60$. From $L - W = 20$ and $L = 60$, it follows that $W = 40$, and so the width of rectangle A is 40 meters.

The correct answer is C.

105. On the number line, the shaded interval is the graph of which of the following inequalities?

(A) $|x| \le 4$

(B) $|x| \le 8$

(C) $|x - 2| \le 4$

(D) $|x - 2| \le 6$

(E) $|x + 2| \le 6$

Algebra Inequalities; Absolute value

The midpoint of the interval from −8 to 4, inclusive, is $\frac{-8+4}{2} = -2$ and the length of the interval from −8 to 4, inclusive, is $4 - (-8) = 12$, so the interval consists of all numbers within a distance of $\frac{12}{2} = 6$ from −2. Using an inequality involving absolute values, this can be described by $|x - (-2)| \le 6$, or $|x + 2| \le 6$.

Alternatively, the inequality $-8 \le x \le 4$ can be written as the conjunction $-8 \le x$ and $x \le 4$. Rewrite this conjunction so that the lower value, −8, and the upper value, 4, are shifted to values that have the same magnitude. This can be done by adding 2 to each side of each inequality, which gives $-6 \le x + 2$ and $x + 2 \le 6$. Thus, $x + 2$ lies between −6 and 6, inclusive, and it follows that $|x + 2| \le 6$.

The correct answer is E.

106. Of all the students in a certain dormitory, $\frac{1}{2}$ are first-year students and the rest are second-year students. If $\frac{4}{5}$ of the first-year students have not declared a major and if the fraction of second-year students who have declared a major is 3 times the fraction of first-year students who have declared a major, what fraction of all the students in the dormitory are second-year students who have not declared a major?

(A) $\frac{1}{15}$

(B) $\frac{1}{5}$

(C) $\frac{4}{15}$

(D) $\frac{1}{3}$

(E) $\frac{2}{5}$

Arithmetic Applied problems

Consider the table below in which T represents the total number of students in the dormitory. Since $\frac{1}{2}$ of the students are first-year students and the rest are second-year students, it follows that $\frac{1}{2}$ of the students are second-year students, and so the totals for the first-year and second-year columns are both $0.5T$. Since $\frac{4}{5}$ of the first-year students have not declared a major, it follows that the middle entry in the first-year column is $\frac{4}{5}(0.5T) = 0.4T$ and the first entry in the first-year column is $0.5T - 0.4T = 0.1T$. Since the fraction of second-year students who have declared a major is 3 times the fraction of first-year students who have declared a major, it follows that the first entry in the second-year column is $3(0.1T) = 0.3T$ and the second entry in the second-year column is $0.5T - 0.3T = 0.2T$. Thus, the fraction of students that are second-year students who have not declared a major is $\frac{0.2T}{T} = 0.2 = \frac{1}{5}$.

	First-year	Second-year	Total
Declared major	$0.1T$	$0.3T$	$0.4T$
Not declared major	$0.4T$	$0.2T$	$0.6T$
Total	$0.5T$	$0.5T$	T

The correct answer is B.

107. If the average (arithmetic mean) of x, y, and z is $7x$ and $x \ne 0$, what is the ratio of x to the sum of y and z?

(A) 1:21

(B) 1:20

(C) 1:6

(D) 6:1

(E) 20:1

Algebra Ratio and proportion

Given that the average of x, y, and z is $7x$, it follows that $\frac{x+y+z}{3} = 7x$, or $x + y + z = 21x$, or $y + z = 20x$. Dividing both sides of the last equation by $20(y + z)$ gives $\frac{1}{20} = \frac{x}{y+z}$, so the ratio of x to the sum of y and z is 1:20.

The correct answer is B.

108. $\frac{(-1.5)(1.2)-(4.5)(0.4)}{30} =$

(A) −1.2
(B) −0.12
(C) 0
(D) 0.12
(E) 1.2

Arithmetic Operations on rational numbers

Simplify the expression.

$$\frac{(-1.5)(1.2)-(4.5)(0.4)}{30} = \frac{-1.80-1.80}{30} = \frac{-3.60}{30} = -0.12$$

The correct answer is B.

109. In the coordinate plane, line k passes through the origin and has slope 2. If points $(3,y)$ and $(x,4)$ are on line k, then $x + y =$

(A) 3.5
(B) 7
(C) 8
(D) 10
(E) 14

Algebra Simple coordinate geometry

Since line k has slope 2 and passes through the origin, the equation of line k is $y = 2x$. If the point $(3,y)$ is on line k, then $y = 2(3) = 6$. If the point $(x,4)$ is on line k, then $4 = 2x$ and so $x = 2$. Therefore, $x + y = 6 + 2 = 8$.

The correct answer is C.

110. If a, b, and c are constants, $a > b > c$, and $x^3 - x = (x - a)(x - b)(x - c)$ for all numbers x, what is the value of b ?

(A) −3
(B) −1
(C) 0
(D) 1
(E) 3

Algebra Simplifying algebraic expressions

Since $(x - a)(x - b)(x - c) = x^3 - x = x(x^2 - 1) = x(x + 1)(x - 1) = (x - 0)(x - 1)(x + 1)$ then a, b, and c are 0, 1, and −1 in some order. Since $a > b > c$, it follows that $a = 1$, $b = 0$, and $c = -1$.

The correct answer is C.

111. Company K's earnings were \$12 million last year. If this year's earnings are projected to be 150 percent greater than last year's earnings, what are Company K's projected earnings this year?

(A) \$13.5 million
(B) \$15 million
(C) \$18 million
(D) \$27 million
(E) \$30 million

Arithmetic Percents

If one quantity x is p percent greater than another quantity y, then $x = y + \left(\frac{p}{100}\right)y$. Let y represent last year's earnings and x represent this year's earnings, which are projected to be 150 percent greater than last year's earnings. Then, $x = y + \left(\frac{150}{100}\right)y = y + 1.5y = 2.5y$. Since last year's earnings were \$12 million, this year's earnings are projected to be 2.5(\$12 million) = \$30 million.

The correct answer is E.

112. $17^3 + 17^4 =$

(A) 17^7
(B) $17^3(18)$
(C) $17^6(18)$
(D) $2(17^3) + 17$
(E) $2(17^3) - 17$

Arithmetic Exponents

Since $17^3 = 17^3 \times 1$ and $17^4 = 17^3 \times 17$, then 17^3 may be factored out of each term. It follows that $17^3 + 17^4 = 17^3(1 + 17) = 17^3(18)$.

The correct answer is B.

113. Jonah drove the first half of a 100-mile trip in x hours and the second half in y hours. Which of the following is equal to Jonah's average speed, in miles per hour, for the entire trip?

(A) $\frac{50}{x+y}$
(B) $\frac{100}{x+y}$
(C) $\frac{25}{x} + \frac{25}{y}$
(D) $\frac{50}{x} + \frac{50}{y}$
(E) $\frac{100}{x} + \frac{100}{y}$

Algebra Applied problems

Using average speed $= \frac{\text{total distance}}{\text{total time}}$, it follows that Jonah's average speed for his entire 100-mile trip is $\frac{100}{x+y}$.

The correct answer is B.

114. What is the greatest number of identical bouquets that can be made out of 21 white and 91 red tulips if no flowers are to be left out? (Two bouquets are identical whenever the number of red tulips in the two bouquets is equal and the number of white tulips in the two bouquets is equal.)

(A) 3
(B) 4
(C) 5
(D) 6
(E) 7

Arithmetic Properties of numbers

Since the question asks for the greatest number of bouquets that can be made using all of the flowers, the number of bouquets will need to be the greatest common factor of 21 and 91. Since $21 = (3)(7)$ and $91 = (7)(13)$, the greatest common factor of 21 and 91 is 7. Therefore, 7 bouquets can be made, each with 3 white tulips and 13 red tulips.

The correct answer is E.

115. In the xy-plane, the points (c,d), $(c,-d)$, and $(-c,-d)$ are three vertices of a certain square. If $c < 0$ and $d > 0$, which of the following points is in the same quadrant as the fourth vertex of the square?

(A) $(-5,-3)$
(B) $(-5,3)$
(C) $(5,-3)$
(D) $(3,-5)$
(E) $(3,5)$

Geometry Coordinate geometry

Because the points (c,d) and $(c,-d)$ lie on the same vertical line (the line with equation $x = c$), one side of the square has length $2d$ and is vertical. Therefore, the side of the square opposite this side has length $2d$, is vertical, and contains the vertex $(-c,-d)$. From this it follows that the remaining vertex is $(-c,d)$, because $(-c,d)$ lies on the same vertical line as $(-c,-d)$ (the line with equation $x = -c$) and these two vertices are a distance $2d$ apart. Because $c < 0$ and $d > 0$, the point $(-c,d)$ has positive x-coordinate and positive y-coordinate. Thus, the point $(-c,d)$ is in Quadrant I. Of the answer choices, only $(3,5)$ is in Quadrant I.

The correct answer is E.

116. For all numbers s and t, the operation $\star$ is defined by $s \star t = (s - 1)(t + 1)$. If $(-2) \star x = -12$, then $x =$

(A) 2
(B) 3
(C) 5
(D) 6
(E) 11

Algebra First-degree equations

The equivalent values established for this problem are $s = -2$ and $t = x$. So, substitute -2 for s and x for t in the given equation:

$$-2 * x = -12$$
$$(-2-1)(x+1) = -12$$
$$(-3)(x+1) = -12$$
$$x+1 = 4$$
$$x = 3$$

The correct answer is B.

117. If the amount of federal estate tax due on an estate valued at \$1.35 million is \$437,000 plus 43 percent of the value of the estate in excess of \$1.25 million, then the federal tax due is approximately what percent of the value of the estate?

A. 30%
B. 35%
C. 40%
D. 45%
E. 50%

Arithmetic Percents; Estimation

The amount of tax divided by the value of the estate is

	$\dfrac{[0.437 + (0.43)(1.35 - 1.25)]\ \cancel{\text{million}}}{1.35\ \cancel{\text{million}}}$	value as fraction
=	$\dfrac{0.437 + (0.43)(0.1)}{1.35}$	arithmetic
=	$\dfrac{0.48}{1.35} = \dfrac{48}{135}$	arithmetic

By long division, $\frac{48}{135}$ is approximately 35.6, so the closest answer choice is 35%.

Alternatively, $\frac{48}{135}$ can be estimated by $\frac{48}{136} = \frac{6}{17} \approx \frac{6}{18} = \frac{1}{3} \approx 33\%$, so the closest answer choice is 35%. Note that $\frac{48}{135}$ is greater than $\frac{48}{136}$, and $\frac{6}{17}$ is greater than $\frac{6}{18}$, so the correct value is greater than 33%, which rules out 30% being the closest.

The correct answer is B.

118. If $\frac{3}{10^4} = x\%$, then $x =$

(A) 0.3
(B) 0.03
(C) 0.003
(D) 0.0003
(E) 0.00003

Arithmetic Percents

Given that $\frac{3}{10^4} = x\%$, and writing $x\%$ as $\frac{x}{100}$, it follows that $\frac{3}{10^4} = \frac{x}{100}$. Multiplying both sides by 100 gives $x = \frac{300}{10^4} = \frac{300}{10,000} = \frac{3}{100} = 0.03$.

The correct answer is B.

119. If a basketball team scores an average (arithmetic mean) of x points per game for n games and then scores y points in its next game, what is the team's average score for the $n + 1$ games?

(A) $\dfrac{nx + y}{n + 1}$
(B) $x + \dfrac{y}{n + 1}$
(C) $x + \dfrac{y}{n}$
(D) $\dfrac{n(x + y)}{n + 1}$
(E) $\dfrac{x + ny}{n + 1}$

Arithmetic Statistics

Using the formula average $= \frac{\text{total points}}{\text{number of games}}$, the average number of points per game for the first n games can be expressed as $x = \frac{\text{total points for } n \text{ games}}{n}$. Solving this equation shows that the total points for n games $= nx$. Then, the total points for $n+1$ games can be expressed as $nx + y$, and the average number of points for $n+1$ games $= \frac{nx+y}{n+1}$.

The correct answer is A.

120. At a certain pizzeria, $\frac{1}{8}$ of the pizzas sold in one week were mushroom and $\frac{1}{3}$ of the remaining pizzas sold were pepperoni. If n of the pizzas sold were pepperoni, how many were mushroom?

(A) $\frac{3}{8}n$

(B) $\frac{3}{7}n$

(C) $\frac{7}{16}n$

(D) $\frac{7}{8}n$

(E) $3n$

Algebra Simplifying algebraic expressions

Let t represent the total number of pizzas sold. Then $\frac{1}{8}t$ represents the number of mushroom pizzas sold, $\frac{7}{8}t$ represents the number of remaining pizzas sold, and $\frac{1}{3}\left(\frac{7}{8}t\right) = \frac{7}{24}t$ represents the number of pepperoni pizzas sold. Then $n = \frac{7}{24}t$, $t = \frac{24}{7}n$, and $\frac{1}{8}t = \frac{1}{8}\left(\frac{24}{7}n\right) = \frac{3}{7}n$. Thus, $\frac{3}{7}n$ mushroom pizzas were sold.

The correct answer is B.

121. What is the value of $2x^2 - 2.4x - 1.7$ for $x = 0.7$?

(A) –0.72

(B) –1.42

(C) –1.98

(D) –2.40

(E) –2.89

Algebra Simplifying algebraic expressions

Work the problem by substituting $x = 0.7$.

$$\begin{aligned} &2x^2 - 2.4x - 1.7 \\ &= 2(0.7)^2 - 2.4(0.7) - 1.7 \\ &= 2(0.49) - 1.68 - 1.7 \\ &= 0.98 - 1.68 - 1.7 \\ &= -2.40 \end{aligned}$$

The correct answer is D.

122. What is the remainder when 3^{24} is divided by 5 ?

(A) 0

(B) 1

(C) 2

(D) 3

(E) 4

Arithmetic Properties of numbers

A pattern in the units digits of the numbers $3, 3^2 = 9, 3^3 = 27, 3^4 = 81, 3^5 = 243$, etc., can be found by observing that the units digit of a product of two integers is the same as the units digit of the product of the units digit of the two integers. For example, the units digit of $3^5 = 3 \times 3^4 = 3 \times 81$ is 3 since the units digit of 3×1 is 3, and the units digit of $3^6 = 3 \times 3^5 = 3 \times 243$ is 9 since the units digit of 3×3 is 9. From this it follows that the units digit of the powers of 3 follow the pattern 3, 9, 7, 1, 3, 9, 7, 1, etc., with a units digit of 1 for $3^4, 3^8, 3^{12}, \ldots, 3^{24}, \ldots$. Therefore, the units digit of 3^{24} is 1. Thus, 3^{24} is 1 more than a multiple of 10, and hence 3^{24} is 1 more than a multiple of 5, and so the remainder when 3^{24} is divided by 5 is 1.

The correct answer is B.

123. If the volume of a ball is 32,490 cubic millimeters, what is the volume of the ball in cubic centimeters? (1 millimeter = 0.1 centimeter)

(A) 0.3249
(B) 3.249
(C) 32.49
(D) 324.9
(E) 3,249

Arithmetic Measurement conversion

Since 1 mm = 0.1 cm, it follows that $1 \text{ mm}^3 = (0.1)^3 \text{ cm}^3 = 0.001 \text{ cm}^3$. Therefore, $32{,}490 \text{ mm}^3 = (32{,}490)(0.001) \text{ cm}^3 = 32.49 \text{ cm}^3$.

The correct answer is C.

124. David used part of $100,000 to purchase a house. Of the remaining portion, he invested $\frac{1}{3}$ of it at 4 percent simple annual interest and $\frac{2}{3}$ of it at 6 percent simple annual interest. If after a year the income from the two investments totaled $320, what was the purchase price of the house?

(A) $96,000
(B) $94,000
(C) $88,000
(D) $75,000
(E) $40,000

Algebra Applied problems; Percents

Let x be the amount, in dollars, that David used to purchase the house. Then David invested $(100{,}000 - x)$ dollars, $\frac{1}{3}$ at 4% simple annual interest and $\frac{2}{3}$ at 6% simple annual interest. After one year the total interest, in dollars, on this investment was $\frac{1}{3}(100{,}000 - x)(0.04) + \frac{2}{3}(100{,}000 - x)(0.06) = 320$. Solve this equation to find the value of x.

$\frac{1}{3}(100{,}000 - x)(0.04) + \frac{2}{3}(100{,}000 - x)(0.06) = 320$	given
$(100{,}000 - x)(0.04) + 2(100{,}000 - x)(0.06) = 960$	multiply both sides by 3
$4{,}000 - 0.04x + 12{,}000 - 0.12x = 960$	distributive property
$16{,}000 - 0.16x = 960$	combine like terms
$16{,}000 - 960 = 0.16x$	add $0.16x - 960$ to both sides
$100{,}000 - 6{,}000 = x$	divide both sides by 0.16
$94{,}000 = x$	

Therefore, the purchase price of the house was $94,000.

The correct answer is B.

125. The cost to rent a small bus for a trip is x dollars, which is to be shared equally among the people taking the trip. If 10 people take the trip rather than 16, how many more dollars, in terms of x, will it cost per person?

(A) $\frac{x}{6}$
(B) $\frac{x}{10}$
(C) $\frac{x}{16}$
(D) $\frac{3x}{40}$
(E) $\frac{3x}{80}$

Algebra Applied problems

If 16 take the trip, the cost per person would be $\frac{x}{16}$ dollars. If 10 take the trip, the cost per person would be $\frac{x}{10}$ dollars. (Note that the lowest common multiple of 10 and 16 is 80.) Thus, if 10 take the trip, the increase in dollars per person would be $\frac{x}{10} - \frac{x}{16} = \frac{8x}{80} - \frac{5x}{80} = \frac{3x}{80}$.

The correct answer is E.

126. Last year Department Store X had a sales total for December that was 4 times the average (arithmetic mean) of the monthly sales totals for January through November. The sales total for December was what fraction of the sales total for the year?

(A) $\frac{1}{4}$

(B) $\frac{4}{15}$

(C) $\frac{1}{3}$

(D) $\frac{4}{11}$

(E) $\frac{4}{5}$

Algebra; Arithmetic Applied problems; Statistics

Let A equal the average sales per month for the first 11 months. The given information about the total sales for the year can then be expressed as $11A + 4A = 15A$. Thus, $4A = (F)(15A)$, where F is the fraction of the sales total for the year that the sales total for December represents. Then $F = \frac{4A}{15A} = \frac{4}{15}$.

The correct answer is B.

127. In the sequence $x_0, x_1, x_2, \ldots, x_n$, each term from x_1 to x_k is 3 greater than the previous term, and each term from x_{k+1} to x_n is 3 less than the previous term, where n and k are positive integers and $k < n$. If $x_0 = x_n = 0$ and if $x_k = 15$, what is the value of n?

(A) 5
(B) 6
(C) 9
(D) 10
(E) 15

Algebra Sequences

Since $x_0 = 0$ and each term from x_1 to x_k is 3 greater than the previous term, then $x_k = 0 + (k)(3)$. Since $x_k = 15$, then $15 = 3k$ and $k = 5$. Since each term from x_{k+1} to x_n is 3 less than the previous term, then $x_n = x_k - (n - k)(3)$. Substituting the known values for x_k, x_n, and k gives $0 = 15 - (n - 5)(3)$, from which it follows that $3n = 30$ and $n = 10$.

The correct answer is D.

128. If $x \neq 2$, then $\frac{3x^2(x-2)-x+2}{x-2} =$

(A) $3x^2 - x + 2$
(B) $3x^2 + 1$
(C) $3x^2$
(D) $3x^2 - 1$
(E) $3x^2 - 2$

Algebra Simplifying algebraic expressions

When simplifying this expression, it is important to note that, as a first step, the numerator must be factored so that the numerator is the product of two or more expressions, one of which is $(x - 2)$. This can be accomplished by rewriting the last two terms of the numerator as $(-1)(x - 2)$. Then

$$\begin{aligned}\frac{3x^2(x-2)-x+2}{x-2} &= \frac{3x^2(x-2)+(-1)(x-2)}{x-2} \\ &= \frac{(x-2)(3x^2+(-1))}{x-2} \\ &= 3x^2+(-1) \\ &= 3x^2-1\end{aligned}$$

The correct answer is D.

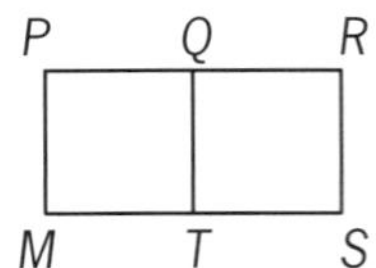

Note: Not drawn to scale.

129. In the figure shown above, line segment QR has length 12, and rectangle $MPQT$ is a square. If the area of rectangular region $MPRS$ is 540, what is the area of rectangular region $TQRS$?

(A) 144
(B) 216
(C) 324
(D) 360
(E) 396

Geometry; Algebra Area; Second-degree equations

Since $MPQT$ is a square, let $MP = PQ = x$. Then $PR = PQ + QR = x + 12$. The area of $MPRS$ can be expressed as $x(x + 12)$. Since the area of $MPRS$ is given to be 540,

$$x(x+12)=540$$
$$x^2+12x=540$$
$$x^2+12x-540=0$$
$$(x-18)(x+30)=0$$
$$x=18 \text{ or } x=-30$$

Since x represents a length and must be positive, $x = 18$. The area of $TQRS$ is then $(12)(18) = 216$.

As an alternative to solving the quadratic equation, look for a pair of positive numbers such that their product is 540 and one is 12 greater than the other. The pair is 18 and 30, so $x = 18$ and the area of $TQRS$ is then $(12)(18) = 216$.

The correct answer is B.

130. Machines A and B always operate independently and at their respective constant rates. When working alone, Machine A can fill a production lot in 5 hours, and Machine B can fill the same lot in x hours. When the two machines operate simultaneously to fill the production lot, it takes them 2 hours to complete the job. What is the value of x ?

(A) $3\frac{1}{3}$

(B) 3

(C) $2\frac{1}{2}$

(D) $2\frac{1}{3}$

(E) $1\frac{1}{2}$

Algebra Applied problems

Since Machine A can fill a production lot in 5 hours, it can fill $\frac{1}{5}$ of the lot in 1 hour. Since Machine B can fill the same production lot in x hours, it can fill $\frac{1}{x}$ of the lot in 1 hour. The two machines operating simultaneously can fill $\frac{1}{5}+\frac{1}{x}$ of the lot in 1 hour. Since it takes them 2 hours to complete the lot together, they can fill $\frac{1}{2}$ of the lot in 1 hour and so $\frac{1}{5}+\frac{1}{x}=\frac{1}{2}$, which can be solved for x as follows:

$$\frac{1}{5}+\frac{1}{x}=\frac{1}{2}$$
$$10x\left(\frac{1}{5}+\frac{1}{x}\right)=10x\left(\frac{1}{2}\right)$$
$$2x+10=5x$$
$$10=3x$$
$$\frac{10}{3}=x$$
$$x=3\frac{1}{3}$$

The correct answer is A.

131. A certain manufacturer sells its product to stores in 113 different regions worldwide, with an average (arithmetic mean) of 181 stores per region. If last year these stores sold an average of 51,752 units of the manufacturer's product per store, which of the following is closest to the total number of units of the manufacturer's product sold worldwide last year?

(A) 10^6

(B) 10^7

(C) 10^8

(D) 10^9

(E) 10^{10}

Arithmetic Estimation

$$\begin{aligned}(113)(181)(51{,}752) &\approx (100)(200)(50{,}000)\\ &= 10^2\times(2\times10^2)\times(5\times10^4)\\ &= (2\times5)\times10^{2+2+4}\\ &= 10^1\times10^8 = 10^9\end{aligned}$$

The correct answer is D.

132. Andrew started saving at the beginning of the year and had saved \$240 by the end of the year. He continued to save and by the end of 2 years had saved a total of \$540. Which of the following is closest to the percent increase in the amount Andrew saved during the second year compared to the amount he saved during the first year?

(A) 11%
(B) 25%
(C) 44%
(D) 56%
(E) 125%

Arithmetic Percents

Andrew saved \$240 in the first year and \$540 – \$240 = \$300 in the second year. The percent increase in the amount Andrew saved in the second year compared to the amount he saved in the first year is $\left(\frac{300-240}{240}\times 100\right)\% = \left(\frac{60}{240}\times 100\right)\% = \left(\frac{1}{4}\times 100\right)\% = 25\%$.

The correct answer is B.

133. Two numbers differ by 2 and sum to S. Which of the following is the greater of the numbers in terms of S?

(A) $\frac{S}{2} - 1$
(B) $\frac{S}{2}$
(C) $\frac{S}{2} + \frac{1}{2}$
(D) $\frac{S}{2} + 1$
(E) $\frac{S}{2} + 2$

Algebra First-degree equations

Let x represent the greater of the two numbers that differ by 2. Then, $x - 2$ represents the lesser of the two numbers. The two numbers sum to S, so $x + (x - 2) = S$. It follows that $2x - 2 = S$, or $2x = S + 2$, or $x = \frac{S}{2} + 1$.

The correct answer is D.

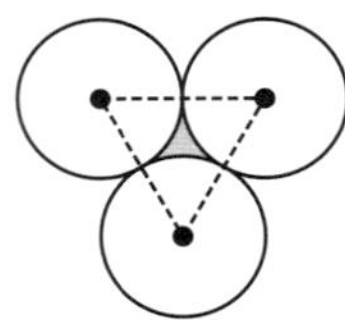

134. The figure shown above consists of three identical circles that are tangent to each other. If the area of the shaded region is $64\sqrt{3} - 32\pi$, what is the radius of each circle?

(A) 4
(B) 8
(C) 16
(D) 24
(E) 32

Geometry Circles; Triangles; Area

Let r represent the radius of each circle. Then the triangle shown dashed in the figure is equilateral with sides $2r$ units long. The interior of the triangle is comprised of the shaded region and three circular sectors. The area of the shaded region can be found as the area of the triangle minus the sum of the areas of the three sectors. Since the triangle is equilateral, its side lengths are in the proportions as shown in the diagram below. The area of the interior of the triangle is $\frac{1}{2}(2r)\left(r\sqrt{3}\right) = r^2\sqrt{3}$.

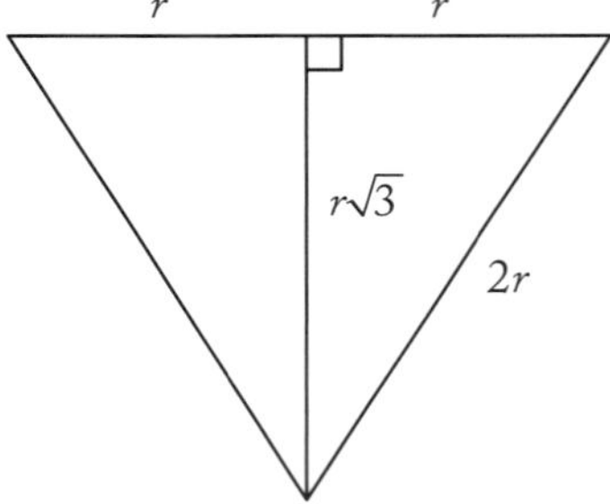

Each of the three sectors has a central angle of 60° because the central angle is an angle of the equilateral triangle. Therefore, the area of each sector is $\frac{60}{360} = \frac{1}{6}$ of the area of the circle. The sum of the areas of the three sectors is then $3\left(\frac{1}{6}\pi r^2\right) = \frac{1}{2}\pi r^2$. Thus, the area of the shaded region is $r^2\sqrt{3}-\frac{1}{2}\pi r^2=r^2\left(\sqrt{3}-\frac{1}{2}\pi\right)$. But, this area is given as $64\sqrt{3}-32\pi=64\left(\sqrt{3}-\frac{1}{2}\pi\right)$. Thus $r^2=64$, and $r=8$.

The correct answer is B.

135. In a numerical table with 10 rows and 10 columns, each entry is either a 9 or a 10. If the number of 9s in the *n*th row is $n-1$ for each *n* from 1 to 10, what is the average (arithmetic mean) of all the numbers in the table?

(A) 9.45
(B) 9.50
(C) 9.55
(D) 9.65
(E) 9.70

Arithmetic Operations with integers

There are $(10)(10)=100$ entries in the table. In rows $1, 2, 3, \ldots, 10$, the number of 9s is $0, 1, 2, \ldots, 9$, respectively, giving a total of $0+1+2+\ldots+9=45$ entries with a 9. This leaves a total of $100-45=55$ entries with a 10. Therefore, the sum of the 100 entries is $45(9)+55(10)=405+550=955$, and the average of the 100 entries is $\frac{955}{100}=9.55$

The correct answer is C.

136. A positive integer *n* is a perfect number provided that the sum of all the positive factors of *n*, including 1 and *n*, is equal to 2*n*. What is the sum of the reciprocals of all the positive factors of the perfect number 28 ?

(A) $\frac{1}{4}$
(B) $\frac{56}{27}$
(C) 2
(D) 3
(E) 4

Arithmetic Properties of numbers

The factors of 28 are 1, 2, 4, 7, 14, and 28. Therefore, the sum of the reciprocals of the factors of 28 is $\frac{1}{1}+\frac{1}{2}+\frac{1}{4}+\frac{1}{7}+\frac{1}{14}+\frac{1}{28}=$

$\frac{28}{28}+\frac{14}{28}+\frac{7}{28}+\frac{4}{28}+\frac{2}{28}+\frac{1}{28}=$

$\frac{28+14+7+4+2+1}{28}=\frac{56}{28}=2.$

The correct answer is C.

137. The infinite sequence $a_1, a_2, \ldots, a_n, \ldots$ is such that $a_1=2$, $a_2=-3$, $a_3=5$, $a_4=-1$, and $a_n=a_{n-4}$ for $n>4$. What is the sum of the first 97 terms of the sequence?

(A) 72
(B) 74
(C) 75
(D) 78
(E) 80

Arithmetic Sequences and series

Because $a_n=a_{n-4}$ for $n>4$, it follows that the terms of the sequence repeat in groups of 4 terms:

Values for n	Values for a_n
1, 2, 3, 4	2, −3, 5, −1
5, 6, 7, 8	2, −3, 5, −1
9, 10, 11, 12	2, −3, 5, −1
13, 14, 15, 16	2, −3, 5, −1

Thus, since $97=24(4)+1$, the sum of the first 97 terms can be grouped into 24 groups of 4 terms each, with one remaining term, which allows the sum to be easily found:

$$(a_1+a_2+a_3+a_4)+(a_5+a_6+a_7+a_8)+\ldots+(a_{93}+a_{94}+a_{95}+a_{96})+a_{97}$$

$$=(2-3+5-1)+(2-3+5-1)+\ldots+(2-3+5-1)+2$$

$$=24(2-3+5-1)+2=24(3)+2=74$$

The correct answer is B.

138. The sequence $a_1, a_2, \ldots, a_n, \ldots$ is such that $a_n = 2a_{n-1} - x$ for all positive integers $n \geq 2$ and for a certain number x. If $a_5 = 99$ and $a_3 = 27$, what is the value of x?

(A) 3
(B) 9
(C) 18
(D) 36
(E) 45

Algebra Sequences and series

An expression for a_5 that involves x can be obtained using $a_3 = 27$ and applying the equation $a_n = 2a_{n-1} - x$ twice, once for $n = 4$ and once for $n = 5$.

$a_4 = 2a_3 - x$	using $a_n = 2a_{n-1} - x$ for $n = 4$
$= 2(27) - x$	using $a_3 = 27$
$a_5 = 2a_4 - x$	using $a_n = 2a_{n-1} - x$ for $n = 5$
$= 2[2(27) - x] - x$	using $a_4 = 2(27) - x$
$= 4(27) - 3x$	combine like terms

Therefore, using $a_5 = 99$, we have

$99 = 4(27) - 3x$	given
$3x = 4(27) - 99$	adding $(3x - 99)$ to both sides
$x = 4(9) - 33$	dividing both sides by 3
$x = 3$	arithmetic

The correct answer is A.

139. A window is in the shape of a regular hexagon with each side of length 80 centimeters. If a diagonal through the center of the hexagon is w centimeters long, then $w =$

(A) 80
(B) 120
(C) 150
(D) 160
(E) 240

Geometry Polygons

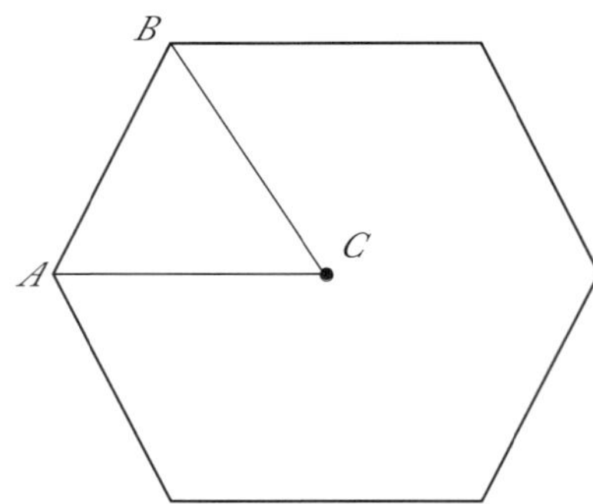

Let A and B be the endpoints of one of the sides of the hexagon and let C be the center of the hexagon. Then the degree measure of $\angle ACB$ is $\frac{360}{6} = 60$ and the sum of the degree measures of $\angle ABC$ and $\angle BAC$ is $180 - 60 = 120$. Also, since $AC = BC$, the degree measures of $\angle ABC$ and $\angle BAC$ are equal. Therefore, the degree measure of each of $\angle ABC$ and $\angle BAC$ is 60. Thus, ΔABC is an equilateral triangle with side length $AB = 80$. It follows that the length of a diagonal through the center of the hexagon is $2(AC) = 2(80) = 160$.

The correct answer is D.

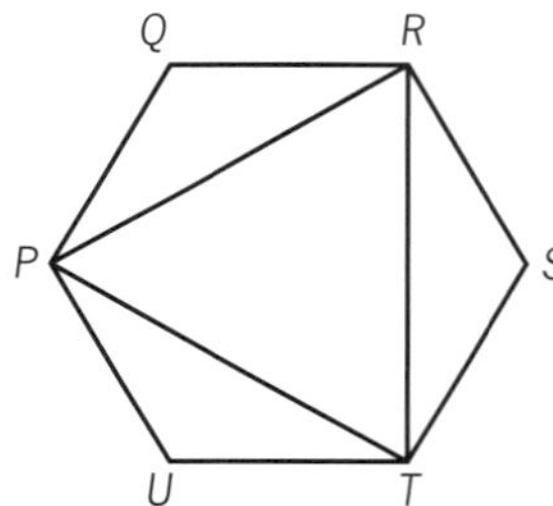

140. In the figure shown, $PQRSTU$ is a regular polygon with sides of length x. What is the perimeter of triangle PRT in terms of x?

(A) $\frac{x\sqrt{3}}{2}$
(B) $x\sqrt{3}$
(C) $\frac{3x\sqrt{3}}{2}$
(D) $3x\sqrt{3}$
(E) $4x\sqrt{3}$

Geometry Polygons

Since $PQRSTU$ is a regular hexagon, ΔPQR, ΔRST, and ΔTUP are the same size and shape, so $PR = RT = TP$ and the perimeter of ΔPRT is $3(PR)$. Note that in the figure above, $PQRSTU$ is partitioned into four triangles. The sum of the degree measures of the interior angles of each triangle is 180°. The total of the degree measures of the interior angles of these four triangles is equal to the sum of the degree measures of the six interior angles of $PQRSTU$. Since $PQRSTU$ is a regular hexagon, each of $\angle UPQ$, $\angle PQR$, $\angle QRS$, $\angle RST$, $\angle STU$, and $\angle TUP$ has the same measure, which is $\frac{(4)(180°)}{6} = 120°$.

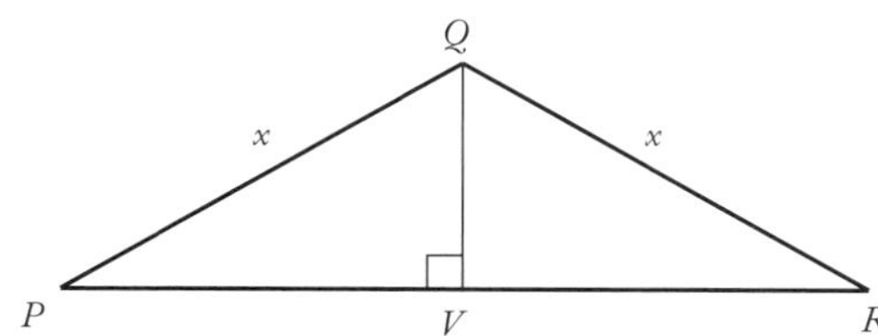

In the figure above, ΔPQR is isosceles with $PQ = QR = x$. The measure of $\angle PQR$ is 120°, and the measure of $\angle P$ = the measure of $\angle R = \frac{180° - 120°}{2} = 30°$. $\overline{QV}$ is perpendicular to $\overline{PR}$ and $PV = VR$. Since ΔPVQ is a 30°–60°–90° triangle, its side lengths are in the ratio $1:\sqrt{3}:2$, and so $PV = \frac{x\sqrt{3}}{2}$ and $PR = x\sqrt{3}$. Therefore, the perimeter of ΔPRT is $3(x\sqrt{3}) = 3x\sqrt{3}$.

The correct answer is D.

141. In a certain medical survey, 45 percent of the people surveyed had the type A antigen in their blood and 3 percent had both the type A antigen and the type B antigen. Which of the following is closest to the percent of those with the type A antigen who also had the type B antigen?

(A) 1.35%

(B) 6.67%

(C) 13.50%

(D) 15.00%

(E) 42.00%

Arithmetic Applied problems; Percents

Let n be the total number of people surveyed. Then, the proportion of the people who had type A who also had type B is $\frac{(3\%)\cancel{n}}{(45\%)\cancel{n}} = \frac{3}{45} = \frac{1}{15}$, which as a percent is approximately 6.67%. Note that by using $\frac{1}{15} = \frac{1}{3} \times \frac{1}{5}$, which equals $\frac{1}{3}$ of 20%, we can avoid dividing by a 2-digit integer.

The correct answer is B.

142. On a certain transatlantic crossing, 20 percent of a ship's passengers held round-trip tickets and also took their cars aboard the ship. If 60 percent of the passengers with round-trip tickets did not take their cars aboard the ship, what percent of the ship's passengers held round-trip tickets?

(A) $33\frac{1}{3}\%$

(B) 40%

(C) 50%

(D) 60%

(E) $66\frac{2}{3}\%$

Arithmetic Percents

Since the number of passengers on the ship is immaterial, let the number of passengers on the ship be 100 for convenience. Let x be the number of passengers that held round-trip tickets. Then, since 20 percent of the passengers held a round-trip ticket and took their cars aboard the ship, $0.20(100) = 20$ passengers held round-trip tickets and took their cars aboard the ship. The remaining passengers with round-trip tickets did not take their cars aboard, and they represent $0.6x$ (that is, 60 percent of the passengers with round-trip tickets). Thus $0.6x + 20 = x$, from which it follows that $20 = 0.4x$, and so $x = 50$. The percent of passengers with round-trip tickets is, then, $\frac{50}{100} = 50\%$.

The correct answer is C.

143. If x and k are integers and $(12^x)(4^{2x+1}) = (2^k)(3^2)$, what is the value of k?

(A) 5
(B) 7
(C) 10
(D) 12
(E) 14

Arithmetic Exponents

Rewrite the expression on the left so that it is a product of powers of 2 and 3.

$$\begin{aligned}(12^x)(4^{2x+1}) &= [(3 \cdot 2^2)^x][(2^2)^{2x+1}] \\ &= (3^x)[(2^2)^x][2^{2(2x+1)}] \\ &= (3^x)(2^{2x})(2^{4x+2}) \\ &= (3^x)(2^{6x+2})\end{aligned}$$

Then, since $(12^x)(4^{2x+1}) = (2^k)(3^2)$, it follows that $(3^x)(2^{6x+2}) = (2^k)(3^2) = (3^2)(2^k)$, so $x = 2$ and $k = 6x + 2$. Substituting 2 for x gives $k = 6(2) + 2 = 14$.

The correct answer is E.

144. If S is the sum of the reciprocals of the 10 consecutive integers from 21 to 30, then S is between which of the following two fractions?

(A) $\frac{1}{3}$ and $\frac{1}{2}$
(B) $\frac{1}{4}$ and $\frac{1}{3}$
(C) $\frac{1}{5}$ and $\frac{1}{4}$
(D) $\frac{1}{6}$ and $\frac{1}{5}$
(E) $\frac{1}{7}$ and $\frac{1}{6}$

Arithmetic Estimation

The value of $\frac{1}{21}+\frac{1}{22}+\frac{1}{23}+\ldots+\frac{1}{30}$ is LESS than $\frac{1}{20}+\frac{1}{20}+\frac{1}{20}+\ldots+\frac{1}{20}$ (10 numbers added), which equals $10\left(\frac{1}{20}\right)=\frac{1}{2}$, and GREATER than $\frac{1}{30}+\frac{1}{30}+\frac{1}{30}+\ldots+\frac{1}{30}$ (10 numbers added), which equals $10\left(\frac{1}{30}\right)=\frac{1}{3}$. Therefore, the value of $\frac{1}{21}+\frac{1}{22}+\frac{1}{23}+\ldots+\frac{1}{30}$ is between $\frac{1}{3}$ and $\frac{1}{2}$.

The correct answer is A.

145. For every even positive integer m, $f(m)$ represents the product of all even integers from 2 to m, inclusive. For example, $f(12) = 2 \times 4 \times 6 \times 8 \times 10 \times 12$. What is the greatest prime factor of $f(24)$?

(A) 23
(B) 19
(C) 17
(D) 13
(E) 11

Arithmetic Properties of numbers

Rewriting $f(24) = 2 \times 4 \times 6 \times 8 \times 10 \times 12 \times 14 \times \ldots \times 20 \times 22 \times 24$ as $2 \times 4 \times 2(3) \times 8 \times 2(5) \times 12 \times 2(7) \times \ldots \times 20 \times 2(11) \times 24$ shows that all of the prime numbers from 2 through 11 are factors of $f(24)$. The next prime number is 13, but 13 is not a factor of $f(24)$ because none of the even integers from 2 through 24 has 13 as a factor. Therefore, the largest prime factor of $f(24)$ is 11.

The correct answer is E.

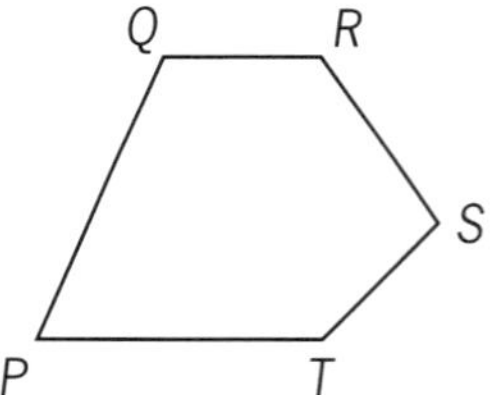

Note: Not drawn to scale.

146. In pentagon $PQRST$, $PQ = 3$, $QR = 2$, $RS = 4$, and $ST = 5$. Which of the lengths 5, 10, and 15 could be the value of PT?

(A) 5 only
(B) 15 only
(C) 5 and 10 only
(D) 10 and 15 only
(E) 5, 10, and 15

Geometry Polygons; Triangles

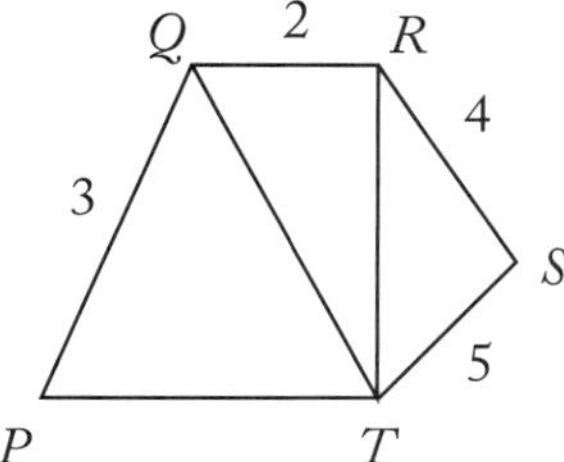

Note: Not drawn to scale.

In the figure above, diagonals $\overline{TQ}$ and $\overline{TR}$ have been drawn in to show ΔTRS and ΔTRQ. Because the length of any side of a triangle must be less than the sum of the lengths of the other two sides, $RT < 5 + 4 = 9$ in ΔTRS, and $QT < RT + 2$ in ΔTRQ. Since $RT < 9$, then $RT + 2 < 9 + 2 = 11$, which then implies $QT < 11$. Now, $PT < QT + 3$ in ΔTQP, and since $QT < 11$, $QT + 3 < 11 + 3 = 14$. It follows that $PT < 14$. Therefore, 15 cannot be the length of $\overline{PT}$ since $15 \nless 14$.

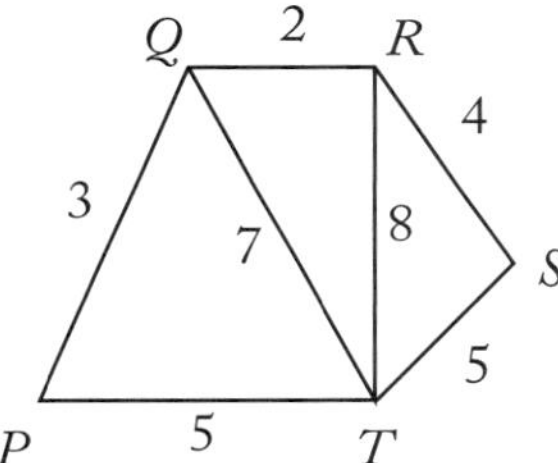

Note: Not drawn to scale.

To show that 5 can be the length of $\overline{PT}$, consider the figure above. For ΔTQP, the length of any side is less than the sum of the lengths of the other two sides as shown below.

$$QT = 7 < 8 = 5 + 3 = PT + PQ$$
$$PQ = 3 < 12 = 5 + 7 = PT + TQ$$
$$PT = 5 < 10 = 3 + 7 = PQ + TQ$$

For ΔRQT, the length of any side is less than the sum of the lengths of the other two sides as shown below.

$$RT = 8 < 9 = 7 + 2 = QT + QR$$
$$RQ = 2 < 15 = 7 + 8 = QT + RT$$
$$QT = 7 < 10 = 2 + 8 = QR + RT$$

For ΔRST, the length of any side is less than the sum of the lengths of the other two sides as shown below.

$$RS = 4 < 13 = 8 + 5 = TR + TS$$
$$RT = 8 < 9 = 5 + 4 = ST + SR$$
$$ST = 5 < 12 = 8 + 4 = TR + RS$$

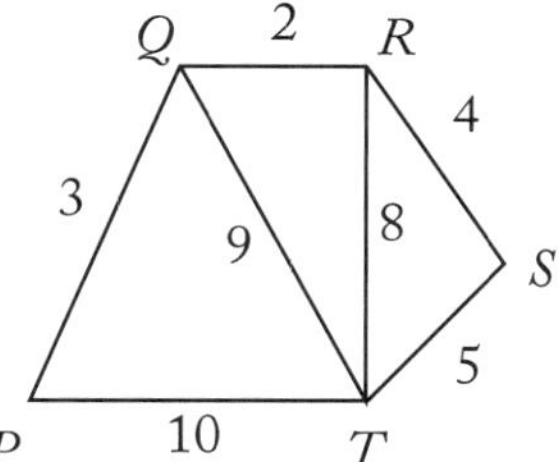

Note: Not drawn to scale.

To show that 10 can be the length of $\overline{PT}$, consider the figure above. For ΔTQP, the length of any side is less than the sum of the lengths of the other two sides as shown below.

$$QT = 9 < 13 = 10 + 3 = PT + PQ$$
$$PQ = 3 < 19 = 10 + 9 = PT + TQ$$
$$PT = 10 < 12 = 3 + 9 = PQ + TQ$$

For ΔRQT, the length of any side is less than the sum of the lengths of the other two sides as shown below.

$$RT = 8 < 11 = 9 + 2 = QT + QR$$
$$RQ = 2 < 17 = 9 + 8 = QT + RT$$
$$QT = 9 < 10 = 2 + 8 = QT + RT$$

For ΔRST, the length of any side is less than the sum of the lengths of the other two sides as shown below.

$$RS = 4 < 13 = 8 + 5 = TR + TS$$
$$RT = 8 < 9 = 5 + 4 = ST + SR$$
$$ST = 5 < 12 = 8 + 4 = TR + RS$$

Therefore, 5 and 10 can be the length of $\overline{PT}$, and 15 cannot be the length of $\overline{PT}$.

The correct answer is C.

3, k, 2, 8, m, 3

147. The arithmetic mean of the list of numbers above is 4. If k and m are integers and $k \neq m$ what is the median of the list?

(A) 2
(B) 2.5
(C) 3
(D) 3.5
(E) 4

Arithmetic Statistics

Since the arithmetic mean $= \dfrac{\text{sum of values}}{\text{number of values}}$, then $\dfrac{3+k+2+8+m+3}{6} = 4$, and so $\dfrac{16+k+m}{6} = 4$, $16 + k + m = 24$, $k + m = 8$. Since $k \neq m$, then either $k < 4$ and $m > 4$ or $k > 4$ and $m < 4$. Because k and m are integers, either $k \leq 3$ and $m \geq 5$ or $k \geq 5$ and $m \leq 3$.

Case (i): If $k \leq 2$, then $m \geq 6$ and the six integers in ascending order are k, 2, 3, 3, m, 8 or k, 2, 3, 3, 8, m. The two middle integers are both 3 so the median is $\dfrac{3+3}{2} = 3$.

Case (ii): If $k = 3$, then $m = 5$ and the six integers in ascending order are 2, k, 3, 3, m, 8. The two middle integers are both 3 so the median is $\dfrac{3+3}{2} = 3$.

Case (iii): If $k = 5$, then $m = 3$ and the six integers in ascending order are 2, m, 3, 3, k, 8. The two middle integers are both 3 so the median is $\dfrac{3+3}{2} = 3$.

Case (iv): If $k \geq 6$, then $m \leq 2$ and the six integers in ascending order are m, 2, 3, 3, k, 8 or m, 2, 3, 3, 8, k. The two middle integers are both 3 so the median is $\dfrac{3+3}{2} = 3$.

The correct answer is C.

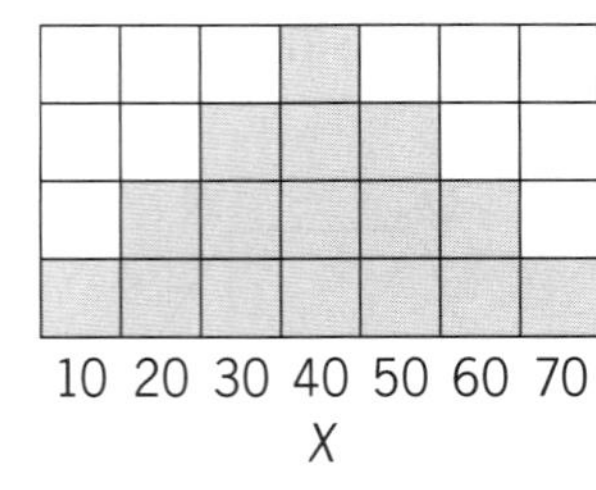

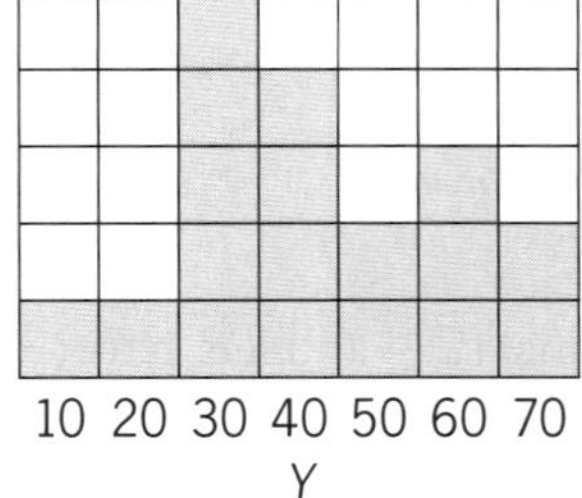

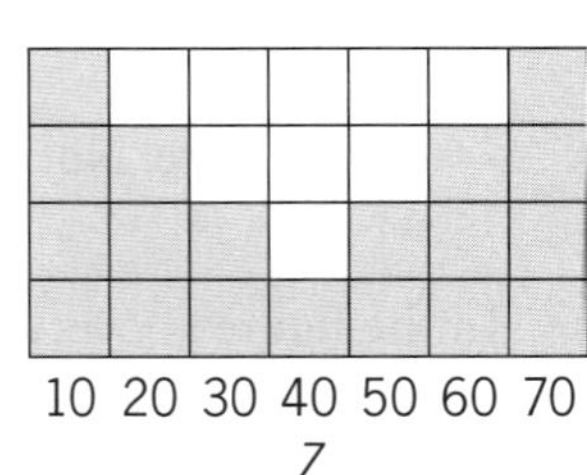

148. If the variables X, Y, and Z take on only the values 10, 20, 30, 40, 50, 60, or 70 with frequencies indicated by the shaded regions above, for which of the frequency distributions is the mean equal to the median?

(A) X only
(B) Y only
(C) Z only
(D) X and Y
(E) X and Z

Arithmetic Statistics

The frequency distributions for both X and Z are symmetric about 40, and thus both X and Z have mean = median = 40. Therefore, any answer choice that does not include both X and Z can be eliminated. This leaves only answer choice E.

The correct answer is E.

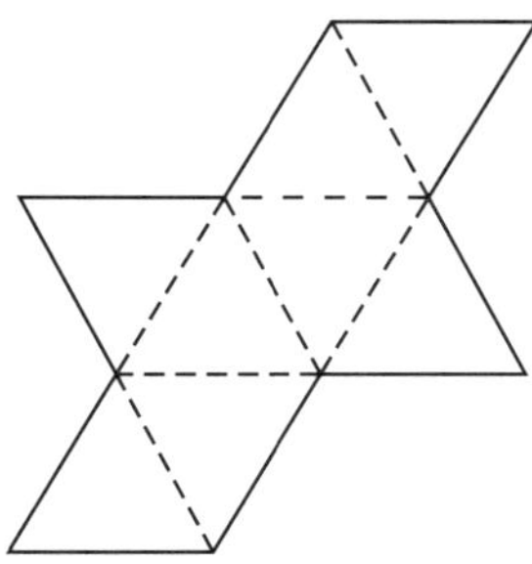

149. When the figure above is cut along the solid lines, folded along the dashed lines, and taped along the solid lines, the result is a model of a geometric solid. This geometric solid consists of 2 pyramids, each with a square base that they share. What is the sum of the number of edges and the number of faces of this geometric solid?

(A) 10
(B) 18
(C) 20
(D) 24
(E) 25

Geometry Solids

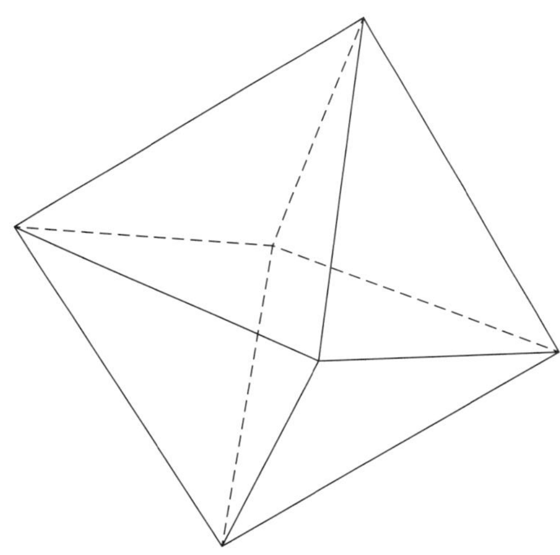

A geometric solid consisting of 2 pyramids, each with a square base that they share, is shown in the figure above. From the figure it can be seen that the solid has 12 edges and 8 faces. Therefore, the sum of the number of edges and the number of faces of the solid is 12 + 8 = 20.

Alternatively, the solid has 7 + 5 = 12 edges because each edge in the solid is generated from either a dashed segment (there are 7 dashed segments) or from a pair of solid segments taped together (there are $\frac{10}{2} = 5$ such pairs of solid segments), and the solid has 8 faces because there are 8 small triangles in the given figure. Therefore, the sum of the number of edges and the number of faces of the solid is 12 + 8 = 20.

The correct answer is C.

$$2x + y = 12$$
$$|y| \le 12$$

150. For how many ordered pairs (x,y) that are solutions of the system above are x and y both integers?

(A) 7
(B) 10
(C) 12
(D) 13
(E) 14

Algebra Absolute value

From $|\,y\,| \le 12$, if y must be an integer, then y must be in the set $S = \{\pm12, \pm11, \pm10, \ldots, \pm3, \pm2, \pm1, 0\}$.
Since $2x + y = 12$, then $x = \frac{12 - y}{2}$. If x must be an integer, then $12 - y$ must be divisible by 2; that is, $12 - y$ must be even. Since 12 is even, $12 - y$ is even if and only if y is even. This eliminates all odd integers from S, leaving only the even integers ±12, ±10, ±8, ±6, ±4, ±2, and 0. Thus, there are 13 possible integer y-values, each with a corresponding integer x-value and, therefore, there are 13 ordered pairs (x,y), where x and y are both integers, that solve the system.

The correct answer is D.

151. The points R, T, and U lie on a circle that has radius 4. If the length of arc RTU is $\frac{4\pi}{3}$ what is the length of line segment RU?

(A) $\frac{4}{3}$

(B) $\frac{8}{3}$

(C) 3

(D) 4

(E) 6

Geometry Circles; Triangles; Circumference

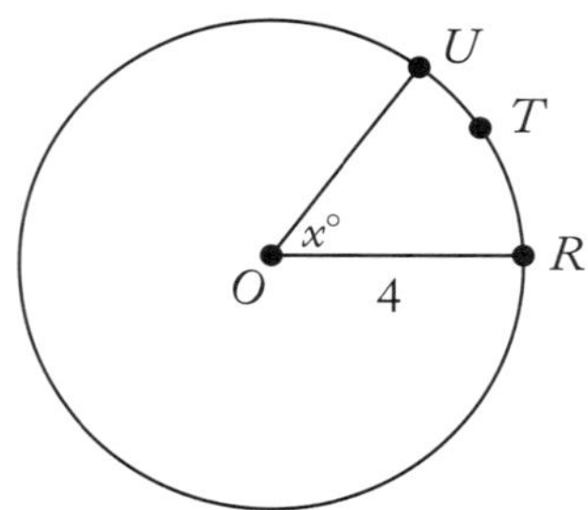

In the figure above, O is the center of the circle that contains R, T, and U and x is the degree measure of $\angle ROU$. Since the circumference of the circle is $2\pi(4) = 8\pi$ and there are 360° in the circle, the ratio of the length of arc RTU to the circumference of the circle is the same as the ratio of x to 360. Therefore, $\frac{\frac{4\pi}{3}}{8\pi} = \frac{x}{360}$. Then $x = \frac{\frac{4\pi}{3}(360)}{8\pi} = \frac{480\pi}{8\pi} = 60$. This means that ΔROU is an isosceles triangle with side lengths $OR = OU = 4$ and vertex angle measuring 60°. The base angles of ΔROU must have equal measures and the sum of their measures must be $180° - 60° = 120°$. Therefore, each base angle measures 60°, ΔROU is equilateral, and $RU = 4$.

The correct answer is D.

152. A certain university will select 1 of 7 candidates eligible to fill a position in the mathematics department and 2 of 10 candidates eligible to fill 2 identical positions in the computer science department. If none of the candidates is eligible for a position in both departments, how many different sets of 3 candidates are there to fill the 3 positions?

(A) 42

(B) 70

(C) 140

(D) 165

(E) 315

Arithmetic Elementary combinatorics

To fill the position in the math department, 1 candidate will be selected from a group of 7 eligible candidates, and so there are 7 sets of 1 candidate each to fill the position in the math department. To fill the positions in the computer science department, any one of the 10 eligible candidates can be chosen for the first position and any of the remaining 9 eligible candidates can be chosen for the second position, making a total of $10 \times 9 = 90$ sets of 2 candidates to fill the computer science positions. But, this number includes the set in which Candidate A was chosen to fill the first position and Candidate B was chosen to fill the second position as well as the set in which Candidate B was chosen for the first position and Candidate A was chosen for the second position. These sets are not different essentially since the positions are identical and in both sets Candidates A and B are chosen to fill the 2 positions. Therefore, there are $\frac{90}{2} = 45$ sets of 2 candidates to fill the computer science positions. Then, using the multiplication principle, there are $7 \times 45 = 315$ different sets of 3 candidates to fill the 3 positions.

The correct answer is E.

153. A survey of employers found that during 1993 employment costs rose 3.5 percent, where employment costs consist of salary costs and fringe-benefit costs. If salary costs rose 3 percent and fringe-benefit costs rose 5.5 percent during 1993, then fringe-benefit costs represented what percent of employment costs at the beginning of 1993 ?

(A) 16.5%
(B) 20%
(C) 35%
(D) 55%
(E) 65%

Algebra; Arithmetic First-degree equations; Percents

Let E represent employment costs, S represent salary costs, and F represent fringe-benefit costs. Then $E = S + F$. An increase of 3 percent in salary costs and a 5.5 percent increase in fringe-benefit costs resulted in a 3.5 percent increase in employment costs. Therefore $1.03S + 1.055F = 1.035E$. But, $E = S + F$, so $1.03S + 1.055F = 1.035(S + F) = 1.035S + 1.035F$.

Combining like terms gives $(1.055 - 1.035)F = (1.035 - 1.03)S$ or $0.02F = 0.005S$. Then, $S = \frac{0.02}{0.005}F = 4F$. Thus, since $E = S + F$, it follows that $E = 4F + F = 5F$. Then, F as a percent of E is $\frac{F}{E} = \frac{F}{5F} = \frac{1}{5} = 20\%$.

The correct answer is B.

154. The subsets of the set {*w*, *x*, *y*} are {*w*}, {*x*}, {*y*}, {*w*, *x*}, {*w*, *y*}, {*x*, *y*}, {*w*, *x*, *y*}, and { } (the empty subset). How many subsets of the set {*w*, *x*, *y*, *z*} contain *w* ?

(A) Four
(B) Five
(C) Seven
(D) Eight
(E) Sixteen

Arithmetic Sets

As shown in the table, the subsets of $\{w, x, y, z\}$ can be organized into two columns, those subsets of $\{w, x, y, z\}$ that do not contain w (left column) and the corresponding subsets of $\{w, x, y, z\}$ that contain w (right column), and each of these collections has the same number of sets. Therefore, there are 8 subsets of $\{w, x, y, z\}$ that contain w.

subsets not containing w	subsets containing w
$\{\ \}$	$\{w\}$
$\{x\}$	$\{w, x\}$
$\{y\}$	$\{w, y\}$
$\{z\}$	$\{w, z\}$
$\{x, y\}$	$\{w, x, y\}$
$\{x, z\}$	$\{w, x, z\}$
$\{y, z\}$	$\{w, y, z\}$
$\{x, y, z\}$	$\{w, x, y, z\}$

The correct answer is D.

155. There are 5 cars to be displayed in 5 parking spaces, with all the cars facing the same direction. Of the 5 cars, 3 are red, 1 is blue, and 1 is yellow. If the cars are identical except for color, how many different display arrangements of the 5 cars are possible?

(A) 20
(B) 25
(C) 40
(D) 60
(E) 125

Arithmetic Elementary combinatorics

There are 5 parking spaces from which 3 must be chosen to display the 3 identical red cars. Thus, there are $\binom{5}{3} = \frac{5!}{3!2!} = 10$ different arrangements of the 3 identical red cars in the parking spaces. There are 2 spaces remaining for displaying the single blue car and 1 space left for displaying the single yellow car. Therefore, there are $(10)(2)(1) = 20$ arrangements possible for displaying the 5 cars in the 5 parking spaces.

The correct answer is A.

156. The number $\sqrt{63-36\sqrt{3}}$ can be expressed as $x+y\sqrt{3}$ for some integers x and y. What is the value of xy?

(A) −18
(B) −6
(C) 6
(D) 18
(E) 27

Algebra Operations on radical expressions

Squaring both sides of $\sqrt{63-36\sqrt{3}} = x + y\sqrt{3}$ gives $63 - 36\sqrt{3} = x^2 + 2xy\sqrt{3} + 3y^2 = (x^2 + 3y^2) + (2xy)\sqrt{3}$, which implies that $-36 = 2xy$, or $xy = -18$. Indeed, if $-36 \neq 2xy$, or equivalently, if $36 + 2xy \neq 0$, then we could write $\sqrt{3}$ as a quotient of the two integers $63 - x^2 - 3y^2$ and $36 + 2xy$, which is not possible because $\sqrt{3}$ is an irrational number. To be more explicit, $63 - 36\sqrt{3} = x^2 + 2xy\sqrt{3} + 3y^2$ implies $63 - x^2 - 3y^2 = (36 + 2xy)\sqrt{3}$, and if $36 + 2xy \neq 0$, then we could divide both sides of the equation $63 - x^2 - 3y^2 = (36 + 2xy)\sqrt{3}$ by $36 + 2xy$ to get $\frac{63 - x^2 - 3y^2}{36 + 2xy} = \sqrt{3}$.

The correct answer is A.

157. There are 10 books on a shelf, of which 4 are paperbacks and 6 are hardbacks. How many possible selections of 5 books from the shelf contain at least one paperback and at least one hardback?

(A) 75
(B) 120
(C) 210
(D) 246
(E) 252

Arithmetic Elementary combinatorics

The number of selections of 5 books containing at least one paperback and at least one hardback is equal to $T - N$, where T is the total number of selections of 5 books and N is the number of selections that do not contain both a paperback and a hardback. The value of T is

$$\binom{10}{5} = \frac{10!}{5!(10-5)!} = \frac{(6)(7)(8)(9)(10)}{(1)(2)(3)(4)(5)}$$

$$= (7)(2)(9)(2) = 252.$$

To find the value of N, first note that no selection of 5 books can contain all paperbacks, since there are only 4 paperback books. Thus, the value of N is equal to the number of selections of 5 books that contain all hardbacks, which is equal to 6 since there are 6 ways that a single hardback can be left out when choosing the 5 hardback books. It follows that the number of selections of 5 books containing at least one paperback and at least one hardback is $T - N = 252 - 6 = 246$.

The correct answer is D.

158. If x is to be chosen at random from the set {1, 2, 3, 4} and y is to be chosen at random from the set {5, 6, 7}, what is the probability that xy will be even?

(A) $\frac{1}{6}$
(B) $\frac{1}{3}$
(C) $\frac{1}{2}$
(D) $\frac{2}{3}$
(E) $\frac{5}{6}$

Arithmetic; Algebra Probability; Concepts of sets

By the principle of multiplication, since there are 4 elements in the first set and 3 elements in the second set, there are (4)(3) = 12 possible products of xy, where x is chosen from the first set and y is chosen from the second set. These products will be even EXCEPT when both x and y are odd. Since there are 2 odd numbers in the first set and 2 odd numbers in the second set, there are (2)(2) = 4 products of x and y that are odd. This means that the remaining 12 − 4 = 8 products are even. Thus, the probability that xy is even is $\frac{8}{12} = \frac{2}{3}$.

The correct answer is D.

159. The function f is defined for each positive three-digit integer n by $f(n) = 2^x 3^y 5^z$, where x, y, and z are the hundreds, tens, and units digits of n, respectively. If m and v are three-digit positive integers such that $f(m) = 9f(v)$, then $m - v =$

(A) 8
(B) 9
(C) 18
(D) 20
(E) 80

Algebra Place value

Let the hundreds, tens, and units digits of m be A, B, and C, respectively; and let the hundreds, tens, and units digits of v be a, b, and c, respectively. From $f(m) = 9f(v)$ it follows that $2^A3^B5^C = 9(2^a3^b5^c) = 3^2(2^a3^b5^c) = 2^a3^{b+2}5^c$. Therefore, $A = a$, $B = b + 2$, and $C = c$. Now calculate $m - v$.

$m - v =$	$(100A + 10B + C) - (100a + 10b + c)$	place value property
$=$	$(100a + 10(b + 2) + c) - (100a + 10b + c)$	obtained above
$=$	$10(b + 2) - 10b$	combine like terms
$=$	$10b + 20 - 10b$	distributive property
$=$	20	combine like terms

The correct answer is D.

160. If $10^{50} - 74$ is written as an integer in base 10 notation, what is the sum of the digits in that integer?

(A) 424
(B) 433
(C) 440
(D) 449
(E) 467

Arithmetic Properties of numbers

$10^2 - 74$	=	100 – 74	=	26
$10^3 - 74$	=	1,000 – 74	=	926
$10^4 - 74$	=	10,000 – 74	=	9,926
$10^5 - 74$	=	100,000 – 74	=	99,926
$10^6 - 74$	=	1,000,000 – 74	=	999,926

From the table above it is clear that $10^{50} - 74$ in base 10 notation will be 48 digits of 9 followed by the digits 2 and 6. Therefore, the sum of the digits of $10^{50} - 74$ is equal to $48(9) + 2 + 6 = 440$.

The correct answer is C.

161. A certain company that sells only cars and trucks reported that revenues from car sales in 1997 were down 11 percent from 1996 and revenues from truck sales in 1997 were up 7 percent from 1996. If total revenues from car sales and truck sales in 1997 were up 1 percent from 1996, what is the ratio of revenue from car sales in 1996 to revenue from truck sales in 1996 ?

(A) 1:2
(B) 4:5
(C) 1:1
(D) 3:2
(E) 5:3

Algebra; Arithmetic First-degree equations; Percents

Let C_{96} and C_{97} represent revenues from car sales in 1996 and 1997, respectively, and let T_{96} and T_{97} represent revenues from truck sales in 1996 and 1997, respectively. A decrease of 11 percent in revenue from car sales from 1996 to 1997 can be represented as $(1 - 0.11)C_{96} = C_{97}$, and a 7 percent increase in revenue from truck sales from 1996 to 1997 can be represented as $(1 + 0.07)T_{96} = T_{97}$. An overall increase of 1 percent in revenue from car and truck sales from 1996 to 1997 can be represented as $C_{97} + T_{97} = (1 + 0.01)(C_{96} + T_{96})$. Then, by substitution of expressions for C_{97} and T_{97} that were derived above, $(1 - 0.11)C_{96} + (1 + 0.07)T_{96} = (1 + 0.01)(C_{96} + T_{96})$ and so $0.89C_{96} + 1.07T_{96} = 1.01(C_{96} + T_{96})$ or $0.89C_{96} + 1.07T_{96} = 1.01C_{96} + 1.01T_{96}$. Then, combining like terms gives $(1.07 - 1.01)T_{96} = (1.01 - 0.89)C_{96}$ or

$0.06T_{96} = 0.12C_{96}$. Thus $\frac{C_{96}}{T_{96}} = \frac{0.06}{0.12} = \frac{1}{2}$. The ratio of revenue from car sales in 1996 to revenue from truck sales in 1996 is 1:2.

The correct answer is A.

162. Becky rented a power tool from a rental shop. The rent for the tool was $12 for the first hour and $3 for each additional hour. If Becky paid a total of $27, excluding sales tax, to rent the tool, for how many hours did she rent it?

(A) 5
(B) 6
(C) 9
(D) 10
(E) 12

Arithmetic Applied problems

Becky paid a total of $27 to rent the power tool. She paid $12 to rent the tool for the first hour and $27 – $12 = $15 to rent the tool for the additional hours at the rate of $3 per additional hour. It follows that she rented the tool for $\frac{15}{3} = 5$ additional hours and a total of $1 + 5 = 6$ hours.

The correct answer is B.

163. If $4 < \frac{7-x}{3}$, which of the following must be true?

I. $5 < x$
II. $|x + 3| > 2$
III. $-(x + 5)$ is positive.

(A) II only
(B) III only
(C) I and II only
(D) II and III only
(E) I, II, and III

Algebra Inequalities

Given that $4 < \frac{7-x}{3}$, it follows that $12 < 7 - x$. Then, $5 < -x$ or, equivalently, $x < -5$.

I. If $4 < \frac{7-x}{3}$, then $x < -5$. If $5 < x$ were true then, by combining $5 < x$ and $x < -5$, it would follow that $5 < -5$, which cannot be true. Therefore, it is not the case that, if $4 < \frac{7-x}{3}$, then Statement I must be true. In fact, Statement I is never true.

II. If $4 < \frac{7-x}{3}$, then $x < -5$, and it follows that $x + 3 < -2$. Since $-2 < 0$, then $x + 3 < 0$ and $|x+3| = -(x+3)$. If $x + 3 < -2$, then $-(x+3) > 2$ and by substitution, $|x + 3| > 2$. Therefore, Statement II must be true for every value of x such that $x < -5$. Therefore, Statement II must be true if $4 < \frac{7-x}{3}$.

III. If $4 < \frac{7-x}{3}$, then $x < -5$ and $x + 5 < 0$. But if $x + 5 < 0$, then it follows that $-(x + 5) > 0$ and so $-(x + 5)$ is positive. Therefore Statement III must be true if $4 < \frac{7-x}{3}$.

The correct answer is D.

164. A certain right triangle has sides of length x, y, and z, where $x < y < z$. If the area of this triangular region is 1, which of the following indicates all of the possible values of y?

(A) $y > \sqrt{2}$
(B) $\frac{\sqrt{3}}{2} < y < \sqrt{2}$
(C) $\frac{\sqrt{2}}{3} < y < \frac{\sqrt{3}}{2}$
(D) $\frac{\sqrt{3}}{4} < y < \frac{\sqrt{2}}{3}$
(E) $y < \frac{\sqrt{3}}{4}$

Geometry; Algebra Triangles; Area; Inequalities

Since x, y, and z are the side lengths of a right triangle and $x < y < z$, it follows that x and y are the lengths of the legs of the triangle and so the area of the triangle is $\frac{1}{2}xy$. But, it is given that the area is 1 and so $\frac{1}{2}xy = 1$. Then, $xy = 2$ and $y = \frac{2}{x}$. Under the assumption that x, y, and z are all positive since they are the side lengths of a triangle, $x < y$ implies $\frac{1}{x} > \frac{1}{y}$ and then $\frac{2}{x} > \frac{2}{y}$. But, $y = \frac{2}{x}$, so by substitution, $y > \frac{2}{y}$, which implies that $y^2 > 2$ since y is positive. Thus, $y > \sqrt{2}$.

Alternatively, if $x < \sqrt{2}$ and $y < \sqrt{2}$ then $xy < 2$. If $x > \sqrt{2}$ and $y > \sqrt{2}$, then $xy > 2$. But, $xy = 2$ so one of x or y must be less than $\sqrt{2}$ and the other must be greater than $\sqrt{2}$. Since $x < y$, it follows that $x < \sqrt{2} < y$ and $y > \sqrt{2}$.

The correct answer is A.

165. On a certain day, a bakery produced a batch of rolls at a total production cost of \$300. On that day, $\frac{4}{5}$ of the rolls in the batch were sold, each at a price that was 50 percent greater than the average (arithmetic mean) production cost per roll. The remaining rolls in the batch were sold the next day, each at a price that was 20 percent less than the price of the day before. What was the bakery's profit on this batch of rolls?

(A) \$150
(B) \$144
(C) \$132
(D) \$108
(E) \$90

Arithmetic Applied problems

Let n be the number of rolls in the batch and p be the average production price, in dollars, per roll. Then the total cost of the batch is $np = 300$ dollars, and the total revenue from selling the rolls in the batch is $\left(\frac{4}{5}n\right)(1.5p) + \left(\frac{1}{5}n\right)(0.8)(1.5p) = \left(\frac{4}{5}n\right)\left(\frac{3}{2}p\right) + \left(\frac{1}{5}n\right)\left(\frac{4}{5}\right)\left(\frac{3}{2}p\right) = \left(\frac{6}{5} + \frac{6}{25}\right)np = \left(\frac{36}{25}\right)np$. Therefore, the profit from selling the rolls in the batch is $\left(\frac{36}{25}\right)np - np = \left(\frac{11}{25}\right)np = \left(\frac{11}{25}\right)(300)$ dollars $= 132$ dollars.

The correct answer is C.

166. A set of numbers has the property that for any number t in the set, $t + 2$ is in the set. If -1 is in the set, which of the following must also be in the set?

I. -3
II. 1
III. 5

(A) I only
(B) II only
(C) I and II only
(D) II and III only
(E) I, II, and III

Arithmetic Properties of numbers

It is given that -1 is in the set and, if t is in the set, then $t + 2$ is in the set.

I. Since $\{-1, 1, 3, 5, 7, 9, 11, \ldots\}$ contains -1 and satisfies the property that if t is in the set, then $t + 2$ is in the set, it is not true that -3 must be in the set.

II. Since -1 is in the set, $-1 + 2 = 1$ is in the set. Therefore, it must be true that 1 is in the set.

III. Since -1 is in the set, $-1 + 2 = 1$ is in the set. Since 1 is in the set, $1 + 2 = 3$ is in the set. Since 3 is in the set, $3 + 2 = 5$ is in the set. Therefore, it must be true that 5 is in the set.

The correct answer is D.

167. A couple decides to have 4 children. If they succeed in having 4 children and each child is equally likely to be a boy or a girl, what is the probability that they will have exactly 2 girls and 2 boys?

(A) $\frac{3}{8}$

(B) $\frac{1}{4}$

(C) $\frac{3}{16}$

(D) $\frac{1}{8}$

(E) $\frac{1}{16}$

Arithmetic Probability

Representing the birth order of the 4 children as a sequence of 4 letters, each of which is B for boy and G for girl, there are 2 possibilities (B or G) for the first letter, 2 for the second letter, 2 for the third letter, and 2 for the fourth letter, making a total of $2^4 = 16$ sequences. The table below categorizes some of these 16 sequences.

# of boys	# of girls	Sequences	# of sequences
0	4	GGGG	1
1	3	BGGG, GBGG, GGBG, GGGB	4
3	1	GBBB, BGBB, BBGB, BBBG	4
4	0	BBBB	1

The table accounts for $1 + 4 + 4 + 1 =$ 10 sequences. The other 6 sequences will have 2Bs and 2Gs. Therefore the probability that the couple will have exactly 2 boys and 2 girls is $\frac{6}{16} = \frac{3}{8}$.

For the mathematically inclined, if it is assumed that a couple has a fixed number of children, that the probability of having a girl each time is p, and that the sex of each child is independent of the sex of the other children, then the number of girls, x, born to a couple with n children is a random variable having the binomial probability distribution. The probability of having exactly x girls born to a couple with n children is given by the formula $\binom{n}{x}p^x(1-p)^{n-x}$. For the problem at hand, it is given that each child is equally likely to be a boy or a girl, and so $p = \frac{1}{2}$. Thus, the probability of having exactly 2 girls born to a couple with 4 children is

$$\binom{4}{2}\left(\frac{1}{2}\right)^2\left(\frac{1}{2}\right)^2 = \frac{4!}{2!2!}\left(\frac{1}{2}\right)^2\left(\frac{1}{2}\right)^2 = (6)\left(\frac{1}{4}\right)\left(\frac{1}{4}\right) = \frac{6}{16} = \frac{3}{8}.$$

The correct answer is A.

168. The closing price of Stock X changed on each trading day last month. The percent change in the closing price of Stock X from the first trading day last month to each of the other trading days last month was less than 50 percent. If the closing price on the second trading day last month was \$10.00, which of the following CANNOT be the closing price on the last trading day last month?

(A) \$3.00

(B) \$9.00

(C) \$19.00

(D) \$24.00

(E) \$29.00

Arithmetic Applied problems; Percents

Let P be the first-day closing price, in dollars, of the stock. It is given that the second-day closing price was $(1 + n\%)P = 10$, so $P = \frac{10}{1+n\%}$, for some value of n such that $-50 < n < 50$. Therefore, P is between $\frac{10}{1+0.50} \approx 6.67$ and $\frac{10}{1-0.50} = 20$. Hence, if Q is the closing price, in dollars, of the stock on the last day, then Q is between $(0.50)(6.67) \approx 3.34$ (50% decrease from the lowest possible first-day closing price) and $(1.50)(20) = 30$ (50% increase from the greatest possible first-day closing price). The only answer choice that gives a number of dollars not between 3.34 and 30 is the first answer choice.

The correct answer is A.

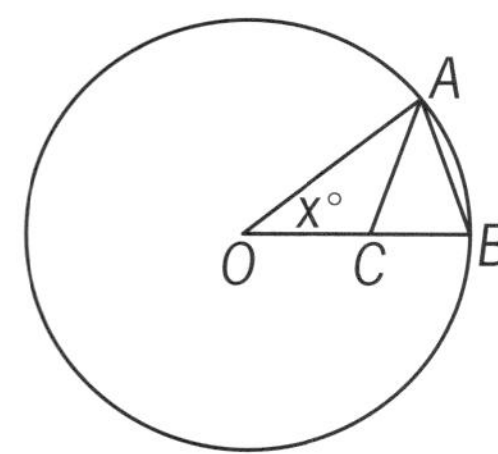

169. In the figure above, point O is the center of the circle and $OC = AC = AB$. What is the value of x?

(A) 40
(B) 36
(C) 34
(D) 32
(E) 30

Geometry Angles

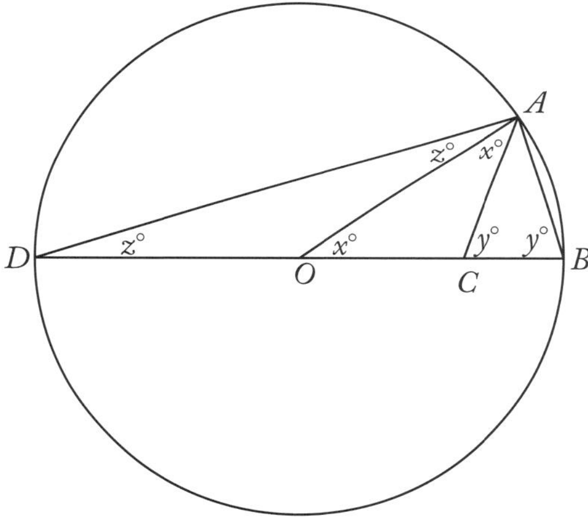

Consider the figure above, where $\overline{DB}$ is a diameter of the circle with center O and $\overline{AD}$ is a chord. Since $OC = AC$, ΔOCA is isosceles and so the base angles, $\angle AOC$ and $\angle OAC$, have the same degree measure. The measure of $\angle AOC$ is given as $x°$, so the measure of $\angle OAC$ is $x°$. Since $AC = AB$, ΔCAB is isosceles and so the base angles, $\angle ACB$ and $\angle ABC$, have the same degree measure. The measure of each is marked as $y°$. Likewise, since $\overline{OD}$ and $\overline{OA}$ are radii of the circle, $OD = OA$, and ΔDOA is isosceles with base angles, $\angle ADO$ and $\angle DAO$, each measuring $z°$. Each of the following statements is true:

(i) The measure of $\angle CAB$ is $180 - 2y$ since the sum of the measures of the angles of ΔCAB is 180.

(ii) $\angle DAB$ is a right angle (because $\overline{DB}$ is a diameter of the circle) and so $z + x + (180 - 2y) = 90$, or, equivalently, $2y - x - z = 90$.

(iii) $z + 90 + y = 180$ since the sum of the measures of the angles of right triangle ΔDAB is 180, or, equivalently, $z = 90 - y$.

(iv) $x = 2z$ because the measure of exterior angle $\angle AOC$ to ΔAOD is the sum of the measures of the two opposite interior angles, $\angle ODA$ and $\angle OAD$.

(v) $y = 2x$ because the measure of exterior angle $\angle ACB$ to ΔOCA is the sum of the measures of the two opposite interior angles, $\angle COA$ and $\angle CAO$.

Multiplying the final equation in (iii) by 2 gives $2z = 180 - 2y$. But, $x = 2z$ in (iv), so $x = 180 - 2y$. Finally, the sum of the measures of the angles of ΔCAB is 180 and so $y + y + x = 180$. Then from (v), $2x + 2x + x = 180$, $5x = 180$, and $x = 36$.

The correct answer is B.

170. An airline passenger is planning a trip that involves three connecting flights that leave from Airports A, B, and C, respectively. The first flight leaves Airport A every hour, beginning at 8:00 a.m., and arrives at Airport B $2\frac{1}{2}$ hours later. The second flight leaves Airport B every 20 minutes, beginning at 8:00 a.m., and arrives at Airport C $1\frac{1}{6}$ hours later. The third flight leaves Airport C every hour, beginning at 8:45 a.m. What is the least total amount of time the passenger must spend between flights if all flights keep to their schedules?

(A) 25 min
(B) 1 hr 5 min
(C) 1 hr 15 min
(D) 2 hr 20 min
(E) 3 hr 40 min

Arithmetic Operations on rational numbers

Since the flight schedules at each of Airports A, B, and C are the same hour after hour, assume that the passenger leaves Airport A at 8:00 and arrives at Airport B at 10:30. Since flights from Airport B leave at 20-minute intervals beginning on the hour, the passenger must wait 10 minutes at Airport B for the flight that leaves at 10:40 and arrives at Airport C $1\frac{1}{6}$ hours or 1 hour 10 minutes later. Thus, the passenger arrives at Airport C at 11:50. Having arrived too late for the 11:45 flight from Airport C, the passenger must wait 55 minutes for the 12:45 flight. Thus, the least total amount of time the passenger must spend waiting between flights is 10 + 55 = 65 minutes, or 1 hour 5 minutes.

The correct answer is B.

171. If n is a positive integer and n^2 is divisible by 72, then the largest positive integer that must divide n is

(A) 6
(B) 12
(C) 24
(D) 36
(E) 48

Arithmetic Properties of numbers

Since n^2 is divisible by 72, $n^2 = 72k$ for some positive integer k. Since $n^2 = 72k$, then $72k$ must be a perfect square. Since $72k = (2^3)(3^2)k$, then $k = 2m^2$ for some positive integer m in order for $72k$ to be a perfect square. Then, $n^2 = 72k = (2^3)(3^2)(2m^2) = (2^4)(3^2)m^2 = [(2^2)(3)(m)]^2$, and $n = (2^2)(3)(m)$. The positive integers that MUST divide n are 1, 2, 3, 4, 6, and 12. Therefore, the largest positive integer that must divide n is 12.

The correct answer is B.

172. A certain grocery purchased x pounds of produce for p dollars per pound. If y pounds of the produce had to be discarded due to spoilage and the grocery sold the rest for s dollars per pound, which of the following represents the gross profit on the sale of the produce?

(A) $(x - y)s - xp$
(B) $(x - y)p - ys$
(C) $(s - p)y - xp$
(D) $xp - ys$
(E) $(x - y)(s - p)$

Algebra Simplifying algebraic expressions; Applied problems

Since the grocery bought x pounds of produce for p dollars per pound, the total cost of the produce was xp dollars. Since y pounds of the produce was discarded, the grocery sold $x - y$ pounds of produce at the price of s dollars per pound, yielding a total revenue of $(x - y)s$ dollars. Then, the grocery's gross profit on the sale of the produce is its total revenue minus its total cost or $(x - y)s - xp$ dollars.

The correct answer is A.

173. If x, y, and z are positive integers such that x is a factor of y, and x is a multiple of z, which of the following is NOT necessarily an integer?

(A) $\frac{x+z}{z}$
(B) $\frac{y+z}{x}$
(C) $\frac{x+y}{z}$
(D) $\frac{xy}{z}$
(E) $\frac{yz}{x}$

Arithmetic Properties of numbers

Since the positive integer x is a factor of y, then $y = kx$ for some positive integer k. Since x is a multiple of the positive integer z, then $x = mz$ for some positive integer m.

Substitute these expressions for x and/or y into each answer choice to find the one expression that is NOT necessarily an integer.

A $\frac{x+z}{z}=\frac{mz+z}{z}=\frac{(m+1)z}{z}=m+1$, which MUST be an integer

B $\frac{y+z}{x}=\frac{y}{x}+\frac{z}{x}=\frac{kx}{x}+\frac{z}{mz}=k+\frac{1}{m}$, which NEED NOT be an integer

Because only one of the five expressions need not be an integer, the expressions given in C, D, and E need not be tested. However, for completeness,

C $\frac{x+y}{z}=\frac{mz+kx}{z}=\frac{mz+k(mz)}{z}=\frac{mz(1+k)}{z}$ $=m(1+k)$, which MUST be an integer

D $\frac{xy}{z}=\frac{(mz)y}{z}=my$, which MUST be an integer

E $\frac{yz}{x}=\frac{(kx)(z)}{x}=kz$, which MUST be an integer

The correct answer is B.

174. Running at their respective constant rates, Machine X takes 2 days longer to produce w widgets than Machine Y. At these rates, if the two machines together produce $\frac{5}{4}w$ widgets in 3 days, how many days would it take Machine X alone to produce $2w$ widgets?

(A) 4

(B) 6

(C) 8

(D) 10

(E) 12

Algebra Applied problems

If x, where $x > 2$, represents the number of days Machine X takes to produce w widgets, then Machine Y takes $x - 2$ days to produce w widgets. It follows that Machines X and Y can produce $\frac{w}{x}$ and $\frac{w}{x-2}$ widgets, respectively, in 1 day and together they can produce $\frac{w}{x}+\frac{w}{x-2}$ widgets in 1 day. Since it is given that, together, they can produce $\frac{5}{4}w$ widgets in 3 days, it follows that, together, they can produce $\frac{1}{3}\left(\frac{5}{4}w\right)=\frac{5}{12}w$ widgets in 1 day. Thus,

$$\frac{w}{x}+\frac{w}{x-2}=\frac{5}{12}w$$
$$\left(\frac{1}{x}+\frac{1}{x-2}\right)w=\frac{5}{12}w$$
$$\left(\frac{1}{x}+\frac{1}{x-2}\right)=\frac{5}{12}$$
$$12x(x-2)\left(\frac{1}{x}+\frac{1}{x-2}\right)=12x(x-2)\left(\frac{5}{12}\right)$$
$$12[(x-2)+x]=5x(x-2)$$
$$12(2x-2)=5x(x-2)$$
$$24x-24=5x^2-10x$$
$$0=5x^2-34x+24$$
$$0=(5x-4)(x-6)$$
$$x=\frac{4}{5}\text{ or }6$$

Therefore, since $x > 2$, it follows that $x = 6$. Machine X takes 6 days to produce w widgets and $2(6) = 12$ days to produce $2w$ widgets.

The correct answer is E.

175. A square wooden plaque has a square brass inlay in the center, leaving a wooden strip of uniform width around the brass square. If the ratio of the brass area to the wooden area is 25 to 39, which of the following could be the width, in inches, of the wooden strip?

I. 1
II. 3
III. 4

(A) I only
(B) II only
(C) I and II only
(D) I and III only
(E) I, II, and III

Geometry Area

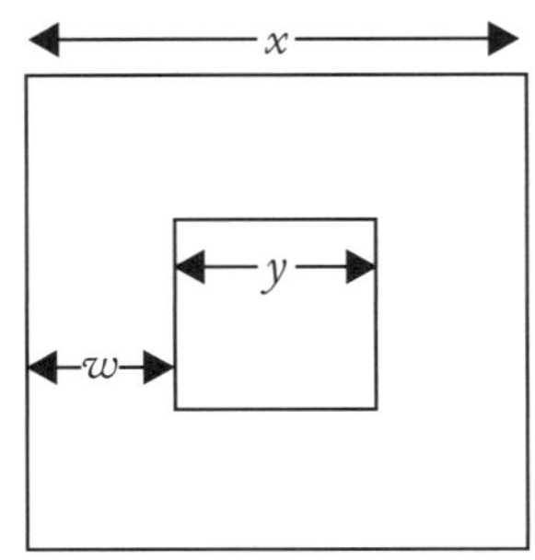

Note: Not drawn to scale.

Let x represent the side length of the entire plaque, let y represent the side length of the brass inlay, and w represent the uniform width of the wooden strip around the brass inlay, as shown in the figure above. Since the ratio of the area of the brass inlay to the area of the wooden strip is 25 to 39, the ratio of the area of the brass inlay to the area of the entire plaque is $\frac{y^2}{x^2} = \frac{25}{25+39} = \frac{25}{64}$. Then, $\frac{y}{x} = \sqrt{\frac{25}{64}} = \frac{5}{8}$ and $y = \frac{5}{8}x$. Also, $x = y + 2w$ and $w = \frac{x-y}{2}$. Substituting $\frac{5}{8}x$ for y into this expression for w gives $w = \frac{x - \frac{5}{8}x}{2} = \frac{\frac{3}{8}x}{2} = \frac{3}{16}x$. Thus,

I. If the plaque were $\frac{16}{3}$ inches on a side, then the width of the wooden strip would be 1 inch, and so 1 inch is a possible width for the wooden strip.

II. If the plaque were 16 inches on a side, then the width of the wooden strip would be 3 inches, and so 3 inches is a possible width for the wooden strip.

III. If the plaque were $\frac{64}{3}$ inches on a side, then the width of the wooden strip would be 4 inches, and so 4 inches is a possible width for the wooden strip.

The correct answer is E.

176. $\dfrac{2\frac{3}{5} - 1\frac{2}{3}}{\frac{2}{3} - \frac{3}{5}} =$

(A) 16
(B) 14
(C) 3
(D) 1
(E) −1

Arithmetic Operations on rational numbers

Work the problem:

$$\frac{2\frac{3}{5} - 1\frac{2}{3}}{\frac{2}{3} - \frac{3}{5}} =$$

$$\frac{\frac{13}{5} - \frac{5}{3}}{\frac{2}{3} - \frac{3}{5}} = \frac{\frac{39-25}{15}}{\frac{10-9}{15}} = \frac{\frac{14}{15}}{\frac{1}{15}} = \frac{14}{15} \times \frac{15}{1} = 14$$

The correct answer is B.

5.0 Data Sufficiency

5.0 Data Sufficiency

Data sufficiency questions appear in the Quantitative section of the GMAT® exam. Multiple-choice data sufficiency questions are intermingled with problem solving questions throughout the section. You will have 75 minutes to complete the Quantitative section of the GMAT exam, or about 2 minutes to answer each question. These questions require knowledge of the following topics:

- Arithmetic
- Elementary algebra
- Commonly known concepts of geometry

Data sufficiency questions are designed to measure your ability to analyze a quantitative problem, recognize which given information is relevant, and determine at what point there is sufficient information to solve a problem. In these questions, you are to classify each problem according to the five fixed answer choices, rather than find a solution to the problem.

Each data sufficiency question consists of a question, often accompanied by some initial information, and two statements, labeled (1) and (2), which contain additional information. You must decide whether the information in each statement is sufficient to answer the question or—if neither statement provides enough information—whether the information in the two statements together is sufficient. It is also possible that the statements, in combination do not give enough information to answer the question.

Begin by reading the initial information and the question carefully. Next, consider the first statement. Does the information provided by the first statement enable you to answer the question? Go on to the second statement. Try to ignore the information given in the first statement when you consider whether the second statement provides information that, by itself, allows you to answer the question. Now you should be able to say, for each statement, whether it is sufficient to determine the answer.

Next, consider the two statements in tandem. Do they, together, enable you to answer the question?

Look again at your answer choices. Select the one that most accurately reflects whether the statements provide the information required to answer the question.

5.1 Test-Taking Strategies

1. **Do not waste valuable time solving a problem.**

   You only need to determine whether sufficient information is given to solve it.

2. **Consider each statement separately.**

   First, decide whether each statement alone gives sufficient information to solve the problem. Be sure to disregard the information given in statement (1) when you evaluate the information given in statement (2). If either, or both, of the statements give(s) sufficient information to solve the problem, select the answer corresponding to the description of which statement(s) give(s) sufficient information to solve the problem.

3. **Judge the statements in tandem if neither statement is sufficient by itself.**

   It is possible that the two statements together do not provide sufficient information. Once you decide, select the answer corresponding to the description of whether the statements together give sufficient information to solve the problem.

4. **Answer the question asked.**

   For example, if the question asks, "What is the value of y ?" for an answer statement to be sufficient, you must be able to find one and only one value for y. Being able to determine minimum or maximum values for an answer (e.g., $y = x + 2$) is not sufficient, because such answers constitute a range of values rather than the specific value of y.

5. **Be very careful not to make unwarranted assumptions based on the images represented.**

   Figures are not necessarily drawn to scale; they are generalized figures showing little more than intersecting line segments and the relationships of points, angles, and regions. For example, if a figure described as a rectangle looks like a square, do not conclude that it is actually a square just by looking at the figure.

If statement 1 is sufficient, then the answer must be **A or D.**

If statement 2 is not sufficient, then the answer must be **A.**

If statement 2 is sufficient, then the answer must be **D.**

If statement 1 is not sufficient, then the answer must be **B, C, or E.**

If statement 2 is sufficient, then the answer must be **B.**

If statement 2 is not sufficient, then the answer must be **C or E.**

If both statements together are sufficient, then the answer must be **C.**

If both statements together are still not sufficient, then the answer must be **E.**

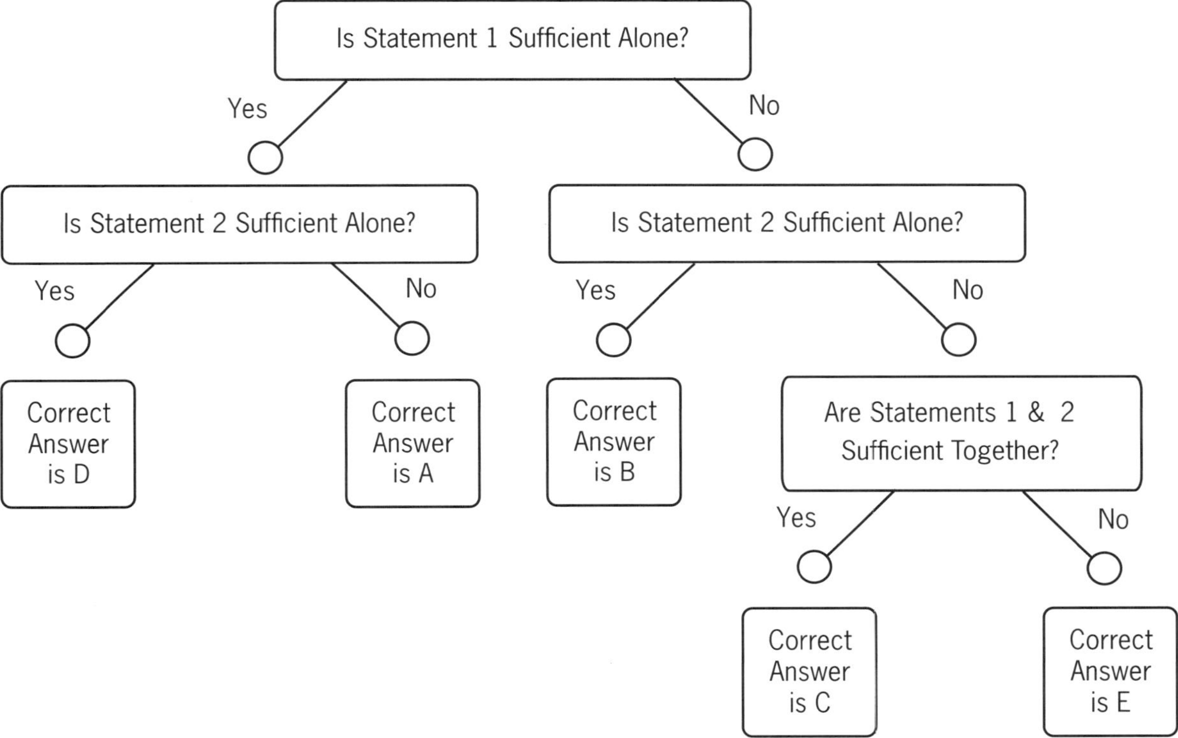

5.2 The Directions

These directions are similar to those you will see for data sufficiency questions when you take the GMAT exam. If you read the directions carefully and understand them clearly before going to sit for the test, you will not need to spend much time reviewing them when you take the GMAT exam.

Each data sufficiency problem consists of a question and two statements, labeled (1) and (2), that give data. You have to decide whether the data given in the statements are *sufficient* for answering the question. Using the data given in the statements *plus* your knowledge of mathematics and everyday facts (such as the number of days in July or the meaning of *counterclockwise*), you must indicate whether the data given in the statements are sufficient for answering the questions and then indicate one of the following answer choices:

(A) Statement (1) ALONE is sufficient, but statement (2) alone is not sufficient to answer the question asked;

(B) Statement (2) ALONE is sufficient, but statement (1) alone is not sufficient to answer the question asked;

(C) BOTH statements (1) and (2) TOGETHER are sufficient to answer the question asked, but NEITHER statement ALONE is sufficient;

(D) EACH statement ALONE is sufficient to answer the question asked;

(E) Statements (1) and (2) TOGETHER are NOT sufficient to answer the question asked, and additional data are needed.

NOTE: In data sufficiency problems that ask for the value of a quantity, the data given in the statements are sufficient only when it is possible to determine exactly one numerical value for the quantity.

Numbers: All numbers used are real numbers.

Figures: A figure accompanying a data sufficiency problem will conform to the information given in the question but will not necessarily conform to the additional information given in statements (1) and (2).

Lines shown as straight can be assumed to be straight and lines that appear jagged can also be assumed to be straight.

You may assume that the positions of points, angles, regions, and so forth exist in the order shown and that angle measures are greater than zero degrees.

All figures lie in a plane unless otherwise indicated.

5.3 Sample Questions

Each data sufficiency problem consists of a question and two statements, labeled (1) and (2), which contain certain data. Using these data and your knowledge of mathematics and everyday facts (such as the number of days in July or the meaning of the word *counterclockwise*), decide whether the data given are sufficient for answering the question and then indicate one of the following answer choices:

A Statement (1) ALONE is sufficient, but statement (2) alone is not sufficient.
B Statement (2) ALONE is sufficient, but statement (1) alone is not sufficient.
C BOTH statements TOGETHER are sufficient, but NEITHER statement ALONE is sufficient.
D EACH statement ALONE is sufficient.
E Statements (1) and (2) TOGETHER are not sufficient.

Note: In data sufficiency problems that ask for the value of a quantity, the data given in the statements are sufficient only when it is possible to determine exactly one numerical value for the quantity.

Example:

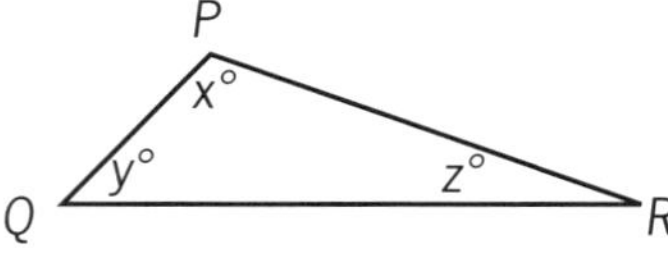

In ΔPQR, what is the value of x ?

(1) $PQ = PR$

(2) $y = 40$

Explanation: According to statement (1) $PQ = PR$; therefore, ΔPQR is isosceles and $y = z$. Since $x + y + z = 180$, it follows that $x + 2y = 180$. Since statement (1) does not give a value for y, you cannot answer the question using statement (1) alone. According to statement (2), $y = 40$; therefore, $x + z = 140$. Since statement (2) does not give a value for z, you cannot answer the question using statement (2) alone. Using both statements together, since $x + 2y = 180$ and the value of y is given, you can find the value of x. Therefore, BOTH statements (1) and (2) TOGETHER are sufficient to answer the questions, but NEITHER statement ALONE is sufficient.

Numbers: All numbers used are real numbers.

Figures:

- Figures conform to the information given in the question, but will not necessarily conform to the additional information given in statements (1) and (2).
- Lines shown as straight are straight, and lines that appear jagged are also straight.
- The positions of points, angles, regions, etc., exist in the order shown, and angle measures are greater than zero.
- All figures lie in a plane unless otherwise indicated.

177. What is the tenths digit of the number d when it is written as a decimal?

   (1) $d = \frac{54}{25}$

   (2) $1{,}000d = 2{,}160$

178. Rita's monthly salary is $\frac{2}{3}$ Juanita's monthly salary. What is their combined monthly salary?

   (1) Rita's monthly salary is \$4,000.

   (2) Either Rita's monthly salary or Juanita's monthly salary is \$6,000.

6 in

179. A framed picture is shown above. The frame, shown shaded, is 6 inches wide and forms a border of uniform width around the picture. What are the dimensions of the viewable portion of the picture?

   (1) The area of the shaded region is 24 square inches.

   (2) The frame is 8 inches tall.

180. What is the value of the integer x ?

   (1) x rounded to the nearest hundred is 7,200.

   (2) The hundreds digit of x is 2.

181. Is $2x > 2y$?

   (1) $x > y$

   (2) $3x > 3y$

182. If p and q are positive, is $\frac{p}{q}$ less than 1 ?

   (1) p is less than 4.

   (2) q is less than 4.

183. In a certain factory, hours worked by each employee in excess of 40 hours per week are overtime hours and are paid for at $1\frac{1}{2}$ times the employee's regular hourly pay rate. If an employee worked a total of 42 hours last week, how much was the employee's gross pay for the hours worked last week?

   (1) The employee's gross pay for overtime hours worked last week was \$30.

   (2) The employee's gross pay for all hours worked last week was \$30 more than for the previous week.

184. If $x > 0$, what is the value of x^5 ?

   (1) $\sqrt{x} = 32$

   (2) $x^2 = 2^{20}$

185. In the quilting pattern shown above, a small square has its vertices on the sides of a larger square. What is the side length, in centimeters, of the larger square?

   (1) The side length of the smaller square is 10 cm.

   (2) Each vertex of the small square cuts 1 side of the larger square into 2 segments with lengths in the ratio of 1:2.

186. Did Insurance Company K have more than \$300 million in total net profits last year?

   (1) Last year Company K paid out \$0.95 in claims for every dollar of premiums collected.

   (2) Last year Company K earned a total of \$150 million in profits from the investment of accumulated surplus premiums from previous years.

187. How many hours would it take Pump A and Pump B working together, each at its own constant rate, to empty a tank that was initially full?

   (1) Working alone at its constant rate, Pump A would empty the full tank in 4 hours 20 minutes.

   (2) Working alone, Pump B would empty the full tank at its constant rate of 72 liters per minute.

188. What is the value of the integer N?

(1) $101 < N < 103$
(2) $202 < 2N < 206$

189. Is zw positive?

(1) $z + w^3 = 20$
(2) z is positive.

190. On the scale drawing of a certain house plan, if 1 centimeter represents x meters, what is the value of x?

(1) A rectangular room that has a floor area of 12 square meters is represented by a region of area 48 square centimeters.
(2) The 15-meter length of the house is represented by a segment 30 centimeters long.

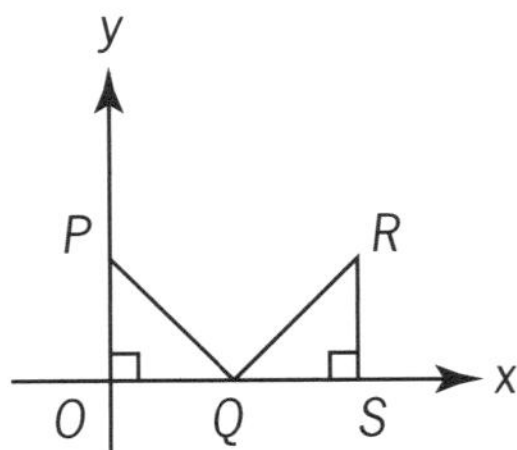

191. In the rectangular coordinate system above, if ΔOPQ and ΔQRS have equal area, what are the coordinates of point R?

(1) The coordinates of point P are (0,12).
(2) $OP = OQ$ and $QS = RS$.

192. If y is greater than 110 percent of x, is y greater than 75 ?

(1) $x > 75$
(2) $y - x = 10$

193. How much did credit-card fraud cost United States banks in year X to the nearest \$10 million?

(1) In year X, counterfeit cards and telephone and mail-order fraud accounted for 39 percent of the total amount that card fraud cost the banks.
(2) In year X, stolen cards accounted for \$158.4 million, or 16 percent, of the total amount that credit-card fraud cost the banks.

194. What is the average (arithmetic mean) of x and y?

(1) The average of x and $2y$ is 10.
(2) The average of $2x$ and $7y$ is 32.

195. What is the value of $\frac{r}{2} + \frac{s}{2}$?

(1) $\frac{r+s}{2} = 5$
(2) $r + s = 10$

196. Is the positive integer n odd?

(1) $n^2 + (n + 1)^2 + (n + 2)^2$ is even.
(2) $n^2 - (n + 1)^2 - (n + 2)^2$ is even.

197. For all x, the expression x^* is defined to be $ax + a$, where a is a constant. What is the value of 2^* ?

(1) $3^* = 2$
(2) $5^* = 3$

198. Is $k + m < 0$?

(1) $k < 0$
(2) $km > 0$

199. A retailer purchased a television set for x percent less than its list price, and then sold it for y percent less than its list price. What was the list price of the television set?

(1) $x = 15$
(2) $x - y = 5$

200. If x and y are positive, is $xy > x + y$?

(1) $x < y$
(2) $2 < x$

201. What is the ratio of c to d?

(1) The ratio of $3c$ to $3d$ is 3 to 4.
(2) The ratio of $c + 3$ to $d + 3$ is 4 to 5.

202. A certain dealership has a number of cars to be sold by its salespeople. How many cars are to be sold?

(1) If each of the salespeople sells 4 of the cars, 23 cars will remain unsold.

(2) If each of the salespeople sells 6 of the cars, 5 cars will remain unsold.

203. A candle company determines that, for a certain specialty candle, the supply function is $p = m_1x + b_1$ and the demand function is $p = m_2x + b_2$, where p is the price of each candle, x is the number of candles supplied or demanded, and m_1, m_2, b_1, and b_2 are constants. At what value of x do the graphs of the supply function and demand function intersect?

(1) $m_1 = -m_2 = 0.005$

(2) $b_2 - b_1 = 6$

204. Some computers at a certain company are Brand X and the rest are Brand Y. If the ratio of the number of Brand Y computers to the number of Brand X computers at the company is 5 to 6, how many of the computers are Brand Y ?

(1) There are 80 more Brand X computers than Brand Y computers at the company.

(2) There is a total of 880 computers at the company.

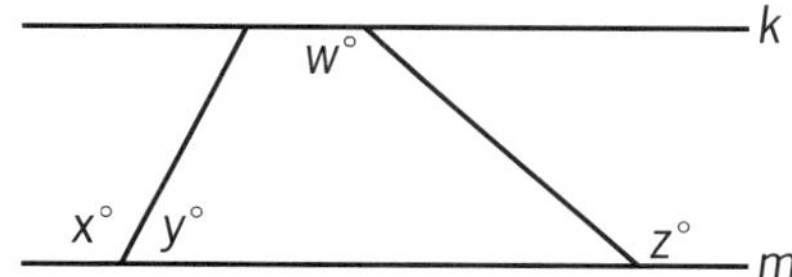

205. In the figure shown, lines k and m are parallel to each other. Is $x = z$?

(1) $x = w$

(2) $y = 180 - w$

206. When the wind speed is 9 miles per hour, the wind-chill factor w is given by

$$w = -17.366 + 1.19t,$$

where t is the temperature in degrees Fahrenheit. If at noon yesterday the wind speed was 9 miles per hour, was the wind-chill factor greater than 0 ?

(1) The temperature at noon yesterday was greater than 10 degrees Fahrenheit.

(2) The temperature at noon yesterday was less than 20 degrees Fahrenheit.

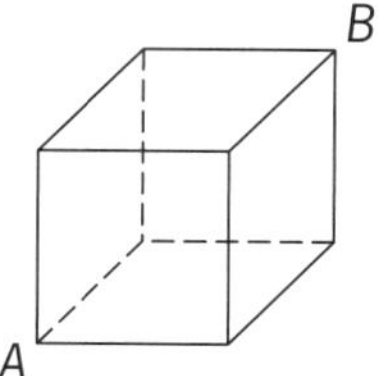

207. What is the volume of the cube above?

(1) The surface area of the cube is 600 square inches.

(2) The length of diagonal AB is $10\sqrt{3}$ inches.

208. Of the 230 single-family homes built in City X last year, how many were occupied at the end of the year?

(1) Of all single-family homes in City X, 90 percent were occupied at the end of last year.

(2) A total of 7,200 single-family homes in City X were occupied at the end of last year.

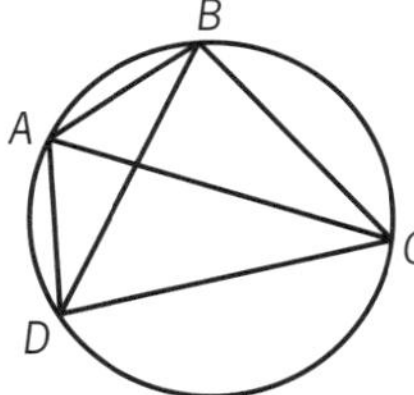

209. In the figure shown, quadrilateral $ABCD$ is inscribed in a circle of radius 5. What is the perimeter of quadrilateral $ABCD$?

(1) The length of AB is 6 and the length of CD is 8.

(2) AC is a diameter of the circle.

210. If x is a positive integer, what is the value of x ?

(1) $x^2 = \sqrt{x}$

(2) $\frac{n}{x} = n$ and $n \neq 0$.

211. Is the median of the five numbers a, b, c, d, and e equal to d?

(1) $a < c < e$

(2) $b < d < c$

212. During a certain bicycle ride, was Sherry's average speed faster than 24 kilometers per hour? (1 kilometer = 1,000 meters)

(1) Sherry's average speed during the bicycle ride was faster than 7 meters per second.

(2) Sherry's average speed during the bicycle ride was slower than 8 meters per second.

213. If x and y are integers, what is the value of x?

(1) $xy = 1$

(2) $x \neq -1$

214. If p, s, and t are positive, is $|ps - pt| > p(s - t)$?

(1) $p < s$

(2) $s < t$

215. Is $x > y$?

(1) $x + y > x - y$

(2) $3x > 2y$

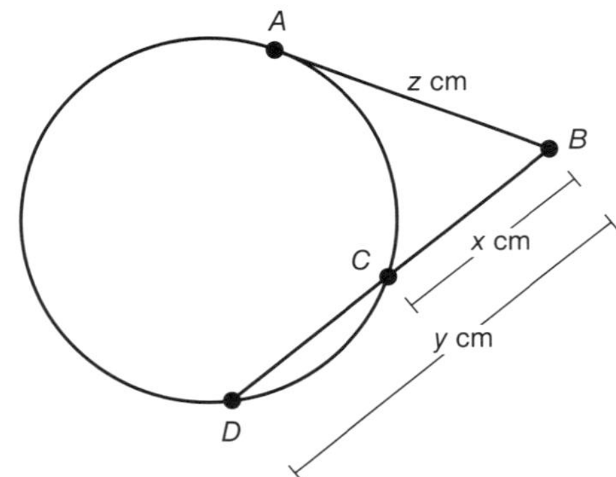

216. In the figure above, $\overline{AB}$, which has length z cm, is tangent to the circle at point A, and $\overline{BD}$, which has length y cm, intersects the circle at point C. If $BC = x$ cm and $z = \sqrt{xy}$, what is the value of x?

(1) $CD = x$ cm

(2) $z = 5\sqrt{2}$

217. The total cost of an office dinner was shared equally by k of the n employees who attended the dinner. What was the total cost of the dinner?

(1) Each of the k employees who shared the cost of the dinner paid \$19.

(2) If the total cost of the dinner had been shared equally by $k + 1$ of the n employees who attended the dinner, each of the $k + 1$ employees would have paid \$18.

218. What is the value of x?

(1) $x + 1 = 2 - 3x$

(2) $\frac{1}{2x} = 2$

219. Is the integer n a prime number?

(1) $24 \leq n \leq 28$

(2) n is not divisible by 2 or 3.

220. What is the sum of the first four terms of sequence S?

(1) After the first two terms of S, the value of each term of S is equal to the average (arithmetic mean) of the last two preceding terms.

(2) The average (arithmetic mean) of the first three terms of S is 10.

221. If x and y are positive integers, what is the remainder when $10^x + y$ is divided by 3?

(1) $x = 5$

(2) $y = 2$

222. What was the amount of money donated to a certain charity?

(1) Of the amount donated, 40 percent came from corporate donations.

(2) Of the amount donated, \$1.5 million came from noncorporate donations.

223. In a certain order, the pretax price of each regular pencil was \$0.03, the pretax price of each deluxe pencil was \$0.05, and there were 50% more deluxe pencils than regular pencils. All taxes on the order are a fixed percent of the pretax prices. The sum of the total pretax price of the order and the tax on the order was \$44.10. What was the amount, in dollars, of the tax on the order?

(1) The tax on the order was 5% of the total pretax price of the order.

(2) The order contained exactly 400 regular pencils.

224. If m is an integer greater than 1, is m an even integer?

(1) 32 is a factor of m.

(2) m is a factor of 32.

225. If the set S consists of five consecutive positive integers, what is the sum of these five integers?

(1) The integer 11 is in S, but 10 is not in S.

(2) The sum of the even integers in S is 26.

226. If $x > 0$, what is the value of x?

(1) $x^3 - x = 0$

(2) $\sqrt[3]{x} - x = 0$

227. Which of the positive numbers x or y is greater?

(1) $y = 2x$

(2) $2x + 5y = 12$

228. A total of 20 amounts are entered on a spreadsheet that has 5 rows and 4 columns; each of the 20 positions in the spreadsheet contains one amount. The average (arithmetic mean) of the amounts in row i is R_i $(1 \le i \le 5)$. The average of the amounts in column j is C_j $(1 \le j \le 4)$. What is the average of all 20 amounts on the spreadsheet?

(1) $R_1 + R_2 + R_3 + R_4 + R_5 = 550$

(2) $C_1 + C_2 + C_3 + C_4 = 440$

229. Was the range of the amounts of money that Company Y budgeted for its projects last year equal to the range of the amounts of money that it budgeted for its projects this year?

(1) Both last year and this year, Company Y budgeted money for 12 projects and the least amount of money that it budgeted for a project was \$400.

(2) Both last year and this year, the average (arithmetic mean) amount of money that Company Y budgeted per project was \$2,000.

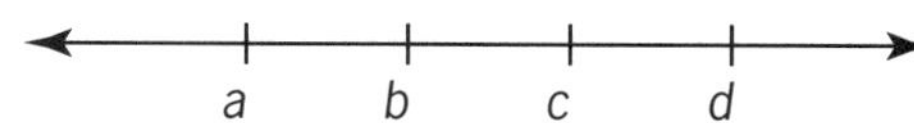

230. If a, b, c, and d are numbers on the number line shown and if the tick marks are equally spaced, what is the value of $a + c$?

(1) $a + b = -8$

(2) $a + d = 0$

231. Is $xm < ym$?

(1) $x > y$

(2) $m < 0$

232. If $y = x^2 - 6x + 9$, what is the value of x?

(1) $y = 0$

(2) $x + y = 3$

233. If $rs \neq 0$, is $\frac{1}{r} + \frac{1}{s} = 4$?

(1) $r + s = 4rs$

(2) $r = s$

234. If x, y, and z are three integers, are they consecutive integers?

(1) $z - x = 2$

(2) $x < y < z$

235. A collection of 36 cards consists of 4 sets of 9 cards each. The 9 cards in each set are numbered 1 through 9. If one card has been removed from the collection, what is the number on that card?

(1) The units digit of the sum of the numbers on the remaining 35 cards is 6.

(2) The sum of the numbers on the remaining 35 cards is 176.

236. In the *xy*-plane, point (r,s) lies on a circle with center at the origin. What is the value of $r^2 + s^2$?

(1) The circle has radius 2.

(2) The point $\left(\sqrt{2},-\sqrt{2}\right)$ lies on the circle.

237. If r, s, and t are nonzero integers, is $r^5s^3t^4$ negative?

(1) rt is negative.

(2) s is negative.

238. Each Type A machine fills 400 cans per minute, each Type B machine fills 600 cans per minute, and each Type C machine installs 2,400 lids per minute. A lid is installed on each can that is filled and on no can that is not filled. For a particular minute, what is the total number of machines working?

(1) A total of 4,800 cans are filled that minute.

(2) For that minute, there are 2 Type B machines working for every Type C machine working.

239. If a and b are constants, what is the value of a ?

(1) $a < b$

(2) $(t - a)(t - b) = t^2 + t - 12$, for all values of t.

240. If x is a positive integer, is $\sqrt{x}$ an integer?

(1) $\sqrt{4x}$ is an integer.

(2) $\sqrt{3x}$ is not an integer.

241. If p, q, x, y, and z are different positive integers, which of the five integers is the median?

(1) $p + x < q$

(2) $y < z$

242. If $w + z = 28$, what is the value of wz ?

(1) w and z are positive integers.

(2) w and z are consecutive odd integers.

243. If $abc \neq 0$, is $\dfrac{\frac{a}{b}}{c} = \dfrac{a}{\frac{b}{c}}$?

(1) $a = 1$

(2) $c = 1$

244. The arithmetic mean of a collection of 5 positive integers, not necessarily distinct, is 9. One additional positive integer is included in the collection and the arithmetic mean of the 6 integers is computed. Is the arithmetic mean of the 6 integers at least 10 ?

(1) The additional integer is at least 14.

(2) The additional integer is a multiple of 5.

245. A certain list consists of 400 different numbers. Is the average (arithmetic mean) of the numbers in the list greater than the median of the numbers in the list?

(1) Of the numbers in the list, 280 are less than the average.

(2) Of the numbers in the list, 30 percent are greater than or equal to the average.

246. In a two-month survey of shoppers, each shopper bought one of two brands of detergent, X or Y, in the first month and again bought one of these brands in the second month. In the survey, 90 percent of the shoppers who bought Brand X in the first month bought Brand X again in the second month, while 60 percent of the shoppers who bought Brand Y in the first month bought Brand Y again in the second month. What percent of the shoppers bought Brand Y in the second month?

(1) In the first month, 50 percent of the shoppers bought Brand X.

(2) The total number of shoppers surveyed was 5,000.

247. If m and n are positive integers, is $m + n$ divisible by 4 ?

(1) m and n are each divisible by 2.

(2) Neither m nor n is divisible by 4.

248. What is the area of rectangular region R?

    (1) Each diagonal of R has length 5.
    (2) The perimeter of R is 14.

249. How many integers n are there such that $r < n < s$?

    (1) $s - r = 5$
    (2) r and s are not integers.

250. If the total price of n equally priced shares of a certain stock was \$12,000, what was the price per share of the stock?

    (1) If the price per share of the stock had been \$1 more, the total price of the n shares would have been \$300 more.
    (2) If the price per share of the stock had been \$2 less, the total price of the n shares would have been 5 percent less.

251. If n is positive, is $\sqrt{n} > 100$?

    (1) $\sqrt{n-1} > 99$
    (2) $\sqrt{n+1} > 101$

252. Is $xy > 5$?

    (1) $1 \leq x \leq 3$ and $2 \leq y \leq 4$.
    (2) $x + y = 5$

253. In Year X, 8.7 percent of the men in the labor force were unemployed in June compared with 8.4 percent in May. If the number of men in the labor force was the same for both months, how many men were unemployed in June of that year?

    (1) In May of Year X, the number of unemployed men in the labor force was 3.36 million.
    (2) In Year X, 120,000 more men in the labor force were unemployed in June than in May.

254. If $x \neq 0$, what is the value of $\left(\frac{x^p}{x^q}\right)^4$?

    (1) $p = q$
    (2) $x = 3$

255. On Monday morning a certain machine ran continuously at a uniform rate to fill a production order. At what time did it completely fill the order that morning?

    (1) The machine began filling the order at 9:30 a.m.
    (2) The machine had filled $\frac{1}{2}$ of the order by 10:30 a.m. and $\frac{5}{6}$ of the order by 11:10 a.m.

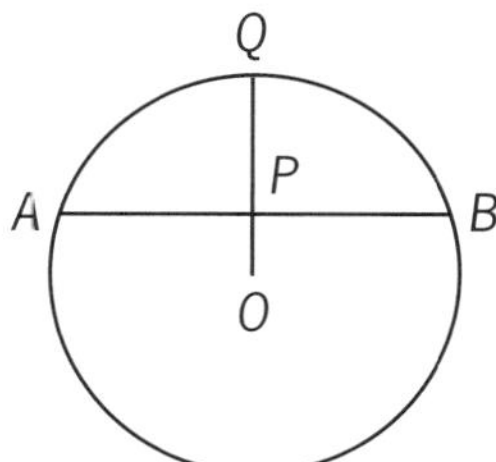

256. What is the radius of the circle above with center O?

    (1) The ratio of OP to PQ is 1 to 2.
    (2) P is the midpoint of chord AB.

257. If a and b are positive integers, what is the value of the product ab?

    (1) The least common multiple of a and b is 48.
    (2) The greatest common factor of a and b is 4.

258. What is the number of 360-degree rotations that a bicycle wheel made while rolling 100 meters in a straight line without slipping?

    (1) The diameter of the bicycle wheel, including the tire, was 0.5 meter.
    (2) The wheel made twenty 360-degree rotations per minute.

259. In the equation $x^2 + bx + 12 = 0$, x is a variable and b is a constant. What is the value of b?

    (1) $x - 3$ is a factor of $x^2 + bx + 12$.
    (2) 4 is a root of the equation $x^2 + bx + 12 = 0$.

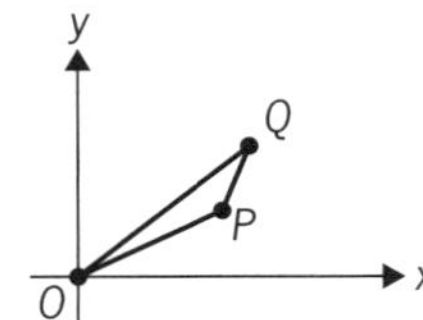

260. In the figure above, line segment OP has slope $\frac{1}{2}$ and line segment PQ has slope 2. What is the slope of line segment OQ ?

(1) Line segment OP has length $2\sqrt{5}$.

(2) The coordinates of point Q are (5,4).

261. In ΔXYZ, what is the length of YZ ?

(1) The length of XY is 3.

(2) The length of XZ is 5.

262. If the average (arithmetic mean) of n consecutive odd integers is 10, what is the least of the integers?

(1) The range of the n integers is 14.

(2) The greatest of the n integers is 17.

263. If x, y, and z are positive numbers, is $x > y > z$?

(1) $xz > yz$

(2) $yx > yz$

264. K is a set of numbers such that

(i) if x is in K, then $-x$ is in K, and

(ii) if each of x and y is in K, then xy is in K.

Is 12 in K ?

(1) 2 is in K.

(2) 3 is in K.

265. If $x^2 + y^2 = 29$, what is the value of $(x - y)^2$?

(1) $xy = 10$

(2) $x = 5$

266. After winning 50 percent of the first 20 games it played, Team A won all of the remaining games it played. What was the total number of games that Team A won?

(1) Team A played 25 games altogether.

(2) Team A won 60 percent of all the games it played.

267. Is x between 0 and 1 ?

(1) x^2 is less than x.

(2) x^3 is positive.

268. If m and n are nonzero integers, is m^n an integer?

(1) n^m is positive.

(2) n^m is an integer.

269. What is the value of xy ?

(1) $x + y = 10$

(2) $x - y = 6$

270. If n is the least of three different integers greater than 1, what is the value of n ?

(1) The product of the three integers is 90.

(2) One of the integers is twice one of the other two integers.

271. Is x^2 greater than x ?

(1) x^2 is greater than 1.

(2) x is greater than -1.

272. Michael arranged all his books in a bookcase with 10 books on each shelf and no books left over. After Michael acquired 10 additional books, he arranged all his books in a new bookcase with 12 books on each shelf and no books left over. How many books did Michael have before he acquired the 10 additional books?

(1) Before Michael acquired the 10 additional books, he had fewer than 96 books.

(2) Before Michael acquired the 10 additional books, he had more than 24 books.

273. If $xy > 0$, does $(x - 1)(y - 1) = 1$?

(1) $x + y = xy$

(2) $x = y$

274. Last year in a group of 30 businesses, 21 reported a net profit and 15 had investments in foreign markets. How many of the businesses did not report a net profit nor invest in foreign markets last year?

(1) Last year 12 of the 30 businesses reported a net profit and had investments in foreign markets.

(2) Last year 24 of the 30 businesses reported a net profit or invested in foreign markets, or both.

275. Is the perimeter of square S greater than the perimeter of equilateral triangle T ?

(1) The ratio of the length of a side of S to the length of a side of T is 4:5.

(2) The sum of the lengths of a side of S and a side of T is 18.

276. If $x + y + z > 0$, is $z > 1$?

(1) $z > x + y + 1$

(2) $x + y + 1 < 0$

277. For all z, $\lceil z \rceil$ denotes the least integer greater than or equal to z. Is $\lceil x \rceil = 0$?

(1) $-1 < x < -0.1$

(2) $\lceil x + 0.5 \rceil = 1$

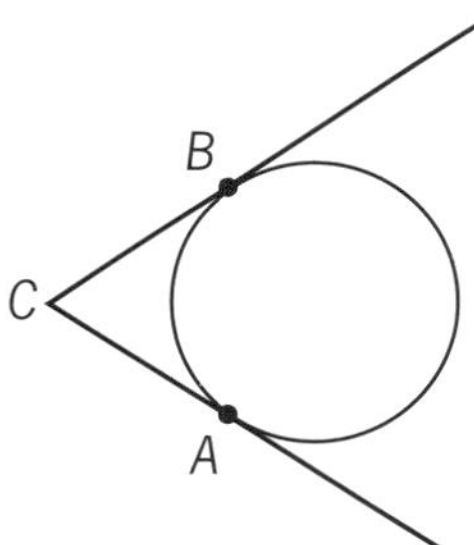

278. The circular base of an above-ground swimming pool lies in a level yard and just touches two straight sides of a fence at points A and B, as shown in the figure above. Point C is on the ground where the two sides of the fence meet. How far from the center of the pool's base is point A ?

(1) The base has area 250 square feet.

(2) The center of the base is 20 feet from point C.

279. If $xy = -6$, what is the value of $xy(x + y)$?

(1) $x - y = 5$

(2) $xy^2 = 18$

280. $[y]$ denotes the greatest integer less than or equal to y. Is $d < 1$?

(1) $d = y - [y]$

(2) $[d] = 0$

281. If N is a positive odd integer, is N prime?

(1) $N = 2^k + 1$ for some positive integer k.

(2) $N + 2$ and $N + 4$ are both prime.

282. If m is a positive integer, then m^3 has how many digits?

(1) m has 3 digits.

(2) m^2 has 5 digits.

283. What is the value of $x^2 - y^2$?

(1) $(x - y)^2 = 9$

(2) $x + y = 6$

284. For each landscaping job that takes more than 4 hours, a certain contractor charges a total of r dollars for the first 4 hours plus $0.2r$ dollars for each additional hour or fraction of an hour, where $r > 100$. Did a particular landscaping job take more than 10 hours?

(1) The contractor charged a total of \$288 for the job.

(2) The contractor charged a total of $2.4r$ dollars for the job.

285. If $x^2 = 2^x$, what is the value of x ?

(1) $2x = \left(\frac{x}{2}\right)^3$

(2) $x = 2^{x-2}$

286. The sequence $s_1, s_2, s_3, \ldots, s_n, \ldots$ is such that $s_n = \frac{1}{n} - \frac{1}{n+1}$ for all integers $n \geq 1$. If k is a positive integer, is the sum of the first k terms of the sequence greater than $\frac{9}{10}$?

(1) $k > 10$

(2) $k < 19$

287. In the sequence S of numbers, each term after the first two terms is the sum of the two immediately preceding terms. What is the 5th term of S ?

(1) The 6th term of S minus the 4th term equals 5.

(2) The 6th term of S plus the 7th term equals 21.

288. If 75 percent of the guests at a certain banquet ordered dessert, what percent of the guests ordered coffee?

(1) 60 percent of the guests who ordered dessert also ordered coffee.

(2) 90 percent of the guests who ordered coffee also ordered dessert.

289. A tank containing water started to leak. Did the tank contain more than 30 gallons of water when it started to leak? (Note: 1 gallon = 128 ounces)

(1) The water leaked from the tank at a constant rate of 6.4 ounces per minute.

(2) The tank became empty less than 12 hours after it started to leak.

290. In the xy-plane, lines k and ℓ intersect at the point (1,1). Is the y-intercept of k greater than the y-intercept of ℓ ?

(1) The slope of k is less than the slope of ℓ.

(2) The slope of ℓ is positive.

291. A triangle has side lengths of a, b, and c centimeters. Does each angle in the triangle measure less than 90 degrees?

(1) The 3 semicircles whose diameters are the sides of the triangle have areas that are equal to 3 cm^2, 4 cm^2, and 6 cm^2, respectively.

(2) $c < a + b < c + 2$

292. Each of the 45 books on a shelf is written either in English or in Spanish, and each of the books is either a hardcover book or a paperback. If a book is to be selected at random from the books on the shelf, is the probability less than $\frac{1}{2}$ that the book selected will be a paperback written in Spanish?

(1) Of the books on the shelf, 30 are paperbacks.

(2) Of the books on the shelf, 15 are written in Spanish.

293. A small school has three foreign language classes, one in French, one in Spanish, and one in German. How many of the 34 students enrolled in the Spanish class are also enrolled in the French class?

(1) There are 27 students enrolled in the French class, and 49 students enrolled in either the French class, the Spanish class, or both of these classes.

(2) One-half of the students enrolled in the Spanish class are enrolled in more than one foreign language class.

294. If S is a set of four numbers w, x, y, and z, is the range of the numbers in S greater than 2 ?

(1) $w - z > 2$

(2) z is the least number in S.

295. Last year $\frac{3}{5}$ of the members of a certain club were males. This year the members of the club include all the members from last year plus some new members. Is the fraction of the members of the club who are males greater this year than last year?

(1) More than half of the new members are male.

(2) The number of members of the club this year is $\frac{6}{5}$ the number of members last year.

296. If a, b, and c are consecutive integers and $0 < a < b < c$, is the product abc a multiple of 8 ?

(1) The product ac is even.

(2) The product bc is a multiple of 4.

297. M and N are integers such that $6 < M < N$. What is the value of N ?

(1) The greatest common divisor of M and N is 6.

(2) The least common multiple of M and N is 36.

298. Stations X and Y are connected by two separate, straight, parallel rail lines that are 250 miles long. Train P and train Q simultaneously left Station X and Station Y, respectively, and each train traveled to the other's point of departure. The two trains passed each other after traveling for 2 hours. When the two trains passed, which train was nearer to its destination?

(1) At the time when the two trains passed, train P had averaged a speed of 70 miles per hour.

(2) Train Q averaged a speed of 55 miles per hour for the entire trip.

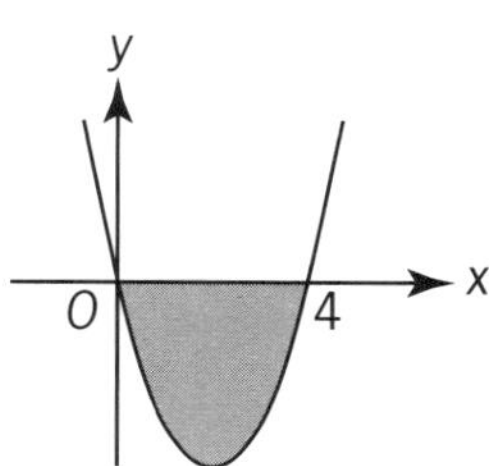

299. In the *xy*-plane shown, the shaded region consists of all points that lie above the graph of $y = x^2 - 4x$ and below the *x*-axis. Does the point (a,b) (not shown) lie in the shaded region if $b < 0$?

(1) $0 < a < 4$

(2) $a^2 - 4a < b$

300. If *a* and *b* are positive integers, is $\sqrt[3]{ab}$ an integer?

(1) $\sqrt{a}$ is an integer.

(2) $b = \sqrt{a}$

5.4 Answer Key

177. D
178. A
179. C
180. E
181. D
182. E
183. A
184. D
185. C
186. E
187. E
188. D
189. E
190. D
191. C
192. A
193. B
194. C
195. D
196. D
197. D
198. C
199. E
200. C
201. A
202. C
203. C
204. D
205. D
206. E
207. D
208. E
209. C
210. D
211. E
212. A
213. C
214. B
215. E
216. C
217. C
218. D
219. A
220. E
221. B
222. C
223. D
224. D
225. D
226. D
227. A
228. D
229. E
230. C
231. C
232. A
233. A
234. C
235. D
236. D
237. E
238. C
239. C
240. A
241. E
242. B
243. B
244. C
245. D
246. A
247. C
248. C
249. C
250. D
251. B
252. E
253. D
254. A
255. B
256. E
257. C
258. A
259. D
260. B
261. E
262. D
263. E
264. C
265. A
266. D
267. A
268. E
269. C
270. C
271. A
272. A
273. A
274. D
275. A
276. B
277. A
278. A
279. B
280. D
281. E
282. E
283. E
284. B
285. D
286. A
287. A
288. C
289. E
290. A
291. A
292. B
293. A
294. A
295. E
296. A
297. C
298. A
299. B
300. B

5.5 Answer Explanations

The following discussion of data sufficiency is intended to familiarize you with the most efficient and effective approaches to the kinds of problems common to data sufficiency. The particular questions in this chapter are generally representative of the kinds of data sufficiency questions you will encounter on the GMAT. Remember that it is the problem solving strategy that is important, not the specific details of a particular question.

177. What is the tenths digit of the number d when it is written as a decimal?

(1) $d = \frac{54}{25}$

(2) $1{,}000d = 2{,}160$

Arithmetic Place value

(1) Given that $d = \frac{54}{25}$, it follows that $d = \frac{54}{25} \times \frac{4}{4} = \frac{216}{100} = 2.16$ and the tenths digit is 1; SUFFICIENT.

(2) Given that $1{,}000d = 2{,}160$, it follows that $d = \frac{2{,}160}{1{,}000} = \frac{216}{100} = 2.16$ and the tenths digit is 1; SUFFICIENT.

The correct answer is D;
each statement alone is sufficient.

178. Rita's monthly salary is $\frac{2}{3}$ Juanita's monthly salary. What is their combined monthly salary?

(1) Rita's monthly salary is \$4,000.

(2) Either Rita's monthly salary or Juanita's monthly salary is \$6,000.

Arithmetic Applied problems

Let R and J be Rita's and Juanita's monthly salaries, respectively, in dollars. It is given that $R = \frac{2}{3}J$. Determine the value of their combined salary, which can be expressed as $R + J = \frac{2}{3}J + J = \frac{5}{3}J$.

(1) Given that $R = 4{,}000$, it follows that $4{,}000 = \frac{2}{3}J$, or $J = \frac{3}{2}(4{,}000) = 6{,}000$. Therefore, $\frac{5}{3}J = \frac{5}{3}(6{,}000) = 10{,}000$; SUFFICIENT.

(2) Given that $R = 6{,}000$ or $J = 6{,}000$, then $J = \frac{3}{2}(6{,}000) = 9{,}000$ or $J = 6{,}000$. Thus, $\frac{5}{3}J = \frac{5}{3}(9{,}000) = 15{,}000$ or $\frac{5}{3}J = \frac{5}{3}(6{,}000) = 10{,}000$, and so it is not possible to determine the value of $\frac{5}{3}J$; NOT sufficient.

The correct answer is A;
statement 1 alone is sufficient.

179. A framed picture is shown above. The frame, shown shaded, is 6 inches wide and forms a border of uniform width around the picture. What are the dimensions of the viewable portion of the picture?

(1) The area of the shaded region is 24 square inches.

(2) The frame is 8 inches tall.

Geometry Area

Let the outer dimensions of the frame be 6 inches by B inches, and let the dimensions of the viewable portion of the picture be a inches by

b inches. Then the area of the frame is the area of the viewable portion and the frame combined minus the area of the viewable portion, which equals $(6B - ab)$ square inches. Determine the values of a and b.

(1) Given that $6B - ab = 24$, then it is not possible to determine the values of a and b. For example, if $B = 8$, $a = 4$, and $b = 6$, then $6B - ab = 6(8) - (4)(6) = 24$. However, if $B = 7$, $a = 3$, and $b = 6$, then $6B - ab = 6(7) - (3)(6) = 24$; NOT sufficient.

(2) Given that $B = 8$, then $6B - ab = 48 - ab$, but it is still not possible to determine the values of a and b; NOT sufficient.

Taking (1) and (2) together, it follows that $6B - ab = 24$ and $B = 8$, and therefore $48 - ab = 24$ and $ab = 24$. Also, letting the uniform width of the border be x inches, the outer dimensions of the frame are $(a + 2x)$ inches $= 6$ inches and $(b + 2x)$ inches $= 8$ inches, from which it follows by subtracting the last two equations that $b - a = 2$. Thus, $b = a + 2$, and so $ab = 24$ becomes $a(a + 2) = 24$, or $a^2 + 2a - 24 = 0$. Factoring gives $(a + 6)(a - 4) = 0$, so $a = -6$ or $a = 4$. Because no dimension of the viewable portion can be negative, it follows that $a = 4$ and $b = a + 2 = 4 + 2 = 6$.

The correct answer is C;
both statements together are sufficient.

180. What is the value of the integer x ?

(1) x rounded to the nearest hundred is 7,200.
(2) The hundreds digit of x is 2.

Arithmetic Rounding

(1) Given that x rounded to the nearest hundred is 7,200, the value of x cannot be determined. For example, x could be 7,200 or x could be 7,201; NOT sufficient.

(2) Given that the hundreds digit of x is 2, the value of x cannot be determined. For example, x could be 7,200 or x could be 7,201; NOT sufficient.

Taking (1) and (2) together is of no more help than either (1) or (2) taken separately because the same examples were used in both (1) and (2).

The correct answer is E;
both statements together are still not sufficient.

181. Is $2x > 2y$?

(1) $x > y$
(2) $3x > 3y$

Algebra Inequalities

(1) It is given that $x > y$. Thus, multiplying both sides by the positive number 2, it follows that $2x > 2y$; SUFFICIENT.

(2) It is given that $3x > 3y$. Thus, multiplying both sides by the positive number $\frac{2}{3}$, it follows that $2x > 2y$; SUFFICIENT.

The correct answer is D;
each statement alone is sufficient.

182. If p and q are positive, is $\frac{p}{q}$ less than 1 ?

(1) p is less than 4.
(2) q is less than 4.

Arithmetic Properties of numbers

(1) Given that p is less than 4, then it is not possible to determine whether $\frac{p}{q}$ is less than 1. For example, if $p = 1$ and $q = 2$, then $\frac{p}{q} = \frac{1}{2}$ and $\frac{1}{2}$ is less than 1. However, if $p = 2$ and $q = 1$, then $\frac{p}{q} = 2$ and 2 is not less than 1; NOT sufficient.

(2) Given that q is less than 4, then it is not possible to determine whether $\frac{p}{q}$ is less than 1. For example, if $p = 1$ and $q = 2$, then $\frac{p}{q} = \frac{1}{2}$ and $\frac{1}{2}$ is less than 1. However, if $p = 2$ and $q = 1$, then $\frac{p}{q} = 2$ and 2 is not less than 1; NOT sufficient.

Taking (1) and (2) together is of no more help than either (1) or (2) taken separately because the same examples were used in both (1) and (2).

The correct answer is E;
both statements together are still not sufficient.

183. In a certain factory, hours worked by each employee in excess of 40 hours per week are overtime hours and are paid for at $1\frac{1}{2}$ times the employee's regular hourly pay rate. If an employee worked a total of 42 hours last week, how much was the employee's gross pay for the hours worked last week?

(1) The employee's gross pay for overtime hours worked last week was \$30.

(2) The employee's gross pay for all hours worked last week was \$30 more than for the previous week.

Arithmetic Applied problems

If an employee's regular hourly rate was $\$R$ and the employee worked 42 hours last week, then the employee's gross pay for hours worked last week was $40R + 2(1.5R)$. Determine the value of $40R + 2(1.5R) = 43R$, or equivalently, the value of R.

(1) Given that the employee's gross pay for overtime hours worked last week was \$30, it follows that $2(1.5R) = 30$ and $R = 10$; SUFFICIENT.

(2) Given that the employee's gross pay for all hours worked last week was \$30 more than for the previous week, the value of R cannot be determined because nothing specific is known about the value of the employee's pay for all hours worked the previous week; NOT sufficient.

The correct answer is A;
statement (1) alone is sufficient.

184. If $x > 0$, what is the value of x^5 ?

(1) $\sqrt{x} = 32$

(2) $x^2 = 2^{20}$

Algebra Exponents

(1) Given that $\sqrt{x} = 32$, it follows that $x = 32^2$ and $x^5 = (32^2)^5$; SUFFICIENT.

(2) Given that $x^2 = 2^{20}$, since x is positive, it follows that $x = \sqrt{2^{20}} = 2^{10}$ and $x^5 = (2^{10})^5$; SUFFICIENT.

The correct answer is D;
each statement alone is sufficient.

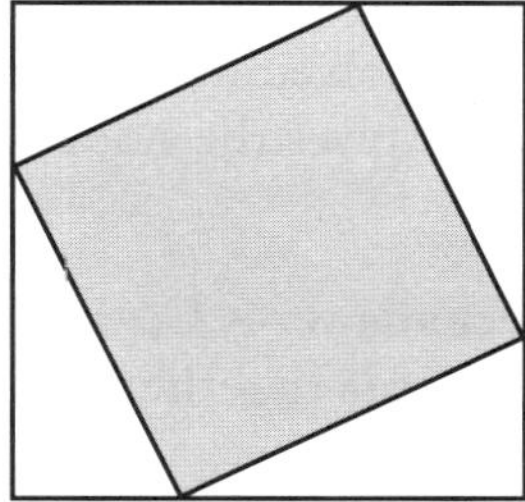

185. In the quilting pattern shown above, a small square has its vertices on the sides of a larger square. What is the side length, in centimeters, of the larger square?

(1) The side length of the smaller square is 10 cm.

(2) Each vertex of the small square cuts 1 side of the larger square into 2 segments with lengths in the ratio of 1:2.

Geometry Triangles; Pythagorean theorem

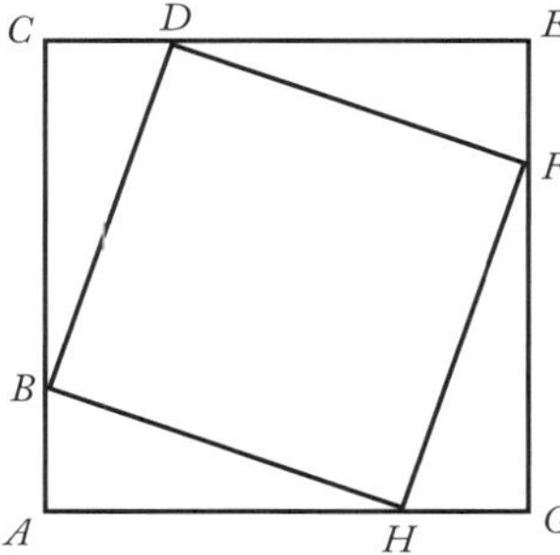

Determine the side length of the larger square or, in the figure above, determine $AG = AH + HG$. Note that ΔBAH, ΔDCB, ΔFED, and ΔHGF are the same size and shape and that $AB = CD = EF = GH$ and $BC = DE = FG = HA$.

(1) This indicates that $HF = 10$, but it is possible that $HG = 6$ and $GF = 8$ $\left(\sqrt{6^2+8^2}=10\right)$, from which it follows that the side length of the larger square is $6 + 8 = 14$, and it is possible that $HG = 1$ and $GF = \sqrt{99}$ $\left(\sqrt{1^2+\left(\sqrt{99}\right)^2}=10\right)$, from which it follows that the side length of the larger square is $1+\sqrt{99}$; NOT sufficient.

(2) This indicates that if $HG = x$, then $AH = 2x$. If $x = 2$, then the side length of the larger square is $2 + 2(2) = 6$, but if $x = 5$, then the side length of the larger square is $5 + 2(5) = 15$; NOT sufficient.

Taking (1) and (2) together, $10=\sqrt{x^2+(2x)^2}$, which can be solved for x. Then taking 3 times the value of x gives the side length of the larger square.

The correct answer is C;
both statements together are sufficient.

186. Did Insurance Company K have more than \$300 million in total net profits last year?

(1) Last year Company K paid out \$0.95 in claims for every dollar of premiums collected.

(2) Last year Company K earned a total of \$150 million in profits from the investment of accumulated surplus premiums from previous years.

Arithmetic Applied problems

Letting R and E, respectively, represent the company's total revenue and total expenses last year, determine if $R - E > \$300$ million.

(1) This indicates that, for $\$x$ in premiums collected, the company paid $\$0.95x$ in claims, but gives no information about other sources of revenue or other types of expenses; NOT sufficient.

(2) This indicates that the company's profits from the investment of accumulated surplus premiums was \$150 million last year, but gives no information about other sources of revenue or other types of expenses; NOT sufficient.

Taking (1) and (2) together gives information on profit resulting from collecting premiums and paying claims as well as profit resulting from investments from accumulated surplus premiums, but gives no indication whether there were other sources of revenue or other types of expenses.

The correct answer is E;
both statements together are still not sufficient.

187. How many hours would it take Pump A and Pump B working together, each at its own constant rate, to empty a tank that was initially full?

(1) Working alone at its constant rate, Pump A would empty the full tank in 4 hours 20 minutes.

(2) Working alone, Pump B would empty the full tank at its constant rate of 72 liters per minute.

Arithmetic Applied problems

Determine how long it would take Pumps A and B working together, each at its own constant rate, to empty a full tank.

(1) This indicates how long it would take Pump A to empty the tank, but gives no information about Pump B's constant rate; NOT sufficient.

(2) This indicates the rate at which Pump B can empty the tank, but without information about the capacity of the tank or Pump A's rate, it is not possible to determine how long both pumps working together would take to empty the tank; NOT sufficient.

Taking (1) and (2) together gives the amount of time it would take Pump A to empty the tank and the rate at which Pump B can empty the tank, but without knowing the capacity of the tank, it is not possible to determine how long the pumps working together would take to empty the tank.

The correct answer is E;
both statements together are still not sufficient.

188. What is the value of the integer N?

(1) $101 < N < 103$
(2) $202 < 2N < 206$

Arithmetic Inequalities

(1) Given that N is an integer and $101 < N < 103$, it follows that $N = 102$; SUFFICIENT.

(2) Given that N is an integer and $202 < 2N < 206$, it follows that $101 < N < 103$ and $N = 102$; SUFFICIENT.

The correct answer is D;
each statement alone is sufficient.

189. Is zw positive?

(1) $z + w^3 = 20$
(2) z is positive.

Arithmetic Properties of numbers

(1) Given that $z + w^3 = 20$, if $z = 1$ and $w = \sqrt[3]{19}$ then $z + w^3 = 20$ and zw is positive. However, if $z = 20$ and $w = 0$, then $z + w^3 = 20$ and zw is not positive; NOT sufficient.

(2) Given that z is positive, if $z = 1$ and $w = \sqrt[3]{19}$, then zw is positive. However, if $z = 20$ and $w = 0$, then zw is not positive; NOT sufficient.

Taking (1) and (2) together is of no more help than either (1) or (2) taken separately because the same examples were used in both (1) and (2).

The correct answer is E;
both statements together are still not sufficient.

190. On the scale drawing of a certain house plan, if 1 centimeter represents x meters, what is the value of x?

(1) A rectangular room that has a floor area of 12 square meters is represented by a region of area 48 square centimeters.
(2) The 15-meter length of the house is represented by a segment 30 centimeters long.

Arithmetic Ratio and proportion

It is given that on the scale drawing, 1 centimeter represents x meters. Determine the value of x. Note that 1 cm^2 represents x^2 m^2.

(1) This indicates that an area of 12 m^2 is represented by an area of 48 cm^2. Then, dividing both 12 and 48 by 48, it follows that an area of $\frac{12}{48} = \frac{1}{4}$ m^2 is represented by an area of $\frac{48}{48} = 1$ cm^2 and so $x^2 = \frac{1}{4}$ or $x = \frac{1}{2}$; SUFFICIENT.

(2) This indicates that a length of 15 m is represented by a length of 30 cm. Then, dividing both 15 and 30 by 30, it follows that a length of $\frac{15}{30} = \frac{1}{2}$ m is represented by a length of $\frac{30}{30} = 1$ cm and so $x = \frac{1}{2}$; SUFFICIENT.

The correct answer is D;
each statement alone is sufficient.

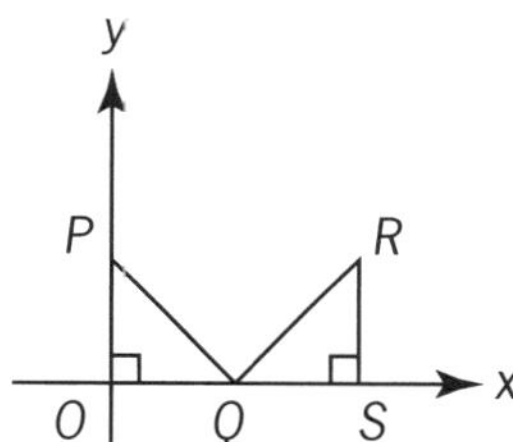

191. In the rectangular coordinate system above, if ΔOPQ and ΔQRS have equal area, what are the coordinates of point R?

(1) The coordinates of point P are (0,12).
(2) $OP = OQ$ and $QS = RS$.

Geometry Coordinate geometry; triangles

Since the area of ΔOPQ is equal to the area of ΔQRS, it follows that $\frac{1}{2}(OQ)(OP) = \frac{1}{2}(QS)(SR)$, or $(OQ)(OP) = (QS)(SR)$. Also, if both OS and SR are known, then the coordinates of point R will be known.

(1) Given that the y-coordinate of P is 12, it is not possible to determine the coordinates of point R. For example, if $OQ = QS = SR = 12$, then the equation $(OQ)(OP) = (QS)(SR)$ becomes $(12)(12) = (12)(12)$, which is true, and the x-coordinate of R is $OQ + QS = 24$ and the y-coordinate of R is $SR = 12$. However, if $OQ = 12$, $QS = 24$, and $SR = 6$, then the equation $(OQ)(OP) = (QS)(SR)$ becomes $(12)(12) = (24)(6)$, which is true, and the x-coordinate of R is $OQ + QS = 36$ and the y-coordinate of R is $SR = 6$; NOT sufficient.

(2) Given that $OP = OQ$ and $QS = RS$, it is not possible to determine the coordinates of point R, since everything given would still be true if all the lengths were doubled, but doing this would change the coordinates of point R; NOT sufficient.

Taking (1) and (2) together, it follows that $OP = OQ = 12$. Therefore, $(OQ)(OP) = (QS)(SR)$ becomes $(12)(12) = (QS)(SR)$, or $144 = (QS)(SR)$. Using $QS = RS$ in the last equation gives $144 = (QS)^2$, or $12 = QS$. Thus, $OQ = QS = SR = 12$ and point R has coordinates (24,12).

The correct answer is C;
both statements together are sufficient.

192. If y is greater than 110 percent of x, is y greater than 75 ?

(1) $x > 75$

(2) $y - x = 10$

Arithmetic; Algebra Percents; Inequalities

(1) It is given that $y > (110\%)\ x = 1.1x$ and $x > 75$.

Therefore, $y > (1.1)(75)$, and so y is greater than 75; SUFFICIENT.

(2) Although it is given that $y - x = 10$, more information is needed to determine if y is greater than 75. For example, if $x = 80$ and $y = 90$, then y is greater than 110 percent of x, $y - x = 10$, and y is greater than 75. However, if $x = 20$ and $y = 30$, then y is greater than 110 percent of x, $y - x = 10$, and y is not greater than 75; NOT sufficient.

The correct answer is A;
statement 1 alone is sufficient.

193. How much did credit-card fraud cost United States banks in year X to the nearest \$10 million?

(1) In year X, counterfeit cards and telephone and mail-order fraud accounted for 39 percent of the total amount that card fraud cost the banks.

(2) In year X, stolen cards accounted for \$158.4 million, or 16 percent, of the total amount that credit-card fraud cost the banks.

Arithmetic Percents

(1) It is given that certain parts of the total fraud cost have a total that is 39% of the total fraud cost, but since no actual dollar amounts are specified, it is not possible to estimate the total fraud cost to the nearest \$10 million; NOT sufficient.

(2) Given that \$158.4 million represents 16% of the total fraud cost, it follows that the total fraud cost equals \$158.4 million divided by 0.16; SUFFICIENT.

The correct answer is B;
statement 2 alone is sufficient.

194. What is the average (arithmetic mean) of x and y ?

(1) The average of x and $2y$ is 10.

(2) The average of $2x$ and $7y$ is 32.

Algebra Statistics

The average of x and y is $\frac{x+y}{2}$, which can be determined if and only if the value of $x + y$ can be determined.

(1) It is given that the average of x and $2y$ is 10. Therefore, $\frac{x+2y}{2} = 10$, or $x + 2y = 20$. Because the value of $x + y$ is desired, rewrite the last equation as $(x + y) + y = 20$, or $x + y = 20 - y$. This shows that the value of $x + y$ can vary. For example, if $x = 20$ and $y = 0$, then $x + 2y = 20$ and $x + y = 20$. However, if $x = 18$ and $y = 1$, then $x + 2y = 20$ and $x + y = 19$; NOT sufficient.

(2) It is given that the average of $2x$ and $7y$ is 32. Therefore, $\frac{2x+7y}{2}=32$, or $2x + 7y = 64$. Because the value of $x + y$ is desired, rewrite the last equation as $2(x + y) + 5y = 64$, or $x+y=\frac{64-5y}{2}$. This shows that the value of $x + y$ can vary. For example, if $x = 32$ and $y = 0$, then $2x + 7y = 64$ and $x + y = 32$. However, if $x = 4$ and $y = 8$, then $2x + 7y = 64$ and $x + y = 12$; NOT sufficient.

Given (1) and (2), it follows that $x + 2y = 20$ and $2x + 7y = 64$. These two equations can be solved simultaneously to obtain the individual values of x and y, which can then be used to determine the average of x and y. From $x + 2y = 20$ it follows that $x = 20 - 2y$. Substituting $20 - 2y$ for x in $2x + 7y = 64$ gives $2(20 - 2y) + 7y = 64$, or $40 - 4y + 7y = 64$, or $3y = 24$, or $y = 8$. Thus, using $x = 20 - 2y$, the value of x is $20 - 2(8) = 4$.

Alternatively, it can be seen that unique values for x and y are determined from (1) and (2) by the fact that the equations $x + 2y = 20$ and $2x + 7y = 64$ represent two nonparallel lines in the standard (x,y) coordinate plane, which have a unique point in common.

The correct answer is C;
both statements together are sufficient.

195. What is the value of $\frac{r}{2}+\frac{s}{2}$?

(1) $\frac{r+s}{2}=5$

(2) $r + s = 10$

Arithmetic Operations with rational numbers

Since $\frac{r}{2}+\frac{s}{2}=\frac{r+s}{2}=\frac{1}{2}(r+s)$, the value of $\frac{r}{2}+\frac{s}{2}$ can be determined exactly when either the value of $\frac{r+s}{2}$ can be determined or the value of $r + s$ can be determined.

(1) It is given that $\frac{r+s}{2}=5$. Therefore, $\frac{r}{2}+\frac{s}{2}=5$; SUFFICIENT.

(2) It is given that $r + s = 10$. Therefore, $\frac{r}{2}+\frac{s}{2}=\frac{1}{2}(r+s)=\frac{1}{2}(10)=5$; SUFFICIENT.

The correct answer is D;
each statement alone is sufficient.

196. Is the positive integer n odd?

(1) $n^2 + (n + 1)^2 + (n + 2)^2$ is even.

(2) $n^2 - (n + 1)^2 - (n + 2)^2$ is even.

Arithmetic Properties of numbers

The positive integer n is either odd or even. Determine if it is odd.

(1) This indicates that the sum of the squares of three consecutive integers, n^2, $(n + 1)^2$, and $(n + 2)^2$, is even. If n is even, then $n + 1$ is odd and $n + 2$ is even. It follows that n^2 is even, $(n + 1)^2$ is odd, and $(n + 2)^2$ is even and, therefore, that $n^2 + (n + 1)^2 + (n + 2)^2$ is odd. But, this contradicts the given information, and so, n must be odd; SUFFICIENT.

(2) This indicates that $n^2 - (n + 1)^2 - (n + 2)^2$ is even. Adding the even number represented by $2(n + 1)^2 + 2(n +2)^2$ to the even number represented by $n^2 - (n + 1)^2 - (n + 2)^2$ gives the even number represented by $n^2 + (n + 1)^2 + (n +2)^2$. This is Statement (1); SUFFICIENT.

The correct answer is D;
each statement alone is sufficient.

197. For all x, the expression x^* is defined to be $ax + a$, where a is a constant. What is the value of 2^* ?

(1) $3^* = 2$

(2) $5^* = 3$

Algebra Linear equations

Determine the value of $2^* = (a)(2) + a = 3a$, or equivalently, determine the value of a.

(1) Given that $3^* = 2$, it follows that $(a)(3) + a = 2$, or $4a = 2$, or $a = \frac{1}{2}$; SUFFICIENT.

(2) Given that $5^* = 3$, it follows that $(a)(5) + a = 3$, or $6a = 3$, or $a = \frac{1}{2}$; SUFFICIENT.

The correct answer is D; each statement alone is sufficient.

198. Is $k + m < 0$?

(1) $k < 0$

(2) $km > 0$

Arithmetic Properties of numbers

(1) Given that k is negative, it is not possible to determine whether $k + m$ is negative. For example, if $k = -2$ and $m = 1$, then $k + m$ is negative. However, if $k = -2$ and $m = 3$, then $k + m$ is not negative; NOT sufficient.

(2) Given that km is positive, it is not possible to determine whether $k + m$ is negative. For example, if $k = -2$ and $m = -1$, then km is positive and $k + m$ is negative. However, if $k = 2$ and $m = 1$, then km is positive and $k + m$ is not negative; NOT sufficient.

Taking (1) and (2) together, k is negative and km is positive, it follows that m is negative. Therefore, both k and m are negative, and hence $k + m$ is negative.

The correct answer is C; both statements together are sufficient.

199. A retailer purchased a television set for x percent less than its list price, and then sold it for y percent less than its list price. What was the list price of the television set?

(1) $x = 15$

(2) $x - y = 5$

Arithmetic Percents

(1) This provides information only about the value of x. The list price cannot be determined using x because no dollar value for the purchase price is given; NOT sufficient.

(2) This provides information about the relationship between x and y but does not provide dollar values for either of these variables; NOT sufficient.

The list price cannot be determined without a dollar value for either the retailer's purchase price or the retailer's selling price. Even though the values for x and y are given or can be determined, taking (1) and (2) together provides no dollar value for either.

The correct answer is E; both statements together are still not sufficient.

200. If x and y are positive, is $xy > x + y$?

(1) $x < y$

(2) $2 < x$

Algebra Inequalities

Determine if $xy > x + y$, where x and y are positive.

(1) This indicates that $x < y$, but does not give enough information to determine if $xy > x + y$. For example, if $x = 3$ and $y = 4$, then $xy = (3)(4) = 12 > 7 = 3 + 4 = x + y$. But if $x = \frac{1}{2}$ and $y = 4$, then $xy = \left(\frac{1}{2}\right)(4) = 2 < 4\frac{1}{2} = \frac{1}{2} + 4 = x + y$; NOT sufficient.

(2) This indicates that $x > 2$, but does not give enough information to determine if $xy > x + y$. For example, if $x = 3$ and $y = 4$, then $xy = (3)(4) = 12 > 7 = 3 + 4 = x + y$. But if $x = 4$ and $y = \frac{1}{2}$, then $xy = (4)\left(\frac{1}{2}\right) = 2 < 4\frac{1}{2} = 4 + \frac{1}{2} = x + y$; NOT sufficient.

Taking (1) and (2) together gives $2 < x < y$. Adding y to all members of the inequality gives $2 + y < x + y < 2y$. Multiplying each member of $2 < x < y$ by y, which is positive, gives

$2y < xy < y^2$. Combining these inequalities gives $2 + y < x + y < 2y < xy$. It follows that $x + y < xy$ or $xy > x + y$.

Alternatively,

$x > 2$	from (2)
$x - 1 > 2 - 1$	subtract 1 from both sides
$\frac{1}{x-1} < \frac{1}{2-1}$	take reciprocals
$\frac{x}{x-1} < \frac{x}{2-1}$	multiply both sides by x, which is positive by (2)
$\frac{x}{x-1} < x$	since $2 - 1 = 1$
$\frac{x}{x-1} < y$	transitive property since $x < y$ by (1)
$x < y(x - 1)$	multiply both sides by $(x - 1)$, which is positive by (2)
$x < xy - y$	distributive property
$x + y < xy$	add y to both sides

The correct answer is C;
both statements together are sufficient.

201. What is the ratio of c to d?

(1) The ratio of $3c$ to $3d$ is 3 to 4.

(2) The ratio of $c + 3$ to $d + 3$ is 4 to 5.

Arithmetic Ratio and proportion

Determine the value of $\frac{c}{d}$.

(1) Given that $\frac{3c}{3d} = \frac{3}{4}$, it follows that $\frac{3c}{3d} = \frac{c}{d} = \frac{3}{4}$; SUFFICIENT.

(2) Given that $\frac{c+3}{d+3} = \frac{4}{5}$, then it is not possible to determine the value of $\frac{c}{d}$. For example, if $c = 1$ and $d = 2$, then $\frac{c+3}{d+3} = \frac{4}{5}$ and $\frac{c}{d} = \frac{1}{2}$. However, if $c = 5$ and $d = 7$, then $\frac{c+3}{d+3} = \frac{8}{10} = \frac{4}{5}$ and $\frac{c}{d} = \frac{5}{7}$; NOT sufficient.

The correct answer is A;
statement (1) alone is sufficient.

202. A certain dealership has a number of cars to be sold by its salespeople. How many cars are to be sold?

(1) If each of the salespeople sells 4 of the cars, 23 cars will remain unsold.

(2) If each of the salespeople sells 6 of the cars, 5 cars will remain unsold.

Algebra Simultaneous equations

Let T be the total number of cars to be sold and S be the number of salespeople. Determine the value of T.

(1) Given that $T = 4S + 23$, it follows that the positive integer value of T can vary, since the positive integer value of S cannot be determined; NOT sufficient.

(2) Given that $T = 6S + 5$, it follows that the positive integer value of T can vary, since the positive integer value of S cannot be determined; NOT sufficient.

(1) and (2) together give a system of two equations in two unknowns. Equating the two expressions for T gives $4S + 23 = 6S + 5$, or $18 = 2S$, or $S = 9$. From this the value of T can be determined by $4(9) + 23$ or $6(9) + 5$.

The correct answer is C;
both statements together are sufficient.

203. A candle company determines that, for a certain specialty candle, the supply function is $p = m_1x + b_1$ and the demand function is $p = m_2x + b_2$, where p is the price of each candle, x is the number of candles supplied or demanded, and m_1, m_2, b_1, and b_2 are constants. At what value of x do the graphs of the supply function and demand function intersect?

(1) $m_1 = -m_2 = 0.005$

(2) $b_2 - b_1 = 6$

Algebra First-degree equations

The graphs will intersect at the value of x such that $m_1x + b_1 = m_2x + b_2$ or $(m_1 - m_2)x = b_2 - b_1$.

(1) This indicates that $m_1 = -m_2 = 0.005$. It follows that $m_1 - m_2 = 0.01$, and so $0.01x = b_2 - b_1$ or $x = 100(b_2 - b_1)$, which can vary as the values of b_2 and b_1 vary; NOT sufficient.

(2) This indicates that $b_2 - b_1 = 6$. It follows that $(m_1 - m_2)x = 6$. This implies that $m_1 \neq m_2$, and so $x = \frac{b_2 - b_1}{m_1 - m_2} = \frac{6}{m_1 - m_2}$, which can vary as the values of m_1 and m_2 vary; NOT sufficient.

Taking (1) and (2) together, $m_1 - m_2 = 0.01$ and $b_2 - b_1 = 6$ and so the value of x is $\frac{6}{0.01} = 600$.

The correct answer is C; both statements together are sufficient.

204. Some computers at a certain company are Brand X and the rest are Brand Y. If the ratio of the number of Brand Y computers to the number of Brand X computers at the company is 5 to 6, how many of the computers are Brand Y ?

(1) There are 80 more Brand X computers than Brand Y computers at the company.

(2) There is a total of 880 computers at the company.

Algebra Simultaneous equations

Let x and y be the numbers of Brand X computers and Brand Y computers, respectively, at the company. Then $\frac{y}{x} = \frac{5}{6}$, or after cross multiplying, $6y = 5x$. Determine the value of y.

(1) Given that $x = 80 + y$, it follows that $5x = 5(80 + y) = 400 + 5y$. Substituting $6y$ for $5x$ on the left side of the last equation gives $6y = 400 + 5y$, or $y = 400$. Alternatively, it can be seen that unique values for x and y are determined by the fact that $6y = 5x$ and $x = 80 + y$ represent the equations of two nonparallel lines in the standard (x,y) coordinate plane, which have a unique point in common; SUFFICIENT.

(2) Given that $x + y = 880$, it follows that $5x + 5y = 5(880)$. Substituting $6y$ for $5x$ on the left side of the last equation gives $6y + 5y = 5(880)$, or $11y = 5(880)$, or $y = 5(80) = 400$. Alternatively, it can be seen that unique values for x and y are determined by the fact that $6y = 5x$ and $x + y = 880$ represent the equations of two nonparallel lines in the standard (x,y) coordinate plane, which have a unique point in common; SUFFICIENT.

The correct answer is D; each statement alone is sufficient.

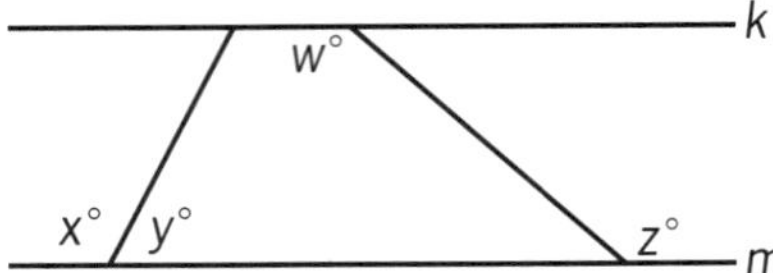

205. In the figure shown, lines k and m are parallel to each other. Is x = z ?

(1) x = w

(2) y = 180 – w

Geometry Angles

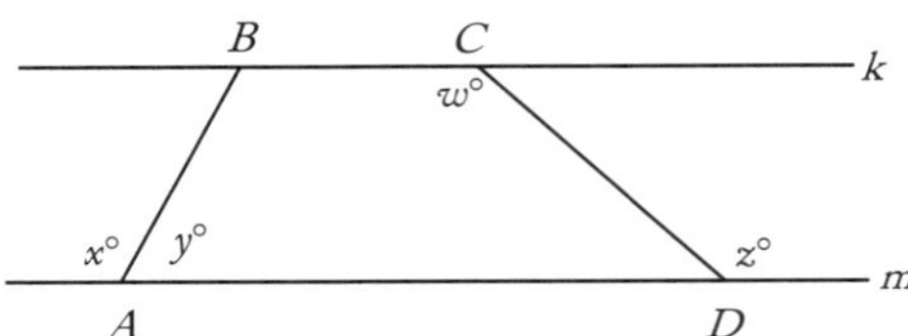

Since lines k and m are parallel, it follows from properties of parallel lines that in the diagram above x is the degree measure of $\angle ABC$ in quadrilateral $ABCD$. Therefore, because $y = 180 - x$, the four interior angles of quadrilateral $ABCD$ have degree measures $(180 - x)$, x, w, and $(180 - z)$.

(1) Given that $x = w$, then because the sum of the degree measures of the angles of the quadrilateral $ABCD$ is 360, it follows that $(180 - x) + x + x + (180 - z) = 360$, or $x - z = 0$, or $x = z$; SUFFICIENT.

(2) Given that $y = 180 - w$, then because $y = 180 - x$, it follows that $180 - w = 180 - x$, or $x = w$. However, it is shown in (1) that $x = w$ is sufficient; SUFFICIENT.

The correct answer is D; each statement alone is sufficient.

206. When the wind speed is 9 miles per hour, the wind-chill factor w is given by

$$w = -17.366 + 1.19t,$$

where t is the temperature in degrees Fahrenheit. If at noon yesterday the wind speed was 9 miles per hour, was the wind-chill factor greater than 0 ?

(1) The temperature at noon yesterday was greater than 10 degrees Fahrenheit.

(2) The temperature at noon yesterday was less than 20 degrees Fahrenheit.

Algebra Applied problems

Determine whether $-17.366 + 1.19t$ is greater than 0.

(1) Given that $t > 10$, it follows that $-17.366 + 1.19t > -17.366 + 1.19(10)$, or $-17.366 + 1.19t > -5.466$. However, it is not possible to determine whether $-17.366 + 1.19t$ is greater than 0. For example, if $t = 19$, then $-17.366 + 1.19t = 5.244$ is greater than 0. However, if $t = 11$, then $-17.366 + 1.19t = -4.276$, which is not greater than 0; NOT sufficient.

(2) Given that $t < 20$, the same examples used in (1) show that it is not possible to determine whether $-17.366 + 1.19t$ is greater than 0; NOT sufficient.

Taking (1) and (2) together is of no more help than either (1) or (2) taken separately because the same examples were used in both (1) and (2).

The correct answer is E;
both statements together are still not sufficient.

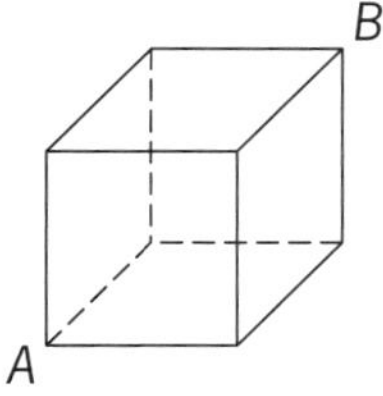

207. What is the volume of the cube above?

(1) The surface area of the cube is 600 square inches.

(2) The length of diagonal AB is $10\sqrt{3}$ inches.

Geometry Volume

This problem can be solved by determining the side length, s, of the cube.

(1) This indicates that $6s^2 = 600$, from which it follows that $s^2 = 100$ and $s = 10$; SUFFICIENT.

(2) To determine diagonal AB, first determine diagonal AN by applying the Pythagorean theorem to ΔAMN: $AN = \sqrt{s^2 + s^2} = \sqrt{2s^2}$. Now determine AB by applying the Pythagorean theorem to ΔANB: $AB = \sqrt{(AN)^2 + (NB)^2} = \sqrt{2s^2 + s^2} = \sqrt{3s^2} = s\sqrt{3}$. It is given that $AB = 10\sqrt{3}$, and so $s = 10$; SUFFICIENT.

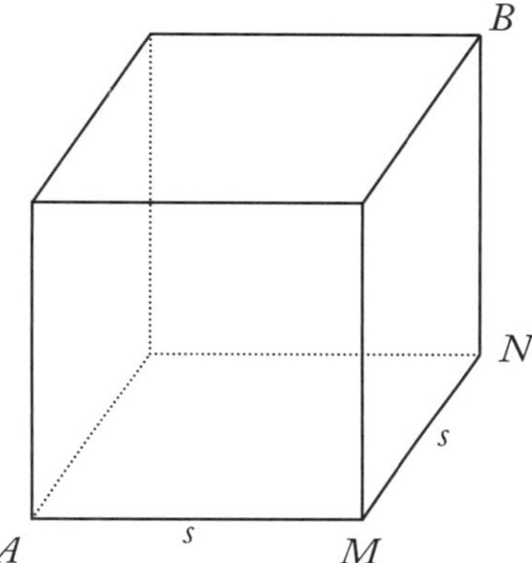

The correct answer is D;
each statement alone is sufficient.

208. Of the 230 single-family homes built in City X last year, how many were occupied at the end of the year?

(1) Of all single-family homes in City X, 90 percent were occupied at the end of last year.

(2) A total of 7,200 single-family homes in City X were occupied at the end of last year.

Arithmetic Percents

(1) The percentage of the occupied single-family homes that were *built* last year is not given, and so the number occupied cannot be found; NOT sufficient.

(2) Again, there is no information about the occupancy of the single-family homes that were *built* last year; NOT sufficient.

Together (1) and (2) yield only the total number of the single-family homes that were occupied. Neither statement offers the needed information as to how many of the single-family homes *built* last year were occupied at the end of last year.

The correct answer is E;
both statements together are still not sufficient.

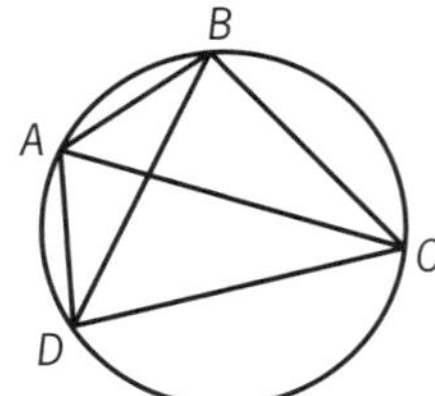

209. In the figure shown, quadrilateral *ABCD* is inscribed in a circle of radius 5. What is the perimeter of quadrilateral *ABCD* ?

(1) The length of *AB* is 6 and the length of *CD* is 8.

(2) *AC* is a diameter of the circle.

Geometry Quadrilaterals; Perimeter; Pythagorean theorem

Determine the perimeter of quadrilateral *ABCD*, which is given by $AB + BC + CD + DA$.

(1) This indicates that $AB = 6$ and $CD = 8$, but gives no information about *BC* or *DA*.

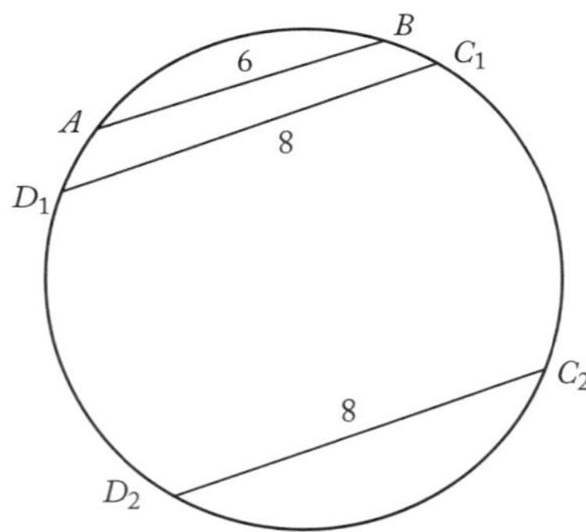

For example, the perimeter of ABC_1D_1 is clearly different than the perimeter of ABC_2D_2 and $\overline{CD}$ could be positioned where $\overline{C_1D_1}$ is on the diagram or it could be positioned where $\overline{C_2D_2}$ is on the diagram; NOT sufficient.

(2) This indicates that $AC = 2(5) = 10$ since *AC* is a diameter of the circle and the radius of the circle is 5. It also indicates that $\angle ABC$ and $\angle ADC$ are right angles since each is inscribed in a semicircle. However, there is no information about *AB*, *BC*, *CD*, or *DA*. For example, if $AB = CD = 6$, then $BC = DA = \sqrt{10^2 - 6^2} = \sqrt{64} = 8$ and the perimeter of *ABCD* is $2(6 + 8) = 28$. However, if $AB = DA = 2$, then $BC = CD = \sqrt{10^2 - 2^2} = \sqrt{96}$ and the perimeter of $ABCD = 2(2 + \sqrt{96})$; NOT sufficient.

Taking (1) and (2) together, ΔABC is a right triangle with $AC = 10$ and $AB = 6$. It follows from the Pythagorean theorem that $BC = \sqrt{10^2 - 6^2} = \sqrt{64} = 8$. Likewise, ΔADC is a right triangle with $AC = 10$ and $CD = 8$. It follows from the Pythagorean theorem that $DA = \sqrt{10^2 - 8^2} = \sqrt{36} = 6$. Thus, the perimeter of quadrilateral *ABCD* can be determined.

The correct answer is C;
both statements together are sufficient.

210. If *x* is a positive integer, what is the value of *x* ?

(1) $x^2 = \sqrt{x}$

(2) $\frac{n}{x} = n$ and $n \neq 0$.

Algebra Operations with radicals

(1) It is given that *x* is a positive integer. Then,

$x^2 = \sqrt{x}$	given
$x^4 = x$	square both sides
$x^4 - x = 0$	subtract *x* from both sides
$x(x-1)(x^2 + x + 1) = 0$	factor left side

Thus, the positive integer value of *x* being sought will be a solution of this equation. One solution of this equation is $x = 0$, which is not a positive integer. Another solution is $x = 1$, which is a positive integer. Also, $x^2 + x + 1$ is a positive integer for all positive integer values of *x*, and so $x^2 + x + 1 = 0$ has no positive integer solutions. Thus, the only possible positive integer value of *x* is 1; SUFFICIENT.

(2) It is given that $n \neq 0$. Then,

$$\begin{aligned} \frac{n}{x} &= n && \text{given} \\ n &= nx && \text{multiply both sides by } x \\ 1 &= x && \text{divide both sides by } n\text{, where } n \neq 0 \end{aligned}$$

Thus, $x = 1$; SUFFICIENT.

The correct answer is D;
each statement alone is sufficient.

211. Is the median of the five numbers a, b, c, d, and e equal to d?

(1) $a < c < e$

(2) $b < d < c$

Arithmetic Statistics

Determine if the median of the five numbers, a, b, c, d, and e, is equal to d.

(1) This indicates that $a < c < e$, but does not indicate a relationship of b and d with a, c, and e. For example, if $a = 5$, $b = 1$, $c = 10$, $d = 7$, and $e = 15$, then $a < c < e$, and d is the median. However, if $a = 5$, $b = 1$, $c = 10$, $d = 2$, and $e = 15$, then $a < c < e$, and a, not d, is the median; NOT sufficient.

(2) This indicates that $b < d < c$, but does not indicate a relationship of a and e with b, d, and c. For example, if $a = 5$, $b = 1$, $c = 10$, $d = 7$, and $e = 15$, then $b < d < c$, and d is the median. However, if $a = 5$, $b = 1$, $c = 10$, $d = 2$, and $e = 15$, then $b < d < c$, and a, not d, is the median; NOT sufficient.

Taking (1) and (2) together is of no more help than either (1) or (2) taken separately since the same examples used to show that (1) is not sufficient also show that (2) is not sufficient.

The correct answer is E;
both statements together are still not sufficient.

212. During a certain bicycle ride, was Sherry's average speed faster than 24 kilometers per hour? (1 kilometer = 1,000 meters)

(1) Sherry's average speed during the bicycle ride was faster than 7 meters per second.

(2) Sherry's average speed during the bicycle ride was slower than 8 meters per second.

Arithmetic Applied problems

This problem can be solved by converting 24 kilometers per hour into meters per second. First, 24 kilometers is equivalent to 24,000 meters and 1 hour is equivalent to 3,600 seconds. Then, traveling 24 kilometers in 1 hour is equivalent to traveling 24,000 meters in 3,600 seconds, or $\frac{24{,}000}{3{,}600} = 6\frac{2}{3}$ meters per second.

(1) This indicates that Sherry's average speed was faster than 7 meters per second, which is faster than $6\frac{2}{3}$ meters per second and, therefore, faster than 24 kilometers per hour; SUFFICIENT.

(2) This indicates that Sherry's average speed was slower than 8 meters per second. Her average speed could have been 7 meters per second (since $7 < 8$), in which case her average speed was faster than $6\frac{2}{3}$ meters per second and, therefore, faster than 24 kilometers per hour. Or her average speed could have been 5 meters per second (since $5 < 8$), in which case her average speed was not faster than $6\frac{2}{3}$ meters per second and, therefore, not faster than 24 kilometers per hour; NOT sufficient.

The correct answer is A;
statement 1 alone is sufficient.

213. If x and y are integers, what is the value of x?

(1) $xy = 1$

(2) $x \neq -1$

Arithmetic Properties of integers

Given that x and y are integers, determine the value of x.

(1) If $x = y = -1$, then $xy = 1$, and if $x = y = 1$, then $xy = 1$; NOT sufficient.

(2) Given that $x \neq -1$, the value of x could be any other integer; NOT sufficient.

Taking (1) and (2) together, since the two possibilities for the value of x are $x = -1$ or $x = 1$ by (1), and $x \neq -1$ by (2), then $x = 1$.

The correct answer is C;
both statements together are sufficient.

214. If p, s, and t are positive, is $|ps - pt| > p(s - t)$?

(1) $p < s$

(2) $s < t$

Algebra Absolute value

Since p is positive, it follows that $|p(s-t)| = |p||s-t| = p|s-t|$. Therefore, the task is to determine if $|s-t| > s-t$. Since $|s-t| = s-t$ if and only if $s - t \geq 0$, it follows that $|s-t| > s-t$ if and only if $s - t < 0$.

(1) This indicates that $p < s$ but does not provide information about the relationship between s and t. For example, if $p = 5$, $s = 10$, and $t = 15$, then $p < s$ and $s < t$, but if $p = 5$, $s = 10$, and $t = 3$, then $p < s$ and $s > t$; NOT sufficient.

(2) This indicates that $s < t$, or equivalently, $s - t < 0$; SUFFICIENT.

The correct answer is B; statement 2 alone is sufficient.

215. Is $x > y$?

(1) $x + y > x - y$

(2) $3x > 2y$

Algebra Inequalities

(1) Given that $x + y > x - y$, it follows that $y > -y$, or $2y > 0$, or $y > 0$. However, nothing is known about the value of x. If $x = 2$ and $y = 1$, then $x + y > x - y$ and the answer to the question is yes. However, if $x = 1$ and $y = 1$, then $x + y > x - y$ and the answer to the question is no; NOT sufficient.

(2) Given that $3x > 2y$, then $x = 2$ and $y = 1$ is possible and the answer to the question is yes. However, if $3x > 2y$, then $x = 1$ and $y = 1$ is also possible and the answer to the question is no; NOT sufficient.

Taking (1) and (2) together is of no more help than either (1) or (2) taken separately because the same examples used to show that (1) is not sufficient also show that (2) is not sufficient.

The correct answer is E; both statements together are still not sufficient.

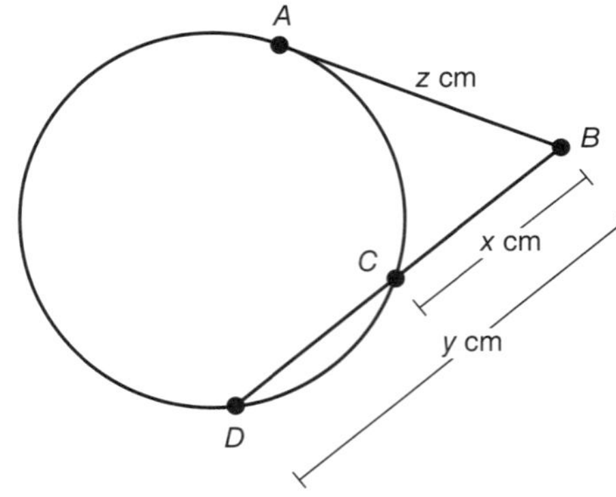

216. In the figure above, $\overline{AB}$, which has length z cm, is tangent to the circle at point A, and $\overline{BD}$, which has length y cm, intersects the circle at point C. If $BC = x$ cm and $z = \sqrt{xy}$, what is the value of x ?

(1) $CD = x$ cm

(2) $z = 5\sqrt{2}$

Geometry Circles

(1) Given that $CD = x$ cm, it is not possible to determine the value of x because all the given information continues to hold when all the parts of the figure increase in length by any given nonzero factor; NOT sufficient.

(2) Given that $z = 5\sqrt{2}$, the value of x will vary when the radius of the circle varies and $\overline{CD}$ is a diameter and thus passes through the center of the circle. To see this, let r be the radius, in centimeters, of the circle and let O be the center of the circle, as shown in the figure below. Then, because $\overline{CD}$ is a diameter, it follows that $CD = 2r$ and $y = x + CD = x + 2r$. Also, ΔOAB is a right triangle and the Pythagorean theorem gives $(OA)^2 + (AB)^2 = (OB)^2$, or $r^2 + (5\sqrt{2})^2 = (x + r)^2$, or $r^2 + 50 = x^2 + 2xr + r^2$, or $x(x + 2r) = 50$, which implies that $xy = z^2$ and $z = \sqrt{xy}$, since $y = x + 2r$ and $z = 5\sqrt{2}$. Therefore, if $z = 5\sqrt{2}$ and $\overline{CD}$ is a diameter, then $z = \sqrt{xy}$ holds, and the value of x can vary.

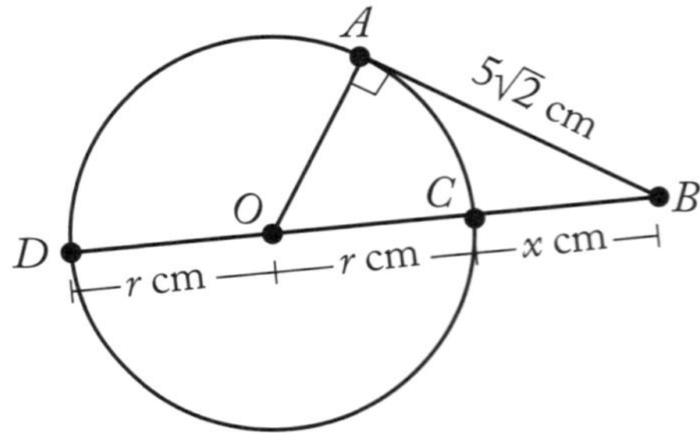

This can be seen by considering the equation $x(x + 2r) = 50$, or $x = \frac{50}{x+2r}$. If the value of r changes slightly to a new value R, then the value of x must also change. Otherwise, there would be two different numbers, namely $\frac{50}{x+2r}$ and $\frac{50}{x+2R}$, equal to each other, which is a contradiction; NOT sufficient.

Taking (1) and (2) together, $y = x + CD = x + x = 2x$ and $z = 5\sqrt{2}$, so $z = \sqrt{xy}$ becomes $5\sqrt{2} = \sqrt{x(2x)}$, or $(5\sqrt{2})^2 = (\sqrt{x(2x)})^2$, or $50 = x(2x)$, or $x^2 = 25$, or $x = 5$.

The correct answer is C;
both statements together are sufficient.

217. The total cost of an office dinner was shared equally by k of the n employees who attended the dinner. What was the total cost of the dinner?

(1) Each of the k employees who shared the cost of the dinner paid \$19.

(2) If the total cost of the dinner had been shared equally by $k + 1$ of the n employees who attended the dinner, each of the $k + 1$ employees would have paid \$18.

Algebra Simultaneous equations

(1) Given that each of the k employees paid \$19, it follows that the total cost of the dinner, in dollars, is $19k$. However, since k cannot be determined, the value of $19k$ cannot be determined; NOT sufficient.

(2) Given that each of $(k + 1)$ employees would have paid \$18, it follows that the total cost of the dinner, in dollars, is $18(k + 1)$. However, since k cannot be determined, the value of $19k$ cannot be determined; NOT sufficient.

Given (1) and (2) together, it follows that $19k = 18(k + 1)$ or $19k = 18k + 18$, or $k = 18$.

Therefore, the total cost of the dinner is $(\$19)k = (\$19)(18)$.

The correct answer is C;
both statements together are sufficient.

218. What is the value of x ?

(1) $x + 1 = 2 - 3x$

(2) $\frac{1}{2x} = 2$

Algebra First- and second-degree equations

(1) Transposing terms gives the equivalent equation $4x = 1$, or $x = \frac{1}{4}$; SUFFICIENT.

(2) Transposing terms gives the equivalent equation $4x = 1$, or $x = \frac{1}{4}$; SUFFICIENT.

The correct answer is D;
each statement alone is sufficient.

219. Is the integer n a prime number?

(1) $24 \le n \le 28$

(2) n is not divisible by 2 or 3.

Arithmetic Properties of numbers

Determine if the integer n is a prime number.

(1) This indicates that n is between 24 and 28, inclusive. It follows that the value of n can be 24, 25, 26, 27, or 28. Each of these is NOT a prime number. Thus, it can be determined that n is NOT a prime number; SUFFICIENT.

(2) This indicates that n is not divisible by 2 or 3. If $n = 7$, then n is not divisible by 2 or 3 and is a prime number. However, if $n = 25$, then n is not divisible by 2 or 3 and is a not prime number since 25 has a factor, namely 5, other than 1 and itself; NOT sufficient.

The correct answer is A;
statement 1 alone is sufficient.

220. What is the sum of the first four terms of sequence S ?

(1) After the first two terms of S, the value of each term of S is equal to the average (arithmetic mean) of the last two preceding terms.

(2) The average (arithmetic mean) of the first three terms of S is 10.

Algebra Statistics

(1) Given that after the first two terms, the value of each term is equal to the average of the last two preceding terms, then the first four terms of the sequence could be 8, 12, 10, and 11, which have a sum of 41. However, the first four terms of the sequence could also be 4, 16, 10, and 13, which have a sum of 43; NOT sufficient.

(2) Given that the average of the first three terms is 10, then the first four terms of the sequence could be 8, 12, 10, and 11, which have a sum of 41. However, the first four terms of the sequence could also be 4, 16, 10, and 13, which have a sum of 43; NOT sufficient.

Taking (1) and (2) together, it is still not possible to determine the sum of the first four terms of the sequence, since the two sequences that were used above in (1) were also used above in (2).

The correct answer is E;
both statements together are still not sufficient.

221. If x and y are positive integers, what is the remainder when $10^x + y$ is divided by 3 ?

(1) $x = 5$

(2) $y = 2$

Arithmetic Properties of numbers

(1) Given that $x = 5$, then $10^x + y = 100{,}000 + y$. More than one remainder is possible when $100{,}000 + y$ is divided by 3. For example, by long division, or by using the fact that $100{,}00 + y = 99{,}999 + (1 + y)$ $= 3(33{,}333) + (1 + y)$, the remainder is 2 when $y = 1$ and the remainder is 0 when $y = 2$; NOT sufficient.

(2) Given that $y = 2$, then $10^x + y = 10^x + 2$. Since the sum of the digits of $10^x + 2$ is 3, which is divisible by 3, it follows that $10^x + 2$ is divisible by 3, and hence has remainder 0 when divided by 3. This can also be seen by writing $10^x + 2$ as $(10^x - 1 + 1) + 2$ $= (10^x - 1) + 1 + 2 = 999 \ldots 99{,}999 + 3$ $= 3(333\ldots33{,}333 + 1)$, which is divisible by 3; SUFFICIENT.

The correct answer is B;
statement 2 alone is sufficient.

222. What was the amount of money donated to a certain charity?

(1) Of the amount donated, 40 percent came from corporate donations.

(2) Of the amount donated, \$1.5 million came from noncorporate donations.

Arithmetic Percents

The statements suggest considering the amount of money donated to be the total of the corporate donations and the noncorporate donations.

(1) From this, only the portion that represented corporate donations is known, with no means of determining the total amount donated; NOT sufficient.

(2) From this, only the dollar amount that represented noncorporate donations is known, with no means of determining the portion of the total donations that it represents; NOT sufficient.

Letting x represent the total dollar amount donated, it follows from (1) that the amount donated from corporate sources can be represented as $0.40x$. Combining the information from (1) and (2) yields the equation $0.40x + \$1{,}500{,}000 = x$, which can be solved to obtain exactly one solution for x.

The correct answer is C;
both statements together are sufficient.

223. In a certain order, the pretax price of each regular pencil was \$0.03, the pretax price of each deluxe pencil was \$0.05, and there were 50% more deluxe pencils than regular pencils. All taxes on the order are a fixed percent of the pretax prices. The sum of the total pretax price of the order and the tax on the order was \$44.10. What was the amount, in dollars, of the tax on the order?

(1) The tax on the order was 5% of the total pretax price of the order.

(2) The order contained exactly 400 regular pencils.

Arithmetic Percents

Let n be the number of regular pencils in the order and let r% be the tax rate on the order as a percent of the pretax price. Then the order contains $1.5n$ deluxe pencils, the total pretax price of the order is

$(\$0.03)n + (\$0.05)(1.5n) = \$0.105n$, and the sum of the total pretax price of the order and the tax on the order is $\left(1+\frac{r}{100}\right)(\$0.105n)$. Given that $\left(1+\frac{r}{100}\right)(\$0.105n) = \$44.10$, what is the value of $\left(\frac{r}{100}\right)(\$0.105n)$?

(1) Given that $r = 5$, then $\left(1+\frac{r}{100}\right)(\$0.105n) = \$44.10$ becomes $(1.05)(0.105n) = 44.10$, which is a first-degree equation that can be solved for n. Since the value of r is known and the value of n can be determined, it follows that the value of $\left(\frac{r}{100}\right)(\$0.105n)$ can be determined; SUFFICIENT.

(2) Given that $n = 400$, then $\left(1+\frac{r}{100}\right)(\$0.105n) = \$44.10$ becomes $\left(1+\frac{r}{100}\right)(0.105)(400) = 44.10$, which is a first-degree equation that can be solved for r. Since the value of r can be determined and the value of n is known, it follows that the value of $\left(\frac{r}{100}\right)(\$0.105n)$ can be determined; SUFFICIENT.

The correct answer is D;
each statement alone is sufficient.

224. If m is an integer greater than 1, is m an even integer?

(1) 32 is a factor of m.

(2) m is a factor of 32.

Arithmetic Properties of numbers

(1) Given that 32 is a factor of m, then each of the factors of 32, including 2, is a factor of m. Since 2 is a factor of m, it follows that m is an even integer; SUFFICIENT.

(2) Given that m is a factor of 32 and m is greater than 1, it follows that $m = 2, 4, 8, 16$, or 32. Since each of these is an even integer, m must be an even integer; SUFFICIENT.

The correct answer is D;
each statement alone is sufficient.

225. If the set S consists of five consecutive positive integers, what is the sum of these five integers?

(1) The integer 11 is in S, but 10 is not in S.

(2) The sum of the even integers in S is 26.

Arithmetic Sequences

(1) This indicates that the least integer in S is 11 since S consists of consecutive integers and 11 is in S, but 10 is not in S. Thus, the integers in S are 11, 12, 13, 14, and 15, and their sum can be determined; SUFFICIENT.

(2) This indicates that the sum of the even integers in S is 26. In a set of 5 consecutive integers, either two of the integers or three of the integers are even. If there are three even integers, then the first integer in S must be even. Also, since $\frac{26}{3} = 8\frac{2}{3}$, the three even integers must be around 8. The three even integers could be 6, 8, and 10, but are not because their sum is less than 26; or they could be 8, 10, and 12, but are not because their sum is greater than 26. Therefore, S cannot contain three even integers and must contain only two even integers. Those integers must be 12 and 14 since $12 + 14 = 26$. It follows that the integers in S are 11, 12, 13, 14, and 15, and their sum can be determined; SUFFICIENT.

Alternately, if n, $n + 1$, $n + 2$, $n + 3$, and $n + 4$ represent the five consecutive integers and three of them are even, then $n + (n + 2) + (n + 4) = 26$, or $3n = 20$, or $n = \frac{20}{3}$, which is not an integer. On the other hand, if two of the integers are even, then $(n + 1) + (n + 3) = 26$, or $2n = 22$, or $n = 11$. It follows that the integers are 11, 12, 13, 14, and 15, and their sum can be determined; SUFFICIENT.

The correct answer is D;
each statement alone is sufficient.

226. If $x > 0$, what is the value of x ?

(1) $x^3 - x = 0$
(2) $\sqrt[3]{x} - x = 0$

Algebra Factoring; Operations with radical expressions

(1) Given that $x^3 - x = 0$, factoring gives $x(x^2 - 1) = x(x - 1)(x + 1) = 0$. Hence, $x = 0$, $x = 1$, or $x = -1$. Since $x > 0$, the value of x cannot be 0 or -1, and so $x = 1$; SUFFICIENT.

(2) Given that $\sqrt[3]{x} - x = 0$, it follows that $\sqrt[3]{x} = x$, or $(\sqrt[3]{x})^3 = x^3$, or $x = x^3$. Therefore, $x^3 - x = 0$ and the discussion in (1) shows that the only positive value of x is $x = 1$; SUFFICIENT.

The correct answer is D;
each statement alone is sufficient.

227. Which of the positive numbers x or y is greater?

(1) $y = 2x$
(2) $2x + 5y = 12$

Algebra Order

(1) Given that x is positive and y is twice the value of x, it follows that y is the greater number. This can be seen algebraically by adding x to both sides of $x > 0$ to get $x + x > x$, or $2x > x$, or $y > x$; SUFFICIENT.

(2) Given that $2x + 5y = 12$, then it is possible that $x = 1$ and $y = 2$, and thus it is possible that y is greater than x. However, it is also possible that $x = 2$ and $y = \frac{8}{5}$, and thus it is possible that x is greater than y; NOT sufficient.

The correct answer is A;
statement 1 alone is sufficient.

228. A total of 20 amounts are entered on a spreadsheet that has 5 rows and 4 columns; each of the 20 positions in the spreadsheet contains one amount. The average (arithmetic mean) of the amounts in row i is R_i ($1 \le i \le 5$). The average of the amounts in column j is C_j ($1 \le j \le 4$). What is the average of all 20 amounts on the spreadsheet?

(1) $R_1 + R_2 + R_3 + R_4 + R_5 = 550$
(2) $C_1 + C_2 + C_3 + C_4 = 440$

Arithmetic Statistics

It is given that R_i represents the average of the amounts in row i. Since there are four amounts in each row, $4R_i$ represents the total of the amounts in row i. Likewise, it is given that C_j represents the average of the amounts in column j. Since there are five amounts in each column, $5C_j$ represents the total of the amounts in column j.

(1) It is given that $R_1 + R_2 + R_3 + R_4 + R_5 = 550$, and so $4(R_1 + R_2 + R_3 + R_4 + R_5) = 4R_1 + 4R_2 + 4R_3 + 4R_4 + 4R_5 = 4(550) = 2{,}200$. Therefore, 2,200 is the sum of all 20 amounts (4 amounts in each of 5 rows), and the average of all 20 amounts is $\frac{2{,}200}{20} = 110$; SUFFICIENT.

(2) It is given that $C_1 + C_2 + C_3 + C_4 = 440$, and so $5(C_1 + C_2 + C_3 + C_4) = 5C_1 + 5C_2 + 5C_3 + 5C_4 = 5(440) = 2{,}200$. Therefore, 2,200 is the sum of all 20 amounts (5 amounts in each of 4 columns), and the average of all 20 amounts is $\frac{2{,}200}{20} = 110$; SUFFICIENT.

The correct answer is D;
each statement alone is sufficient.

229. Was the range of the amounts of money that Company Y budgeted for its projects last year equal to the range of the amounts of money that it budgeted for its projects this year?

(1) Both last year and this year, Company Y budgeted money for 12 projects and the least amount of money that it budgeted for a project was $400.
(2) Both last year and this year, the average (arithmetic mean) amount of money that Company Y budgeted per project was $2,000.

Arithmetic Statistics

Let G_1 and L_1 represent the greatest and least amounts, respectively, of money that Company Y budgeted for its projects last year, and let G_2 and L_2 represent the greatest and least amounts, respectively, of money that Company Y budgeted for its projects this year. Determine if the range of the amounts of money Company Y budgeted for its projects last year is equal to the range of amounts budgeted for its projects this year; that is, determine if $G_1 - L_1 = G_2 - L_2$.

(1) This indicates that $L_1 = L_2 = \$400$, but does not give any information about G_1 or G_2; NOT sufficient.

(2) This indicates that the average amount Company Y budgeted for its projects both last year and this year was \$2,000 per project, but does not give any information about the least and greatest amounts that it budgeted for its projects either year; NOT sufficient.

Taking (1) and (2) together, it is known that $L_1 = L_2 = \$400$ and that the average amount Company Y budgeted for its projects both last year and this year was \$2,000 per project, but there is no information about G_1 or G_2. For example, if, for each year, Company Y budgeted \$400 for each of 2 projects and \$2,320 for each of the 10 others, then (1) and (2) are true and the range for each year was \$2,320 – \$400 = \$1,920. However, if, last year, Company Y budgeted \$400 for each of 2 projects and \$2,320 for each of the 10 others, and, this year, budgeted \$400 for each of 11 projects and \$19,600 for 1 project, then (1) and (2) are true, but the range for last year was \$1,920 and the range for this year was \$19,600 – \$400 = \$19,200.

The correct answer is E;
both statements together are still not sufficient.

230. If a, b, c, and d are numbers on the number line shown and if the tick marks are equally spaced, what is the value of a + c ?

(1) a + b = −8

(2) a + d = 0

Algebra Sequences

It is given that the distance between a and b is the same as the distance between b and c, which is the same as the distance between c and d. Letting q represent this distance, then $b = a + q$, $c = a + 2q$, and $d = a + 3q$. The value of $a + c$ can be determined if the value of $a + (a + 2q) = 2a + 2q$ can be determined.

(1) It is given that $a + b = -8$. Then, $a + (a + q) = 2a + q = -8$. From this, the value of $2a + 2q$ cannot be determined. For example, the values of a and q could be −5 and 2, respectively, or they could be −6 and 4, respectively; NOT sufficient.

(2) It is given that $a + d = 0$. Then, $a + (a + 3q) = 2a + 3q = 0$. From this, the value of $2a + 2q$ cannot be determined. For example, the values of a and q could be −3 and 2, respectively, or they could be −6 and 4, respectively; NOT sufficient.

Taking (1) and (2) together, adding the equations, $2a + q = -8$ and $2a + 3q = 0$ gives $4a + 4q = -8$ and so $2a + 2q = \frac{-8}{2} = -4$.

The correct answer is C;
both statements together are sufficient.

231. Is $xm < ym$?

(1) $x > y$

(2) $m < 0$

Algebra Inequalities

(1) Given that $x > y$, the inequality $xm < ym$ can be true (for example, if $m = -1$, then $xm < ym$ becomes $-x < -y$, or $x > y$, which is true by assumption) and it is possible that the inequality $xm < ym$ can be false (for example, if $m = 0$, then $xm < ym$ becomes $0 < 0$, which is false); NOT sufficient.

(2) Given that $m < 0$, the inequality $xm < ym$ can be true (for example, if $m = -1$, $x = 2$, and $y = 1$, then $xm < ym$ becomes $-2 < -1$, which is true) and it is possible that the inequality $xm < ym$ can be false (for example, if $m = -1$, $x = 1$, and $y = 2$, then $xm < ym$ becomes $-1 < -2$, which is false); NOT sufficient.

Taking (1) and (2) together, multiplying both sides of the inequality $x > y$ by m reverses the inequality sign (since $m < 0$), which gives $xm < ym$.

The correct answer is C;
both statements together are sufficient.

232. If $y = x^2 - 6x + 9$, what is the value of x ?

(1) $y = 0$

(2) $x + y = 3$

Algebra Second-degree equations

Given that $y = x^2 - 6x + 9 = (x - 3)^2$, what is the value of x ?

(1) Given that $y = 0$, it follows that $(x - 3)^2 = 0$, or $x = 3$; SUFFICIENT.

(2) Given that $x + y = 3$, or $y = 3 - x$, then $x = 3$ and $y = 0$ are possible, since $y = (x - 3)^2$ becomes $0 = (3 - 3)^2$, which is true, and $y = 3 - x$ becomes $0 = 3 - 3$, which is true. However, $x = 2$ and $y = 1$ are also possible, since $y = (x - 3)^2$ becomes $1 = (2 - 3)^2$, which is true, and $y = 3 - x$ becomes $1 = 3 - 2$, which is true; NOT sufficient.

Note: The values for x and y used in (2) above can be found by solving $(x - 3)^2 = 3 - x$, which can be rewritten as $x^2 - 6x + 9 = 3 - x$, or $x^2 - 5x + 6 = 0$, or $(x - 3)(x - 2) = 0$.

The correct answer is A;
statement 1 alone is sufficient.

233. If $rs \neq 0$, is $\frac{1}{r} + \frac{1}{s} = 4$?

(1) $r + s = 4rs$

(2) $r = s$

Algebra First- and second-degree equations

(1) Dividing each side of the equation $r + s = 4rs$ by rs gives $\frac{r+s}{rs} = \frac{4rs}{rs}$, or $\frac{r}{rs} + \frac{s}{rs} = \frac{4rs}{rs}$, or $\frac{1}{s} + \frac{1}{r} = 4$; SUFFICIENT.

(2) If $r = s = \frac{1}{2}$ then $\frac{1}{r} + \frac{1}{s} = 4$, but if $r = s = 1$, then $\frac{1}{s} + \frac{1}{r} = 2$; NOT sufficient.

The correct answer is A;
statement 1 alone is sufficient.

234. If x, y, and z are three integers, are they consecutive integers?

(1) $z - x = 2$

(2) $x < y < z$

Arithmetic Properties of numbers

(1) Given $z - x = 2$, it is possible to choose y so that x, y, and z are consecutive integers (for example, $x = 1$, $y = 2$, and $z = 3$) and it is possible to choose y so that x, y, and z are not consecutive integers (for example, $x = 1$, $y = 4$, and $z = 3$); NOT sufficient.

(2) Given that $x < y < z$, the three integers can be consecutive (for example, $x = 1$, $y = 2$, and $z = 3$) and the three integers can fail to be consecutive (for example, $x = 1$, $y = 3$, and $z = 4$); NOT sufficient.

Using (1) and (2) together, it follows that y is the unique integer between x and z and hence the three integers are consecutive.

The correct answer is C;
both statements together are sufficient.

235. A collection of 36 cards consists of 4 sets of 9 cards each. The 9 cards in each set are numbered 1 through 9. If one card has been removed from the collection, what is the number on that card?

(1) The units digit of the sum of the numbers on the remaining 35 cards is 6.

(2) The sum of the numbers on the remaining 35 cards is 176.

Arithmetic Properties of numbers

The sum $1 + 2 + \ldots + 9$ can be evaluated quickly by several methods. One method is to group the terms as $(1 + 9) + (2 + 8) + (3 + 7) + (4 + 6) + 5$, and therefore the sum is $(4)(10) + 5 = 45$. Thus, the sum of the numbers on all 36 cards is $(4)(45) = 180$.

(1) It is given that the units digit of the sum of the numbers on the remaining 35 cards is 6. Since the sum of the numbers on all 36 cards is 180, the sum of the numbers on the remaining 35 cards must be 179, 178, 177, …, 171, and of these values, only 176 has a units digit of 6. Therefore, the number on the card removed must be $180 - 176 = 4$; SUFFICIENT.

(2) It is given that the sum of the numbers on the remaining 35 cards is 176. Since the sum of the numbers on all 36 cards is 180, it follows that the number on the card removed must be $180 - 176 = 4$ SUFFICIENT.

The correct answer is D;
each statement alone is sufficient.

236. In the *xy*-plane, point (r,s) lies on a circle with center at the origin. What is the value of $r^2 + s^2$?

(1) The circle has radius 2.

(2) The point $\left(\sqrt{2},-\sqrt{2}\right)$ lies on the circle.

Geometry Simple coordinate geometry

Let R be the radius of the circle. A right triangle with legs of lengths $|r|$ and $|s|$ can be formed so that the line segment with endpoints (r,s) and $(0,0)$ is the hypotenuse. Since the length of the hypotenuse is R, the Pythagorean theorem for this right triangle gives $R^2 = r^2 + s^2$. Therefore, to determine the value of $r^2 + s^2$, it is sufficient to determine the value of R.

(1) It is given that $R = 2$; SUFFICIENT.

(2) It is given that $\left(\sqrt{2},-\sqrt{2}\right)$ lies on the circle. A right triangle with legs each of length $\sqrt{2}$ can be formed so that the line segment with endpoints $\left(\sqrt{2},-\sqrt{2}\right)$ and $(0,0)$ is the hypotenuse. Since the length of the hypotenuse is the radius of the circle, which is R, where $R^2 = r^2 + s^2$, the Pythagorean theorem for this right triangle gives $R^2 = \left(\sqrt{2}\right)^2 + \left(\sqrt{2}\right)^2 = 2 + 2 = 4$. Therefore, $r^2 + s^2 = 4$; SUFFICIENT.

The correct answer is D;
each statement alone is sufficient.

237. If r, s, and t are nonzero integers, is $r^5s^3t^4$ negative?

(1) rt is negative.

(2) s is negative.

Arithmetic Properties of numbers

Since $r^5s^3t^4 = (rt)^4rs^3$ and $(rt)^4$ is positive, $r^5s^3t^4$ will be negative if and only if rs^3 is negative, or if and only if r and s have opposite signs.

(1) It is given that rt is negative, but nothing can be determined about the sign of s. If the sign of s is the opposite of the sign of r, then $r^5s^3t^4 = (rt)^4rs^3$ will be negative. However, if the sign of s is the same as the sign of r, then $r^5s^3t^4 = (rt)^4rs^3$ will be positive; NOT sufficient.

(2) It is given that s is negative, but nothing can be determined about the sign of r. If r is positive, then $r^5s^3t^4 = (rt)^4rs^3$ will be negative. However, if r is negative, then $r^5s^3t^4 = (rt)^4rs^3$ will be positive; NOT sufficient.

Given (1) and (2), it is still not possible to determine whether r and s have opposite signs. For example, (1) and (2) hold if r is positive, s is negative, and t is negative, and in this case r and s have opposite signs. However, (1) and (2) hold if r is negative, s is negative, and t is positive, and in this case r and s have the same sign.

The correct answer is E;
both statements together are still not sufficient.

238. Each Type A machine fills 400 cans per minute, each Type B machine fills 600 cans per minute, and each Type C machine installs 2,400 lids per minute. A lid is installed on each can that is filled and on no can that is not filled. For a particular minute, what is the total number of machines working?

(1) A total of 4,800 cans are filled that minute.

(2) For that minute, there are 2 Type B machines working for every Type C machine working.

Algebra Simultaneous equations

(1) Given that 4,800 cans were filled that minute, it is possible that 12 Type A machines, no Type B machines, and 2 Type C machines were working, for a total of 14 machines, since (12)(400) + (0)(600) = 4,800 and (2)(2,400) = 4,800. However, it is also possible that no Type A machines, 8 Type B machines, and 2 Type C machines were working, for a total of 10 machines, since (0)(400) + (8)(600) = 4,800 and (2)(2,400) = 4,800; NOT sufficient.

(2) Given that there are 2 Type B machines working for every Type C machine working, it is possible that there are 6 machines working—3 Type A machines, 2 Type B machines, and 1 Type C machine. This gives 3(400) + 2(600) = 2,400 cans and 1(2,400) = 2,400 lids. It is also possible that there are 12 machines working—6 Type A machines, 4 Type B machines, and 2 Type C machines. This gives 6(400) + 4(600) = 4,800 cans and 2(2,400) = 4,800 lids; NOT sufficient.

Taking (1) and (2) together, since there were 4,800 cans filled that minute, there were 4,800 lids installed that minute. It follows that 2 Type C machines were working that minute, since (2)(2,400) = 4,800. Since there were twice this number of Type B machines working that minute, it follows that 4 Type B machines were working that minute. These 4 Type B machines filled (4)(600) = 2,400 cans that minute, leaving 4,800 – 2,400 = 2,400 cans to be filled by Type A machines. Therefore, the number of Type A machines working that minute was $\frac{2,400}{400} = 6$, and it follows that the total number of machines working that minute was 2 + 4 + 6 = 12.

The correct answer is C;
both statements together are sufficient.

239. If a and b are constants, what is the value of a ?

(1) $a < b$

(2) $(t - a)(t - b) = t^2 + t - 12$, for all values of t.

Algebra Second-degree equations

(1) Given that $a < b$, it is not possible to determine the value of a. For example, $a < b$ is true when $a = 1$ and $b = 2$, and $a < b$ is true when $a = 2$ and $b = 3$; NOT sufficient.

(2) By factoring, what is given can be expressed as $(t - a)(t - b) = (t + 4)(t - 3)$, so either $a = -4$ and $b = 3$, or $a = 3$ and $b = -4$; NOT sufficient.

Taking (1) and (2) together, the relation $a < b$ is satisfied by only one of the two possibilities given in the discussion of (2) above, namely $a = -4$ and $b = 3$. Therefore, the value of a is –4.

The correct answer is C;
both statements together are sufficient.

240. If x is a positive integer, is $\sqrt{x}$ an integer?

(1) $\sqrt{4x}$ is an integer.

(2) $\sqrt{3x}$ is not an integer.

Algebra Radicals

(1) It is given that $\sqrt{4x} = n$, or $4x = n^2$, for some positive integer n. Since $4x$ is the square of an integer, it follows that in the prime factorization of $4x$, each distinct prime factor is repeated an even number of times. Therefore, the same must be true for the prime factorization of x, since the prime factorization of x only differs from the prime factorization of $4x$ by two factors of 2, and hence by an even number of factors of 2; SUFFICIENT.

(2) Given that $\sqrt{3x}$ is not an integer, it is possible for $\sqrt{x}$ to be an integer (for example, $x = 1$) and it is possible for $\sqrt{x}$ to not be an integer (for example, $x = 2$); NOT sufficient.

The correct answer is A;
statement 1 alone is sufficient.

241. If p, q, x, y, and z are different positive integers, which of the five integers is the median?

(1) $p + x < q$

(2) $y < z$

Arithmetic Statistics

Since there are five different integers, there are two integers greater and two integers less than the median, which is the middle number.

(1) No information is given about the order of y and z with respect to the other three numbers; NOT sufficient.

(2) This statement does not relate y and z to the other three integers; NOT sufficient.

Because (1) and (2) taken together do not relate p, x, and q to y and z, it is impossible to tell which is the median. For example, if $p = 3$, $x = 4$, $q = 8$, $y = 9$, and $z = 10$, then the median is 8, but if $p = 3$, $x = 4$, $q = 8$, $y = 1$, and $z = 2$, then the median is 3.

The correct answer is E;
both statements together are still not sufficient.

242. If $w + z = 28$, what is the value of wz?

(1) w and z are positive integers.

(2) w and z are consecutive odd integers.

Arithmetic Arithmetic operations

(1) The fact that w and z are both positive integers does not allow the values of w and z to be determined because, for example, if $w = 20$ and $z = 8$, then $wz = 160$, and if $w = 10$ and $z = 18$, then $wz = 180$; NOT sufficient.

(2) Since w and z are consecutive odd integers whose sum is 28, it is reasonable to consider the possibilities for the sum of consecutive odd integers: $\ldots, (-5) + (-3) = -8$, $(-3) + (-1) = -4$, $(-1) + 1 = 0$, $1 + 3 = 4, \ldots$, $9 + 11 = 20$, $11 + 13 = 24$, $13 + 15 = 28$, $15 + 17 = 32, \ldots$. From this list it follows that only one pair of consecutive odd integers has 28 for its sum, and hence there is exactly one possible value for wz.

This problem can also be solved algebraically by letting the consecutive odd integers w and z be represented by $2n + 1$ and $2n + 3$, where n can be any integer. Since $28 = w + z$, it follows that

$28 = (2n+1)+(2n+3)$	
$28 = 4n+4$	simplify
$24 = 4n$	subtract 4 from both sides
$6 = n$	divide both sides by 4

Thus, $w = 2(6) + 1 = 13$, $z = 2(6) + 3 = 15$, and hence exactly one value can be determined for wz; SUFFICIENT.

The correct answer is B;
statement 2 alone is sufficient.

243. If $abc \neq 0$, is $\dfrac{\frac{a}{b}}{c} = \dfrac{a}{\frac{b}{c}}$?

(1) $a = 1$

(2) $c = 1$

Algebra Fractions

Since $\dfrac{\frac{a}{b}}{c} = \dfrac{a}{b} \div c = \dfrac{a}{b} \times \dfrac{1}{c} = \dfrac{a}{bc}$ and $\dfrac{a}{\frac{b}{c}} = a \div \dfrac{b}{c} = a \times \dfrac{c}{b} = \dfrac{ac}{b}$, it is to be determined whether $\dfrac{a}{bc} = \dfrac{ac}{b}$.

(1) Given that $a = 1$, the equation to be investigated, $\dfrac{a}{bc} = \dfrac{ac}{b}$, is $\dfrac{1}{bc} = \dfrac{c}{b}$. This equation can be true for some nonzero values of b and c (for example, $b = c = 1$) and

false for other nonzero values of b and c (for example, $b = 1$ and $c = 2$); NOT sufficient.

(2) Given that $c = 1$, the equation to be investigated, $\frac{a}{bc} = \frac{ac}{b}$, is $\frac{a}{b} = \frac{a}{b}$. This equation is true for all nonzero values of a and b; SUFFICIENT.

The correct answer is B; statement 2 alone is sufficient.

244. The arithmetic mean of a collection of 5 positive integers, not necessarily distinct, is 9. One additional positive integer is included in the collection and the arithmetic mean of the 6 integers is computed. Is the arithmetic mean of the 6 integers at least 10 ?

(1) The additional integer is at least 14.

(2) The additional integer is a multiple of 5.

Arithmetic Statistics

Since the arithmetic mean of the 5 integers is 9, the sum of the 5 integers divided by 5 is equal to 9, and hence the sum of the 5 integers is equal to $(5)(9) = 45$. Let x be the additional positive integer. Then the sum of the 6 integers is $45 + x$, and the arithmetic mean of the 6 integers is $\frac{45+x}{6}$. Determine whether $\frac{45+x}{6} \geq 10$, or equivalently, whether $45 + x \geq 60$, or equivalently, whether $x \geq 15$.

(1) Given that $x \geq 14$, then x could equal 14 and $x \geq 15$ is not true, or x could equal 15 and $x \geq 15$ is true; NOT sufficient.

(2) Given that x is a multiple of 5, then x could equal 10 and $x \geq 15$ is not true, or x could equal 15 and $x \geq 15$ is true; NOT sufficient.

Taking (1) and (2) together, then x is a multiple of 5 that is greater than or equal to 14, and so x could equal one of the numbers 15, 20, 25, 30, ... Each of these numbers is greater than or equal to 15.

The correct answer is C; both statements together are sufficient.

245. A certain list consists of 400 different numbers. Is the average (arithmetic mean) of the numbers in the list greater than the median of the numbers in the list?

(1) Of the numbers in the list, 280 are less than the average.

(2) Of the numbers in the list, 30 percent are greater than or equal to the average.

Arithmetic Statistics

In a list of 400 numbers, the median will be halfway between the 200th and the 201st numbers in the list when the numbers are ordered from least to greatest.

(1) This indicates that 280 of the 400 numbers in the list are less than the average of the 400 numbers. This means that both the 200th and the 201st numbers, as well as the median, are less than the average and, therefore, that the average is greater than the median; SUFFICIENT.

(2) This indicates that $(0.3)(400) = 120$ of the numbers are greater than or equal to the average. This means that the other $400 - 120 = 280$ numbers are less than the average, which is the same as the information in (1); SUFFICIENT.

The correct answer is D; each statement alone is sufficient.

246. In a two-month survey of shoppers, each shopper bought one of two brands of detergent, X or Y, in the first month and again bought one of these brands in the second month. In the survey, 90 percent of the shoppers who bought Brand X in the first month bought Brand X again in the second month, while 60 percent of the shoppers who bought Brand Y in the first month bought Brand Y again in the second month. What percent of the shoppers bought Brand Y in the second month?

(1) In the first month, 50 percent of the shoppers bought Brand X.

(2) The total number of shoppers surveyed was 5,000.

Arithmetic Percents

This problem can be solved by using the following contingency table where A and B represent, respectively, the number of shoppers who bought

Brand X and the number of shoppers who bought Brand Y in the first month; C and D represent, respectively, the number of shoppers who bought Brand X and the number of shoppers who bought Brand Y in the second month; and T represents the total number of shoppers in the survey. Also in the table, $0.9A$ represents the 90% of the shoppers who bought Brand X in the first month and also bought it in the second month, and $0.1A$ represents the $(100 - 90)\% = 10\%$ of the shoppers who bought Brand X in the first month and Brand Y in the second month. Similarly, $0.6B$ represents the 60% of the shoppers who bought Brand Y in the first month and also bought it in the second month, and $0.4B$ represents the $(100 - 60)\% = 40\%$ of the shoppers who bought Brand Y in the first month and Brand X in the second month.

		Second Month		
		X	Y	Total
First Month	X	$0.9A$	$0.1A$	A
	Y	$0.4B$	$0.6B$	B
	Total	C	D	T

Determine the value of $\frac{D}{T}$ as a percentage.

(1) This indicates that 50% of the shoppers bought Brand X in the first month, so $A = 0.5T$. It follows that the other 50% of the shoppers bought Brand Y in the first month, so $B = 0.5T$. Then, $D = 0.1A + 0.6B = 0.1(0.5T) + 0.6(0.5T) = 0.05T + 0.30T = 0.35T$. It follows that $\frac{D}{T} = \frac{0.35T}{T} = 0.35$, which is 35%; SUFFICIENT.

(2) This indicates that $T = 5{,}000$, as shown in the following table:

		Second Month		
		X	Y	Total
First Month	X	$0.9A$	$0.1A$	A
	Y	$0.4B$	$0.6B$	B
	Total	C	D	5,000

But not enough information is given to be able to determine D or D as a percentage of 5,000; NOT sufficient.

The correct answer is A;
statement 1 alone is sufficient.

247. If m and n are positive integers, is $m + n$ divisible by 4 ?

(1) m and n are each divisible by 2.

(2) Neither m nor n is divisible by 4.

Arithmetic Properties of numbers

Determine whether the sum of the positive integers m and n is divisible by 4.

(1) It is given that m is divisible by 2 and n is divisible by 2. If, for example, $m = 2$ and $n = 2$, then each of m and n is divisible by 2 and $m + n = 2 + 2 = 4$, which is divisible by 4. However, if $m = 2$ and $n = 4$, then each of m and n is divisible by 2 and $m + n = 2 + 4 = 6$, which is not divisible by 4; NOT sufficient.

(2) It is given that neither m nor n is divisible by 4. If, for example, $m = 3$ and $n = 5$, then neither m nor n is divisible by 4 and $m + n = 3 + 5 = 8$, which is divisible by 4. On the other hand, if $m = 3$ and $n = 6$, then neither m nor n is divisible by 4 and $m + n = 3 + 6 = 9$, which is not divisible by 4; NOT sufficient.

Taking (1) and (2) together, m is not divisible by 4, so $m = 4q + r$, where q is a positive integer and $0 < r < 4$. However, m is divisible by 2, so r must be even. Since the only positive even integer less than 4 is 2, then $r = 2$ and $m = 4q + 2$. Similarly, since n is divisible by 2 but not by 4, $n = 4s + 2$. It follows that $m + n = (4q + 2) + (4s + 2) = 4q + 4s + 4 = 4(q + s + 1)$, and $m + n$ is divisible by 4.

The correct answer is C;
both statements together are sufficient.

248. What is the area of rectangular region R?

(1) Each diagonal of R has length 5.

(2) The perimeter of R is 14.

Geometry Rectangles

Let L and W be the length and width of the rectangle, respectively. Determine the value of LW.

(1) It is given that a diagonal's length is 5. Thus, by the Pythagorean theorem, it follows that $L^2 + W^2 = 5^2 = 25$. The value of LW cannot be determined, however, because $L = \sqrt{15}$ and $W = \sqrt{10}$ satisfy $L^2 + W^2 = 25$ with $LW = \sqrt{150}$, and $L = \sqrt{5}$ and $W = \sqrt{20}$ satisfy $L^2 + W^2 = 25$ with $LW = \sqrt{100}$; NOT sufficient.

(2) It is given that $2L + 2W = 14$, or $L + W = 7$, or $L = 7 - W$. Therefore, $LW = (7 - W)W$, which can vary in value. For example, if $L = 3$ and $W = 4$, then $L + W = 7$ and $LW = 12$. However, if $L = 2$ and $W = 5$, then $L + W = 7$ and $LW = 10$; NOT sufficient.

Given (1) and (2) together, it follows from (2) that $(L + W)^2 = 7^2 = 49$, or $L^2 + W^2 + 2LW = 49$. Using (1), 25 can be substituted for $L^2 + W^2$ to obtain $25 + 2LW = 49$, or $2LW = 24$, or $LW = 12$. Alternatively, $7 - W$ can be substituted for L in $L^2 + W^2 = 25$ to obtain the quadratic equation $(7 - W)^2 + W^2 = 25$, or $49 - 14W + W^2 + W^2 = 25$, or $2W^2 - 14W + 24 = 0$, or $W^2 - 7W + 12 = 0$. The left side of the last equation can be factored to give $(W - 4)(W - 3) = 0$. Therefore, $W = 4$, which gives $L = 7 - W = 7 - 4 = 3$ and $LW = (3)(4) = 12$, or $W = 3$, which gives $L = 7 - W = 7 - 3 = 4$ and $LW = (4)(3) = 12$. Since $LW = 12$ in either case, a unique value for LW can be determined.

The correct answer is C;
both statements together are sufficient.

249. How many integers n are there such that $r < n < s$?

(1) $s - r = 5$

(2) r and s are not integers.

Arithmetic Properties of numbers

(1) The difference between s and r is 5. If r and s are integers (e.g., 7 and 12), the number of integers between them (i.e., n could be 8, 9, 10, or 11) is 4. If r and s are not integers (e.g., 6.5 and 11.5), then the number of integers between them (i.e., n could be 7, 8, 9, 10, or 11) is 5. No information is given that allows a determination of whether s and r are integers; NOT sufficient.

(2) No information is given about the difference between r and s. If $r = 0.4$ and $s = 0.5$, then r and s have no integers between them. However, if $r = 0.4$ and $s = 3.5$, then r and s have 3 integers between them; NOT sufficient.

Using the information from both (1) and (2), it can be determined that, because r and s are not integers, there are 5 integers between them.

The correct answer is C;
both statements together are sufficient.

250. If the total price of n equally priced shares of a certain stock was \$12,000, what was the price per share of the stock?

(1) If the price per share of the stock had been \$1 more, the total price of the n shares would have been \$300 more.

(2) If the price per share of the stock had been \$2 less, the total price of the n shares would have been 5 percent less.

Arithmetic Arithmetic operations; Percents

Since the price per share of the stock can be expressed as $\frac{\$12,000}{n}$, determining the value of n is sufficient to answer this question.

(1) A per-share increase of \$1 and a total increase of \$300 for n shares of stock mean together that $n(\$1) = \$300$. It follows that $n = 300$; SUFFICIENT.

(2) If the price of each of the n shares had been reduced by \$2, the total reduction in price would have been 5 percent less or 0.05(\$12,000). The equation $2n = 0.05(\$12{,}000)$ expresses this relationship. The value of n can be determined to be 300 from this equation; SUFFICIENT.

The correct answer is D; each statement alone is sufficient.

251. If n is positive, is $\sqrt{n} > 100$?

(1) $\sqrt{n-1} > 99$

(2) $\sqrt{n+1} > 101$

Algebra Radicals

Determine if $\sqrt{n} > 100$ or equivalently, if $n > (100)(100) = 10{,}000$.

(1) Given that $\sqrt{n-1} > 99$, or equivalently, $n - 1 > (99)(99)$, it follows from

$$\begin{aligned}(99)(99) &= 99(100-1)\\ &= 9{,}900-99\\ &= 9{,}801\end{aligned}$$

that $\sqrt{n-1} > 99$ is equivalent to $n - 1 > 9{,}801$, or $n > 9{,}802$. Since $n > 9{,}802$ allows for values of n that are greater than 10,000 and $n > 9{,}802$ allows for values of n that are not greater than 10,000, it cannot be determined if $n > 10{,}000$; NOT sufficient.

(2) Given that $\sqrt{n+1} > 101$, or equivalently, $n + 1 > (101)(101)$, it follows from

$$\begin{aligned}(101)(101) &= 101(100+1)\\ &= 10{,}100+101\\ &= 10{,}201\end{aligned}$$

that $\sqrt{n+1} > 101$ is equivalent to $n + 1 > 10{,}201$, or $n > 10{,}200$. Since $10{,}200 > 10{,}000$, it can be determined that $n > 10{,}000$; SUFFICIENT.

The correct answer is B; statement 2 alone is sufficient.

252. Is $xy > 5$?

(1) $1 \le x \le 3$ and $2 \le y \le 4$.

(2) $x + y = 5$

Algebra Inequalities

(1) While it is known that $1 \le x \le 3$ and $2 \le y \le 4$, xy could be $(3)(4) = 12$, which is greater than 5, or xy could be $(1)(2) = 2$, which is not greater than 5; NOT sufficient.

(2) Given that $x + y = 5$, xy could be 6 (when $x = 2$ and $y = 3$), which is greater than 5, and xy could be 4 (when $x = 1$ and $y = 4$), which is not greater than 5; NOT sufficient.

Both (1) and (2) together are not sufficient since the two examples given in (2) are consistent with both statements.

The correct answer is E; both statements together are still not sufficient.

253. In Year X, 8.7 percent of the men in the labor force were unemployed in June compared with 8.4 percent in May. If the number of men in the labor force was the same for both months, how many men were unemployed in June of that year?

(1) In May of Year X, the number of unemployed men in the labor force was 3.36 million.

(2) In Year X, 120,000 more men in the labor force were unemployed in June than in May.

Arithmetic Percents

Since 8.7 percent of the men in the labor force were unemployed in June, the number of unemployed men could be calculated if the total number of men in the labor force was known. Let t represent the total number of men in the labor force.

(1) This implies that for May $(8.4\%)t = 3{,}360{,}000$, from which the value of t can be determined; SUFFICIENT.

(2) This implies that $(8.7\% - 8.4\%)t = 120{,}000$ or $(0.3\%)t = 120{,}000$. This equation can be solved for t; SUFFICIENT.

The correct answer is D; each statement alone is sufficient.

254. If $x \neq 0$, what is the value of $\left(\frac{x^p}{x^q}\right)^4$?

(1) $p = q$

(2) $x = 3$

Arithmetic; Algebra Arithmetic operations; Simplifying expressions

(1) Since $p = q$, it follows that $\left(\frac{x^p}{x^q}\right)^4 = \left(\frac{x^p}{x^p}\right)^4 = (1)^4$; SUFFICIENT.

(2) Since $x = 3$ (and, therefore, $x \neq 1$) and the values of p or q are unknown, the value of the expression $\left(\frac{x^p}{x^q}\right)^4$ cannot be determined; NOT sufficient.

The correct answer is A; statement 1 alone is sufficient.

255. On Monday morning a certain machine ran continuously at a uniform rate to fill a production order. At what time did it completely fill the order that morning?

(1) The machine began filling the order at 9:30 a.m.

(2) The machine had filled $\frac{1}{2}$ of the order by 10:30 a.m. and $\frac{5}{6}$ of the order by 11:10 a.m.

Arithmetic Arithmetic operations

(1) This merely states what time the machine began filling the order; NOT sufficient.

(2) In the 40 minutes between 10:30 a.m. and 11:10 a.m., $\frac{5}{6} - \frac{1}{2} = \frac{1}{3}$ of the order was filled. Therefore, the entire order was completely filled in $3 \times 40 = 120$ minutes, or 2 hours. Since half the order took 1 hour and was filled by 10:30 a.m., the second half of the order, and thus the entire order, was filled by 11:30 a.m.; SUFFICIENT.

The correct answer is B; statement 2 alone is sufficient.

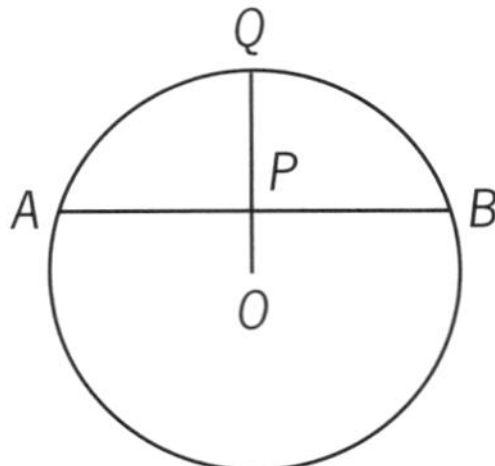

256. What is the radius of the circle above with center *O* ?

(1) The ratio of *OP* to *PQ* is 1 to 2.

(2) *P* is the midpoint of chord *AB*.

Geometry Circles

(1) It can be concluded only that the radius is 3 times the length of *OP*, which is unknown; NOT sufficient.

(2) It can be concluded only that $AP = PB$, and the chord is irrelevant to the radius; NOT sufficient.

Together, (1) and (2) do not give the length of any line segment shown in the circle. In fact, if the circle and all the line segments were uniformly expanded by a factor of, say, 5, the resulting circle and line segments would still satisfy both (1) and (2). Therefore, the radius of the circle cannot be determined from (1) and (2) together.

The correct answer is E; both statements together are still not sufficient.

257. If *a* and *b* are positive integers, what is the value of the product *ab* ?

(1) The least common multiple of *a* and *b* is 48.

(2) The greatest common factor of *a* and *b* is 4.

Arithmetic Properties of numbers

Determine the value of the product of positive integers *a* and *b*.

(1) This indicates that the least common multiple (lcm) of *a* and *b* is 48, which means that 48 is the least integer that is a multiple of both *a* and *b*. If $a = 24$ and $b = 16$, then the multiples of *a* are 24, 48, 72, . . ., and the multiples of *b* are 16, 32, 48, 64, ... So, 48 is the lcm of 24 and 16, and $ab = (24)(16)$. However, if $a = 48$ and $b = 16$, then the multiples of *a* are 48, 96, . . ., and the multiples of *b* are 16, 32, 48, 64,

.... So, 48 is the lcm of 48 and 16, and ab = (48)(16); NOT sufficient.

(2) This indicates that 4 is the greatest common factor (gcf) of a and b, which means that 4 is the greatest integer that is a factor of both a and b. If $a = 4$ and $b = 4$, then 4 is the gcf a and b, and $ab = (4)(4)$. However, if $a = 4$ and $b = 16$, then 4 is the gcf of a and b, and $ab = (4)(16)$; NOT sufficient.

Taking (1) and (2) together, each of a and b is a multiple of 4 (which means that each of a and b is divisible by 4) and 48 is a multiple of each of a and b (which means that 48 is divisible by each of a and b). It follows that the only possible values for a and b are 4, 8, 12, 16, 24, and 48. The following table shows all possible pairs of these values and that only 4 of them ($a = 4$ and $b = 48$, $a = 12$ and $b = 16$, $a = 16$ and $b = 12$, $a = 48$ and $b = 4$), satisfy both (1) and (2).

		b					
		4	**8**	**12**	**16**	**24**	**48**
a	**4**	lcm is 4, not 48	lcm is 8, not 48	lcm is 12, not 48	lcm is 16, not 48	lcm is 24, not 48	lcm is 48, gcf is 4
	8	lcm is 8, not 48	lcm is 8, not 48	lcm is 24, not 48	gcf is 8, not 4	gcf is 8, not 4	gcf is 8, not 4
	12	lcm is 12, not 48	lcm is 24, not 48	gcf is 12, not 4	lcm is 48, gcf is 4	gcf is 12, not 4	gcf is 12, not 4
	16	lcm is 16, not 48	gcf is 8, not 4	lcm is 48, gcf is 4	gcf is 16, not 4	gcf is 8, not 4	gcf is 16, not 4
	24	lcm is 24, not 48	gcf is 8, not 4	gcf is 12, not 4	gcf is 8, not 4	gcf is 24, not 4	gcf is 24, not 4
	48	lcm is 48, gcf is 4	gcf is 8, not 4	gcf is 12, not 4	gcf is 16, not 4	gcf is 24, not 4	gcf is 48, not 4

In each case where both (1) and (2) are satisfied, $ab = 192$.

Alternatively,

(1) Using prime factorizations, since the least common multiple of a and b is 48 and $48 = 2^4 \cdot 3^1$, it follows that $a = 2^p \cdot 3^q$, where $p \leq 4$ and $q \leq 1$, and $b = 2^r \cdot 3^s$, where $r \leq 4$ and $s \leq 1$. Since the least common multiple of two positive integers is the product of the highest power of each prime in the prime factorizations of the two integers, one of p or r must be 4 and one of q or s must be 1. If, for example, $p = 4$, $q = 1$, and $r = s = 0$, then $a = 2^4 \cdot 3^1 = 48$, $b = 2^0 \cdot 3^0 = 1$, and $ab = (48)(1) = 48$. However, if $p = 4$, $q = 1$, $r = 4$, and $s = 1$, then $a = 2^4 \cdot 3^1 = 48$, $b = 2^4 \cdot 3^1 = 48$, and $ab = (48)(48) = 2{,}304$; NOT sufficient.

(2) If $a = 4$ and $b = 4$, then the greatest common factor of a and b is 4 and $ab = (4)(4) = 16$. However, if $a = 4$ and $b = 12$, then the greatest common factor of a and b is 4 and $ab = (4)(12) = 48$; NOT sufficient.

Taking (1) and (2) together, by (1), $a = 2^p \cdot 3^q$, where $p \leq 4$ and $q \leq 1$, and $b = 2^r \cdot 3^s$, where $r \leq 4$ and $s \leq 1$. Since the least common multiple of two positive integers is the product of the highest power of each prime in the prime factorizations of the two integers, exactly one of p or r must be 4 and the other one must be 2. Otherwise, either the least common multiple of a and b would not be 48 or the greatest common factor would not be 4. Likewise, exactly one of q or s must be 1 and the other one must be 0. The following table gives all possible combinations of values for p, q, r, and s along with corresponding values of a, b, and ab.

p	q	r	s	$a = 2^p \cdot 3^q$	$b = 2^r \cdot 3^s$	ab
2	0	4	1	$2^2 \cdot 3^0 = 4$	$2^4 \cdot 3^1 = 48$	192
2	1	4	0	$2^2 \cdot 3^1 = 12$	$2^4 \cdot 3^0 = 16$	192
4	0	2	1	$2^4 \cdot 3^0 = 16$	$2^2 \cdot 3^1 = 12$	192
4	1	2	0	$2^4 \cdot 3^1 = 48$	$2^2 \cdot 3^0 = 4$	192

In each case, $ab = 192$.

The correct answer is C;
both statements together are sufficient.

258. What is the number of 360-degree rotations that a bicycle wheel made while rolling 100 meters in a straight line without slipping?

(1) The diameter of the bicycle wheel, including the tire, was 0.5 meter.

(2) The wheel made twenty 360-degree rotations per minute.

Geometry Circles

For each 360-degree rotation, the wheel has traveled a distance equal to its circumference. Given either the circumference of the wheel or the means to calculate its circumference, it is thus possible to determine the number of times the circumference of the wheel was laid out along the straight-line path of 100 meters.

(1) The circumference of the bicycle wheel can be determined from the given diameter using the equation $C = \pi d$, where d = the diameter; SUFFICIENT.

(2) The speed of the rotations is irrelevant, and no dimensions of the wheel are given; NOT sufficient.

The correct answer is A; statement 1 alone is sufficient.

259. In the equation $x^2 + bx + 12 = 0$, x is a variable and b is a constant. What is the value of b ?

(1) $x - 3$ is a factor of $x^2 + bx + 12$.

(2) 4 is a root of the equation $x^2 + bx + 12 = 0$.

Algebra First- and second-degree equations

(1) Method 1: If $x - 3$ is a factor, then $x^2 + bx + 12 = (x - 3)(x + c)$ for some constant c. Equating the constant terms (or substituting $x = 0$), it follows that $12 = -3c$, or $c = -4$. Therefore, the quadratic polynomial is $(x - 3)(x - 4)$, which is equal to $x^2 - 7x + 12$, and hence $b = -7$.

Method 2: If $x - 3$ is a factor of $x^2 + bx + 12$, then 3 is a root of $x^2 + bx + 12 = 0$. Therefore, $3^2 + 3b + 12 = 0$, which can be solved to get $b = -7$.

Method 3: The value of b can be found by long division:

$$\begin{array}{r} x + (b+3) \\ x - 3 \overline{\smash{)}\, x^2 + bx + 12} \\ \underline{x^2 - 3x } \\ (b+3)x + 12 \\ \underline{(b+3)x - 3b - 9} \\ 3b + 21 \end{array}$$

These calculations show that the remainder is $3b + 21$. Since the remainder must be 0, it follows that $3b + 21 = 0$, or $b = -7$; SUFFICIENT.

(2) If 4 is a root of the equation, then 4 can be substituted for x in the equation $x^2 + bx + 12 = 0$, yielding $4^2 + 4b + 12 = 0$. This last equation can be solved to obtain a unique value for b; SUFFICIENT.

The correct answer is D; each statement alone is sufficient.

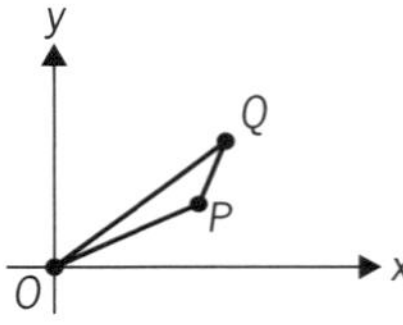

260. In the figure above, line segment OP has slope $\frac{1}{2}$ and line segment PQ has slope 2. What is the slope of line segment OQ ?

(1) Line segment OP has length $2\sqrt{5}$.

(2) The coordinates of point Q are (5,4).

Geometry Coordinate geometry

Let P have coordinates (a,b) and Q have coordinates (x,y). Since the slope of $\overline{OP}$ is $\frac{1}{2}$, it follows that $\frac{b-0}{a-0} = \frac{1}{2}$, or $a = 2b$. What is the slope of $\overline{OQ}$?

(1) Given that $\overline{OP}$ has length $2\sqrt{5}$, it follows from the Pythagorean theorem that $a^2 + b^2 = \left(2\sqrt{5}\right)^2$, or $(2b)^2 + b^2 = 20$, or $5b^2 = 20$. The only positive solution of this equation is $b = 2$, and therefore $a = 2b = 4$ and the coordinates of P are $(a,b) = (4,2)$.

However, nothing is known about how far Q is from P. If Q is close to P, then the slope of $\overline{OQ}$ will be close to $\frac{1}{2}$ (the slope of $\overline{OP}$), and if Q is far from P, then the slope of $\overline{OQ}$ will be close to 2 (the slope of $\overline{PQ}$). To be explicit, since the slope of $\overline{PQ}$ is 2, it follows that $\frac{y-2}{x-4} = 2$, or $y = 2x - 6$. Choosing $x = 4.1$ and $y = 2(4.1) - 6 = 2.2$ gives $(x,y) = (4.1,2.2)$, and the slope of $\overline{OQ}$ is $\frac{2.2}{4.1}$, which is close to $\frac{1}{2}$. On the other hand, choosing $x = 100$ and $y = 2(100) - 6 = 194$ gives $(x,y) = (100,194)$, and the slope of $\overline{OQ}$ is $\frac{194}{100}$, which is close to 2; NOT sufficient.

(2) Given that the coordinates of point Q are (5,4), it follows that the slope of $\overline{OQ}$ is $\frac{4-0}{5-0} = \frac{4}{5}$; SUFFICIENT.

The correct answer is B;
statement 2 alone is sufficient.

261. In ΔXYZ, what is the length of YZ?

(1) The length of XY is 3.

(2) The length of XZ is 5.

Geometry Triangles

Given the length of one side of a triangle, it is known that the sum of the lengths of the other two sides is greater than that given length. The length of either of the other two sides, however, can be any positive number.

(1) Only the length of one side, XY, is given, and that is not enough to determine the length of YZ; NOT sufficient.

(2) Again, only the length of one side, XZ, is given and that is not enough to determine the length of YZ; NOT sufficient.

Even by using the triangle inequality stated above, only a range of values for YZ can be determined from (1) and (2). If the length of side YZ is represented by k, then it is known both that $3 + 5 > k$ and that $3 + k > 5$, or $k > 2$. Combining these inequalities to determine the length of k yields only that $8 > k > 2$.

The correct answer is E;
both statements together are still not sufficient.

262. If the average (arithmetic mean) of n consecutive odd integers is 10, what is the least of the integers?

(1) The range of the n integers is 14.

(2) The greatest of the n integers is 17.

Arithmetic Statistics

Let k be the least of the n consecutive odd integers. Then the n consecutive odd integers are $k, k + 2, k + 4, \ldots, k + 2(n - 1)$, where $k + 2(n - 1)$ is the greatest of the n consecutive odd integers and $[k + 2(n - 1)] - k = 2(n - 1)$ is the range of the n consecutive odd integers. Determine the value of k.

(1) Given that the range of the odd integers is 14, it follows that $2(n - 1) = 14$, or $n - 1 = 7$, or $n = 8$. It is also given that the average of the 8 consecutive odd integers is 10, and so, $\frac{k+(k+2)+(k+4)+\ldots+(k+14)}{8} = 10$ from which a unique value for k can be determined; SUFFICIENT.

(2) Given that the greatest of the odd integers is 17, it follows that the n consecutive odd integers can be expressed as $17, 17 - 2, 17 - 4, \ldots, 17 - 2(n - 1)$. Since the average of the n consecutive odd integers is 10, then

$$\frac{17+(17-2)+(17-4)+\ldots+[17-2(n-1)]}{n} = 10,$$

or

$$17+(17-2)+(17-4)+\ldots+[17-2(n-1)] = 10n \text{ (i)}$$

The n consecutive odd integers can also be expressed as $k, k + 2, k + 4, \ldots, k + 2(n - 1)$.

Since the average of the n consecutive odd integers is 10, then

$$\frac{k+(k+2)+(k+4)+\ldots+[k+2(n-1)]}{n} = 10,$$

or

$$k+(k+2)+(k+4)+\ldots+[k+2(n-1)]=10n \text{ (ii)}$$

Adding equations (i) and (ii) gives

$$(17+k)+(17+k)+(17+k)+\ldots+(17+k)=20n$$
$$n(17+k)=20n$$
$$17+k=20$$
$$k=3$$

Alternatively, because the numbers are consecutive odd integers, they form a data set that is symmetric about its average, and so the average of the numbers is the average of the least and greatest numbers. Therefore, $10=\frac{k+17}{2}$, from which a unique value for k can be determined; SUFFICIENT.

The correct answer is D;
each statement alone is sufficient.

263. If x, y, and z are positive numbers, is $x>y>z$?

(1) $xz>yz$

(2) $yx>yz$

Algebra Inequalities

(1) Dividing both sides of the inequality by z yields $x>y$. However, there is no information relating z to either x or y; NOT sufficient.

(2) Dividing both sides of the inequality by y yields only that $x>z$, with no further information relating y to either x or z; NOT sufficient.

From (1) and (2) it can be determined that x is greater than both y and z. Since it still cannot be determined which of y or z is the least, the correct ordering of the three numbers also cannot be determined.

The correct answer is E;
both statements together are still not sufficient.

264. K is a set of numbers such that

(i) if x is in K, then $-x$ is in K, and

(ii) if each of x and y is in K, then xy is in K.

Is 12 in K?

(1) 2 is in K.

(2) 3 is in K.

Arithmetic Properties of numbers

(1) Given that 2 is in K, it follows that K could be the set of all real numbers, which contains 12. However, if K is the set $\{\ldots,-16,-8,-4,-2,2,4,8,16,\ldots\}$, then K contains 2 and K satisfies both (i) and (ii), but K does not contain 12. To see that K satisfies (ii), note that K can be written as $\{\ldots,-2^4,-2^3,-2^2,-2^1,2^1,2^2,2^3,2^4,\ldots\}$, and thus a verification of (ii) can reduce to verifying that the sum of two positive integer exponents is a positive integer exponent; NOT sufficient.

(2) Given that 3 is in K, it follows that K could be the set of all real numbers, which contains 12. However, if K is the set $\{\ldots,-81,-27,-9,-3,3,9,27,81,\ldots\}$, then K contains 3 and K satisfies both (i) and (ii), but K does not contain 12. To see that K satisfies (ii), note that K can be written as $\{\ldots,-3^4,-3^3,-3^2,-3^1,3^1,3^2,3^3,3^4,\ldots\}$, and thus a verification of (ii) can reduce to verifying that the sum of two positive integer exponents is a positive integer exponent; NOT sufficient.

Given (1) and (2), it follows that both 2 and 3 are in K. Thus, by (ii), $(2)(3)=6$ is in K. Therefore, by (ii), $(2)(6)=12$ is in K.

The correct answer is C;
both statements together are sufficient.

265. If $x^2+y^2=29$, what is the value of $(x-y)^2$?

(1) $xy=10$

(2) $x=5$

Algebra Simplifying algebraic expressions

Since $(x - y)^2 = (x^2 + y^2) - 2xy$ and it is given that $x^2 + y^2 = 29$, it follows that $(x - y)^2 = 29 - 2xy$. Therefore, the value of $(x - y)^2$ can be determined if and only if the value of xy can be determined.

(1) Since the value of xy is given, the value of $(x - y)^2$ can be determined; SUFFICIENT.

(2) Given only that $x = 5$, it is not possible to determine the value of xy. Therefore, the value of $(x - y)^2$ cannot be determined; NOT sufficient.

The correct answer is A;
statement 1 alone is sufficient.

266. After winning 50 percent of the first 20 games it played, Team A won all of the remaining games it played. What was the total number of games that Team A won?

(1) Team A played 25 games altogether.

(2) Team A won 60 percent of all the games it played.

Arithmetic Percents

Let r be the number of the remaining games played, all of which the team won. Since the team won $(50\%)(20) = 10$ of the first 20 games and the r remaining games, the total number of games the team won is $10 + r$. Also, the total number of games the team played is $20 + r$. Determine the value of r.

(1) Given that the total number of games played is 25, it follows that $20 + r = 25$, or $r = 5$; SUFFICIENT.

(2) It is given that the total number of games won is $(60\%)(20 + r)$, which can be expanded as $12 + 0.6r$. Since it is also known that the number of games won is $10 + r$, it follows that $12 + 0.6r = 10 + r$. Solving this equation gives $12 - 10 = r - 0.6r$, or $2 = 0.4r$, or $r = 5$; SUFFICIENT.

The correct answer is D;
each statement alone is sufficient.

267. Is x between 0 and 1 ?

(1) x^2 is less than x.

(2) x^3 is positive.

Arithmetic Arithmetic operations

(1) Since x^2 is always nonnegative, it follows that here x must also be nonnegative, that is, greater than or equal to 0. If $x = 0$ or 1, then $x^2 = x$. Furthermore, if x is greater than 1, then x^2 is greater than x. Therefore, x must be between 0 and 1; SUFFICIENT.

(2) If x^3 is positive, then x is positive, but x can be any positive number; NOT sufficient.

The correct answer is A;
statement 1 alone is sufficient.

268. If m and n are nonzero integers, is m^n an integer?

(1) n^m is positive.

(2) n^m is an integer.

Arithmetic Properties of numbers

It is useful to note that if $m > 1$ and $n < 0$, then $0 < m^n < 1$, and therefore m^n will not be an integer. For example, if $m = 3$ and $n = -2$, then $m^n = 3^{-2} = \frac{1}{3^2} = \frac{1}{9}$.

(1) Although it is given that n^m is positive, m^n can be an integer or m^n can fail to be an integer. For example, if $m = 2$ and $n = 2$, then $n^m = 2^2 = 4$ is positive and $m^n = 2^2 = 4$ is an integer. However, if $m = 2$ and $n = -2$, then $n^m = (-2)^2 = 4$ is positive and $m^n = 2^{-2} = \frac{1}{2^2} = \frac{1}{4}$ is not an integer; NOT sufficient.

(2) Although it is given that n^m is an integer, m^n can be an integer or m^n can fail to be an integer. For example, if $m = 2$ and $n = 2$, then $n^m = 2^2 = 4$ is an integer and $m^n = 2^2 = 4$ is an integer. However, if $m = 2$ and $n = -2$, then $n^m = (-2)^2 = 4$ is an integer and $m^n = 2^{-2} = \frac{1}{2^2} = \frac{1}{4}$ is not an integer; NOT sufficient.

Taking (1) and (2) together, it is still not possible to determine if m^n is an integer, since the same examples are used in both (1) and (2) above.

The correct answer is E;
both statements together are still not sufficient.

269. What is the value of xy ?

(1) $x + y = 10$

(2) $x - y = 6$

Algebra First- and second-degree equations; Simultaneous equations

(1) Given $x + y = 10$, or $y = 10 - x$, it follows that $xy = x(10 - x)$, which does not have a unique value. For example, if $x = 0$, then $xy = (0)(10) = 0$, but if $x = 1$, then $xy = (1)(9) = 9$; NOT sufficient.

(2) Given $x - y = 6$, or $y = x - 6$, it follows that $xy = x(x - 6)$, which does not have a unique value. For example, if $x = 0$, then $xy = (0)(-6) = 0$, but if $x = 1$, then $xy = (1)(-5) = -5$; NOT sufficient.

Using (1) and (2) together, the two equations can be solved simultaneously for x and y. One way to do this is by adding the two equations, $x + y = 10$ and $x - y = 6$, to get $2x = 16$, or $x = 8$. Then substitute into either of the equations to obtain an equation that can be solved to get $y = 2$. Thus, xy can be determined to have the value $(8)(2) = 16$. Alternatively, the two equations correspond to a pair of nonparallel lines in the (x,y) coordinate plane, which have a unique point in common.

The correct answer is C; both statements together are sufficient.

270. If n is the least of three different integers greater than 1, what is the value of n ?

(1) The product of the three integers is 90.

(2) One of the integers is twice one of the other two integers.

Arithmetic Operations with integers

Given that n is the least of three different integers n, p, and q, where $1 < n < p < q$, determine the value of n.

(1) This indicates that the product of the three integers is 90. The integers could be 2, 5, and 9 since $(2)(5)(9) = 90$, and n would be 2. However, the integers could be 3, 5, and 6 since $(3)(5)(6) = 90$, and n would be 3; NOT sufficient.

(2) This indicates that one of the integers is twice one of the others. It could be that $p = 2n$, or $q = 2n$, or $q = 2p$. For example, if $n = 2, p = 4$, and $q = 5$, then $p = 2n$, and the value of n would be 2. If $n = 3, p = 4$, and $q = 6$, then $q = 2n$, and the value of n would be 3; NOT sufficient.

Taking (1) and (2) together, if $p = 2n$, then $npq = (n)(2n)(q) = 90$, or $n^2q = 45$. It follows that $n = 3, p = (2)(3) = 6$, and $q = 5$. The value of n is 3. If $q = 2n$, then $npq = (n)(p)(2n) = 90$ or $n^2p = 45$. It follows that $n = 3, p = 5$, and $q = (2)(3) = 6$. The value of n is 3. If $q = 2p$, then $npq = (n)(p)(2p) = 90$ or $np^2 = 45$. It follows that $n = 5, p = 3$, and $q = (2)(3) = 6$, and this case can be eliminated because n is not the least of the three integers. Therefore, the value of n is 3.

Alternatively, taking (1) and (2) together, the integers n, p, and q are among 2, 3, 5, 6, 9, 10, 15, 18, 30, and 45 since they are factors of 90 from (1). Because all three integers are different and $90 = (2)(3)(15) = (2)(3^2)(5)$, n, p, and q must be among the integers 2, 3, 5, 9, 10, and 15. Only two pairs of these integers satisfy (2): 3 and 6 since $6 = (2)(3)$ and 5 and 10 since $10 = (2)(5)$. However, for each possible value for n, $(n)(5)(10) > 90$. Therefore, the only pair that satisfies both (1) and (2) is 3 and 6, and the third integer is then $\frac{90}{(3)(6)} = 5$. Thus, the value of n is 3.

The correct answer is C; both statements together are sufficient.

271. Is x^2 greater than x ?

(1) x^2 is greater than 1.

(2) x is greater than -1.

Arithmetic; Algebra Exponents; Inequalities

(1) Given $x^2 > 1$, it follows that either $x > 1$ or $x < -1$. If $x > 1$, then multiplying both sides of the inequality by the positive number x gives $x^2 > x$. On the other hand, if $x < -1$, then x is negative and x^2 is positive (because $x^2 > 1$), which also gives $x^2 > x$; SUFFICIENT.

(2) Given $x > -1$, x^2 can be greater than x (for example, $x = 2$) and x^2 can fail to be greater than x (for example, $x = 0$); NOT sufficient.

The correct answer is A; statement 1 alone is sufficient.

272. Michael arranged all his books in a bookcase with 10 books on each shelf and no books left over. After Michael acquired 10 additional books, he arranged all his books in a new bookcase with 12 books on each shelf and no books left over. How many books did Michael have before he acquired the 10 additional books?

(1) Before Michael acquired the 10 additional books, he had fewer than 96 books.

(2) Before Michael acquired the 10 additional books, he had more than 24 books.

Arithmetic Properties of numbers

If x is the number of books Michael had before he acquired the 10 additional books, then x is a multiple of 10. After Michael acquired the 10 additional books, he had $x + 10$ books and $x + 10$ is a multiple of 12.

(1) If $x < 96$, where x is a multiple of 10, then $x = 10, 20, 30, 40, 50, 60, 70, 80,$ or 90 and $x + 10 = 20, 30, 40, 50, 60, 70, 80, 90,$ or 100. Since $x + 10$ is a multiple of 12, then $x + 10 = 60$ and $x = 50$; SUFFICIENT.

(2) If $x > 24$, where x is a multiple of 10, then x must be one of the numbers 30, 40, 50, 60, 70, 80, 90, 100, 110, …, and $x + 10$ must be one of the numbers 40, 50, 60, 70, 80, 90, 100, 110, 120, …. Since there is more than one multiple of 12 among these numbers (for example, 60 and 120), the value of $x + 10$, and therefore the value of x, cannot be determined; NOT sufficient.

The correct answer is A; statement 1 alone is sufficient.

273. If $xy > 0$, does $(x - 1)(y - 1) = 1$?

(1) $x + y = xy$

(2) $x = y$

Algebra First- and second-degree equations

By expanding the product $(x - 1)(y - 1)$, the question is equivalent to whether $xy - y - x + 1 = 1$, or $xy - y - x = 0$, when $xy > 0$.

(1) If $x + y = xy$, then $xy - y - x = 0$, and hence by the remarks above, $(x - 1)(y - 1) = 1$; SUFFICIENT.

(2) If $x = y$, then $(x - 1)(y - 1) = 1$ can be true $(x = y = 2)$ and $(x - 1)(y - 1) = 1$ can be false $(x = y = 1)$; NOT sufficient.

The correct answer is A; statement 1 alone is sufficient.

274. Last year in a group of 30 businesses, 21 reported a net profit and 15 had investments in foreign markets. How many of the businesses did not report a net profit nor invest in foreign markets last year?

(1) Last year 12 of the 30 businesses reported a net profit and had investments in foreign markets.

(2) Last year 24 of the 30 businesses reported a net profit or invested in foreign markets, or both.

Arithmetic Concepts of sets

Consider the Venn diagram below in which x represents the number of businesses that reported a net profit and had investments in foreign markets. Since 21 businesses reported a net profit, $21 - x$ businesses reported a net profit only. Since 15 businesses had investments in foreign markets, $15 - x$ businesses had investments in foreign markets only. Finally, since there is a total of 30 businesses, the number of businesses that did not report a net profit and did not invest in foreign markets is $30 - (21 - x + x + 15 - x) = x - 6$.

Determine the value of $x - 6$, or equivalently, the value of x.

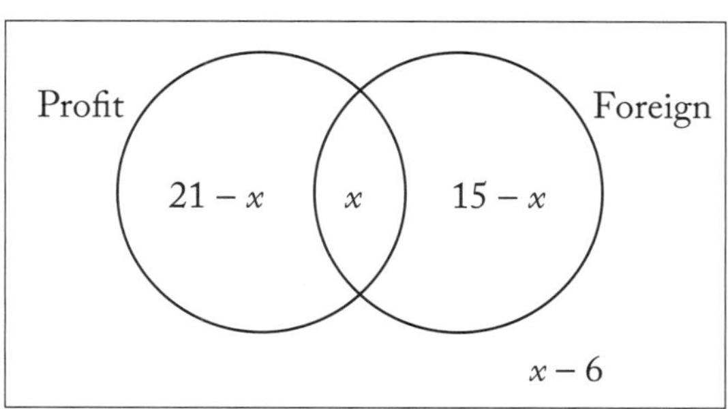

(1) It is given that $12 = x$; SUFFICIENT.

(2) It is given that $24 = (21 - x) + x + (15 - x)$. Therefore, $24 = 36 - x$, or $x = 12$.

Alternatively, the information given is exactly the number of businesses that are not among those to be counted in answering the question posed in the problem, and therefore the number of businesses that are to be counted is $30 - 24 = 6$; SUFFICIENT.

The correct answer is D; each statement alone is sufficient.

275. Is the perimeter of square S greater than the perimeter of equilateral triangle T ?

(1) The ratio of the length of a side of S to the length of a side of T is 4:5.

(2) The sum of the lengths of a side of S and a side of T is 18.

Geometry Perimeter

Letting s and t be the side lengths of square S and triangle T, respectively, the task is to determine if $4s > 3t$, which is equivalent (divide both sides by $4t$) to determining if $\frac{s}{t} > \frac{3}{4}$.

(1) It is given that $\frac{s}{t} = \frac{4}{5}$. Since $\frac{4}{5} > \frac{3}{4}$, it follows that $\frac{s}{t} > \frac{3}{4}$; SUFFICIENT.

(2) Many possible pairs of numbers have the sum of 18. For some of these (s,t) pairs it is the case that $\frac{s}{t} > \frac{3}{4}$ (for example, $s = t = 9$), and for others of these pairs it is not the case that $\frac{s}{t} > \frac{3}{4}$ (for example, $s = 1$ and $t = 17$); NOT sufficient.

The correct answer is A; statement 1 alone is sufficient.

276. If $x + y + z > 0$, is $z > 1$?

(1) $z > x + y + 1$

(2) $x + y + 1 < 0$

Algebra Inequalities

(1) The inequality $x + y + z > 0$ gives $z > -x - y$. Adding this last inequality to the given inequality, $z > x + y + 1$, gives $2z > 1$, or $z > \frac{1}{2}$, which suggests that (1) is not sufficient. Indeed, z could be 2 ($x = y = 0$ and $z = 2$ satisfy both $x + y + z > 0$ and $z > x + y + 1$), which is greater than 1, and z could be $\frac{3}{4}$ ($x = y = -\frac{1}{4}$ and $z = \frac{3}{4}$ satisfy both $x + y + z > 0$ and $z > x + y + 1$), which is not greater than 1; NOT sufficient.

(2) It follows from the inequality $x + y + z > 0$ that $z > -(x + y)$. It is given that $x + y + 1 < 0$, or $(x + y) < -1$, or $-(x + y) > 1$. Therefore, $z > -(x + y)$ and $-(x + y) > 1$, from which it follows that $z > 1$; SUFFICIENT.

The correct answer is B; statement 2 alone is sufficient.

277. For all z, $\lceil z \rceil$ denotes the least integer greater than or equal to z. Is $\lceil x \rceil = 0$?

(1) $-1 < x < -0.1$

(2) $\lceil x + 0.5 \rceil = 1$

Algebra Operations with real numbers

Determining if $\lceil x \rceil = 0$ is equivalent to determining if $-1 < x \le 0$. This can be inferred by examining a few representative examples, such as $\lceil -1.1 \rceil = -1$, $\lceil -1 \rceil = -1$, $\lceil -0.9 \rceil = 0$, $\lceil -0.1 \rceil = 0$, $\lceil 0 \rceil = 0$, and $\lceil 0.1 \rceil = 1$.

(1) Given $-1 < x < -0.1$, it follows that $-1 < x \le 0$, since $-1 < x \le 0$ represents all numbers x that satisfy $-1 < x < -0.1$ along with all numbers x that satisfy $-0.1 \le x \le 0$; SUFFICIENT.

(2) Given $\lceil x + 0.5 \rceil = 1$, it follows from the same reasoning used just before (1) above that this equality is equivalent to $0 < x + 0.5 \le 1$, which in turn is equivalent to $-0.5 < x \le 0.5$. Since from among these values of x it is possible for $-1 < x \le 0$ to be true (for example, $x = -0.1$) and it is possible for $-1 < x \le 0$ to be false (for example, $x = 0.1$), it cannot be determined if $\lceil x \rceil = 0$; NOT sufficient.

The correct answer is A; statement 1 alone is sufficient.

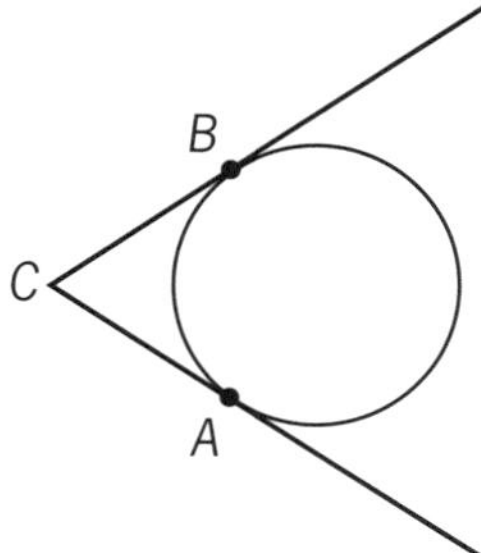

278. The circular base of an above-ground swimming pool lies in a level yard and just touches two straight sides of a fence at points A and B, as shown in the figure above. Point C is on the ground where the two sides of the fence meet. How far from the center of the pool's base is point A?

(1) The base has area 250 square feet.

(2) The center of the base is 20 feet from point C.

Geometry Circles

Let Q be the center of the pool's base and r be the distance from Q to A, as shown in the figure below.

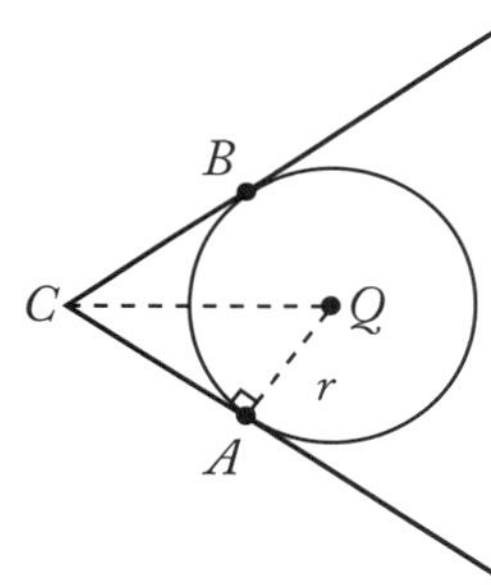

Since A is a point on the circular base, QA is a radius (r) of the base.

(1) Since the formula for the area of a circle is area $= \pi r^2$, this information can be stated as $250 = \pi r^2$ or $\sqrt{\frac{250}{\pi}} = r$; SUFFICIENT.

(2) Since $\overline{CA}$ is tangent to the base, ΔQAC is a right triangle. It is given that $QC = 20$, but there is not enough information to use the Pythagorean theorem to determine the length of $\overline{QA}$; NOT sufficient.

The correct answer is A; statement 1 alone is sufficient.

279. If $xy = -6$, what is the value of $xy(x + y)$?

(1) $x - y = 5$

(2) $xy^2 = 18$

Algebra First- and second-degree equations

By substituting –6 as the value of xy, the question can be simplified to "What is the value of $-6(x + y)$?"

(1) Adding y to both sides of $x - y = 5$ gives $x = y + 5$. When $y + 5$ is substituted for x in the equation $xy = -6$, the equation yields $(y + 5)y = -6$, or $y^2 + 5y + 6 = 0$. Factoring the left side of this equation gives $(y + 2)(y + 3) = 0$. Thus, y may have a value of –2 or –3. Since a unique value of y is not determined, neither the value of x nor the value of xy can be determined; NOT sufficient.

(2) Since $xy^2 = (xy)y$ and $xy^2 = 18$, it follows that $(xy)y = 18$. When –6 is substituted for xy, this equation yields $-6y = 18$, and hence $y = -3$. Since $y = -3$ and $xy = -6$, it follows that $-3x = -6$, or $x = 2$. Therefore, the value of $x + y$, and hence the value of $xy(x + y) = -6(x + y)$ can be determined; SUFFICIENT.

The correct answer is B; statement 2 alone is sufficient.

280. $[y]$ denotes the greatest integer less than or equal to y. Is $d < 1$?

(1) $d = y - [y]$

(2) $[d] = 0$

Algebra Operations with real numbers

(1) It is given $d = y - [y]$. If y is an integer, then $y = [y]$, and thus $y - [y] = 0$, which is less than 1. If y is not an integer, then y lies between two consecutive integers, the smaller of which is equal to $[y]$. Since each of these two consecutive integers is at a distance of less than 1 from y, it follows that $[y]$ is at a distance of less than 1 from y, or $y - [y] < 1$. Thus, regardless of whether y is an integer or y is not an integer, it can be determined that $d < 1$; SUFFICIENT.

(2) It is given that $[d] = 0$, which is equivalent to $0 \le d < 1$. This can be inferred by examining a few representative examples, such as $[-0.1] = -1$, $[0] = 0$, $[0.1] = 0$, $[0.9] = 0$, and $[1.1] = 1$. From $0 \le d < 1$, it follows that $d < 1$; SUFFICIENT.

The correct answer is D;
each statement alone is sufficient.

281. If N is a positive odd integer, is N prime?

(1) $N = 2^k + 1$ for some positive integer k.
(2) $N + 2$ and $N + 4$ are both prime.

Arithmetic Properties of numbers

Determine whether the positive odd integer N is prime.

(1) This indicates that $N = 2^k + 1$ for some positive integer k. If $k = 1$, then $N = 2^1 + 1 = 3$ and N is prime. However, if $k = 3$, then $N = 2^3 + 1 = 9$ and N is not prime; NOT sufficient.

(2) This indicates that both $N + 2$ and $N + 4$ are prime. If $N = 3$, then $N + 2 = 5$ and $N + 4 = 7$ are both prime and N is prime. However, if $N = 9$, then $N + 2 = 11$ and $N + 4 = 13$ are both prime and N is not prime; NOT sufficient.

Taking (1) and (2) together is of no more help than (1) and (2) taken separately since the same examples were used to show that neither (1) nor (2) is sufficient.

The correct answer is E;
both statements together are still not sufficient.

282. If m is a positive integer, then m^3 has how many digits?

(1) m has 3 digits.
(2) m^2 has 5 digits.

Arithmetic Properties of numbers

(1) Given that m has 3 digits, then m could be 100 and $m^3 = 1{,}000{,}000$ would have 7 digits, or m could be 300 and $m^3 = 27{,}000{,}000$ would have 8 digits; NOT sufficient.

(2) Given that m^2 has 5 digits, then m could be 100 (because $100^2 = 10{,}000$ has 5 digits) or m could be 300 (because $300^2 = 90{,}000$ has 5 digits). In the former case, $m^3 = 1{,}000{,}000$ has 7 digits and in the latter case, $m^3 = 27{,}000{,}000$ has 8 digits; NOT sufficient.

Given (1) and (2), it is still possible for m to be 100 or for m to be 300, and thus m^3 could have 7 digits or m^3 could have 8 digits.

The correct answer is E;
both statements together are still not sufficient.

283. What is the value of $x^2 - y^2$?

(1) $(x - y)^2 = 9$
(2) $x + y = 6$

Algebra Second-degree equations

Determine the value of $x^2 - y^2$.

(1) This indicates that $(x - y)^2 = 9$. It follows that $x - y = -3$ or $x - y = 3$, which gives information about the value of $x - y$ but not specific information about the value of x, y, or $x^2 - y^2$. For example, if $x = \frac{9}{2}$ and $y = \frac{3}{2}$, then $(x - y)^2 = \left(\frac{9}{2} - \frac{3}{2}\right)^2 = 9$ and $x^2 - y^2 = \frac{81}{4} - \frac{9}{4} = 18$. But if $x = \frac{3}{2}$ and $y = \frac{9}{2}$, then $(x - y)^2 = \left(\frac{3}{2} - \frac{9}{2}\right)^2 = 9$ and $x^2 - y^2 = \frac{9}{4} - \frac{81}{4} = -18$; NOT sufficient.

(2) This indicates that $x + y = 6$ but does not give specific information about the value of x, y, or $x^2 - y^2$. For example, if $x = \frac{9}{2}$ and $y = \frac{3}{2}$, then $x + y = \frac{9}{2} + \frac{3}{2} = 6$ and $x^2 - y^2 = \frac{81}{4} - \frac{9}{4} = 18$. But if $x = \frac{3}{2}$ and $y = \frac{9}{2}$, then $x + y = \frac{3}{2} + \frac{9}{2} = 6$ and $x^2 - y^2 = \frac{9}{4} - \frac{81}{4} = -18$; NOT sufficient.

Taking (1) and (2) together is of no more help than (1) and (2) taken separately since the same examples were used to show that neither (1) nor (2) is sufficient.

Alternatively, note that $x^2 - y^2 = (x - y)(x + y)$. From (1), $x - y = \pm 3$, and from (2), $x + y = 6$. Therefore, taking (1) and (2) together allows for both $x^2 - y^2 = (3)(6) = 18$ and $x^2 - y^2 = (-3)(6) = -18$.

The correct answer is E;
both statements together are still not sufficient.

284. For each landscaping job that takes more than 4 hours, a certain contractor charges a total of r dollars for the first 4 hours plus $0.2r$ dollars for each additional hour or fraction of an hour, where $r > 100$. Did a particular landscaping job take more than 10 hours?

(1) The contractor charged a total of \$288 for the job.

(2) The contractor charged a total of $2.4r$ dollars for the job.

Algebra Applied problems

If y represents the total number of hours the particular landscaping job took, determine if $y > 10$.

(1) This indicates that the total charge for the job was \$288, which means that $r + 0.2r(y - 4) = 288$. From this it cannot be determined if $y > 10$. For example, if $r = 120$ and $y = 11$, then $120 + 0.2(120)(7) = 288$, and the job took more than 10 hours. However, if $r = 160$ and $y = 8$, then $160 + 0.2(160)(4) = 288$, and the job took less than 10 hours; NOT sufficient.

(2) This indicates that $r + 0.2r(y - 4) = 2.4r$, from which it follows that

$r + 0.2ry - 0.8r = 2.4r$	use distributive property
$0.2ry = 2.2r$	subtract $(r - 0.8r)$ from both sides
$y = 11$	divide both sides by $0.2r$

Therefore, the job took more than 10 hours; SUFFICIENT.

The correct answer is B; statement 2 alone is sufficient.

285. If $x^2 = 2^x$, what is the value of x?

(1) $2x = \left(\frac{x}{2}\right)^3$

(2) $x = 2^{x-2}$

Algebra Exponents

Given $x^2 = 2^x$, determine the value of x. Note that $x \neq 0$ because $0^2 = 0$ and $2^0 = 1$.

(1) This indicates that $2x = \left(\frac{x}{2}\right)^3$, so $2x = \frac{x^3}{8}$ and $16x = x^3$. Since $x \neq 0$, then $16 = x^2$, so $x = -4$ or $x = 4$. However, $(-4)^2 = 16$ and $2^{-4} = \frac{1}{16}$, so $x \neq -4$. Therefore, $x = 4$; SUFFICIENT.

(2) This indicates that $x = 2^{x-2}$, so $x = \frac{2^x}{2^2}$ and $4x = 2^x$. Since it is given that $x^2 = 2^x$, then $4x = x^2$ and, because $x \neq 0$, it follows that $x = 4$; SUFFICIENT.

The correct answer is D; each statement alone is sufficient.

286. The sequence $s_1, s_2, s_3, \ldots, s_n, \ldots$ is such that $s_n = \frac{1}{n} - \frac{1}{n+1}$ for all integers $n \geq 1$. If k is a positive integer, is the sum of the first k terms of the sequence greater than $\frac{9}{10}$?

(1) $k > 10$

(2) $k < 19$

Arithmetic Sequences

The sum of the first k terms can be written as

$$\left(\frac{1}{1} - \frac{1}{2}\right) + \left(\frac{1}{2} - \frac{1}{3}\right) + \ldots + \left(\frac{1}{k-1} - \frac{1}{k}\right) + \left(\frac{1}{k} - \frac{1}{k+1}\right)$$

$$= 1 + \left(-\frac{1}{2} + \frac{1}{2}\right) + \left(-\frac{1}{3} + \frac{1}{3}\right) + \ldots + \left(-\frac{1}{k} + \frac{1}{k}\right) - \frac{1}{k+1}$$

$$= 1 - \frac{1}{k+1}.$$

Therefore, the sum of the first k terms is greater than $\frac{9}{10}$ if and only if $1 - \frac{1}{k+1} > \frac{9}{10}$, or $1 - \frac{9}{10} > \frac{1}{k+1}$, or $\frac{1}{10} > \frac{1}{k+1}$. Multiplying both sides of the last inequality by $10(k + 1)$ gives the equivalent condition $k + 1 > 10$, or $k > 9$.

(1) Given that $k > 10$, then it follows that $k > 9$; SUFFICIENT.

(2) Given that $k < 19$, it is possible to have $k > 9$ (for example, $k = 15$) and it is possible to not have $k > 9$ (for example, $k = 5$); NOT sufficient.

The correct answer is A; statement 1 alone is sufficient.

287. In the sequence S of numbers, each term after the first two terms is the sum of the two immediately preceding terms. What is the 5th term of S?

(1) The 6th term of S minus the 4th term equals 5.

(2) The 6th term of S plus the 7th term equals 21.

Arithmetic Sequences

If the first two terms of sequence S are a and b, then the remaining terms of sequence S can be expressed in terms of a and b as follows.

n	nth term of sequence S
1	a
2	b
3	$a + b$
4	$a + 2b$
5	$2a + 3b$
6	$3a + 5b$
7	$5a + 8b$

For example, the 6th term of sequence S is $3a + 5b$ because $(a + 2b) + (2a + 3b) = 3a + 5b$. Determine the value of the 5th term of sequence S, that is, the value of $2a + 3b$.

(1) Given that the 6th term of S minus the 4th term of S is 5, it follows that $(3a + 5b) - (a + 2b) = 5$. Combining like terms, this equation can be rewritten as $2a + 3b = 5$, and thus the 5th term of sequence S is 5; SUFFICIENT.

(2) Given that the 6th term of S plus the 7th term of S is 21, it follows that $(3a + 5b) + (5a + 8b) = 21$. Combining like terms, this equation can be rewritten as $8a + 13b = 21$. Letting e represent the 5th term of sequence S, this last equation is equivalent to $4(2a + 3b) + b = 21$, or $4e + b = 21$, which gives a direct correspondence between the 5th term of sequence S and the 2nd term of sequence S. Therefore, the 5th term of sequence S can be determined if and only if the 2nd term of sequence S can be determined. Since the 2nd term of sequence S cannot be determined, the 5th term of sequence S cannot be determined. For example, if $a = 1$ and $b = 1$, then $8a + 13b = 8(1) + 13(1) = 21$ and the 5th term of sequence S is $2a + 3b = 2(1) + 3(1) = 5$. However, if $a = 0$ and $b = \frac{21}{13}$, then

$$8a + 13b = 8(0) + 13\left(\frac{21}{13}\right) = 21$$

and the 5th term of sequence S is

$$2a + 3b = 2(0) + 3\left(\frac{21}{13}\right) = \frac{63}{13};$$ NOT sufficient.

The correct answer is A; statement 1 alone is sufficient.

288. If 75 percent of the guests at a certain banquet ordered dessert, what percent of the guests ordered coffee?

(1) 60 percent of the guests who ordered dessert also ordered coffee.

(2) 90 percent of the guests who ordered coffee also ordered dessert.

Arithmetic Concepts of sets; Percents

Consider the Venn diagram below that displays the various percentages of 4 groups of the guests. Thus, x percent of the guests ordered both dessert and coffee and y percent of the guests ordered coffee only. Since 75 percent of the guests ordered dessert, $(75 - x)$% of the guests ordered dessert only. Also, because the 4 percentages represented in the Venn diagram have a total sum of 100 percent, the percentage of guests who did not order either dessert or coffee is $100 - [(75 - x) + x + y] = 25 - y$. Determine the percentage of guests who ordered coffee, or equivalently, the value of $x + y$.

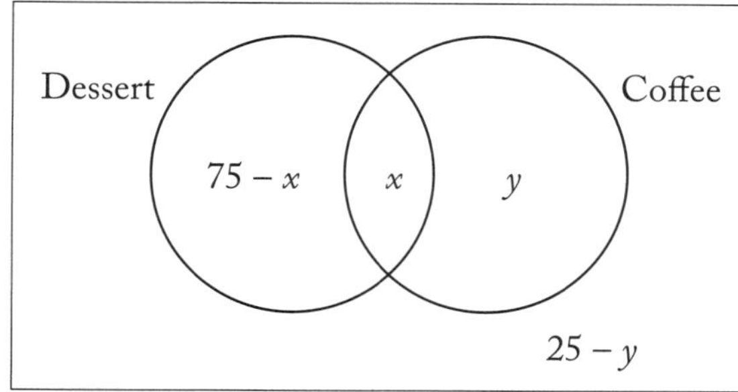

(1) Given that x is equal to 60 percent of 75, or 45, the value of $x + y$ cannot be determined; NOT sufficient.

(2) Given that 90 percent of $x + y$ is equal to x, it follows that $0.9(x + y) = x$, or $9(x + y) = 10x$. Therefore, $9x + 9y = 10x$, or $9y = x$. From this the value of $x + y$ cannot be determined. For example, if $x = 9$ and $y = 1$, then all 4 percentages in the Venn diagram are between 0 and 100, $9y = x$, and $x + y = 10$. However, if $x = 18$ and $y = 2$, then all 4 percentages in the Venn diagram are between 0 and 100, $9y = x$, and $x + y = 20$; NOT sufficient.

Given both (1) and (2), it follows that $x = 45$ and $9y = x$. Therefore, $9y = 45$, or $y = 5$, and hence $x + y = 45 + 5 = 50$.

The correct answer is C;
both statements together are sufficient.

289. A tank containing water started to leak. Did the tank contain more than 30 gallons of water when it started to leak? (Note: 1 gallon = 128 ounces)

(1) The water leaked from the tank at a constant rate of 6.4 ounces per minute.

(2) The tank became empty less than 12 hours after it started to leak.

Arithmetic Rate problems

(1) Given that the water leaked from the tank at a constant rate of 6.4 ounces per minute, it is not possible to determine if the tank leaked more than 30 gallons of water. In fact, any nonzero amount of water leaking from the tank is consistent with a leakage rate of 6.4 ounces per minute, since nothing can be determined about the amount of time the water was leaking from the tank; NOT sufficient.

(2) Given that the tank became empty in less than 12 hours, it is not possible to determine if the tank leaked more than 30 gallons of water because the rate at which water leaked from the tank is unknown. For example, the tank could have originally contained 1 gallon of water that emptied in exactly 10 hours or the tank could have originally contained 31 gallons of water that emptied in exactly 10 hours; NOT sufficient.

Given (1) and (2) together, the tank emptied at a constant rate of

$$\left(6.4\frac{\text{oz}}{\text{min}}\right)\left(60\frac{\text{min}}{\text{hr}}\right)\left(\frac{1}{128}\frac{\text{gal}}{\text{oz}}\right) = \frac{(64)(6)}{128}\frac{\text{gal}}{\text{hr}} =$$

$\frac{(64)(6)}{(64)(2)}\frac{\text{gal}}{\text{hr}} = 3\frac{\text{gal}}{\text{hr}}$ for less than 12 hours.

If t is the total number of hours the water leaked from the tank, then the total amount of water emptied from the tank, in gallons, is $3t$, which is therefore less than $(3)(12) = 36$. From this it is not possible to determine if the tank originally contained more than 30 gallons of water. For example, if the tank leaked water for a total of 11 hours, then the tank originally contained $(3)(11)$ gallons of water, which is more than 30 gallons of water. However, if the tank leaked water for a total of 2 hours, then the tank originally contained $(3)(2)$ gallons of water, which is not more than 30 gallons of water.

The correct answer is E;
both statements together are still not sufficient.

290. In the xy-plane, lines k and ℓ intersect at the point $(1,1)$. Is the y-intercept of k greater than the y-intercept of ℓ?

(1) The slope of k is less than the slope of ℓ.

(2) The slope of ℓ is positive.

Algebra Coordinate geometry

Let m_1 and m_2 represent the slopes of lines k and ℓ, respectively. Then, using the point-slope form for the equation of a line, an equation of line k can be determined: $y - 1 = m_1(x - 1)$, or $y = m_1x + (1 - m_1)$. Similarly, an equation for line ℓ is $y = m_2x + (1 - m_2)$. Determine if $(1 - m_1) > (1 - m_2)$, or equivalently if $m_1 < m_2$.

(1) This indicates that $m_1 < m_2$; SUFFICIENT.

(2) This indicates that $m_2 > 0$. If $m_1 = -1$, for example, then $m_1 < m_2$, but if $m_2 = 4$ and $m_1 = 5$, then $m_1 > m_2$; NOT sufficient.

The correct answer is A; statement 1 alone is sufficient.

291. A triangle has side lengths of a, b, and c centimeters. Does each angle in the triangle measure less than 90 degrees?

(1) The 3 semicircles whose diameters are the sides of the triangle have areas that are equal to 3 cm^2, 4 cm^2, and 6 cm^2, respectively.

(2) $c < a + b < c + 2$

Geometry Triangles; Pythagorean theorem

Given a triangle with sides of lengths a, b, and c centimeters, determine whether each angle of the triangle measures less than 90°. Assume that the vertices of the triangle are A, B, and C and that a is the side length of the side opposite $\angle A$, b is the side length of the side opposite $\angle B$, and c is the side length of the side opposite $\angle C$, where $a \le b \le c$.

Note that for a right triangle, $a^2 + b^2 = c^2$. However, if $a^2 + b^2 > c^2$, then the triangle is acute (i.e., a triangle with each angle measuring less than 90°). This is illustrated by the following figures.

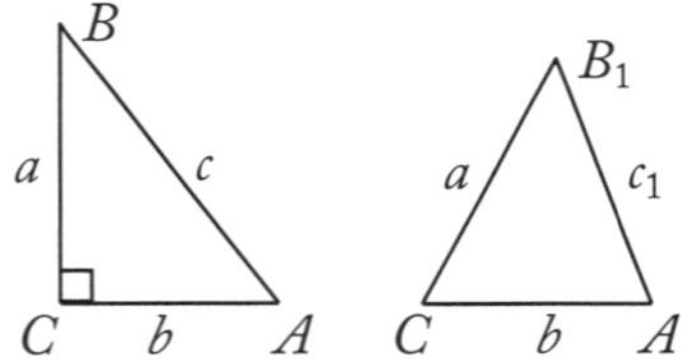

ΔBCA on the left is a right triangle with sides $BC = a$, $CA = b$, and $AB = c$, where $a^2 + b^2 = c^2$ by the Pythagorean theorem. The triangle on the right, ΔB_1CA, has sides $B_1C = a$, $CA = b$, and $AB_1 = c_1$. Clearly $AB = c > AB_1 = c_1$, so $c^2 > c_1^2$. Since $a^2 + b^2 = c^2$ and $c^2 > c_1^2$, it follows that $a^2 + b^2 > c_1^2$, and ΔB_1CA is clearly an acute triangle.

(1) This indicates that the areas of the 3 semicircles whose diameters are the sides of the triangle are 3 cm^2, 4 cm^2, and 6 cm^2, respectively. Then, because "respectively" implies that a is the diameter of the semicircle with area 3 cm^2, b is the diameter of the semicircle with area 4 cm^2, and c is the diameter of the semicircle with area 6 cm^2, as shown below, then $3 = \frac{1}{2}\pi\left(\frac{a}{2}\right)^2$ from which it follows that $a^2 = \frac{24}{\pi}$. Similarly, $b^2 = \frac{32}{\pi}$, and $c^2 = \frac{48}{\pi}$.

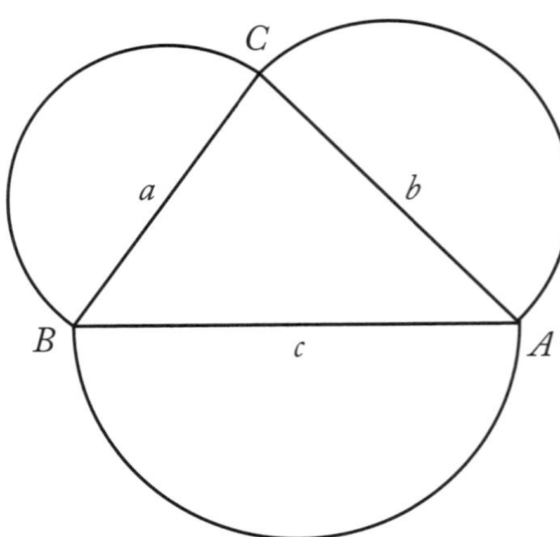

Because $a^2 + b^2 = \frac{24}{\pi} + \frac{32}{\pi} = \frac{56}{\pi} > \frac{48}{\pi} = c^2$, the angle with greatest measure (i.e., the angle at C) is an acute angle, which implies that each angle in the triangle is acute and measures less than 90°; SUFFICIENT.

(2) This indicates that $c < a + b < c + 2$. If $a = 1$, $b = 1$, and $c = 1$, then $1 < 1 + 1 < 1 + 2$. It follows that the triangle is equilateral; therefore, each angle measures less than 90°. However, if $a = 1$, $b = 1$, and $c = \sqrt{2}$, then $\sqrt{2} < 1 + 1 < \sqrt{2} + 2$, but $1^2 + 1^2 = (\sqrt{2})^2$ and the triangle is a right triangle; NOT sufficient.

The correct answer is A; statement 1 alone is sufficient.

292. Each of the 45 books on a shelf is written either in English or in Spanish, and each of the books is either a hardcover book or a paperback. If a book is to be selected at random from the books on the shelf, is the probability less than $\frac{1}{2}$ that the book selected will be a paperback written in Spanish?

(1) Of the books on the shelf, 30 are paperbacks.

(2) Of the books on the shelf, 15 are written in Spanish.

Arithmetic Probability

(1) This indicates that 30 of the 45 books are paperbacks. Of the 30 paperbacks, 25 could be written in Spanish. In this case, the probability of randomly selecting a paperback book written in Spanish is $\frac{25}{45} > \frac{1}{2}$. On the other hand, it is possible that only 5 of the paperback books are written in Spanish. In this case, the probability of randomly selecting a paperback book written in Spanish is $\frac{5}{45} < \frac{1}{2}$; NOT sufficient.

(2) This indicates that 15 of the books are written in Spanish. Then, at most 15 of the 45 books on the shelf are paperbacks written in Spanish, and the probability of randomly selecting a paperback book written in Spanish is at most $\frac{15}{45} < \frac{1}{2}$; SUFFICIENT.

The correct answer is B; statement 2 alone is sufficient.

293. A small school has three foreign language classes, one in French, one in Spanish, and one in German. How many of the 34 students enrolled in the Spanish class are also enrolled in the French class?

(1) There are 27 students enrolled in the French class, and 49 students enrolled in either the French class, the Spanish class, or both of these classes.

(2) One-half of the students enrolled in the Spanish class are enrolled in more than one foreign language class.

Arithmetic Sets

Given that 34 students are enrolled in the Spanish class, how many students are enrolled in both the Spanish and French classes? In other words, given that $x + y = 34$ in the diagram below, what is the value of y?

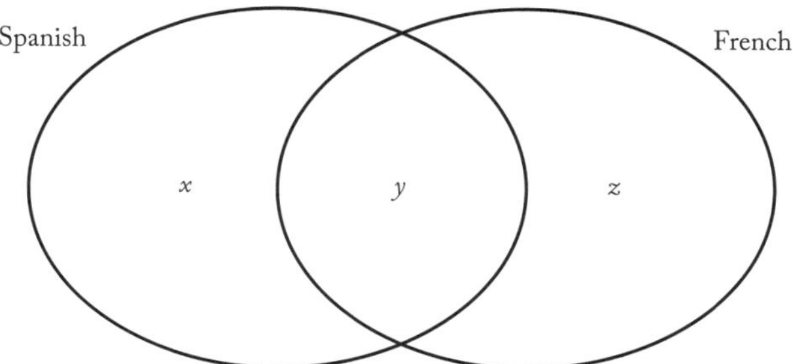

(1) It is given that $y + z = 27$ and $x + y + z = 49$. Adding the equations $x + y = 34$ and $y + z = 27$ gives $x + 2y + z = 34 + 27 = 61$, or $y + (x + y + z) = 61$. Since $x + y + z = 49$, it follows that $y + 49 = 61$, or $y = 12$; SUFFICIENT.

(2) Given that half the students enrolled in the Spanish class are enrolled in more than one foreign language class, then it is possible that no students are enrolled in the French and German classes only and 17 students are enrolled in both the Spanish and French classes. On the other hand, it is also possible that there are 17 students enrolled in the French and German classes only and no students enrolled in both the Spanish and French classes; NOT sufficient.

The correct answer is A; statement 1 alone is sufficient.

294. If S is a set of four numbers w, x, y, and z, is the range of the numbers in S greater than 2 ?

(1) $w - z > 2$

(2) z is the least number in S.

Arithmetic Statistics

The range of the numbers w, x, y, and z is equal to the greatest of those numbers minus the least of those numbers.

(1) This reveals that the difference between two of the numbers in the set is greater than 2, which means that the range of the four numbers must also be greater than 2; SUFFICIENT.

(2) The information that z is the least number gives no information regarding the other numbers or their range; NOT sufficient.

The correct answer is A; statement 1 alone is sufficient.

295. Last year $\frac{3}{5}$ of the members of a certain club were males. This year the members of the club include all the members from last year plus some new members. Is the fraction of the members of the club who are males greater this year than last year?

(1) More than half of the new members are male.

(2) The number of members of the club this year is $\frac{6}{5}$ the number of members last year.

Arithmetic Operations with fractions

Let L represent the number of members last year; N the number of new members added this year; and x the number of members added this year who are males. It is given that $\frac{3}{5}$ of the members last year were males. It follows that the number of members who are male this year is $\frac{3}{5}L + x$. Also, the total number of members this year is $L + N$. Determine if $\frac{\frac{3}{5}L + x}{L + N} > \frac{3}{5}$, or equivalently, determine if $3L + 5x > 3L + 3N$ or simply if $x > \frac{3}{5}N$.

(1) This indicates that $x > \frac{1}{2}N$. If, for example, $N = 20$ and $x = 11$, then $11 > \frac{1}{2}(20) = 10$, but $11 \not> \frac{3}{5}(20) = 12$. On the other hand, if $N = 20$ and $x = 16$, then $16 > \frac{1}{2}(20) = 10$, and $16 > \frac{3}{5}(20) = 12$; NOT sufficient.

(2) This indicates that $L + N = \frac{6}{5}L$. It follows that $N = \frac{1}{5}L$. If, for example, $L = 100$, then $N = \frac{1}{5}(100) = 20$. If $x = 11$, then $11 \not> \frac{3}{5}(20) = 12$. On the other hand, if $x = 16$, then $16 > \frac{1}{2}(20) = 10$, and $16 > \frac{3}{5}(20) = 12$; NOT sufficient.

Taking (1) and (2) together is of no more help than (1) and (2) taken separately since the same examples were used to show that neither (1) nor (2) is sufficient.

The correct answer is E; both statements together are still not sufficient.

296. If a, b, and c are consecutive integers and $0 < a < b < c$, is the product abc a multiple of 8 ?

(1) The product ac is even.

(2) The product bc is a multiple of 4.

Arithmetic Operations with integers

Determine whether the product of three consecutive positive integers, a, b and c, where $a < b < c$, is a multiple of 8.

Since a, b, and c are consecutive integers, then either both a and c are even and b is odd, or both a and c are odd and b is even.

(1) This indicates that at least one of a or c is even, so both a and c are even. Since, when counting from 1, every fourth integer is a multiple of 4, one integer of the pair of consecutive even integers a and c is a multiple of 4. Since the other integer of the pair is even, the product ac is a multiple of 8, and, therefore, abc is a multiple of 8; SUFFICIENT.

(2) This indicates that bc is a multiple of 4. If $b = 3$ and $c = 4$, then $a = 2$ and $bc = 12$, which is a multiple of 4. In this case, $abc = (2)(3)(4) = 24$, which is a multiple of 8. However, if $b = 4$ and $c = 5$, then $a = 3$ and $bc = 20$, which is a multiple of 4. In this case, $abc = (3)(4)(5) = 60$, which is not a multiple of 8; NOT sufficient.

The correct answer is A; statement 1 alone is sufficient.

297. M and N are integers such that $6 < M < N$. What is the value of N?

(1) The greatest common divisor of M and N is 6.

(2) The least common multiple of M and N is 36.

Arithmetic Properties of numbers

(1) Given that the greatest common divisor (GCD) of M and N is 6 and $6 < M < N$, then it is possible that $M = (6)(5) = 30$ and $N = (6)(7) = 42$. However, it is also possible that $M = (6)(7) = 42$ and $N = (6)(11) = 66$; NOT sufficient.

(2) Given that the least common multiple (LCM) of M and N is 36 and $6 < M < N$, then it is possible that $M = (4)(3) = 12$ and $N = (9)(2) = 18$. However, it is also possible that $M = (4)(3) = 12$ and $N = (9)(4) = 36$; NOT sufficient.

Taking (1) and (2) together, it follows that 6 is a divisor of M and M is a divisor of 36. Therefore, M is among the numbers 6, 12, 18, and 36. For the same reason, N is among the numbers 6, 12, 18, and 36. Since $6 < M < N$, it follows that M cannot be 6 or 36 and N cannot be 6. Thus, there are three choices for M and N such that $M < N$. These three choices are displayed in the table below, which indicates why only one of the choices, namely $M = 12$ and $N = 18$, satisfies both (1) and (2).

M	N	GCD	LCM
12	18	6	36
12	36	12	36
18	36	18	36

The correct answer is C;
both statements together are sufficient.

298. Stations X and Y are connected by two separate, straight, parallel rail lines that are 250 miles long. Train P and train Q simultaneously left Station X and Station Y, respectively, and each train traveled to the other's point of departure. The two trains passed each other after traveling for 2 hours. When the two trains passed, which train was nearer to its destination?

(1) At the time when the two trains passed, train P had averaged a speed of 70 miles per hour.

(2) Train Q averaged a speed of 55 miles per hour for the entire trip.

Arithmetic Applied problems; Rates

(1) This indicates that Train P had traveled $2(70) = 140$ miles when it passed Train Q. It follows that Train P was $250 - 140 = 110$ miles from its destination and Train Q was 140 miles from its destination, which means that Train P was nearer to its destination when the trains passed each other; SUFFICIENT.

(2) This indicates that Train Q averaged a speed of 55 miles per hour for the entire trip, but no information is given about the speed of Train P. If Train Q traveled for 2 hours at an average speed of 55 miles per hour and Train P traveled for 2 hours at an average speed of 70 miles per hour, then Train P was nearer to its destination when the trains passed. However, if Train Q traveled for 2 hours at an average speed of 65 miles per hour and Train P traveled for 2 hours at an average speed of 60 miles per hour, then Train Q was nearer to its destination when the trains passed. Note that if Train Q traveled at $\frac{(120)(55)}{140} = 47\frac{1}{7}$ miles per hour for the remainder of the trip, then its average speed for the whole trip was 55 miles per hour; NOT sufficient.

The correct answer is A;
statement 1 alone is sufficient.

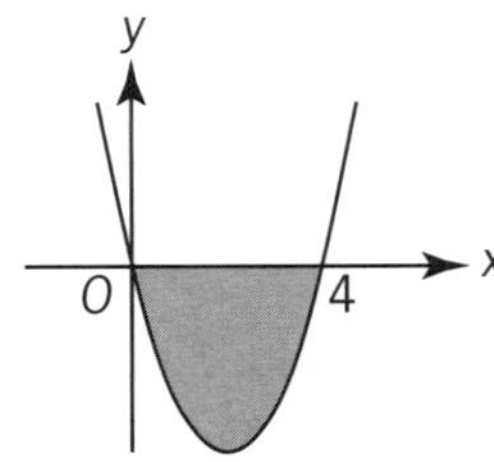

299. In the *xy*-plane shown, the shaded region consists of all points that lie above the graph of $y = x^2 - 4x$ and below the *x*-axis. Does the point (a,b) (not shown) lie in the shaded region if $b < 0$?

(1) $0 < a < 4$

(2) $a^2 - 4a < b$

Algebra Coordinate geometry

In order for (a,b) to lie in the shaded region, it must lie above the graph of $y = x^2 - 4x$ and below the *x*-axis. Since $b < 0$, the point (a,b) lies below the *x*-axis. In order for (a,b) to lie above the graph of $y = x^2 - 4x$, it must be true that $b > a^2 - 4a$.

(1) This indicates that $0 < a < 4$. If $a = 2$, then $a^2 - 4a = 2^2 - 4(2) = -4$, so if $b = -1$, then $b > a^2 - 4a$ and (a,b) is in the shaded region. But if $b = -5$, then $b < a^2 - 4a$ and (a,b) is not in the shaded region; NOT sufficient.

(2) This indicates that $b > a^2 - 4a$, and thus, (a,b) is in the shaded region; SUFFICIENT.

The correct answer is B; statement 2 alone is sufficient.

300. If *a* and *b* are positive integers, is $\sqrt[3]{ab}$ an integer?

(1) $\sqrt{a}$ is an integer.

(2) $b = \sqrt{a}$

Arithmetic Properties of numbers

(1) Given that $\sqrt{a}$ is an integer, then $a = 4$ is possible. If, in addition $b = 1$, then $\sqrt[3]{ab} = \sqrt[3]{4}$ is not an integer. However, if, in addition $b = 2$, then $\sqrt[3]{ab} = \sqrt[3]{8} = 2$ is an integer; NOT sufficient.

(2) Given that $b = \sqrt{a}$, then $\sqrt[3]{ab} = \sqrt[3]{a\sqrt{a}} = \sqrt[3]{\sqrt{a}^3} = \sqrt{\sqrt[3]{a}^3} = \sqrt{a} = b$ is an integer; SUFFICIENT.

The correct answer is B; statement 2 alone is sufficient.

Appendix A Answer Sheets

Problem Solving Answer Sheet

1.
2.
3.
4.
5.
6.
7.
8.
9.
10.
11.
12.
13.
14.
15.
16.
17.
18.
19.
20.
21.
22.
23.
24.
25.
26.
27.
28.
29.
30.
31.
32.
33.
34.
35.
36.
37.
38.
39.
40.
41.
42.
43.
44.
45.
46.
47.
48.
49.
50.
51.
52.
53.
54.
55.
56.
57.
58.
59.
60.
61.
62.
63.
64.
65.
66.
67.
68.
69.
70.
71.
72.
73.
74.
75.
76.
77.
78.
79.
80.
81.
82.
83.
84.
85.
86.
87.
88.
89.
90.
91.
92.
93.
94.
95.
96.
97.
98.
99.
100.
101.
102.
103.
104.
105.
106.
107.
108.
109.
110.
111.
112.
113.
114.
115.
116.
117.
118.
119.
120.
121.
122.
123.
124.
125.
126.
127.
128.
129.
130.
131.
132.
133.
134.
135.
136.
137.
138.
139.
140.
141.
142.
143.
144.
145.
146.
147.
148.
149.
150.
151.
152.
153.
154.
155.
156.
157.
158.
159.
160.
161.
162.
163.
164.
165.
166.
167.
168.
169.
170.
171.
172.
173.
174.
175.
176.

Data Sufficiency Answer Sheet

177.
178.
179.
180.
181.
182.
183.
184.
185.
186.
187.
188.
189.
190.
191.
192.
193.
194.
195.
196.
197.
198.
199.
200.
201.
202.
203.
204.
205.
206.
207.
208.
209.
210.
211.
212.
213.
214.
215.
216.
217.
218.
219.
220.
221.
222.
223.
224.
225.
226.
227.
228.
229.
230.
231.
232.
233.
234.
235.
236.
237.
238.
239.
240.
241.
242.
243.
244.
245.
246.
247.
248.
249.
250.
251.
252.
253.
254.
255.
256.
257.
258.
259.
260.
261.
262.
263.
264.
265.
266.
267.
268.
269.
270.
271.
272.
273.
274.
275.
276.
277.
278.
279.
280.
281.
282.
283.
284.
285.
286.
287.
288.
289.
290.
291.
292.
293.
294.
295.
296.
297.
298.
299.
300.

Notes

Notes

Notes

Notes

Notes

Notes

Notes

Notes

Notes

Notes

Notes

Notes

Notes

Notes

Notes

Notes

Notes